T0347243

RESOURCES FOR THE FUTURE LIBRARY COLLECTION
URBAN AND REGIONAL ECONOMICS

Volume 6

Public Economics and the Quality of Life

Full list of titles in the set
URBAN AND REGIONAL ECONOMICS

Public Economics and the Quality of Life

Lowdon Wingo and Alan Evans

Washington, DC • London

First published in 1977 by The Johns Hopkins University Press for Resources for the Future

This edition first published in 2011 by RFF Press, an imprint of Earthscan

First edition © The Johns Hopkins University Press 1977
This edition © Earthscan 1977, 2011

Earthscan LLC, 1616 P Street, NW, Washington, DC 20036, USA
Earthscan Ltd, Dunstan House, 14a St Cross Street, London EC1N 8XA, UK
Earthscan publishes in association with the International Institute for Environment and Development

For more information on RFF Press and Earthscan publications, see www. rffpress.org and www.earthscan.co.uk or write to earthinfo@earthscan.co.uk

ISBN: 978-1-61726-076-6 (Volume 6)
ISBN: 978-1-61726-008-7 (Urban and Regional Economics set)
ISBN: 978-1-61726-000-1 (Resources for the Future Library Collection)

A catalogue record for this book is available from the British Library

Publisher's note

The publisher has made every effort to ensure the quality of this reprint, but points out that some imperfections in the original copies may be apparent.

At Earthscan we strive to minimize our environmental impacts and carbon footprint through reducing waste, recycling and offsetting our CO_2 emissions, including those created through publication of this book. For more details of our environmental policy, see www.earthscan.co.uk.

Public Economics and the Quality of Life

Public Economics
and the Quality of Life

edited by

Lowdon Wingo and Alan Evans

*Published for Resources for the Future
and the Centre for Environmental Studies
by The Johns Hopkins University Press,
Baltimore and London*

Library of Congress Catalog Card Number 76-47393

ISBN 0-8018-1941-5

Library of Congress Cataloging in Publication Data will be found
on the last printed page of this book.

Contents

Contributors

PETER BOHM
Professor, Department of Economics, University of Stockholm, Stockholm, Sweden

ANTHONY J. CULYER
Assistant Director, Institute of Social and Economic Research, University of York, Heslington, York, England

DAVID DONNISON
Chairman, Supplementary Benefits Committee, Department of Health and Social Security, London, England

ALAN EVANS
Research Officer, Centre for Environmental Studies, London, England

EDWIN T. HAEFELE
Professor, Department of Political Science and School of Public and Urban Policy, University of Pennsylvania, Philadelphia, Pennsylvania

BRUCE W. HAMILTON
Assistant Professor, Department of Political Economy, Johns Hopkins University, Baltimore, Maryland

IRVING HOCH
Fellow, Resources for the Future, Washington, D.C.

ROBERT A. LEONE
Associate Professor, Harvard Business School, Harvard University, Cambridge, Massachusetts

JOHN R. MEYER
Professor, Harvard Business School, Harvard University, Cambridge, Massachusetts

HERBERT C. MORTON
Director, Public Affairs, Resources for the Future, Washington, D.C.

MANCUR OLSON
Professor, Department of Economics, University of Maryland, College Park, Maryland, and Consultant, Resources for the Future, Washington, D.C.

DAVID W. PEARCE
Professor of Political Economy, University of Aberdeen, Aberdeen, Scotland

A. MITCHELL POLINSKY
Assistant Professor, Department of Economics, Harvard University, Cambridge, Massachusetts

DANIEL L. RUBINFELD
Assistant Professor, Department of Economics, University of Michigan, Ann Arbor, Michigan

MICHAEL WHITBREAD
Economic Adviser, Department of the Environment, London, England

ALAN WILLIAMS
Professor, Institute of Social and Economic Research, University of York, Heslington, York, England

LOWDON WINGO
Professor and Director, School of Urban and Regional Planning, University of Southern California, Los Angeles

Preface

If "redistribution" was the dominant political theme of the 1960s, that of the 1970s has been most assuredly "quality." On the first day of the decade, President Nixon signed into law legislation creating the Council on Environmental Quality, and later that same year the National Goals Research Group brought forth its report *Toward Balanced Growth: Quantity with Quality,* which argued that "growth now should be directed toward achieving the higher social goal of improving the quality of human life." In February 1972 the Speaker of the House of Representatives, Carl Albert, urged support of the Rural Development Act of 1972, contending that "a broad enhancement of the quality of life in rural America is contemplated in this bill." And Gerald Ford's Second Biennial Report on National Growth and Development opened with a slightly different tone: "There has been much talk in recent years about the impact of future growth on the quality of American life. . . . [but] growth is not something which affects the quality of our lives; it is the measure of that effect." State capitols, county courthouses, and city halls have picked up the theme; the prospect of greater affluence concerns the voter less than his sense of the deterioration of important qualities of his life.

Anticipating this political preoccupation with quality, Resources for the Future early turned its attention to key quality issues arising from the abuse of the environment in an articulate work by Orris C. Herfindahl and Allen V. Kneese, entitled *Quality of the Environment: An Economic Approach to Some Problems in Using Land, Water, and Air,* which was published in 1965. A year later RFF published its forum volume, *Environmental Quality in a Growing Economy,* edited by Henry Jarrett, which was followed in 1969 by Harvey Perloff's *The Quality of the Urban Environment.* It was not a large conceptual leap from a focus on elements of the physical environment to a concern with the more general qualitative characteristics of the human environment.

The idea for this book grew out of this intellectual history, in which I participated. It first found expression in my Donald J. Robertson Memorial Lecture at the University of Glasgow in September 1972.[1] In this lecture I sought to relate the poorly articulated normative concerns of physical and environmental planners to the intellectual tools, old and new, with which economists were addressing policy issues. This theme, it turned out, was also of interest to London's Centre for Environmental Studies and especially to my colleague Alan Evans.

It did not take us long to discover that the topic, properly defined, commanded a broad interest among practitioners and theoreticians identified with the so-called policy sciences. If "the quality of life" is taken as a synonym for *real* consumption, the gratification resulting from an individual's interaction with his *total* environment, then public policy to improve the quality of life would have to deal with *real* production—all of those dimensions of the environment that bear on individual welfare. These range from the conventional private consumption goods of the marketplace to so-called public goods, which can only be consumed collectively.

In recent years, literature dealing with the quality of life has appeared in such diverse fields as sociology, psychology, marketing, ecology, architecture, and urban design. The principal concepts to emerge from this literature have important analogues in the policy sciences. Clearly, the current interest of many psychologists in human perception and motivation has its counterpart in the economist's interest in consumer behavior and utility theory. The physical planner's engagement with institutional and organizational tools to redress environmental shortfalls is mirrored by the economist's preoccupation with breakdowns in the institutions of exchange (which he refers to as "market failure"). The planner's normative pursuit of a "best" environment for human growth and happiness finds kindred expression in the economist's concept of "welfare."

Awareness of this underlying, policy-oriented conceptual structure led Resources for the Future in Washington and the Centre for Environmental Studies in London to join in an effort to endow the concept of quality of life with a richer policy and analytical content. Under their auspices, an International Research Conference on Public Policy and the Quality of Life in Cities was convened in New Orleans, January 2–7, 1975, bringing together economists, political scientists, planners,

---

[1] Later published as Lowdon Wingo, "The Quality of Life: Toward a Microeconomic Definition," *Urban Studies* vol. 10, no. 1 (February 1973) pp. 3–18.

and others engaged in research and policy activities related to quality of life issues. While British and American viewpoints and experience were most strongly represented, other participants spoke from the Swedish, French, Australian, and OECD perspectives. Save one, the papers in this volume evolved from that conference. The exception, Herbert Morton's paper on "Reflections on the Quality of Working Life," was solicited when we became aware that this major public policy sector was not represented among the materials presented at the conference.

While the authors of the papers in this volume are well known in their own fields and so do much to establish the credibility of the quality of life as a viable public policy construct, we would be remiss if we did not mention other distinguished participants in the conference, whose contributions and critical evaluations are represented in the content and quality of the papers making up this volume. These include Christian Averous, Mark Blaug, Otto Davis, Richard Easterlin, David Eversley, Colin Gannon, Harvey Garn, Anthony Harrison, Peter Hall, Werner Hirsch, Dick Netzer, Paul Portney, and Harry Verwaygen. My young colleague Charles Sawyer made a special contribution to the success of the conference.

The conference, in my judgment, helped to establish the policy relevance of quality of life concepts, while its participants maintained a caution not always found among economists and their coreligionists in the policy sciences when they deal with this protean subject. If this volume succeeds in conveying some of this caution, and the complexities of the issues, then the conference will have been most valuable indeed.

In the long run, it may even contribute to a more sophisticated understanding of the interaction between man and his environment, and to a broader synthesis of concepts and methods among the policy sciences, the behavioral sciences, and the environmental sciences.

Lowdon Wingo
School of Urban and Regional Planning
University of Southern California

June 1977

Introduction: Can Public Policy Improve the Quality of Life?

ALAN EVANS AND LOWDON WINGO

Policy Aspects of the Quality of Life

IN recent years increasing concern has been voiced over the consequences and prospects of continuing economic growth. E. J. Mishan's *The Costs of Economic Growth* (1967) has become a rallying point for many who contend that increases in gross national product lead inevitably to increased pollution, congestion, and other external diseconomies which counter the apparent increase in economic welfare. In response, Nordhaus and Tobin (1972) have tried to measure the extent of this reduction in welfare at the macroeconomic level; Easterlin (1973) and King (1974) have provided alternative indicators of differences in economic welfare; at the microeconomic level, Walters (1975) has attempted to obtain better measures of the incidence of these diseconomies, and Griffin (1974) has attempted the same for the costs of controlling them. Baumol and Oates (1971) have sought to devise more effective methods of control.

Another contingent identified with Forrester (1971), Meadows and coauthors (1972), and the Club of Rome has argued that the finiteness of world resources limits the growth of gross *world* product and makes the case for policies aimed at achieving zero growth rates. Wilfred Beckerman's *In Defense of Economic Growth* (1975) accuses these "eco-doomsters" of ignorance of the facts of economic life—to wit, the processes by which a relatively plentiful good will be substituted for another which is becoming scarce, the implications of discounting, and the fact that the quantity of "known" resources of any natural material is defined by the costliness of exploration and the technology of extraction.

J. K. Galbraith's *The Affluent Society* (1958) and *The New Industrial State* (1967) take the position that the developed economies

1

have passed the stage at which the basic needs of their populations for food, clothing, and shelter can be easily met, and that in reality industrial output is determined by manipulating the wants of the consumer through advertising and those of the government through political lobbying in the military-industrial complex. Indeed, once the basic needs of the population have been met, further increases in the gross national product through the production of goods which consumers and governments have been made to want may not increase welfare in any meaningful sense: such production preempts public expenditure on amenities which would in fact be "preferred" by the population. Hence, there is "private affluence and public squalor."

Each of these arguments converges on the conclusion that less importance should be attached to the production and consumption of goods and more to the other aspects of human experience. Preoccupation with the quantity of private goods consumed should give way to a larger concern for those relationships between the individual and his environment encompassed by the concept of the "quality of life." The precise nature of the quality of life is not easily specified. Lowdon Wingo identifies the quality of life as a function of market failure, the social character of consumption, and the mediating role of social choice processes in his discussion in this volume. David Donnison, by contrast, relates the quality of life to the objectives of government social policy —levels of health, welfare, and education, as well as the distribution of income. What is clear is that, as Wingo points out, it is now incumbent on policy makers to take into account the impact governmental measures will have on the quality of life. But why should the quality of life assume such importance at this time? Why should we *now* be so concerned about pollution when by all accounts pollution in the industrial cities of the nineteenth century was so much more oppressive?

Surely the explanation lies in the fact that in the developed economies the basic needs of the population have been largely met. All those lines of argument set out above are in a sense a product of an affluent society. If the basic needs of food, shelter, and clothing have not been provided, it is difficult to argue that the benefits of any increase in production are outweighed by increases in congestion and pollution, or that natural resources should be conserved for future populations, or that the demand for increased production is being created and manipulated by the producers. That all three of these views are features of a wealthy society can be inferred from the fact that they are generally given short shrift by the poor within the developed economies and by the leaders of the underdeveloped economies, both regarding economic growth as needed to provide the basic necessities they currently lack. Furthermore, in the developed economies, economic growth and technological development have made it possible to achieve a variety of qualitative improvements in the environment at comparatively low social costs.

Pollution in nineteenth-century England must have had the same inevitability as the law of gravity—one could not repeal it, one could only seek the least troublesome way to live with it. Increasingly, now, we know that what stands between us and the environmental qualities we seek are not technical barriers but institutional constraints, not so much matters of science but of art in the rearrangement of institutions and social processes. The requirements of technology, the distribution of rights, and the wants of the public need to be articulated. Economics, the law, and the electorate will all delineate the quality of life to which the public will have access. If these areas overlap in some matter affecting the quality of life, and the law and technology permit it, an opportunity exists for the political will to choose an improvement in this quality. While David Donnison's contribution to this book examines how the specialist properly works to advance the quality of life, Edwin T. Haefele analyzes the characteristics of a properly functioning political system in which the public, however constrained by traditions and the state of technique, remains sovereign. Haefele's civil calculus becomes a tool for reducing the institutional barriers which obstruct the proper exercise of social choice.

The decreasing importance of goods and commodities and the increasing importance of subjective responses of individuals to their environment can also be seen in the structural changes which have been taking place in the developed economies. For years it has been predicted that increasing productivity (economic growth) resulting from technical change and the accumulation of capital would allow great reductions in the time spent in work and present people with a growing leisure problem, as the four, three, or even two-day week became normal. In fact, things haven't quite turned out like that. It is true that hours of work have generally fallen, but the rate of decrease has been fairly slow. Economic progress has instead resulted in an improvement in the conditions of work, the quality of life at the workplace, a topic which is briefly discussed by Herbert Morton in this volume. Part of this change has resulted from a shift in employment out of manufacturing industry and into services (and a shift within manufacturing industry from production itself to office work). In part, labor is being transferred from the more easily mechanized to the less easily mechanized jobs (Baumol, 1967), but this shift is also a response to satiation in the provision of manufactured goods, and to the fact that when increases in leisure time do occur, they result in an increased demand for services and "experiential environments" to be "consumed" in that leisure time. Things as such—goods or commodities—become less important over time, and services, qualities, and all kinds of externalities and other "nonmarket" goods become more important. The demand for such "qualities" appears to be highly income elastic: the demand for qualitative improvements increases disproportionately as income increases. As evidence, Walters (1975) calculates that the income elasticity of demand for quiet is in the region of 1.7 to 2.0, a relatively high figure. While his cross-sectional data offer evidence that quiet is more highly valued by the rich than the poor within a society, it suggests the plausibility, also, of the proposition that as incomes generally increase, quiet will become generally more highly valued. Studies of the incidence of air quality improvements suggest the same conclusions.

The major difficulty with a concept such as the quality of life is measurement, which in one way or another is the concern of almost all the papers in this volume. Whereas we can easily measure physical *quantities* and changes in such quantities, even with the index number problem of measuring aggregate changes, it is much more difficult to measure *qualities* and changes in qualities, let alone aggregate them, since the subjective problems, which can be relegated to the pricing processes when dealing with quantities, enter at an earlier stage in the case of qualities. While it may be unarguable that the quantity of a good produced has increased, whether a change in quality is a change for better or worse is a matter of taste. Further complicating this problem is the fact that the components of "the quality of life" almost necessarily have the character of nontraded and nontradable goods.

Economic Attributes of the Quality of Life

The economist cannot, however, sit on the sidelines leaving others to do the dirty jobs he is too fastidious to touch. If improving the quality of life is to be a goal of policy makers, then the policy maker will be served well by advice from economists on the means of attaining that goal. The initial reaction of most economists to this role is that the necessary tools lie in applied welfare economics, since improvements in the quality of life are almost necessarily defined at the microeconomic level. While the major economic problems of the past forty or fifty years have been essentially macroeconomic—general and regional unemployment, inflation (in more or less that temporal order)—advice on economic policy to improve the quality of life must involve the assessment of the microeconomic impact of particular policies. The usual method of assessment is some form of cost–benefit analysis, which has become quite highly developed in the past fifteen or twenty years, particularly in the new branches of applied economics—the economics of health and education, urban economics, and the economics of the environment —as well as in the older field of transportation economics.

The assessment and comparison of the costs and benefits of a policy may, however, be regarded as an inadequate measure of improvements in the quality of life. In this volume, for example, Alan Williams takes the measurement of the quality of life of the elderly, and argues that the apparatus of Paretian welfare economics is of little help in this instance. The quality of life of the elderly, in his view, should not in fact be measured by assessing the financial worth of any environmental change to them, but by the use of some measure of the state of health of the person, since "pain-free survival" is of overriding importance for this age group. Williams believes that economists will, however, have something to contribute regarding the construction of this measure because of their experience in gauging the importance of trading off one cost or benefit against another, in this case one kind of pain against another.

Cost–benefit analysis identifies a policy as acceptable if the aggregate financial value of the proposed improvements in people's welfare outweighs that of the decreases. But, in almost all cases, some people must be net gainers and others net losers. Should one take other differences between these two populations into account? A. J. Culyer's article argues that a too thoroughgoing application of cost–benefit analysis to the choice of policies can damage the quality of life by cutting across what he calls, following Tarasovsky, the "Cherished Illusions" of the population—that the police will protect the population equally or that the medical services will treat each patient equally well. The widespread, straightforward application of cost–benefit analysis could demolish these illusions by implying that the police should protect the goods of the rich or the lives of the young more assiduously than the goods of the poor or the lives of the elderly, or that expenditure on medical treatment accorded to a person might depend on his value to the community. Culyer here supports concern for the plight of the aged in a world governed by efficiency conditions.

The more usual charge against cost–benefit analysis as the basis for choosing policy is its perversity in matters of equity: the net losers from a policy may already be, in some sense, worse off than the net gainers and one would therefore prefer to make them better rather than worse off. In Culyer's view, the economist should remain silent on distributional questions, for the sake of both professional modesty and logical consistency, presenting the results of a cost–benefit analysis, if one is to be used, to the policy maker and allowing him to make his own choice on grounds of equity. David Pearce, on the other hand, argues against the sanctity of judgments based on Paretian welfare economics, contending that the effects of alternative welfare judgments should be made clear to policy makers.

Suppose, however, that one is willing to set these problems aside and to attempt to determine the optimal policy, taking into account its costs and benefits; how does one go about estimating the costs and benefits to the persons affected? One alternative is a direct approach; one can ask people how much they are willing to pay for alternative policies, a procedure discussed by Peter Bohm and also by Michael Whitbread.

A second alternative is to attempt to estimate directly the costs arising from the absence of these policies. Thus, Mitchell Polinsky and Daniel Rubinfeld suggest two direct methods to measure the costs of pollution: *health studies*, which seek to determine the relationship between improvements in the environment and human health and then place a dollar value on these health improvements; and *cost studies*, which seek to ascertain the extra costs created by environmental disamenities, such as the physical damage to buildings attributable to polluted air. The difficulty with these methods is that they are partial and complementary rather than competitive.

One has to measure the value of all types of health improvements *and* the value of all types of physical damage and one may never be sure that some other cost has not been missed. Moreover, aesthetic improvements cannot be so measured; the aesthetic value to the population of a less polluted environment must be found by some other means, and added to the other costs. Similarly, certain types of environmental improvement cannot be measured in this way; for example, if a noise is below a certain level there is no physical or physiological damage, even though the noise may be unpleasant.

A third strategy estimates the costs and benefits indirectly by finding out what valuation people put on a nontraded good by examining their behavior with respect to that and some other good which is traded. In transport project assessment, this method has been used to evaluate savings in travel time by studying people's behavior in choosing between faster but more expensive and slower but cheaper travel modes. With respect to pollution, Polinsky and Rubinfeld suggest two indirect methods; *wage rate studies*, which seek to determine the wage differences among urban areas for a given quality labor necessary to compensate for urban disamenities; and *property value studies* which seek to determine the relationship between property values and environmental amenities in order to predict change in aggregate property values (interpreted as willingness to pay) resulting from an environmental improvement.

Examples of both these methods appear in this volume. They suffer from one disadvantage in common with simply asking people: they assume that people know the value to themselves of some difference in their circumstances, and this may not be the case. For instance, Pearce cites cadmium as an example of a pollutant which may be observed to have both spatial and temporal effects on people far from its source because it can be transported and because it can be stored. If persons who may suffer from it are unaware of the risk, then they will make no allowance for it in choosing among jobs at different wage rates and houses at different prices. An associated disadvantage of measuring environmental differences by measuring differences between wage rates or property values, or both, is that the measure will be correct only if the different property or labor markets are in equilibrium. If the differences between property values and/or wage levels are felt to be incorrect, then people will migrate between areas. This migration has itself been used as an indicator of environmental differences, for example, by Lave, Lave, and Seskin (1974) who explained intraurban migration by environmental differences between U.S. cities and their suburbs. But if there is migration because of these differences, then the property or labor markets cannot be in equilibrium, and if they were in equilibrium there would be no migration.

Moreover, Alan Evans makes the case that migration resulting from environmental differences may result in the elimination of these differences under conditions of equilibrium. If people migrating to environmentally favored areas degrade the environment for themselves and others because of the higher density in the favored area, then local environmental improvements may be countered by in-migration and the resulting changes in property values will reflect the market consequences of both this environmental improvement and the in-migration. It might thus be difficult, in equilibrium, to obtain a true assessment of the worth of an environmental improvement unless there are controls on in-migration. But Hamilton's empirical study of the effect of zoning on the progressivity of the property tax shows that controls raise difficult problems with respect to equity and deliberate redistribution as a feature of the quality of life in a developed economy.

While property values are more usually used to estimate the value of differences between residential areas *within* urban areas, wage levels are usually used to estimate the value of differences *between* urban areas within a nation. The latter offers the more difficult problem. In particular, while it may be relatively easy to specify the valued differences among various residential areas, it may be difficult to specify these differences for urban areas: Thus, Meyer and Leone, and Hoch are preoccupied with the search for plausible variables. It is also more difficult to demonstrate equilibrium in the national labor market, given the long periods over which migration among regions has occurred.

Moreover, the residents of an area may pay lower prices for land because of its unfavorable attributes. The owner of the land has to accept these lower prices because he has no choice; he cannot move the land. If the residents of an urban area wish to be paid higher wages for living in that area, firms may be under no compulsion to pay these higher wages if their location is not fixed, so they must be getting some benefit. This benefit may be merely the ability to pollute (for which the firm partially compensates residents by paying higher wages); but if it is not, then the differences between the urban areas must not only be environmental attributes affecting consumers, but also the sort of qualities which affect firms.

We must conclude that the declining importance of consumer goods and the increasing importance of the nontraded experiences contributing to "the quality of life" will not make life easier for economists, but rather the reverse. At a macroeconomic level, economic welfare cannot be measured by crude statistics such as gross national product but must, as Olson shows, be adjusted to take into account, at the least, the most obvious external effects. At the microeconomic level, welfare economics ceases to be an academic exercise and assumes greater importance as a tool of government. Moreover, the role of government itself becomes greater. If the production of goods is of primary importance, then there are well-known arguments suggesting that information need only be minimal. In a wealthy society, as the consumption of goods tends toward satiation, then, as we argued earlier, externalities become more and more important. But, as Pearce argues in his paper, it is necessary for government to intervene to ensure the optimal regulation of these external effects, so that greater intervention becomes necessary. Nearly all of the papers in this book are concerned with economics as a tool of government to ensure that this regulation is optimal. It is also true, however, that the political process itself becomes more important both because of the necessity to intervene and the necessity to reflect the wishes of the public.

References

Baumol, William J. 1967. "Macroeconomics of Unbalanced Growth," *American Economic Review* vol. LVII, no. 3 (June) pp. 415–426.

————, and Wallace E. Oates. 1975. *The Theory of Environmental Policy: Externalities, Public Outlays and the Quality of Life* (Englewood Cliffs, N.J., Prentice-Hall).

Beckerman, Wilfred. 1975. *Two Cheers for the Affluent Society, A Spirited Defense of Economic Growth* (New York, St. Martin's Press).

Easterlin, Richard A. 1973. "Does Money Buy Happiness?" *The Public Interest* vol. 30 (Winter) pp. 3–10.

Forrester, Jay W. 1971. *World Dynamics* (Cambridge, Mass., Wright-Allen).

Galbraith, John Kenneth. 1958. *The Affluent Society* (Boston, Houghton Mifflin).

————. 1967. *The New Industrial State* (Boston, Houghton Mifflin).

Griffin, James. 1974. "An Econometric Evaluation of Sulfur Taxes," *Journal of Political Economy* vol. 82, no. 4 (July/August) pp. 669–688.

King, Mervyn A. 1974. "Economic Growth and Social Development—A Statistical Investigation," *Review of Income and Wealth* Series 20, no. 3 (September) pp. 251–272.

Lave, Lester B., Judith R. Lave, and Eugene P. Seskin. 1974. "Migration and Urban Change," in J. G. Rothenberg and Ian G. Heggie, eds., *Transport and the Urban Environment* (London, Macmillan).

Meadows, Donella H., Dennis L. Meadows, Jorgen Randers, and William W. Behrens III. 1972. *The Limits to Growth*. A Report for the Club of Rome's project on the Predicament of Mankind (New York, Universe Books).

Mishan, E. J. 1967. *The Costs of Economic Growth* (London, Staples Press).

Nordhaus, William D., and James Tobin. 1972. "Is Growth Obsolete?" in National Bureau of Economic Research, 50th Anniversary Colloquium, vol. 5, *Economic Growth* (New York, NBER).

Walters, Alan A. 1975. *Noise and Prices* (London, Oxford University Press).

Wingo, Lowdon. 1973. "The Quality of Life: Toward A Microeconomic Definition," *Urban Studies* vol. 10, no. 1 (February) pp. 3–18.

PART I

1
Objective, Subjective, and Collective Dimensions of the Quality of Life

LOWDON WINGO

1. Introduction

"QUALITY" has become the byword in American public policy in the 1970s, succeeding "poverty" in the '60s and "growth" in the preceding decade. We appear to have become relatively more interested in "better" than in "more," which a society can afford to do once it has "enough." And what could be of greater interest to any of us than "life"? In this context "quality" is a normative concept—the quality of life is seen as being good or bad, as improving or deteriorating, as being better in some cases than in others. The term "life," however, may be misleading. Here, it refers to *human* life. Even so, for some it would mean the interactions of the vital processes which define "being alive"; for us, rather, it refers to the human being as an *experiencer*, for it is this dimension of life that underlies collective behavior and, as a consequence, collective welfare. And in this sense it becomes the focus of our attention.

The concept of the quality of life offers scholars a basis for expanding comparatively restricted positive and normative models of human behavior in the direction of more comprehensive propositions about how people and groups pursue their well-being. Finding, testing, and agreeing upon such propositions are tasks for the behavioral sciences; evaluating them is a task for social ethics. At present, the neoclassical model of economic behavior is the most accessible conceptual apparatus we have to integrate testable propositions about behavior with normative judgments about the outcomes of such behavior. It contends that when

The overall support of this project by Resources for the Future is gratefully acknowledged, as is the special and valuable contribution of Charles Sawyer in the preparation of this manuscript.

13

confronted with divisible and excludable goods reflecting the true costs of production, the individual behavior of a set of consumers, each of whom pursues his own self-interest, has perfect knowledge of the characteristics and prices of all relevant goods and equal access to them, and is indifferent to the consumption behavior of all others, leads inexorably to a "best" employment of such goods, that is, that producing the greatest possible volume of gratification to the consumers. Since in reality consumption and production conditions diverge in varying degrees from these propositions, the *raison d'être* of public policy, an economist might argue, is to repair, or compensate for these "imperfections"—to goad society into acting as though the neoclassical model were real and its optimum the *summum bonum*.

A postulate that underlies basic economic theory is that human behavior is rational in that it is governed by self-interest, that is, by the *hedonistic* quality of experience.[1] Thus, one framework for defining the quality of life is not unfamiliar. The neoclassical economic model deals with consumption, that is, experiences dependent on the use of scarce resources (or increased entropy, if you prefer). A model of the quality of life will, accordingly, have an intimate relationship to models of microeconomic behavior.

For those reluctant to accept so simple a view of man and what is significant in his experiential environment, a more appealing approach to policy may specify that the model "fit" more closely observed dimensions of the "real" world and then proceed by successively relaxing the conditions of the neoclassical model to propagate models of greater generality. For example, we could allow for interdependence among consumers by dropping the individualistic postulate of neoclassical economic behavior, which would lead us to look beyond the model of individual preferences to the social context of consumption. We could, further, relax the specification that the relevant goods be tradable, which would require going beyond final consumption of market goods to other kinds of human experience and behavioral responses. In addition to firms, consumers, goods, prices, and markets as basic elements, a quality of life paradigm will need to deal more generally with normatively distinguished "experiences," social organization, quasi-markets, and social gains or losses, and include the behavior of political institutions and, hence, policy. A model of this sort, however, could end up being so diffuse, so complex, or so general that it would contribute little either to an understanding of behavior or to an evaluation of its consequences; it would, in fact, be empty and formal.

---

[1] That is, the capacity of an experience to give pleasure or pain to the experiencer.

Recent work on the environment and externalities has led, indeed, to some revision of the standard neoclassical model: the acquisition of a good via the market is *not* isomorphic with consumption, and consumption is not isomorphic with gratification. Nevertheless, such an analogue offers a plan for this paper: the external and internal dimensions of this relationship can be studied as the "objective–subjective" dimensions of experience, and especially the type of experience called consumption. We can then examine the objective conditions which elicit normatively identifiable responses in the individual; that is, we can examine some of the *supply* conditions of the quality of life. Then we can pursue the definitional question through some examination of the relevant subjective, or *demand*, conditions underlying responses to changes in the objective conditions. Finally, we will briefly look at the impact of collective institutions on the quality of life.

2. Aspects of the Quality of Life "Objectively" Defined

Specification of the supply characteristics of the quality of life can be generated from successive relaxations of the ideal case described by the conditions of the neoclassical model of economic behavior. We can begin with Isard's criticism that a crucial implied condition of the neoclassical model is that no cost be incurred by producers or consumers between successive stages of production or between the production of final goods and their consumption. There are no transfer costs, transportation is free, space is fictitious. If one relaxes this condition by allowing for positive transfer costs, the neoclassical model becomes a special case of a more general "space economy" model in which the location of consumption and production activities becomes an essential dimension (Isard, 1956).

Within this more general model, in recent years much of microeconomic analysis has been preoccupied with the locational behavior of profit-maximizing firms confronting distribution of markets and resource sources. Spatial equilibrium is defined by $P_{ik} = (MC)_{ik}$, where P_{ik} refers to the price of good k at place i; in this expression the marginal cost of k at i reflects both the technological and spatial margins and defines for each good a set of market areas. The spatial distribution of natural resources and population is exogenous. Disturbances in the distribution equilibrium can arise from (1) changes in production conditions stemming from the effect of technological change on the spatial MC surfaces and hence on the structure of market areas, or changes in location patterns caused by different sets of resource inputs, or (2) changes in demand conditions caused by changing population distributions, secular shifts in the structure of consumer preferences, or relative changes in prices or disposable income.

Up to this point, a modification of the neoclassical model is of marginal interest in quality of life terms. If labor is perfectly mobile and exclusively motivated by the consumption of market goods, wages for similar work will be equal everywhere, and no one will have any incentive to change labor markets (migrate). But this would be true only if the ratio of the wage rate to labor's marginal physical product were the same everywhere, a condition satisfied either where producing centers are the same size or where no costs or benefits are uniquely associated with urban scale. Clearly, all centers of production are *not* the same size.

What, then, is there to disturb the relationship between the wage rate and labor's marginal physical product? If the labor input is construed to be the product of a technology assembling and organizing labor skills at the production site, then labor input is an intermediate good, and the wage becomes payment for the intermediate good, "labor." The production costs of labor, then, will include not only the opportunity costs to each individual of the time, energy, and attention required by his job, but also the daily costs of transferring labor from home to work. Urban rent theory argues that land values will vary inversely with transportation costs, or distance, from the center to the margin of the city. Since that distance will tend to vary with size of city, the sum of an individual's rent and commuting costs for similar housing types and densities will also vary with size of city.[2] If, then, labor's marginal physical product is everywhere the same, the wage rate will vary with city size. As a pecuniary diseconomy of scale, this variation in labor costs will counter the technological economies of urban scale from industry to industry. With perfect mobility among settlements then, the worker in the *large* city will obviously value the additional time required for commuting less than the increment in wages; the reverse is true for the worker in the smaller community: each finds his best balance between income and leisure.

Thus, the space economy—with economies of scale in production and diseconomies of urban scale with respect to labor—is automatically differentiated by qualities which engage individual preference systems in different ways. Given a free and knowledgeable opportunity to do so, each person would make the locational choice most consistent with his relative valuation of leisure, living space (or density), and income. At equilibrium, wages would *not* be equal among cities, but would reflect

[2] The case here is made only with respect to rent and transfer costs. Hoch (1972) has made it more generally for all diseconomies of urban scale.

differences in the composition of local labor forces in terms of individual preferences for money, time, and space.

While most location theory treats production and consumption in terms of *physical* resource inputs, Harvey Perloff has pointed out that general environmental conditions are frequently treated as consumption goods, which he has referred to as *amenity* resources (Perloff and coauthors, 1960; Perloff and Wingo, 1961). Coastlines, benign climatic conditions, and access to unusual or appealing landscapes enter into utility functions as readily as do more conventional market goods. The massive shift of the U.S. population toward the West and South during the past century and the more recent emptying out of the American heartland suggest the value of these environmental goods. At equilibrium, then, wage rates will also vary from place to place according to the valuation of these amenity resources at the margin.

Now, some of these goods are becoming increasingly rival (i.e., subject to congestion). Many of the early attractions of California have been lost through the impact of rapid population growth. Seeing its prospective future in California's recent past, Oregon, like several other states, is seeking explicit policies to discourage further population growth in order to preserve its amenity resources. Clearly, the individual pursuit of these goods over an extended period has substantially affected the nature of the quality of life in the United States.

Treating amenity resources as "nonproduced" public goods suggests a relaxation of yet another condition of the neoclassical model. Let us now consider publicly produced, local, *nonrival* public goods, such as education, personal security, or public health, which are characterized by lack of segregability and, hence, joint consumption, and which are characteristically produced by local governmental units responding to the preferences of their constituencies. In a well-known article, Charles Tiebout reasoned that if enough jurisdictions offered enough variety in the composition, quality, and tax prices of such goods, a consumer could treat each jurisdiction as though it were a composite but conventional good and then choose to "buy" the mix he most prefers by locating his household in the jurisdiction offering this mix.[3] To the extent that some jurisdictional bundles were *strongly* preferred, one would expect such preferences to be capitalized into the jurisdiction's land values, as the pressure of demand generates "rivalness" through the limitations of space in which to increase the number of dwelling units. Hence, although most such goods are nonrival technologically, they become rival through space limitations in the jurisdiction, and the degree

---

[3] Taking into consideration access costs to his place of work, of course. See Tiebout (1956).

of rivalry will be reflected in its land values. Tiebout's space economy of nonrival goods admits of no such limitations and would be in equilibrium if all residents were assigned to jurisdictions such that no one could improve his own welfare by changing location among jurisdictions.

Up to this point in our examination, the mechanism for pursuing improvements in the quality of life beyond market goods has been the quasi-market process of mobility, which responds to differential income and amenity attributes, modified by variations in transportation costs. But, as Hirschman (1970) has pointed out, actors on the economic stage of the market have three fundamental options: to stay and participate (i.e., to consume), to exit, or to use "voice" to express their dissatisfaction. Mobility involves an exit–stay decision that depends on one's awareness of opportunities for welfare gains that are sufficiently great to compensate for the perceived disutilities of relocation, but it offers no options to the dissatisfied consumer who finds no rewarding opportunities to relocate.

Clearly, the array of such nonrival public goods is not independent of the way in which jurisdictions are organized in space, nor of the preferences of their constituencies. These are determined by the collective choice mechanisms that the larger society has made available. The social constitution may acknowledge consumer sovereignty over local public goods and empower localities to divert some of the local social product for the production of such goods, while prescribing decision rules for aggregating community preferences; or it may define such goods to be uniquely invested with the interests of the larger society—to be *merit* goods—to be produced by the larger society and allocated by some egalitarian rule among its component parts. The first case describes the U.S. federal system, the latter the unitary systems characterizing Western Europe. In short, societies provide for a voice option in the production of local public goods, if for no other reason than to reduce the instability and inefficiency introduced by exclusive use of the exit option in the individual pursuit of a "best" feasible composite local good.

Since the output of public goods in the U.S. federal system depends on both the constitutional rule for aggregating preferences within jurisdictions and the composition of those preferences, any process affecting the composition of preferences will affect the output of public goods. Thus, distribution of the population among jurisdictions in such a way as to maximize homogeneity of preference for public goods in each jurisdiction would maximize welfare since all agree that in such a case the goods and their opportunity costs would produce the highest utility level for each individual. By contrast, if the constituents in each jurisdiction exhibit heterogeneous tastes, any outcome will leave dissatisfied many persons who, in the absence of loyalty to the locale or hope of reconstituting the output of public goods, would have incentive to migrate to a more compatible jurisdiction. Buchanan and Goetz (1972) have argued that while equilibrium is possible in a metropolitan region with the complementary exercise of voice and exit options, spatial variations in rents and transport costs contradict optimality conditions. McGuire (1972) has countered that such costs can be construed as the prices of access to these sets of local public goods. Indeed, the long-run equilibrium should be characterized by a large *heterogeneous* set of small *homogeneous* communities in each labor market area. Under these circumstances, large urban regions would have the same kind of advantage over smaller urban settlements that the large integrated supermarket has over the corner grocery—a more extensive array of (such composite local public) goods more efficiently purveyed.

We can now reintroduce the quality of rivalness as characterizing these composite goods, which implies that all members of all jurisdictions have a direct welfare interest in individual migration decisions. For example, if jurisdictions A and B are subject to increasing diseconomies of scale, the migrant who moves from A to B benefits the inhabitants of A by reducing by one unit the demand for its public goods and so improving the quality of those goods, and imposes a loss of welfare on the residents of B.[4] It would be to A's interest to bribe him to leave and B's to bribe him not to come. Migration is, hence, the great leveler with respect to rival public goods offered by a specified set of jurisdictions, so long as the act of migrating imposes differential costs and benefits on various constituencies. Since freedom of movement is fundamental to our system, and since factor mobility is directly related to allocative efficiency, society would pay a substantial welfare cost if it chose indiscriminately to restrict mobility to eliminate these unhappy external effects: we cannot forget that almost three and a half centuries of American history have been dominated by the assertion of the exit option in political and economic life.

The concept of the consumption club developed by Buchanan (1965) suggests a theoretical approach to the problem. If all jurisdictions declared themselves to be clubs charging new members (migrants) an initiation fee sufficient to compensate other club members for their loss of welfare at the margin, and if the charter of each club required it to

---

[4] Assuming, of course, that these qualitative gains and losses are not offset by the concurrent movement of his fiscal resources. The inhabitants of A may, indeed, be worse off if the apportioned loss of tax revenues is greater than the value of the improvement in the quality of the local public goods, and vice versa.

refund to the resigning member an amount equal to the gains his departure would bring to other members, then his move would be externality free: no community would gain or lose as a result of his decision and he would then make a substantially more rational consumption decision.

In the absence of such a mechanism, however, one can expect constituencies to act to protect the quality of their public goods. Unable to assess rational initiation fees, they tax entry indirectly by imposing restrictive regulations—zoning, housing, sanitation, taxes on real estate transactions, or limitations on new construction. While the end of such devices is frequently to maintain the public good of social homogeneity, they are also directed toward restricting growth and change which would erode the quality of highly rival local public goods. Integrated sets of such policies are now referred to as local "growth policies," designed to restrain, as far as the judicial processes permit, growing pressure on the community's quality of life.

The condition of rivalness seriously complicates the use of the neoclassical model in dealing with the quality of life. Individualistic behavior and a high degree of access to environmental or localized public goals will result in some combination of quality degradation and cost escalation. It follows that the control of the quality of such goods depends not only on the level of physical output, or capacity, but on the systematic regulation of their consumption by some formal or informal group. Once the relevant collective action and supporting institutions are launched, the level of gratification of no member can be viewed as independent of that of any other. This brings us around to examine the correspondence of the economist's concept of the utility function with the psychosocial processes which relate motivation to consumption behavior.

3. Subjective Dimensions of the Quality of Life

A definition of the quality of life can appropriately be compounded from the insights into human behavior provided by concepts from psychology and sociology. Here we may distinguish those focusing upon the internal state of the individual from those concentrating on the relations among individuals. In the first case, one's quality of life may be simply taken as a synonym for one's *happiness*, the nature of which has been the subject of twenty-five centuries of Western philosophical discourse, and the elusiveness of which has inspired the Eastern philosophical tradition.

If we take "happiness" to refer to so simple a thing as the gratification of human appetites and material aspirations, what is the origin of such a preference system? Cybernetically, it can be seen as a program that translates experience into action, but who is the programmer? Economic theory asks us to assume that individual preference programs are established extrabehaviorally and are relatively fixed—that they are given. Such assumptions would not preclude preference programs modified by learning, that is, by the systematic accumulation of experience. If God, the gene pool, and learning are the sole sources of the individual preference program, human behavior will be consistent with the individualistic postulate of economic theory.

It is only when the analyst has to allow for the fact that the preference program of one consumer depends on those of others, or that it can be reprogrammed deliberately from the outside, that the simplicity of the economist's conceptual structure is compromised. The normative qualities of the neoclassical system no longer hold: the consumer is no longer sovereign, but subject to *other* sovereignties—of producers through advertising, of governments through propaganda, of neighbors and associates as collectivities through the social disciplines which such groups impose on their members. He is constantly being reprogrammed as governments educate him and deliver collective services, as new commodities and services offer increasingly specialized kinds of gratification, as he perceives more and more the experiential requirements of preferred life-styles. Thus, needs, wants, whims, desires, drives, demands, and other preference-oriented constructs characterize the human preference system, which is in continuous flux because the human personality exists in a social environment that is constantly reordering experience and experiential opportunities.

The neoclassical model does not require that all consumers be carbon copies: diversity among individual preference structures does not compromise economic man, nor does some modest exogenous drift in his marginal rates of substitution. What the model does require is additivity among individual preference structures, to make conventional concepts of demand credible, and to preserve the normative qualities of the individual vote in the marketplace. If, on the other hand, I derive pleasure or pain from A's consumption of good J, then A's resulting gratification, or consumer surplus, is not an exact measure of the gains and losses to society from that act of consumption. Indeed, if A *knows* of my pleasure or pain, he may moderate his consumption according to some nonhedonic ethos—"do unto others as you would have them do unto you." If, furthermore, A knows that I know that he knows that his consumption of J can give me pleasure or pain, A will then be guided in part by the state of his affect for me in his consumption of J. Or I will *interpret* A's consumption of J to reflect the state of his affect for me. If A is a smoker and I am not, then A's pleasure from enjoying an after-dinner cigarette must be offset against my discomfort. If A knows of my discomfort, he may not even light up. If he knows that I know he knows of my discomfort, then he has good reason to believe that I will interpret his lighting up as an act of personal aggression from which consequences may flow which A might want to avoid. Where such consequences or "consumption externalities" exist, consumption is a *social*, not an individual act: not only does it affect the gratifications of other persons than the consumer, but it takes on social meaning in the relations of individuals to each other.[5]

Social consumption becomes, in fact, a mode of communication within and among social groupings. Obviously, to drive a Rolls-Royce is to use a symbol to communicate to the world one's identification with a social elite; a youth in ragged jeans may be no less concerned with social communication. When consumption takes on social meaning, it is no longer possible to say with conviction that the surplus gratifications received by the individual consumer represent the net change in the welfare of society, nor even to say the same after netting out conceptually all of the consumption externalities. Consumption as social communication goes beyond hedonism and the socially additive calculus of pleasure and pain; it is an act of communion, which, in conjunction with others, simultaneously individuates and collectivizes the consumer. It is the symbolic role of consumption in this individuation/collectivization process that advertising and marketing activities have richly understood.

From an analytical point of view, what is important is the fact that the normative qualities of social consumption transcend the hedonic gratifications of consumption and its externalities; at the micro level they are involved in the success with which the individual realizes a role in society complementary to his self-image, and at the macro level, in the success with which society organizes those roles to permit self-images to mature and be realized. The individualistic postulate of the economist cannot be sustained in those sectors of consumptive experience where hedonically motivated behavior cannot account for the amount and kind of consumption, for in these cases consumption is a means to other ends for which we have developed no such elegant normative calculus.

A nonradical translation of these propositions can be found in Kelvin Lancaster's reformulation of consumption theory following suggestions advanced by Stigler, Morishima, Becker, and others (Lancaster, 1966).

---

[5] While this point did not escape Marx, Veblen (1899) at the turn of the century analyzed the role of conspicuous consumption as a social rather than an individualistic form of behavior.

Much consumer behavior cannot be explained by the contention that the individual preference structure consists of normative distinctions among *goods* in consumption—indeed, people could be shown to have many different motives in similar consumption behavior. So something must intervene between the *act* of consumption and the structure of gratification, and that something must be associated directly with human preferences. Lancaster calls that something "characteristics," which appear to be much more related to subjectively defined wants or needs. "Goods" are, then, the inputs into "activities" which produce "characteristics," and activities can be expressed as matrices of coefficients. This formulation added versatility to consumption theory in its ability to deal with consumer behavior in relation to public goods as well as conventional market or private goods. It also suggested that new levels of complexity in the relationship between goods and human gratification were properly in the domain of economic analysis because the hedonic mechanisms were more complex than utility theory had anticipated. Lancaster here does not specifically treat the problem of interdependent utility functions or the nonhedonic calculus required to deal with social consumption.

The interesting contribution that emerges from Lancaster and others is the opportunity to see consumption behavior in other than hedonic terms, a fact which has critical implications for the integration of economic behavior in more general models of social behavior. Behavior can be most simply described by a combination of the hedonic calculus and memory. Such a combination (1) provides for a classification of experiences into those which are to be sought and those which are to be avoided; and (2) tags certain kinds of experience as anticipatory to those to be sought or avoided and programs (conditions) them to trigger avoidance-attraction behavior. On such a conceptual structure rests much of behavioral psychology. For the economist, the avoidance-attraction program becomes a calculus in which the hedonic value of any prospective consumptive experience (good) is precise and stable. It follows, then, that if all consumptive experiences are characterized by pleasure or pain, the hedonist will maximize the net balance of pleasure, which is to say that he will find a pattern of consumption such that the experiences of another "unit" of pain (disutility, say, of labor) will be equated with a comparable quantity of pleasure (utility, say, of consumption made possible by the marginal disutility of labor).

Lancaster's "consumption technology" allows the consumption of goods to be related to a more erudite view of social behavior. In the first place, the qualities that enter into the individual's preference system can be defined by the social context in which the individual lives. The hope of Heaven, the high regard of one's fellows, the requirements of institutional roles, privacy, these are "metagoods" around which motivation is organized and for the production of which goods are consumed. Such metagoods are, for us, the dimensions of the quality of life.

In the second place, Lancaster's preference system structures his C-(for "characteristics") spaces. This expresses the dependence of the individual's quality of life on the utilization of his resources of time, skill, experience, and intelligence to achieve some best or better mix of these dimensions of the quality of life. A home in the country is more than a flow of housing services; it has, in addition, technological relations to privacy, intimacy with nature, prestige, indeed, to spirituality.

Social consumption then, has as its principal objective social communion. For the consumptive act to be symbolic, it must be rich in meaning for the consumer. Not only must he know and experience the significance of the act of consumption, but that understanding must be widely shared. The artifacts with which I embellish my home, the schools to which I send my children, how I spend my holidays—all are messages I transmit to a social audience as much as they are acts of self-gratification. But each of us must be confident that he knows what the message will "mean" to the audience.

Social consumption is part of a social language which is defined external to the individual, and it is his facility with that language which makes him ultimately a social being and a personality in the fullest sense. While consumption theory has not pursued the individual beyond hedonism, any concept of the quality of life which limits itself to hedonism in dealing with the quality of human experience will ultimately be found to be little more than a sentimental synonym for economic welfare.

The social context of consumption, then, cannot easily be disengaged from the experiential quality of life. Certainly there must be a high degree of stability in social behavior for social communication to take place; one must not only know what he means by his behavior but have confidence that others understand what it is that he is trying to communicate. Values, mores, and customs provide the language and the stability out of which more formal social processes and institutions may be maintained. This social language must be extensively shared if society is to be able to decide on the distribution of goods that do not fit into the neoclassical model of consumption behavior.

4. A Note on Collective Institutions and the Quality of Life

Neoclassical economic man exists in a world that lacks a government to deflect him from his utility-maximizing course. By some accounts, it is only because his single-minded behavior as a producer or consumer sometimes affects the welfare of others that government need exist at all. But the fact of government underlies any discourse about the quality of life; indeed, we look to it to reorganize society's incentives to improve the quality of our experience, and we expect it to do so by being sensitive to the interdependence of our gratifications. We accept the fact that the collective power of government to manipulate the environment sets up the rules by which each person plays the utility-maximizing game. Rivalness of goods and the social context of individual gratifications make the behavior of government a necessary element in any model of the quality of life.

Three principal functions of government need to be specified in such a model:

1. Definition of property. Government continuously distinguishes which goods are to be treated as common, public, or private. While this is not a completely discretionary choice, public policy has a wide latitude in determining the property status of societal goods. Common property becomes reclassified as public when symptoms of rivalness begin to show, as in the early history of American public lands, or in the more recent history of air quality regulation. While public property frequently becomes redefined as private when governments convey individual rights to the use of property in the public domain, private property is continuously being redefined to reflect a more general collective interest. The continuing controversy over the regulation of strip mining in the United States is a case in point, as was the British socialization of development rights after the war. This governmental function defines the market or quasi-market processes which give individuals or groups access to society's output.

2. Determination of the bill of public goods—pure, impure, local, and national. The way society mobilizes its collective choice processes will delimit the variety, quality, and costs of major components of the quality of life. While some goods are technologically pure and national, others become public goods at the national level through public policies that make them ubiquitous. More recently, the trend has been toward a larger role for local public goods in the total array of the public sector output, a consequence of what has come to be known as the New Federalism. More generally, a social constitution, written or unwritten, (1) defines the jurisdictional structure of government, (2) distributes the authority to produce public goods, and (3) specifies the way in which resources may be mobilized for that purpose.

3. Bounding of the private goods sector. Government not only creates the environment for the private economy, but influences the

distribution of the benefits accruing from private sector production. It may define some goods as pernicious (heroin and pornography) and others benign (medicine and recreation). It can encourage or discourage innovation and determine the incidence of costs to be borne by consumers and nonconsumers.

The nature of public goods, the socialization of individual gratifications, and the mediating role of social choice processes embedded in the institutions of government are, then, essential elements in the definition of the quality of life. Bridging the gulf between each person's experiential environment and his motivations and gratifications poses no little challenge to interdisciplinary research and philosophical speculation. For a society dedicated to improving the quality of individual lives, sensitivity to this relationship is an essential condition of public policy.

References

Buchanan, James M. 1965. "An Economic Theory of Clubs," *Economica* New Series, vol. 32, no. 135 (February) pp. 1–14.

———, and Charles J. Goetz. 1972. "Efficiency Limits of Fiscal Mobility: An Assessment of the Tiebout Model," *Journal of Public Economics* vol. 1, no. 1, pp. 25–43.

Hirschman, A. E. 1970. *Exit, Voice and Loyalty* (Cambridge, Mass., Harvard University Press).

Hoch, Irving. 1972. "Income and City Size," *Urban Studies* vol. 9, no. 3 (October) pp. 299–328.

Isard, Walter. 1956. *Location and Space Economy* (Cambridge, Mass., MIT Press).

Lancaster, Kelvin J. 1966. "A New Approach to Consumer Theory," *Journal of Political Economy* vol. 74, no. 2 (April) pp. 132–157.

Maslow, Abraham H. 1970. *Motivation and Personality* 2nd ed. (New York, Harper & Row) pp. 149 ff.

McGuire, Martin. 1972. "Private Good Clubs and Public Good Clubs: Economic Models of Group Formation," *Swedish Journal of Economics* vol. 74, no. 1 (March) pp. 84–99.

Perloff, Harvey S., and Lowdon Wingo, Jr. 1961. "Natural Resource Endowment and Regional Economic Growth," in Joseph J. Spengler, ed., *Natural Resources and Economic Growth* (Baltimore, Johns Hopkins University Press for Resources for the Future).

———, Edgar S. Dunn, Jr., Eric E. Lampard, and Richard F. Muth. 1960. *Regions, Resources and Economic Growth* (Baltimore,

Johns Hopkins University Press for Resources for the Future) pp. 471–475.

Tiebout, Charles. 1956. "A Pure Theory of Local Expenditures," *Journal of Political Economy* vol. 64, no. 5 (October).

U.S. Environmental Protection Agency. 1973. *The Quality of Life Concept: A Potential New Tool for Decision Makers* (Washington, EPA).

Veblen, Thorstein. 1899. *The Theory of the Leisure Class* (New York, Macmillan).

2
Variations in the Quality of Urban Life Among Cities and Regions

IRVING HOCH

1. Introduction

THIS paper examines variations in the quality of urban life among cities and regions by relating various measures of well-being to urban scale, which is primarily measured by population size, and to regional dummy variables. The unit of observation is usually the Standard Metropolitan Statistical Area (SMSA), which, in most cases, corresponds well to what we usually mean by "urban area." This paper continues a line of inquiry reported in several previous papers (Hoch, 1972a, b; 1974a in particular). The central thesis of the work is that the quality of life declines, on net, with increases in urban scale, which is defined to embrace both population size and density. As a consequence, workers must be paid higher money wages to compensate for the decline in quality and to achieve equivalent real income in all places.

Quality of life is defined here as encompassing both money and nonpecuniary components under the argument that one can often be traded for the other; for example, rent can be traded for travel time, or a person can spend more on cleaning or live under dirtier conditions as particulate air pollution increases.

It seems plausible that increases in money cost with urban scale primarily involve rent increases, which in turn affect most consumption items by way of multiplier effects. Many nonpecuniary costs stem from crowding, or the effects of density, but I see population size as the primary scale variable, for with larger size there will be a bidding up of land values and rents, more intensive use of the land, and hence, higher

---

Judith Drake served as research assistant on the work for this project and developed data and carried out computations for a number of the tables in this paper.

density. There are nonpecuniary benefits as well as costs of scale, generally a consequence of increased specialization and division of labor, but I read the evidence as showing that nonpecuniary costs outweigh benefits.

Of course, observed money differentials in wages between places may involve disequilibrium as well as, or instead of, compensatory payments. In fact, in the following section I interpret the evidence to mean that lower wage rates in the South are primarily the result of disequilibrium rather than compensation for a higher quality of life resulting from better climate. But I interpret other evidence as indicating that urban scale differentials are primarily compensatory in nature, since they seem remarkably stable over time, and appear to bear no particular relation to population growth rate.

An equilibrium model underlies my thesis. It assumes there is a long-run upward-sloping supply of labor that holds for all urban areas, with equilibrium for each area determined by that supply curve plus the specific local demand curve reflecting each area's specific production function. Hence, large urban areas have become large because they are relatively more efficient, the reverse of the argument that they are more efficient because they are large.[1] Such areas must pay higher wage rates to compensate for the quality deterioration that occurs with size, as expressed in the upward-sloping labor supply curve.

The bulk of this paper presents empirical evidence for my thesis. Section 2 is a detailed documentation of the effect of urban size and region on wage rates and per capita incomes. Section 3 considers some of the factors that explain the urban and regional wage differentials established in section 2. The last part of the paper, section 4, briefly presents some implications of the results.

In the empirical work, the emphasis is on urban size, rather than density, as the primary variable of interest, because population size turned out to be much more important than density in explaining wage differentials. The empirical work primarily involves estimation by single equation regression, under the argument that population size, at a point in time, is essentially exogenous. Future work may well involve the development of simultaneous relationships, but the present simpler and more economic approach appears to be defensible in terms of both theoretical rationale and empirical results obtained.

---

[1] Gordon Cameron (1973, p. 24) has argued that "few dispute that the large city is highly productive and thereby generates high incomes." But I interpret my results to mean the large city is large because it is productive, and is not necessarily productive because it is large. Further, "high" incomes must be generated if workers are to locate and remain in large cities.

The definition of quality of life employed here, essentially corresponding to personal welfare, seemed most useful and convenient in the present context. Lowdon Wingo (1973 and chapter 1, this volume) presents a cogent discussion of the issues and policy implications of alternative definitions. In particular, Wingo's preferred definition stresses the environmental (both physical and social) and interpersonal aspects of the quality of life concept. This paper, in effect, takes tastes and preferences as given; Wingo's concern with the social processes involved in the formation of tastes and preferences points up the implicit assumption employed here, and may lead to refinement and generalization through relaxation of that assumption.

2. Evidence on Wage and Income Differentials

This section presents evidence on the existence of wage and income differentials that increase with urban scale and region, and the magnitudes of those differentials. By tapping a number of diverse sources of information, some inferences can also be made on the way the differentials have varied by group and over time, and of more importance, on why those differentials occur. The sources of information employed include data on (1) the wages of individuals who have migrated, by size of place of origin and destination; (2) the wages of persons in well-defined occupations with rather precise standards of work performance; (3) per capita incomes over an extended time period (1929–72), and (4) incomes of families and unrelated individuals by race and poverty area classification within large metropolitan areas. The sample units for the last three data sources were individual metropolitan areas, so results are obtained by both population size and regional classifications.

Some of the inferences that emerge are: (1) the existence of a North–South wage differential of around 7 percent, and a population differential that increases by about 9 percent per magnitude of population; (2) stronger differentials for blacks than for whites, and for women than for men; (3) the likelihood that the southern differential primarily reflects a relative "oversupply" of unskilled to skilled labor, in process of reduction over time, rather than climate; (4) the likelihood that disequilibrium explained some of the population size differential between 1929 and 1950, but that compensatory payments are the major explanation since that time; (5) some evidence that differentials by size of place hold across income classes, though the differentials may become stronger for higher income classes.

Wages for the Same Persons in Different Locales

The Social Security Administration maintains an annual 1 percent sample of all social security records, the same social security numbers being selected for inclusion each year. It is therefore possible to compare wages for covered workers in different time periods. Such a comparison was carried out by the Bureau of Economic Analysis for migrants and nonmigrants in 1960 and 1965, cross-classified by size of locale at origin and destination. Three location classifications were employed: non-SMSA's, SMSA's with populations between 50,000 and 500,000; and SMSA's with populations over 500,000. Table 1 presents some of the results of this comparison, with data on numbers of workers, and on 1965 mean wage relative to 1960 mean wage for each class. The 1965 to 1960 wage ratio was around 1.25 for nonmigrants, with little variation among the three population size classes.

Similarly, those migrants who moved to a destination locale with population in the same size class as their origin had a wage ratio around 1.35, again with little variation between classes. Hence, for these subsets, migrants improved their economic position relative to nonmigrants by about 8 percent (135/125 = 1.08).[2]

Migrants moving from one size class to another showed differences in the 1965 to 1960 wage ratio which increased monotonically with population size for all cases. Specific numerical values for the progressions appear in the last section of table 1, using the non-SMSA ratio as base. Thus, for workers whose origin was an SMSA of 500,000 or over, the relative 1965 to 1960 wage ratios at the respective destinations were 100, 104.5, 107.3, moving from the non-SMSA through the small SMSA to the large SMSA classification, respectively. (Explicitly, we have 123.6/123.6, 129.2/123.6 and 132.6/123.6, with all fractions multiplied by 100.) The results for this case are quite close to the progression obtained by averaging over the three cases, which was 100, 104.3, and 107.8.

This procedure involves the assumption that the groups of migrants from a given origin are homogeneous, so that wage differentials at different destinations are completely explainable by quality of life differences at the destinations. This seems defensible on a first-approximation basis. However, some strong differences in pattern appear between migrants classified by race and sex, as shown in table 2. For

---

[2] The 1965 consumer price index relative to that for 1960 was 1.057, so most of the wage increases involved real gains. Some of these gains probably reflect the time pattern of earnings over the individual's working life.

Table 1.   Wages in 1965 Relative to 1960 for Migrants and
Nonmigrants by Location in 1960 and in 1965

(population and worker figures in thousands)

Location in 1960 by population of place	Interstate migrants—location in 1965 by population of place			Nonmigrants as of 1965 *(located in same place as in 1960)*
	Non-SMSA	SMSA 50— <500	SMSA ≥500	
	(1) Number of workers			
Non-SMSA	376.3	210.0	484.8	7,676.4
SMSA, 50— <500	186.9	150.1	410.6	5,661.5
SMSA, >500	481.7	357.5	1,509.8	18,740.4
	(2) (1965 mean wage)/(1960 mean wage) × 100			
Non-SMSA	135.4	145.2	146.5	127.0
SMSA, 50— <500	134.9	136.7	145.5	125.5
SMSA, >500	123.6	129.2	132.6	124.3
	(3) 1965–60 wage ratio on non-SMSA base (%)			
Non-SMSA	100.0	107.2	108.2	NDC[a]
SMSA, 50— <500	100.0	101.3	107.8	NDC
SMSA, >500	100.0	104.5	107.3	NDC
Simple average over all locales	100.0	104.3	107.8	NDC

Source: U.S. Department of Commerce, Bureau of Economic Analysis, Regional Information System. "Migration Matrix" dated January 18, 1973. Matrix based on the Social Security Administration's continuous work history sample. "Migration Matrix" was an enclosure, in letter from David Cartwright of BEA to Irving Hoch, March 13, 1973.

[a] Not directly comparable because nonmigrant values in (2) correspond to migrant entries along main diagonal. It is worth noting that the ratio of nonmigrant entries to that of migrants who remained in the same size classification was, respectively, 0.938, 0.918, and 0.937 (obtained by 127.0/135.4; 125.5/136.7; and 124.3/132.6). These ratios are consistent across size classes, indicating that migrants improved their wages more than did nonmigrants, and that the percentage improvement was about the same in each size class.

each category of a white–black, male–female cross-classification, table 2 presents the 1965 to 1960 wage ratio on the non-SMSA base, averaged over the three location cases (as was done in the last line in table 1). It turns out that blacks have a much stronger differential by size than do whites, and that the female differential for the largest size class is considerably above the male for both races. A plausible explanation for the racial difference can involve underlying differences in regional patterns of migration streams, with strong movement of whites from north to south, and of blacks from south to north. Since wages for the same work are lower in the south than the north, presumably reflecting persistent differences in cost of living by regions, this long-term differential should reduce the 1965 to 1960 wage ratio for whites

Table 2.   1965 to 1960 Wage Ratio on Non-SMSA Base
Averaged over Locales for Race-Sex Groupings

	Wage ratio on non-SMSA base			
Grouping	Non-SMSA	SMSA 50 – <500 thousand	SMSA ≥500 thousand	Number of migrants in thousands
All	100.0	104.3	107.8	4,167.7
White males	100.0	104.1	105.9	2,897.9
White females	100.0	104.0	114.1	925.0
Black males	100.0	113.2	120.2	256.8
Black females	100.0	110.2	131.4	88.0

Source: Derived from data in "Migration Matrix" cited in table 1.

and increase it for blacks. In particular, if blacks tend to move from smaller places in the South to larger places in the North, while whites do the opposite, we can explain the differences in pattern in table 2. Accounting for region of origin and destination, then, is likely to increase the urban size differential for whites and reduce it for blacks. In addition, it is possible that the initial wage disequilibrium was stronger for blacks than for whites. That kind of explanation may be involved in the sex differences, as well; perhaps female employment opportunities showed greatest improvement in large places during the period.

Wage Rates for Specific Occupations

The Bureau of Labor Statistics Area Wage Surveys contain data across SMSA's on well-defined occupations, whose work characteristics are described by quite specific standards, so that there should be little or no problem of difference in labor quality between places. These data were employed to carry out a detailed examination of the effect of SMSA population size and regions on wage rates by using a regression equation of the form:

$$W = a + b (\log P) + cS \qquad (1)$$

where W is wage rate for specific occupation, P is SMSA population in thousands, and S is a dummy variable for region, SMSA's in the South taking on a value of 1, and all other SMSA's taking on a value of 0.

In practice, equation (1) was estimated for twenty-five individual occupations, organized into three samples covering specific years in the period 1966–70. Further, standardized wage rates were employed to make comparisons easier, all wage observations for a given occupation being divided by the average wage rate for the occupation and then multiplied by 100, so that all results are on a base of 100 percent. Table 3 presents the results for the twenty-five cases, exhibiting for each occupation its average hourly wage deflated to a 1960 base, the estimated coefficients for the standardized wage using equation (1), the corresponding t ratios, $\bar{R}^2$'s, and sample sizes (numbers of SMSA's for which data were available). The t ratios were generally quite high, the log of SMSA population being statistically significant at the 10 percent level in all cases, while the southern dummy was statistically significant in 22 of the 25 equations. The coefficients for log SMSA population ranged from 5.0 to 16.0, with the bulk of the cases falling between 7.0 and 12.0; the coefficient for the South was always negative, but showed more spread, ranging from −2.0 to −23.5.

Table 4 presents average values of the coefficients of equation (1) for all occupations and for various groupings of occupations. On average, the coefficient for log population was 9.4, indicating an increase in wages of 9.4 percent for the same work with each increasing magnitude of population. Given the base standardized wage of 75.08 (corresponding to a population of 1,000), the application of the average coefficients implies that an SMSA of 10 million population in the North will have a wage of 112.72, or 1.50 the base. The average coefficient for the South was −7.4, indicating that the same work receives 7 percent less pay in the South than in the North.

The pattern of results in table 4 suggested that the estimated coefficients might be related to employee characteristics. To test this, the 25 standardized coefficients for log of population and for the South (in table 3) were each related to four explanatory variables: MALE, UNION, BLUE-COLLAR and dollar WAGE, where the first three variables are dummies, and the last is deflated hourly wage, shown in the first column of table 3. The dummy variable definitions were: male = 1, female = 0; union = 1, nonunion = 0; blue-collar = 1, white-collar = 0. (The union–nonunion dichotomy occurred in sample I for the building trades; in all other cases, it was assumed the occupations were nonunion.) Two of the variables were statistically significant for each coefficient, with these results:

$$\text{LOGPOP COEFFICIENT} = 10.880 - 2.634 \text{ MALE} + 4.471 \text{ UNION}$$
$$\phantom{\text{LOGPOP COEFFICIENT} = } (12.337) \quad (2.548) \qquad (3.290)$$

$$\text{SOUTH COEFFICIENT} = -14.002 - 7.772 \text{ BLUE-COLLAR} + 3.813 \text{ WAGE}$$
$$\phantom{\text{SOUTH COEFFICIENT} = } (4.569) \quad (4.844) \qquad\qquad (3.325)$$

The t ratios appear in parentheses beneath the estimated parameters, with all above the 5 percent significance level.

The results indicate that the effect of population on wages is stronger (1) for female than for male occupations, and (2) for union than for nonunion occupations. The first result reinforces the inference drawn from the social security sample (table 2), while the second contradicts a common argument that unions tend to establish uniform wage rates across all places.[3] Admittedly, the present result is specific to building trade unions; however, since union political power generally appears to increase with urban size, it seems plausible that economic power will also increase.

The results for the South coefficient may have considerable import for analysis and policy; they show that the southern negative wage differential was stronger for blue-collar than for white-collar occupations, and decreased as the average rate of pay increased. Low-paid, and presumably low-skilled occupations received relatively much lower rates of pay in the South than the North, while high-paid, high-skilled occupations were paid almost as much in the South as in the North. (In table 3, laborer's wage rates in the South are 23 percent below the U.S. average, while those for accounting clerk, class A, and registered nurse are only 2 percent below the U.S. average.) This suggests a much larger relative supply of low-skilled than of high-skilled labor in the South than the North, and is probably the core of the explanation for the reverse migration streams of whites and blacks to and from the South. Money wages for skilled labor that are a few percentage points lower in the South than in the North will in real terms be some percentage points higher in the South. Available evidence indicates that the cost-of-living differential between North and South is about 7 percent,[4] approximately equal to the average differential obtained for wages in table 4. Given the variation in the wage differential by occupation, we can infer that much of the cost-of-living differential stems from the lower wages of unskilled labor, rather than from such factors as climate differences. Insofar as the North–South differential involves a long-term disequilibrium in process of slow elimination, we can predict a steady reduction over time in the amount of the differential.

An extension of the wage analysis based on equation (1) supports the argument that climate explains only a small part of the North–South wage differential, and leads to some modification of the estimate of the effect of population on wages. That work is reported in detail

---

[3] Wilbur Thompson (1968, p. 15) has argued "with the spread of unionism comes the drive for uniform wage rates throughout the country to buttress labor's bargaining power. . . . For workers to quote the same wage for all places is for them to give up all influence on the selection of the place of work."

[4] That estimate is developed in section 3 employing 1971 data, and a similar result was found using 1967 data.

Table 3. Relation of Wage Rates to Population and Southern Region, for 25 Occupations

Sample and occupation	Deflated average hourly wage (1960 base)	Standardized[a] coefficients in wage equation			t ratios		$\bar{R}^2$ (Adjusted R^2)	Sample size (number of SMSA's)
		Constant	Log SMSA pop.	South[b]	Log SMSA pop.	South		
Sample I (1966)								
Maintenance (nonunion)								
Carpenter	$2.87	78.16	8.04	−5.95	2.82	2.30	0.20	50
Electrician	3.05	82.28	6.39	−3.62	2.80	1.75	0.16	50
Painter	2.80	85.60	5.75	−8.02	1.84	2.84	0.17	50
Union building trades								
Carpenter	3.84	67.26	12.07	−9.05	5.28	4.38	0.51	50
Electrician	4.22	73.36	9.83	−7.48	5.75	4.84	0.56	50
Painter	3.54	53.99	16.25	−6.11	5.40	2.24	0.42	50
Sample II (1969)								
Male								
Janitor	1.83	90.16	5.72	−20.85	2.08	7.89	0.43	86
Laborer	2.21	79.61	9.75	−23.47	3.97	9.92	0.58	86
Auto mechanic	2.98	72.48	10.84	−10.10	6.59	6.38	0.50	86

Female							
Accounting clerk, A	2.32	75.78	8.93	−3.26	5.37	2.04	0.27	86
Keypunch operator, B	1.82	67.94	12.08	−6.61	6.68	3.80	0.41	86
Stenographer, general	1.96	68.79	11.47	−3.80	6.70	2.30	0.37	86
Switchbd.-receptionist	1.81	63.38	13.59	−5.66	10.44	4.52	0.61	86
Typist, class B	1.68	75.03	9.50	−6.12	6.16	4.12	0.39	86
Sample III (1970)							
Computer operator, B	2.67	80.34	7.23	−5.29	3.38	2.40	0.25	48
Computer programmer, B	3.56	79.03	7.29	−3.25	4.67	2.13	0.36	43
Draftsman, A	3.71	76.10	8.42	−2.66	3.85	1.35	0.17	71
Draftsman, B	3.08	74.52	9.37	−4.12	5.46	2.50	0.30	82
Draftsman, C	2.50	82.67	6.67	−6.27	3.38	3.57	0.24	76
Accounting clerk, A, male	2.86	86.03	5.09	−2.21	2.22	1.04	0.05	66
Office boy	1.71	76.11	8.81	−6.39	4.51	3.74	0.37	74
Registered nurse, female	2.92	71.98	9.71	−2.07	4.71	1.03	0.24	62
Machinist	3.09	67.03	12.20	−6.83	5.91	3.54	0.39	77
Shipping clerk	2.41	74.91	9.47	−8.14	3.77	3.30	0.24	74
Trucker, power forklift	2.34	74.54	10.89	−17.51	4.61	7.90	0.52	83

a All observations for given occupation divided by average wage for occupation, and then multiplied by 100, so standardized wage is on base of 100 percent.

b Dummy variable. SMSA's in southern region take on value of 1, all other SMSA's take on value of 0 for the variable.

Table 4.   Average Values of Coefficients of Wage Relations
for All Occupations and for Groupings of Occupations

			Average values of coefficients for		
Category	No. of cases	Average wage ($)	Constant	Log SMSA population	South
All occupations	25	2.71	75.08	9.41	−7.39
Sample I	6	3.39	73.44	9.72	−6.71
Sample II	8	2.08	74.15	10.23	−9.99
Sample III	11	2.80	76.66	8.65	−5.89
Nonunion building trades	3	2.91	82.01	6.73	−5.86
Union building trades	3	3.87	64.87	12.72	−7.55
Low-paid blue-collar[a]	4	2.20	79.80	8.96	−17.49
High-paid blue-collar[b]	2	3.04	69.76	11.52	−8.47
Low-paid white-collar[c]	5	1.80	70.25	11.09	−5.72
High-paid white-collar[d]	8	2.95	78.31	7.84	−3.64

[a] Janitor; laborer; shipping clerk; trucker, forklift operator. Wage < $2.50.
[b] Auto mechanic, machinist. Wage > $2.50.
[c] Includes office boy and all female occupations in sample II except accounting clerk A.
[d] All other occupations in samples II and III. Wage > $2.00.

elsewhere (Hoch, 1974b); to summarize it here, equation (1) was expanded by bringing in additional explanatory variables, including several measures of climate, and a number of nonclimate variables, including other regional dummy variables, percent of population that was black, growth in population, and some measures of population density.

One of the regional dummies employed was the Confederacy (that is, the states that seceded from the Union during the Civil War), covering a more restricted set of places than the South, and the product of the Confederacy times percent black was introduced to account for possible interaction between region and race. Density was measured by central city population density (in thousands of persons per square mile), and by a high density variable, set at zero for densities below 10,000 per square mile, and at observed density for readings above the 10,000 figure.

The climate and racial composition variables generally had a good deal of explanatory power, in terms of the number of equations in which they were statistically significant; the density and growth variables, on the other hand, were relatively weak. The results are summarized in table 5, which aggregates the twenty-five individual equations into averages for each of the three samples (see table 3).

The coefficient for the log of SMSA population drops somewhat relative to the results in tables 3 and 4, though the variable was statistically significant in most of the underlying equations. Variables

Table 5.   Average Results by Sample for Extended Wage Equations
(Coefficients for Variables Appearing in Equations)

Independent variable	Sample I	Sample II	Sample III
Constant	100.4158	319.0014	168.3957
Region			
Northeast	−6.2550	−1.9163	−2.9615
North Central	—	2.3882	—
South	−5.3656	−4.9790	−4.9314
West	—	0.7943	0.6896
Confederacy[a]	—	−1.7791	−2.6567
Pacific Southwest	—	5.9755	—
Percent black	0.3543	0.2985	0.2744
Confederacy × percent black	−0.3300	−0.2839	−0.2503
Log SMSA population	6.7512	5.8881	5.6715
City density	—	—	−0.0977
High city density	—	0.1097	0.0121
Growth in SMSA pop. 1960–70	—	—	0.0232
Summer temperature	−0.2591	−5.3874	−1.5365
Square of summer temp./100	—	2.8768	0.4816
Winter temperature	0.0993	0.1694	−0.0640
Square of winter temp./100	—	−0.2705	0.2168
Precipitation	−0.0947	−1.4948	−1.0885
(Precip. × summer temp.)/100	—	2.0497	1.3275
Wind velocity	—	0.1230	0.8001

Source: Irving Hoch with Judith Drake, "Wages, Climate and the Quality of Life," *Journal of Environmental Economics and Management* vol. 1, no. 4, p. 283, table 6.
Note: Units of measure: SMSA population and density in thousands; summer temperature in °F, July average; winter temperature in °F, January average; precipitation in inches, annual average; wind velocity in average miles per hour.
— Not applicable because variable does not enter equation.
[a] The states of Alabama, Arkansas, Florida, Georgia, Louisiana, Mississippi, North Carolina, South Carolina, Tennessee, Texas, and Virginia.

that were not statistically significant were omitted from those underlying equations, and so were excluded in forming the averages shown in table 5. Bringing the log of population into all equations, and again averaging yields these estimates of its average coefficient:

Sample I	6.751
Sample II	5.958
Sample III	6.003
All	6.168

Although the occupations have not been weighted according to their share of the U.S. or urban labor force, and some occupational types may not be adequately represented, the consistency of results lends support to the hope that the average value of 6.2 is close to the result that would emerge, given proper weighting.

Table 6. Ratio of Wages in South to North
Before and After Accounting for Climate Effects

Occupational group[a]	Ratio of wages in South to North		Number of occupations
	Before climate effects	*After climate effects*	
Blue-collar			
Low wage	0.835	0.873	4
High wage	0.930	0.932	8
White-collar			
Low wage	0.944	0.951	5
High wage	0.965	0.954	8
All occupations	0.929	0.933	25

[a] As defined in table 4.

The drop in average from 9.4 in table 4 to 6.2 here shows the effect of the other explanatories, including some effect due to both density and percent black, both well correlated with population size. Hence, wages for the same work are estimated to increase by 6 percent for each magnitude of population, when we control for the other explanatories. In particular, this can be interpreted as the increase in wages for white employees only, paralleling the black–white differential found in table 2.

The possibility that climate differences might be a source for the North–South wage differential was investigated by comparing wage predictions by region before and after the climate variables were introduced. If climate were involved, it would tend to replace the South in the equations, and reduce the differentials in predicted wage. Thus, let $W = A + bS$, where W is predicted wage, S is the southern dummy variable, A denotes the effect attributable to all other variables, and A and b are estimates obtained from the regression equation. Then W for both North and South was calculated before and after the climate and other variables were introduced, extending equation (1). In the former case, A contains only the effect of log of population, while in the latter it contains the effect of all other variables, including all of the climate variables. Then the predicted wage for the South as a fraction of that for the North was calculated for the before and after cases, respectively, with results shown in table 6. Accounting for climate yields a small reduction in the North–South differential, primarily concentrated in the low-wage, blue-collar occupations. This may occur because climate affects working conditions more in those occupations than in others, with working conditions, as well as living conditions affecting the wage differential. The relatively minor effect attributable to climate receives support from another application of the extended equations. The squared term for summer temperature and the interaction between summer temperature and precipitation implied an optimal temperature in some of the equations (which occurred where money wages were at a minimum). Generally, the South deviated considerably from this optimal condition, being too hot and humid.

Per Capita Income in Metropolitan Areas

The U.S. Bureau of Economic Analysis (1967 to present) of the Department of Commerce annually publishes tables of aggregate and per capita income for all metropolitan areas (SMSA's). It is of some interest to examine how per capita income varies by SMSA population size and region. Results should differ from the results for wages because of (1) differences in labor force quality and (2) differences in the composition of income (wage versus nonwage forms of income) that occur between places. Results are also subject to some minor distortions because of changing definitions over time; for example, the number of SMSA's increases and individual SMSA's are enlarged by the addition of outlying counties. Finally, sample coverage varies considerably between the two sources. Despite these problems, the much greater time span covered by the income data is a considerable advantage. Thus, table 7 presents per capita incomes relative to that for all SMSA counties over the period 1929 through 1972, by population size class and major region. (The population size class refers to the specific year, so that an individual SMSA can move from one class to another, over time.) The general pattern fits expectations, with a general increase in per capita income with SMSA size and a persistent North–South differential. It is also clear that over time there has been a narrowing of the difference between SMSA and non-SMSA counties, some reduction of the North–South differential, and perhaps some narrowing of the population size differential. The last conclusions can be made more firm by inspection of table 8, which exhibits the results for equations relating the log of deflated per capita income to the log of SMSA population and regional dummies for a number of individual years. The constant term can be interpreted as "base" income that holds for a population of 1,000 persons in the northeastern region, which is used as base for the regional dummies. The increase in the constant's value over time is indicative of the rise in real income in the United States. The elasticity, α, exhibits the percent increase in per capita income that occurs, given a percentage increase in population size. It is noteworthy that this elasticity decreases from 1929 to 1950, falling from 0.11 to around 0.07, and then is quite stable, with small variations around the latter figure. The average over the nine observations from 1950 through

Table 7. Per Capita Income Relative to Per Capita Income Averaged over All SMSA Counties, by Population Size Class and Region, over Time

Population size class (SMSA pop. in thousands)	1929	1940	1950	1959	1962	1965	1967	1969	1972
				North					
0–< 250	0.784	0.831	0.914	0.903	0.912	0.899	0.887	0.874	0.878
250–< 500	0.875	0.918	0.921	0.919	0.906	0.913	0.912	0.898	0.920
500–<1,000	1.007	1.007	1.019	0.981	0.984	0.967	0.961	0.957	0.969
1,000–<2,500	1.118	1.170	1.065	1.049	1.043	1.018	1.021	1.012	0.998
2,500–<8,000	1.148	1.126	1.084	1.114	1.120	1.120	1.115	1.119	1.125
≥8,000 NYC	1.486	1.303	1.207	1.214	1.250	1.233	1.242	1.247	1.265
				South					
0–< 250	0.564	0.616	0.735	0.726	0.724	0.741	0.758	0.769	0.775
250–< 500	0.773	0.785	0.805	0.788	0.777	0.801	0.798	0.803	0.814
500–<1,000	0.735	0.812	0.884	0.833	0.805	0.823	0.847	0.869	0.902
1,000–<2,500	—	—	—	0.983	0.925	0.924	0.931	0.928	0.956
				U.S. Nonmetropolitan					
Non-SMSA counties	0.432	0.462	0.625	0.656	0.677	0.696	0.703	0.708	0.743

Source: Derived from data in *Survey of Current Business*, May 1969, 19–33 (for 1940); May 1971, 20–31 (for 1929, 1950–69), and May 1974, 6–75 (for 1972). Number of SMSA's in samples by date of source: 1969 data: 221, 1971 data: 231, 1974 data: 251.
— Not applicable.

1972 is 0.0695. This implies that if population increases by an order of magnitude, per capita income increases by 17 percent. For the 1950 through 1972 period, the range obtained for this effect is 16 to 18 percent (antilog 0.0662 = 1.16, and antilog 0.0721 = 1.18). This contrasts with a 1929 effect of 29 percent, and a 1940 effect of 25 percent per order of magnitude increase in population. The southern region was the dominant region, in terms of statistical significance, and the southern effect shows a pattern of continual increase, moving from 0.74 to a bit over 0.90 of the northeast base. The West, on the other hand, shows a pattern of decline, though there is a fairly pronounced reversal in 1972. The North Central region shows a much more variable pattern, though a consistent pattern of decline toward 1.00 occurs from its 1965 value of 1.07. All of these regional patterns seem consistent with a process of regional equilibration, all regions tending to move toward 1.00, though 1.00 may not be the exact final equilibrium point, if there are differences in the quality of life between regions in terms of climate or natural hazard. Both factors apply to California, which includes a large part of the western population; better climate might drive the California equilibrium below 1.00, but the earthquake hazard would

Table 8.   Results for Log of Deflated Per Capita Income Related to
Log of Population and Region

Year	Antilog constant term: C	Elasticity α	Standard error for α	Antilog region dummy coefficient South: S	Antilog region dummy coefficient North Central: NC	Antilog region dummy coefficient West: W	R² Explained variance	Number of SMSA's in sample
1929	766	0.1129	0.0146	0.743	1.003	1.043	0.491	231
1940	872	0.0967	0.0150	0.759	0.993	1.029	0.430	221
1950	1283	0.0662	0.0116	0.858	1.081	1.062	0.375	231
1959	1434	0.0721	0.0086	0.857	1.056	1.044	0.504	231
1962	1566	0.0671	0.0088	0.836	1.039	1.029	0.498	231
1965	1670	0.0700	0.0085	0.873	1.070	0.997	0.469	231
1966	1737	0.0704	0.0085	0.881	1.061	0.985	0.445	231
1967	1826	0.0688	0.0084	0.881	1.047	0.974	0.421	231
1968	1891	0.0687	0.0080	0.897	1.038	0.971	0.410	231
1969	1896	0.0719	0.0078	0.896	1.034	0.961	0.428	231
1972	2116	0.0703	0.0069	0.906	1.028	0.997	0.451	251

Source: Same as table 7.
Results from equation of form:

$$\log A = c + s + nc + w + \alpha \log P, \text{ so}$$

antilog form is $A = C(S)(NC)(W)P^{\alpha}$, where A = per capita income for individual SMSA deflated by consumer price index on 1957–59 base; P = SMSA population in thousands; s, nc and w = regional dummy variables for South, North Central, and West regions, respectively, with Northeast set = 0; $S = 10^s$, etc., c = constant, with $C = 10^c$.

tend to drive it up again. (We might even speculate that the increase in the western effect between 1969 and 1972 was due in part to the impact of the Los Angeles earthquake of 1971.)

If we employ an equation for income of the same form as that used for wages, corresponding to equation (1) and tables 3 and 4, with per capita income related to log population and the South, we obtain table 9, with results roughly the same as those in table 8. (Though containing essentially the same information, tables 8 and 9 afford somewhat different perspectives.) With per capita incomes on a percentage basis, the overall average equaling 100 percent, we find in table 9 that an increase of one magnitude of population increases per capita income by 26 percent in 1929, by 23 percent in 1940, and by roughly 16 percent in the years thereafter. The southern differential declines in absolute terms, moving from −27 percent in 1929 to about −10 percent in 1972. The magnitudes for the latter year are somewhat higher than the estimates of 9.4 percent and −7.4 percent for log of population and the South, respectively, obtained from the wage equations (table 4), but the difference can probably be explained by differences in sample coverage, likely lack of homogeneity of labor, and differences in mix

Table 9.   Results for Deflated Per Capita Income Related to Log of
Population and the South (in Standardized Terms)

		Coefficient for		t Ratio for		
Year	Constant term	Log SMSA pop.	South	Log SMSA pop.	South	$\bar{R}^2$
1929	53.24	26.30	−26.67	9.02	9.22	0.494
1940	58.38	22.63	−24.56	7.53	8.70	0.434
1950	76.58	13.05	−18.69	5.40	8.62	0.356
1959	67.92	15.95	−17.98	8.75	11.05	0.514
1965	67.94	15.33	−15.86	8.38	9.67	0.465
1969	62.90	16.48	−10.94	9.67	7.12	0.431
1972	63.66	16.12	−10.65	10.94	8.04	0.473

Source: Same as table 7.

Results from equation of form:

$$A = c + a \log P + bS$$

where A is deflated per capita income, P is SMSA population in thousands and S is the southern region dummy. Coefficients were divided by the average of A over all SMSA's, and then multiplied by 100, so that results refer to percentages of the average of A over all SMSA's.

of factors of production, between regions and population size classes, noted earlier.

Assuming a general correspondence between the income and wage relations, we can make the following inferences:

1. The process of regional equilibration has continued throughout the period, with reduction of regional differentials continuing to occur.

2. The differential by urban population size narrowed between 1929 and 1950, perhaps involving a movement toward an equilibrium. However, since that time, the differential has been remarkably stable, suggesting that equilibrium between SMSA's of different size has been more or less attained, with the differential interpreted as compensation for both greater money and psychic costs of living with urban size.

Certainly, the differential appears to bear little relation to population growth, since middle-sized SMSA's had highest rates of growth, for metropolitan areas in the 1960–70 period, and the ten largest metropolitan areas have had little population growth since 1970, with a number losing population.[5]

Parenthetically, it is of some interest to compare the results of this section with those of Meyer and Leone, which were based on similar hypotheses and methods, and are reported in chapter 3 in this volume. The first section of their paper builds on the work of Nordhaus and Tobin (1972), employing SMSA's rather than counties, and the key result of their tables 2 through 4 is that population density and total population coefficients sum to a "remarkably stable" total of around

[5] Based on data in U.S. Bureau of the Census (1971, 1973).

0.07 to 0.08. This is essentially the same estimate obtained here for population in table 8. In both equations the log of deflated income is regressed on measures of urban scale in log form. The use of regional dummies in table 8 is a parallel to the Meyer and Leone employment of individual SMSA cost-of-living deflators, for most of the SMSA cost-of-living differential seems attributable to regional (North–South) differences. The correspondence in estimates occurs despite some difference in the income employed (personal income per capita versus median family income), and considerable difference in sample size (over 200 versus 39). Some other consistencies emerge. Thus, the coefficient for percent black population is positive in both their results and mine in table 5, though that table also shows considerable regional interaction for the variable. However, the results for the Meyer and Leone wage equations (their tables 5 through 7) diverge from those obtained here, and are hardly encouraging, given the underlying hypotheses. The elasticity sums for population and density are generally small and *negative*. It seems likely that colinearity is the explanation, since the sign of "percent urban" is invariably opposite that of the scale variables, the *t* ratios for percent urban and population are usually quite low, and a strong correlation between those variables seems likely. It might be useful to redo the regressions, dropping percent urban from the equations.

Some other features of the Meyer–Leone analysis merit comment. Migration rate is used as an independent variable, but is likely to be an effect, rather than a cause of wage differentials. Again, there is good evidence that air pollution and crime rate are functions of urban scale (Hoch, 1972b, 1974b); hence, their inclusion in the equations should account for some of the scale effect, so that the estimated coefficient for the latter variable applies to a "residual" component covering all other disamenities. This can explain why there is a fall in the scale effect between their table 2 and their table 4. Finally, the basic consistency of results for their income measure and that employed here suggests that differences in sample size do not greatly affect estimates, so that differences between wage and income results here are probably the consequences of differences in distribution of factors of production and labor quality by size of place.

Income of Families and Individuals by Race and Poverty Area Classification Within Metropolitan Areas

Given the basic thesis of this paper, we would expect that the money income of poor people, as well as that of rich people, would increase with population size. This implies that the "poverty line," or an income standard, also ought to increase with urban size. The evidence on wages supports the argument, of course, since wage rates for both low and high wage occupations increased with urban size at about the same rate, there being no significant difference in the size effect as a function of wage rates. Some additional evidence appears in tables 10 and 11, based on special census tabulations carried out for the Office of Economic Opportunity. For 97 large SMSA's in 1969, census tracts with a "poverty rate" of 20 percent or more were designated as poverty areas, the definition of poverty being the standard one employed by government agencies. All other census tracts were designated as "remaining areas." For the two sets of areas, a number of tabulations were made, including data on average incomes of families and unrelated individuals, by race. Table 10 lists the money averages for these groupings, by SMSA population size, and table 11 presents the same information in relative terms, by dividing each column entry (for a particular area, race, and household category) by the overall average for that column. (These relatives are not directly compared to earlier tables because of differences in composition of the samples; the absence of small SMSA's here shifts all values up, so that the base value of 100 occurs at a larger population.) Besides average income, tables 10 and 11 also present average public assistance income of households receiving it.

There are a number of problems involved in interpreting these tables, of course; for example, nonpoor, as well as poor people, live in poverty areas, and the converse holds for "remaining" areas. Notwithstanding the problems, there seems general confirmation of the pattern of increasing incomes with population size for all household, race, and poverty area classes, although some inconsistencies do occur. For white families in poverty areas, there seems little in the way of an upward trend in income with size; New York City is often anomalous; and public assistance income in the South shows a decrease in the highest size class. It is possible that average family size declines with urban size, which would explain why income of white unrelated individuals in poverty areas shows more of a size effect than does that of white families. There is also some evidence that increases in the cost of living with urban size are more pronounced for higher than for lower income families (see section 3).

Several factors may explain the New York City results, which, for average income often show a decline relative to the preceding class. To some extent, this may reflect rent control, with implicit (imputed) income accruing to tenants not having been counted. To some extent, this may reflect considerably higher public assistance levels in the New York City SMSA which probably cause some in-migration of poor people to the area. The public assistance differential for New York City is considerably higher than its corresponding wage or income differential, while that for the South seems greater in terms of negative differential. Considering such differences, Kenneth Arrow (1970, p. 21) has argued:

> The fiscal problems of the cities stem in part from the fact that they have been more responsive to the demands for justice to the poor. To cite one figure, aid for a family of four with dependent children totals $250 a month in New York City and $35 a month in Mississippi, with cost-of-living factors explaining only a small part of that difference.

We can speculate that other, less virtuous motives, could be involved. An increase in number of welfare recipients could be in the interest of the welfare bureaucracy,[6] or of the local political party then in power,[7] or even of the city of New York, if the policy brought an increase in population, on net, and if increased population size yielded net benefits in terms of increased national political power or increased state and federal aid. The last item may seem the weakest of the putative causes if we accept Long's argument (1972, pp. 117, 118) that the city is "desperately concerned to hold business and middle- and stable-working class among its inhabitants." But Long proceeds to turn the argument around, suggesting that the central city is in the process of finding a new role as "an Indian reservation or poor farm moved downtown," with "suburbanized keepers paid by society to keep the Indian reservation in order and off its conscience." This might be extended to yield the argument that other cities have an interest in New York City serving as the prime specialist in the welfare function.

3. Evidence on Bads and Goods with Urban Size

This section briefly considers evidence on factors explaining the wage differential with population size. In short, the evidence suggests that cost of living, as measured by a conventional market-basket index, probably explains about half the differential, with the remainder accounted for by the *net* effect of psychic bads over psychic goods that are a function of urban size. A chain of inferences is involved, of

---

[6] Norton Long (1972, p. 115) citing Lyle Fitch and William Baumol, notes the vulnerability of the large city to municipal employee pressure, including "maintenance and increase in the number of jobs."

[7] An editorial on welfare problems ties them to "policies aimed deliberately at forging a political power base built on welfare fund recipients." *Wall Street Journal* December 31, 1974, p. 6.

Table 10. Incomes of Households by Race and Poverty Area Classification for Region and Population Size Classes, 1969

SMSA population size in thousands	Families				Unrelated individuals				Number of SMSA's in sample
	Poverty areas		Remaining areas		Poverty areas		Remaining areas		
	White	Black	White	Black	White	Black	White	Black	
Average income in North									
250–< 500	8,265	6,304	11,938	8,884	3,338	2,763	4,521	3,751	15
500–<1,000	8,235	6,785	12,311	9,304	3,313	2,864	5,065	3,980	19
1,000–<2,500	8,145	6,713	12,816	9,522	3,458	2,966	4,974	3,915	18
2,500–<9,000	8,806	7,099	14,257	10,222	3,993	3,389	5,806	4,499	7
≥9,000	6,893	6,837	14,569	10,087	3,304	3,474	6,177	4,430	1
Average income in South									
250–< 500	8,086	5,499	11,356	6,849	3,166	2,086	4,589	2,278	20
500–<1,000	7,716	5,884	11,820	7,883	3,383	2,350	4,825	2,777	11
1,000–<2,500	8,248	5,878	12,569	8,046	3,596	2,496	5,243	2,913	6
Average public assistance income of households receiving public assistance in North									
250–< 500	1,332	1,440	1,243	743	749	464	905	187	15
500–<1,000	1,582	1,630	1,221	1,558	803	922	859	469	19
1,000–<2,500	1,483	1,579	1,206	1,540	914	920	914	637	18
2,500–<9,000	1,636	1,906	1,279	1,656	1,047	1,146	973	1,091	7
≥9,000	2,390	2,291	1,630	2,048	1,359	1,421	1,200	1,453	1
Average public assistance income of households receiving public assistance in South									
250–< 500	858	891	810	673	626	569	664	97	20
500–<1,000	964	1,093	860	909	743	729	746	419	11
1,000–<2,500	845	884	798	852	650	693	676	575	6

Source: Derived from data in special census tabulations of 97 SMSA's for Office of Economic Opportunity obtained from Industrial and Social Branch, National Archives, 1974.

Poverty areas: Census tracts with a poverty rate of 20 percent or more.

Table 11. Relative Incomes of Households by Race and Poverty Area Classification for Region and Population Size Classes, 1969

SMSA population size in thousands	Families				Unrelated individuals			
	Poverty areas		Remaining areas		Poverty areas		Remaining areas	
	White	Black	White	Black	White	Black	White	Black
Average income in North relative to all SMSA income average								
250–< 500	1.013	1.001	0.973	1.032	0.985	1.035	0.920	1.096
500–<1,000	1.009	1.077	1.003	1.081	0.978	1.073	1.030	1.163
1,000–<2,500	0.998	1.066	1.044	1.106	1.021	1.111	1.012	1.144
2,500–<9,000	1.079	1.127	1.162	1.187	1.179	1.269	1.181	1.315
≥9,000	0.845	1.086	1.187	1.172	0.975	1.301	1.257	1.295
Average income in South relative to all SMSA income average								
250–< 500	0.991	0.873	0.925	0.796	0.934	0.781	0.933	0.666
500–<1,000	0.945	0.934	0.963	0.916	0.999	0.880	0.981	0.812
1,000–<2,500	1.011	0.933	1.024	0.935	1.061	0.935	1.067	0.852
Average public assistance income in North relative to all SMSA's								
250–< 500	1.047	1.060	1.152	0.651	0.952	0.607	1.098	0.429
500–<1,000	1.244	1.199	1.132	1.365	1.020	1.207	1.042	1.076
1,000–<2,500	1.166	1.162	1.118	1.350	1.161	1.204	1.109	1.461
2,500–<9,000	1.286	1.403	1.185	1.451	1.330	1.500	1.181	2.502
≥9,000	1.879	1.686	1.511	1.795	1.727	1.860	1.456	3.333
Average public assistance income in South relative to all SMSA's								
250–< 500	0.675	0.656	0.751	0.590	0.795	0.745	0.806	0.222
500–<1,000	0.758	0.804	0.797	0.797	0.944	0.954	0.905	0.961
1,000–<2,500	0.664	0.650	0.740	0.747	0.826	0.907	0.820	1.319

Source: Table 10 column entries divided by corresponding average over all 97 SMSA's.

course. First, the wage differential is interpreted as fully compensatory rather than involving some element of disequilibrium payments above long-run market equilibrium. Next, it is assumed that available evidence on cost of living is accurate, though there is some reason to suspect there may be some understatement of conventional market-basket costs with urban size. Finally, it is argued that the difference between wage and cost-of-living increases with urban size *must* involve a net excess of psychic bads over goods. Certainly, there are good things that occur as urban areas grow large; but the evidence suggests they are outweighed by the bad, for how else can we explain the net wage differential that occurs? Some future effort could be devoted to attempts to attach weights to the various goods and bads involved, in effect, further extending equation (1).

Oded Izraeli (1973), in fact, has carried out a commendable first approximation for such an analysis and Meyer and Leone's introduction of a variety of explanatory variables (chapter 3) also fits under this heading. However, a very large number of factors may enter the analysis, and the analyst is faced with formidable problems of data limitation, simultaneity, multicollinearity, and specification error. These problems appear to occur for both the Izraeli and the Meyer and Leone efforts, and are likely to hold for a considerable time into the future.

Finally, the preferences revealed by wage differentials occur at the margin. Fritz Machlup (1974, p. 96), has argued that there must be a tradeoff between physical and cultural suffocation: "some people [do] not mind breathing bad air if only they [can] listen to an opera or watch a dirty peep show. The indifference curves for these goods and bads [are] different for different people." This suggests that wage differentials may change if we move far enough away from the margin established by the "average" consumer, or the "typical" migrant. It also suggests that people who are "specialized" to a particular size of locale, or more specifically, to a particular place, obtain a species of "rent," which is not likely to enter into any form of national income or welfare accounting.

Urban Bads

The Bureau of Labor Statistics has issued limited series on comparative costs of living for 38 SMSA's and four nonmetropolitan urban areas, covering each major census region. (Data on Honolulu and Anchorage are also included, but were not utilized here because of the special circumstances of those places.) Data for 1971 were utilized to derive equations in which a standardized total budget for a family of four was related to the log of population and the South. Standardization was attained by employing the U.S. urban average as a base of 100. Budget totals include consumption; social security and all income taxes; and gifts and contributions, insurance, and occupational expenses. Results appear in table 12 as regression estimates obtained for low, middle, and high income families, which were then pooled to obtain a composite estimate, employing weights derived from Census Bureau data.[8]

The southern differential of −7.8 percent squares well with the estimate of −7.4 percent obtained from the wage equations (table 4). The effect for log of population increases with income class, and to some extent this reflects the effect of income taxes, whose increase with population size is somewhat more pronounced than the increase for consumption (which is exclusive of taxes). Of course, with progressive income taxes, a compensatory income payment will lead to higher taxes and, hence, the need for an additional compensatory increment in income. The stronger cost-of-living effect with higher income may explain why poverty areas showed less size effect than remaining areas in tables 10 and 11. The weighted average for the coefficient of log of population is 4.86, roughly half the magnitude for the variable in the relation for wages in table 4, which was 9.41. Hence, it seems proper to infer that increases in cost of living account for about half of the increase in money wages with urban size. This may be something of an understatement because the BLS budgets satisfy "prevailing community standards" (Groom, 1967) so that housing costs are on a housing unit basis rather than on a cost per square foot basis; more generally, the budgets involve an index of total expenditure (price times quantity), rather than a pure price index. Again, transportation costs in large metropolitan areas are shown as about the same as the average for all urban areas, based on the availability of public transit in the large areas (U.S. Bureau of Labor Statistics, 1972). But auto insurance data indicate that such insurance increases considerably with urban size. For example, 1972 New York state data on assigned risk insurance (poor risks who must be insured by being assigned to a pool of insurers) shows a New York City rate about twice that for small upstate communities, with the premium costs about $200 versus $90. (Although assigned risks are high risk cases, other data in the source document indicate that their premiums are not grossly above the average, with their differential amounting to perhaps 20 percent above the average.) The New York state data were employed in a more extended analysis by regressing the assigned risk insurance premiums for 77 communities on the following significant population characteristics: log of SMSA

[8] The weights applied were 0.22, 0.37, and 0.41, respectively, based on data appearing in U.S. Bureau of the Census (1970).

Table 12. Standardized Budgets (Cost-of-Living Indexes) Related to Population Size and Southern Region, for Three Levels of Living, Autumn 1971

Variable	Coefficients				t ratios		
	Weighted average[a]	Lower budget[b]	Intermediate budget[b]	Higher budget[b]	Lower budget	Intermediate budget	Higher budget
Constant	86.389	92.075	87.643	82.207	32.189	25.320	21.207
Log SMSA pop.	4.860	3.008	4.541	6.141	3.178	3.964	4.787
South	−7.775	−6.181	−8.425	−8.043	4.139	4.663	3.970
$\bar{R}^2$	—	0.393	0.479	0.487	—	—	—

Source: Derived from data in U.S. Bureau of Labor Statistics, *Autumn 1971 Urban Family Budgets*, news release USDL-72-240, 1972.
[a] Weighted average obtained by applying weights of 0.22, 0.37, and 0.41, respectively, to lower, intermediate, and higher budget.
[b] Budgets refer to annual expenditures by four-person urban family with average expenditures of $7,214; $10,971, and $15,905 for the respective cases.
— Not applicable.

Table 13. Results for Regression of Automobile Insurance Rates on
Population Characteristics, New York State, 1972

(*population and density in thousands*)

Variable	Coefficient	t Ratio	Average values[a]
Constant	42.593	1.757	—
Log SMSA population	49.001	3.801	2.856
Central city density	−6.168	3.236	10.841
Local population	0.018	3.047	180.243
Local density	0.634	2.098	6.312
Distance to central city of SMSA (in miles)	−0.316	1.908	20.247
Outer suburb or rural locale (dummy)	−16.809	3.811	0.403
New York SMSA (dummy)	41.703	1.994	0.221

Source: Derived from assigned risk premium data for March 1972 listed in New York Insurance Dept., *Competition Among Automobile Insurers in New York State,* 1972.

Note: $\bar{R}^2 = 0.69$.

[a] Average for insurance premium = $119.

population, in thousands; the density of the central city of the SMSA, in thousands; the local city population, in thousands; the local density, in thousands; distance of the community to the SMSA's central city, in miles; a dummy variable for locations in the outer suburbs or in rural areas; and a dummy variable for the New York City SMSA. The local city was defined as that closest to the given locale, with the individual boroughs of New York City used for communities within the city. An assumed minimum population of 5,000 and density of 2,000 were assigned to rural communities, and the largest urban center within 50 miles was treated as surrogate SMSA for communities not located within metropolitan areas. Employing the log of SMSA population only, these results were obtained:

premium = $56.56 + 21.87$ log SMSA pop., t ratio = 5.23, $\bar{R}^2 = 0.25$

Table 13 exhibits results when all significant variables are brought into the equation. All of the coefficients show costs increasing with urbanization and urban scale, save for central city density, with a negative coefficient, perhaps accounting for some nonlinearity in the relationship.

The roughly half of the urban wage differential not accounted for by cost-of-living increases can thus be hypothesized to account for money costs not picked up in the conventional cost-of-living index, or for the net of nonmarket costs over benefits, with urban size. Some of the latter are time costs of the journey to work, air pollution and noise, and the psychic costs of crime not covered by insurance premiums. I have developed some detailed evidence on each of these cost components in previous papers (Hoch, 1972a, b; 1974a, b) and note that all show strong correlations with urban size and density. However, in the case of crime rates, the observed increases in rates with urban size may overstate risks. When a number of other variables are introduced, effects attributable to urban scale (population size and density) are considerably reduced. Many of these other variables account for race, ethnic, and group composition. Now, there is considerable evidence that much crime is intraracial, and perhaps intragroup generally, so that risk facing a member of a specific group may not vary much by urban size. Robbery appears to be an exception, with relatively higher black commission and white victimization for that crime, perhaps reflecting higher heroin addiction rates for blacks, and greater availability of heroin in large cities. Table 14 summarizes my evidence on crime rates, with the first part of the table showing "raw" crime rates by population size class. The table's second part shows the rates as a function of urban scale effects only, all other variables (and average disturbances) held constant, with these rates obtained from fitted regression equations, and excluding estimated interactions that occur for percent black population and population size in the case of assault and robbery. The final part of the table brings in those interactions; the marked increase for robbery in this last section, and the literature on heroin and crime are the source of my conjectures on robbery. In particular, Hunt (1974) has developed evidence that the sequence of peak use of heroin is a function of city size; number of new users peaked first in the larger cities, and then peaked in medium-sized cities, and is still on an uptrend in places under 500,000 population. Brown and Silverman (1972) find a significant positive relationship between heroin prices and crimes devoted to "revenue-raising" in New York City, which has a considerably greater addict population than other cities (perhaps as much as half the total addict population). Their results for eight other major cities were not so clear-cut, however. The influence of other factors that are omitted is almost always a problem with crime statistics and may explain the lack of tidiness in these results. For example, table 14 shows a considerable attenuation of crime rates as related to scale when other factors are taken into account; in fact, homicide and rape show some declines for the largest size classes in the second section of the table. This primarily reflects the influence of density, which generally had a negative coefficient in the fitted equations.

Urban Goods

Many things improve as urban size increases, so there are benefits as well as costs of urban scale. These should enter most utility functions—

Table 14.   Index Numbers of 1970 Crime Rates, Observed versus Estimates as
Functions of Scale Effects Only

(*population in thousands*)

Population class	Homicide	Rape	Robbery	Assault	Burglary	Larceny	Auto theft
	Indexes of observed data *(Sample average = 100)*						
0–< 250	84.85	73.92	61.62	84.58	80.10	88.74	61.39
250–< 500	94.38	88.80	67.30	95.00	93.79	91.16	74.95
500–<1,000	100.04	96.19	90.78	96.11	102.24	103.92	120.02
1,000–<2,500	117.60	133.58	151.65	111.91	116.44	115.10	128.41
2,500–<9,000	132.61	154.35	251.52	134.17	125.59	114.63	170.85
≥9,000 (NYC)	137.87	105.76	470.35	177.84	156.36	156.37	199.63
	Indexes of estimates as functions of scale effects only, *excluding % black-size interactions*						
0–< 250	96.16	91.83	94.47	103.92	94.19	102.70	73.06
250–< 500	96.11	96.16	95.74	97.48	97.30	97.85	86.32
500–<1,000	98.73	98.19	103.61	99.06	104.96	107.69	117.00
1,000–<2,500	109.69	121.24	102.42	101.48	102.20	98.05	119.03
2,500–<9,000	107.48	66.00	116.59	101.70	102.54	80.15	119.14
≥9,000	98.04	64.83	136.75	125.89	135.68	117.83	107.86
	Indexes of estimates as functions of scale effects only, *including % black-size interactions*						
0–< 250	—	—	79.60	100.70	—	—	—
250–< 500	—	—	80.29	95.78	—	—	—
500–<1,000	—	—	97.05	99.39	—	—	—
1,000–<2,500	—	—	133.63	103.74	—	—	—
2,500–<9,000	—	—	168.14	107.10	—	—	—
≥9,000	—	—	299.19	133.96	—	—	—

Source: Irving Hoch, "Factors in Urban Crime," *Journal of Urban Economics* vol. 1, no. 2 (1974) p. 218.
— Not applicable.

most people prefer greater choice to less, and usually have option demand, at least, for specialized services that can be available only in a large enough market.

Some examination of the availability of specialized services was carried out by relating information on museums, "things to do," and good restaurants to urban size. Table 15 shows this relation for employment in museums, and number of museums by category in terms of average number per SMSA, and average number per 100,000 persons, based on a sample of 224 SMSA's. There are marked, and statistically significant, increases in the first set with size; but there tend to be decreases in the second, though these are not statistically significant. I would hazard the guess that, on net, the advantage clearly lies with increased size. The resident of the New York SMSA has 36 art museums he may visit, though the number per capita in the area is about half that

Table 15. Museums Per Metropolitan Area, and Number Per 100,000 Persons, by SMSA Population Size, 1972

SMSA population size class (pop. in thousands)	Employment in museums (persons)	Museum category				
		Art museums	Science museums	General museums	Specialized museums	Historical museums
		Average number per SMSA				
0–< 250	9.444	0.899	0.687	0.576	0.293	1.465
250–< 500	15.678	1.424	1.051	0.932	0.509	2.746
500–<1,000	33.939	2.545	2.212	1.576	1.636	5.667
1,000–<2,500	51.000	3.680	4.320	1.880	2.080	7.000
2,500–<9,000	198.857	14.143	11.143	5.857	6.741	29.857
≥9,000 (NYC)	440.000	36.000	24.000	11.000	19.000	63.000
		Average number per 100,000 persons				
0–< 250	6.44	0.654	0.489	0.416	0.198	0.980
250–< 500	4.80	0.439	0.325	0.287	0.156	0.865
500–<1,000	4.92	0.384	0.299	0.227	0.238	0.819
1,000–<2,500	3.45	0.253	0.299	0.139	0.138	0.462
2,500–<9,000	5.19	0.365	0.281	0.149	0.173	0.765
≥9,000 (NYC)	3.82	0.313	0.208	0.095	0.165	0.547

Source: Derived from data in American Association of Museums and Crowell-Collier Educational Corp., *The Official Museum Directory, 1973,* Skokie, Ill: New Register Publishing Co., 1973.

for SMSA's with less than 250,000 population. But the resident of the latter area has only 0.9 of a museum (on average) that he may visit.

Of course, the distance to any *one* museum is probably greater for the resident of the larger than of the smaller area. But the distance to two or more will be appreciably less, if the resident of the small SMSA has to go out of town to visit more than one museum.

In table 16, a similar pattern occurs for information on "things to do," and numbers of good restaurants, ranked from one to five stars, as listed in the Mobil Travel Guides for 1974, with 209 SMSA's in the sample. The smallest SMSA grouping affords its inhabitant or visitor approximately 10 "things to do" (local sights worth seeing, etc.), in contrast to 180 for the New York City area, with a monotonic increase in between. Similarly, the number of restaurants per SMSA increases monotonically for every star category. The number per 100,000 persons shows a sharp decline with size for things to do, but for good restaurants, there is generally first a decline and then an increase, though the point of upturn is itself a function of restaurant quality, generally occurring sooner (at lower population size) the higher the quality. For two-star restaurants and above, New York City has by far the greatest number per 100,000 persons. To summarize, the larger the SMSA, the greater the choice, but people in small places often have the greatest opportunities on a per capita basis. In the case of fine restaurants, however, New York City leads in both measures.

A final example of a good increasing with urban size is that of unemployment level, which for both 1960 and 1970 shows a mild decline when it is related to urban size alone, but shows a much more pronounced decline when it is related to urban size and a number of other variables. Table 17 shows regression results under this procedure, in which explanatory variables appear if they are statistically significant at the 10 percent level, or cause other variables to become statistically significant. The log of SMSA population is statistically significant in 1970, and close to significance in 1960, with negative coefficients in both years. Table 18 exhibits unemployment rates by SMSA population size before and after accounting for the effect of other variables, that is, the latter figures are obtained by holding all other variables constant while only SMSA size varies. Thus, there is a strong suggestion here that unemployment is reduced as urban size increases, other things being equal. (This may be small consolation to ethnic and racial groups with higher than average unemployment rates who also tend to concentrate in large urban areas—perhaps because their employment opportunities are better there, also.)

Table 16. "Things to Do" and Good Restaurants per Metropolitan Area, and Number per 100,000 Persons, 1974

SMSA population size class (pop. in thousands)	Number of SMSA's	Things to do	Restaurant by quality				
			1* Better than average	2* Very good	3* Excellent	4* Outstanding	5* One of best in country
			Average number per SMSA				
0–< 250	100	9.450	0.940	1.960	0.430	0.030	0
250–< 500	59	14.729	1.763	3.678	0.797	0.102	0
500–<1,000	33	23.727	2.485	7.455	2.030	0.182	0.030
1,000–<2,500	25	33.560	4.720	14.240	6.200	0.880	0.040
2,500–<9,000	7	93.143	11.286	47.429	18.857	3.857	0.143
≥9,000 (NYC)	1	180.000	69.000	181.000	63.000	16.000	2.000
			Average number per 100,000 persons				
0–< 250	100	6.718	0.682	1.360	0.284	0.017	0
250–< 500	59	4.541	0.560	1.163	0.251	0.037	0
500–<1,000	33	3.471	0.356	1.066	0.284	0.025	0.005
1,000–<2,500	25	2.330	0.344	1.015	0.437	0.066	0.003
2,500–<9,000	7	2.339	0.284	1.154	0.447	0.101	0.005
≥9,000	1	1.562	0.599	1.570	0.546	0.139	0.017

Source: Derived from data in *Mobil Travel Guides*, 7 volumes covering United States, Chicago, Ill.: Rand McNally & Co., 1974. (Coverage is for all places listed falling within SMSA's).

Table 17.   Results for Regressions of Unemployment on
Explanatory Variables, 1960 and 1970

	Coefficients		t ratios	
	1970	*1960*	*1970*	*1960*
Constant	7.769	5.831	8.317	4.114
Log SMSA population	−1.258	−0.683	3.590	1.534
Growth in pop. (%)	−0.014	−0.025	1.526	2.830
Northeast	−0.576	0.674	1.876	1.484
Confederacy	−1.131	−1.229	2.894	2.024
South	—	1.940	—	3.162
West	2.079	2.270	4.625	3.417
Ethnic (%)	0.073	0.059	2.393	2.329
Foreign-born (%)	0.080	—	1.437	—
American Indian (%)	0.523	—	1.792	—
Japanese (%)	−0.136	−0.101	2.806	1.563
Black (%)	0.055	—	3.000	—
Male primary individuals (%)[a]	−0.541	−1.020	1.850	2.157
Age 65+ (%)	—	0.285	—	2.674
$\bar{R}^2$	0.337	0.308	—	—

Sources: Table derived from data in following sources: Unemployment from annual
Manpower Report of the President, table TD6, 1972 and 1962 issues; other variables
from U.S. Bureau of the Census, U.S. Census of Population, 1960 and 1970.
— Not applicable because variable does not enter equation.
[a] Persons who live alone or with nonrelations only.

On Combining Goods and Bads in a Predictive Equation

In the introduction to this section it was noted that an attempt could be
made to allocate the urban size wage differential among its presumed
sources by extending equation (1) to include important goods and bads
as explanatory variables. But the brief survey of some of those goods
and bads suggests this will not be easy because of the large numbers of
variables and interrelationships involved. Oded Izraeli's (1973) ex-
ploratory work is a case in point. For a sample of sixty-seven observations on wages of laborers in SMSA's, he related wages deflated by the
cost-of-living index to nine explanatories. Because cost-of-living data
were available for only thirty-nine observations, he filled in the gaps by
estimate. Significant explanatories included population; air pollution,
as measured by sulfates; climate, as measured by winter temperature; the
property tax rate; and regional net migration. All had a positive sign,
except for a negative coefficient for winter temperature. Nonsignficant
variables included expenditures for local government services per
capita; median age; an aggregate measure of crime, fire, and accident
hazard; and unemployment rate. The first two of these had *t* ratios that
were nearly significant, while *t* ratios for the last two were quite low. A
number of problems seem apparent: among them are (1) the hazard

Table 18.   Estimated Unemployment Rates by SMSA Population Size,
Before and After Accounting for Other Variables

SMSA population size in thousands	Before accounting for other variables (%)		After accounting for other variables (%)	
	1970	1960	1970	1960
(1) 0–< 250	4.748	5.758	5.013	5.840
(2) 250–< 500	4.780	6.044	5.041	5.909
(3) 500–<1,000	4.112	5.203	4.151	5.266
(4) 1,000–<2,500	4.584	5.400	4.170	5.506
(5) 2,500–<9,000	4.486	5.383	3.351	5.250
(6) ≥ 9,000 (NYC)	4.000	5.300	2.535	4.638
All	4.553	5.645	4.553	5.645

Source: Derived from table 17.

variable seems too aggregate a measure; (2) sulfates and winter temperature each serve as proxies for a large number of variables, and this seems questionable; further, sulfates are highly correlated with urban density (Hoch, 1972b), and the latter variable is not included in the equation; (3) regional net migration is likely to be a function rather than a determinant of relative wage rates.

In general, since many goods and bads are highly correlated with urban size or density, or both, multicollinearity will be a problem in the attempt to measure causal components of the wage differential. But results to date appear good enough to encourage further work along these lines.

4. Conclusions

The occurrence of compensatory wage differentials with increases in urban scale has a number of implications, and several of them will be considered in this concluding section.

1. Many advocates of the redirection of migrants from large places, or the "decanting" of persons already there, often base their argument on likely reductions in nonpecuniary aspects of the quality of life that occur with size, but the argument neglects the existence of compensation in the form of higher money income. Often, the redirection argument is put in more sophisticated terms by using a marginal cost formulation: inmigrants impose external (or social) marginal costs that exceed the average benefits they derive. In effect, the argument implies that a curve marginal to the labor supply curve should be used in deriving "optimal" population size. But I think this involves sophistry, as well as sophistication, for new demanders always raise price, as new suppliers always lower it, in a situation that does not involve perfect elasticity. I believe

that the use of a marginal social cost criterion in such situations corresponds to a monopoly solution, which is hardly Pareto optimal. Analogously, newcomers to a specific labor market will lower wages, so that a "marginal social cost" is imposed on workers previously employed in that market; accounting for this marginal cost in effect generates a marginal revenue curve based on the demand for labor (or average revenue). The intersection of marginal revenue and supply, rather than demand and supply, yields a monopolistic, rather than a competitive, solution on the labor market.

2. Although my thesis and underlying model assume equilibrium, I recognize that the real world is generally only in the process of moving to an equilibrium, at best, and, of more importance, that an equilibrium is not necessarily an optimum. On the first point, it is plausible that many, perhaps most, urban areas are not in equilibrium; yet the evidence suggests that since 1950, at least, the system of cities probably has not deviated far from an equilibrium, or, at any rate, disequilibrium does not seem to be related to urban size. On the second point, improper pricing of common property resources can cause considerable deviations from optimality. If proper pricing occurred for air pollution, for example, it most likely would lead to population redistribution. I believe this would involve large places growing larger, on the basis of Izraeli's result that money wages increase with pollution, and noting that air pollution increases with urban scale; this implies that a reduction in air pollution will cause current money wages to be above the long-term equilibrium for the new situation, causing an influx of labor, which will be more pronounced the larger the area. (An important incidental note is that policy differences often stem from differences in drawing the line between private property and common property.)

3. There is likely to be a good deal of money illusion in making comparisons between places of different size, for compensatory money payments are often neglected. This can have unfortunate consequences for both analysis and policy. The definition and measurement of poverty is an important case in point. Defining a poverty level in fixed dollar terms will understate poverty in the North relative to the South, and in large places relative to small. This point appears to have escaped Daniel P. Moynihan in his advocacy of the Family Assistance Plan.[9] It is possible that some of the opposition to the plan involved at least an intuitive awareness of the flaw in measurement.

4. It is possible to devise an estimate of the portion of total personal income that compensates for the costs and disamenities of urban life. If

---

[9] In particular, see Moynihan's (1973) discussion on pp. 326 and 352–356, and the Passell and Ross review (1973, p. 16).

we employ as our base the relative money income at a population of 1,000, we can then deflate money income to this base by using the parameter estimates of table 4. At that population, the money wage relative is estimated as 75 on an SMSA average of 100. (It seems noteworthy that this corresponds to the nonmetropolitan income relative of 74.3 in table 7.) Table 19 shows the deflation process for 1972 income by SMSA size class and region. (The southern wage differential was retained in the deflation process, so the southern base was 67.7.) The resultant deflated total SMSA income is 0.715 of the original money income, with ratios of 0.712 for the North and 0.724 for the South. For total U.S. personal income, the ratio of deflated to undeflated income is 0.776, so the "cost" of urbanization is estimated to be 0.224 in 1972.[10]

The primary concern of this paper has been to furnish empirical documentation for its central thesis. A number of diverse sources of data yielded a rather consistent pattern of results. Thus, both the southern wage and cost-of-living differential were estimated as around 7 percent. The wage differential for urban size was estimated as 9.4 percent per order of magnitude of population, in contrast to a cost-of-living differential of around 4.9 percent, roughly half that for wages. The difference was interpreted as compensation for the net of nonpecuniary costs over benefits with size. The differentials for per capita income were greater in absolute magnitude than those for wages, amounting to 16 percent per order of magnitude for urban size, and 10 percent for the North–South differential. This was interpreted as reflecting differing mixes of factors and of labor quality, by size of place. The income results suggest a progressive narrowing of regional income differentials by migration, while the wage results indicate that most of the North–South differential can be explained as a long-term disequilibrium phenomenon. A number of differences in size effect emerged between groups, in terms of unionization, sex, race, and income category; these merit further investigation. It is to be hoped that utilization of information on the

---

[10] In Hoch (1974a, p. 89) I employed a non-SMSA money income base of 0.90, rather than 0.75, based on data in Fuchs (1967), and as a consequence, estimated the cost of urbanization as only 0.133 of U.S. income in 1969. The present estimate might be refined by estimating the average population size for the nonmetropolitan population (here treated as 1,000) and using that population as the source of the corresponding money income base. Both the present and the prior estimate in Hoch (1974a) appear to be above the corresponding Nordhaus–Tobin estimate and considerably above the Meyer–Leone estimate (chapter 3). Some of the differences may reflect differences in base, as was the case for my alternative estimates. Perhaps most of the differences reflect differences in estimated scale effects (Nordhaus–Tobin) or the effects of employing the percent urban measure (Meyer–Leone).

Table 19. Deflated Personal Income on Nonmetropolitan Base, 1972

Region and population size class (pop. in thousands)	Total personal income in millions of dollars[a]	Quality-of-life index	Income deflator	Deflated personal income in millions of dollars[a]	Ratio of deflated to undeflated income
Nonmetropolitan	198,972	75.08[b] 67.69[b]	1.000	198,972.0	1.000
SMSA's—North					
0–< 250	39,635	95.56	1.273	31,135.1	
250–< 500	59,383	98.84	1.316	45,123.9	
500–<1,000	73,818	101.77	1.355	54,477.5	
1,000–<2,500	154,013	105.01	1.399	110,087.9	
2,500–<9,000	195,364	109.47	1.458	133,994.5	
≥9,000	60,674	112.70	1.501	40,422.4	
All SMSA's, North	582,887			415,241.3	0.712
SMSA's—South					
0–< 250	28,386	87.94	1.299	21,852.2	
250–< 500	30,858	91.53	1.352	22,824.0	
500–<1,000	42,873	94.51	1.396	30,711.3	
1,000–<2,500	45,616	97.94	1.447	31,524.5	
All SMSA's, South	147,733			106,912.0	0.724
SMSA total	730,620			522,153.3	0.715
U.S. total	929,592			721,125.3	0.776

Sources: Income data from Survey of Current Business, May 1974; quality-of-life index numbers from table 4; income deflator obtained by dividing quality-of-life index by northern and southern base index, for respective regions.
  a Income in Hawaii and Alaska excluded.
  b Northern base = 75.08, southern base = 67.69.

urban size and regional differentials will be of considerable help in analyzing group differences in income and welfare, and as indicated in the initial part of this section, in a variety of analytic and policy applications.

References

Arrow, Kenneth J. 1970. "The Effects of the Price System and Market on Urban Economic Development," in *Urban Processes* (Washington, Urban Institute) p. 21.

Brown, George F., Jr., and Lester P. Silverman. 1974. "The Retail Price of Heroin: Estimation and Applications," *Journal of the American Statistical Association* vol. 69, no. 347, pp. 595–606.

Cameron, Gordon. 1973. *The Relevance to the U.S. of British and French Regional Population Strategies*. Urban and Regional Studies Discussion Paper No. 8. (Glasgow, University of Glasgow.)

Fuchs, Victor R. 1967. *Differentials in Hourly Earnings by Region and City Size, 1959*. Occasional Paper 101. (New York, National Bureau of Economic Research).

Groom, Phyllis. 1967. "A New City Worker's Family Budget," *Monthly Labor Review* vol. 90, no. 11, p. 1.

Hoch, Irving. 1972a. "Income and City Size," *Urban Studies* vol. 9, no. 3, pp. 299–328.

———. 1972b. "Urban Scale and Environmental Quality," in Ronald G. Ridker, ed., *Population, Resources and the Environment*, Commission on Population Growth and the American Future, Research Reports, vol. III, pp. 235–284.

———. 1974a. "Inter-urban Differences in the Quality of Life," in J. G. Rothenberg and Ian G. Heggie, eds., *Transport and the Urban Environment*, (London, Macmillan) pp. 54–90.

———. 1974b. "Factors in Urban Crime," *Journal of Urban Economics* vol. 1, no. 2, pp. 184–229.

———, with Judith Drake. 1974c. "Wages, Climate and the Quality of Life," *Journal of Environmental Economics and Management* vol. 1, no. 4, pp. 268–295.

Hunt, Leon G. 1974. "Recent Spread of Heroin Use in the United States," *American Journal of Public Health* vol. 74 (suppl.) pp. 16–23.

Izraeli, Oded. 1973. "Differentials in Nominal Wages and Prices Between Cities" (Ph.D. dissertation, Department of Economics, University of Chicago, 1973).

Long, Norton E. 1972. *The Unwalled City* (New York, Basic Books) pp. 111–118.

Machlup, Fritz. 1974. Comments made at International Economic Association Conference, cited in J. G. Rothenberg and Ian G. Heggie, eds., *Transport and the Urban Environment* (London, Macmillan) p. 96.

Moynihan, Daniel P. 1973. *The Politics of a Guaranteed Income* (New York, Random House) pp. 326 and 352–356.

Nordhaus, William D., and James Tobin. 1972. "Is Growth Obsolete?" in National Bureau of Economic Research, 50th Anniversary Colloquium, vol. 5, *Economic Growth* (New York, NBER).

Passell, Peter, and Leonard Ross. 1973. Book review of Daniel P. Moynihan's *The Politics of a Guaranteed Income*, in *The New York Times Book Review Section*, January 14, 1973, p. 16.

Thompson, Wilbur. 1968. *National Growth and its Distribution* (Washington, U.S. Department of Agriculture) p. 15.

U.S. Bureau of Economic Analysis. 1967 to present. "Local Area Personal Income," in *Survey of Current Business*.

U.S. Bureau of Labor Statistics. 1972. *Autumn 1971 Urban Family Budgets*. News release USDL-72-240.

U.S. Bureau of the Census. 1970. *Current Population Reports*. Series P-60, no. 75, December 14, 1970, table 8.

———. 1971. *U.S. Census of Population: 1970, Number of Inhabitants, Final Report*, PC(1)-A1 U.S. Summary.

———. 1973. "Estimate of Population of Metropolitan Areas, 1971 and 1972," in *Current Population Reports, Population Estimates and Projections*. Series P-25, no. 505 (September).

Wingo, Lowdon. 1973. "The Quality of Life: Toward a Microeconomic Definition," *Urban Studies* vol. 10, no. 1, pp. 3–18.

3

The Urban Disamenity Revisited

JOHN R. MEYER AND ROBERT A. LEONE

1. Introduction

IN an important pioneer effort undertaken a few years ago, William Nordhaus and James Tobin (1972) made a number of suggestions on how the national income accounts might be restructured to better reflect economic welfare. Their welfare-oriented approach contrasted with the traditional concern of national income measurement—gauging the aggregate level of market activity within an economy. The purposes of their enterprise were (1) to see to what extent the national income accounts could be used for constructing a more meaningful measure of economic welfare without resorting to massive or highly controversial supplementary measurement efforts, and (2) to test the extent to which simple market measures as embodied in the national income accounts may have been misleading about "the true progress" contributed by economic growth over the past few decades.

As one small part of their effort, Nordhaus and Tobin attempted to define and estimate a quantity called the "urban disamenity." This disamenity was meant to reflect losses in economic welfare that might have been sustained by society because of the general processes of population growth and urban agglomeration. To measure this phenomenon, they suggested that money income differentials realized by those residing in rural and urban locales could be contrasted, the idea being that extra income is required by those residing in urban areas to compensate them for the disamenities of such locations. They hypothesized that in equilibrium, given "costless" mobility, people of the same skills would everywhere realize the same real level of income or satisfactions. Thus, if the impact of nonmarket externalities (e.g., crime, pollution, and so on) on one location were particularly adverse and not fully reflected in lower local real estate or other prices (perhaps

This paper was prepared with the assistance of Anne Hill.

because industrial or commercial or other needs kept the prices high), then wages or salaries or other compensation would require an offsetting adjustment to maintain the equilibrium among labor markets.

It should be stressed that the Nordhaus and Tobin effort to measure the "urban disamenity" was a very small part of perhaps the first serious quantitative attempt to demonstrate how the national income and product accounts might be adjusted to better measure economic and social welfare. Broadly speaking, they made two classes of adjustment to existing gross national product (GNP) figures. First, they made corrections for increased real product flows which merely maintain but do not necessarily increase the flow of the ultimate service they are designed to provide (e.g., expenditures for police, fire, and protective services). Second, they attempted to account for the role of nonmarket activities, including the valuation of increased leisure time, the change in composition of nonworking time, the valuation of household chores, and so on. Their "urban disamenity" calculation is only one of several nonmarket adjustments to national income measures they considered.

Measuring the value of amenities or the "good life" is an exceedingly difficult problem. Prior efforts to infer valuation without direct market data have been based on studies of health effects, opportunity costs, and wage and property value differentials.[1] Many of the same problems and difficulties confront them all.

This paper focuses on the particular problem of using income or wage or salary data to estimate or establish the existence of the urban disamenity, utilizing the framework laid down by Nordhaus and Tobin. Thus, in the next section we turn to a summarization and critique of the Tobin and Nordhaus effort. We follow in section 3 with a report of some alternative estimates, hopefully somewhat improved, that we have constructed using essentially their concepts and procedures. In section 4 we expand the discussion somewhat beyond Nordhaus and Tobin to the issue of whether differential incidences are observable in the extent to which any urban disamenity is experienced by different groups in society. In section 5 we return to the focus of Nordhaus and Tobin, using the various empirical coefficients we have estimated to reassess the extent of the urban disamenity "correction" that might be made to the

[1] See *Air Quality and Automobile Emissions Control,* a report by the Coordinating Committee on Air Quality Standards, National Academy of Sciences, to the Committee on Public Works, U.S. Senate, September 1974, 93-24, for an application of all four of these approaches. While the NAS study was the first to employ all these approaches simultaneously, Lave and Seskin (1970) produced the seminal health study, while Ridker and Henning (1967) pioneered the property value approach. The Tobin and Nordhaus wage study helped motivate the NAS investigation of wage differentials.

national income accounts. Finally, in section 6 our major findings and conclusions are set forth.

2. The Nordhaus–Tobin Model of Urban Disamenities

Nordhaus and Tobin seek to measure "urban disamenity" by the co-efficients obtained from regressing median family money income real-ized in a specific geographic area on total population of the area, the density of that population, the percentage of the population classified as "urban," and a set of variables controlling for characteristics that might be expected to influence income but which are unrelated to the basic urbanization and population relationships. Examples of these other in-fluences are differences in the human capital embodied in the labor forces in different regions, disequilibrium in the local labor market, and the percent of the local population classified as black.[2]

As noted above, Nordhaus and Tobin imply that real compensation from both market and nonmarket activities in a highly mobile society, such as that of the United States, should be roughly equal at the margin when markets with the same labor skills or human capital are in equi-librium. Since equilibrium may or may not exist at a given point in time, they incorporate reflections of potential labor market disequilibrium, namely net markets and the age structure of the labor force, to correct for these possibilities. A complete listing of their variables as well as a summary of their basic regression findings are shown in table 1.[3]

As table 1 also indicates, Nordhaus and Tobin used several different samples for estimating their basic regression equation. Specifically, the county is their basic unit of observation and they attempt to control for various kinds of extraneous characteristics by using regional subsamples, such as the counties of the three southern New England states and New York, New Mexico, and Wisconsin as separate state samples. As can be seen from table 1, rather different results were obtained from regressions on data for these different samples or states. Indeed, there is even a remarkable amount of sign reversal for the coefficients pertaining to the basic population, density, and urbanization variables crucial to their evaluation of the urban disamenity.

The appropriateness of their model can be questioned as well. To begin, is *median personal (money) income* the best measure of differen-tials necessary to compensate people for living and working in what are environmentally less attractive areas? At a minimum, it could be argued

[2] Nordhaus and Tobin, perhaps wisely, include this variable without much elaboration as to its representation.

[3] Nordhaus and Tobin, 1972, pp. 48–49, table A-13.

Table 1. Nordhaus–Tobin Original Estimates with Log Median Family Income as the Dependent Variable Using County Data

County data source	Sample areas				
	Mass, R.I., Conn.	New Mexico	New York	Wisconsin	Indiana
Migration rate	0.00045	−0.00029	0.0012	0.002	0.0017
	(0.24)	(−0.58)	(0.25)	(2.6)	(2.4)
Population Negro	−0.0089	−0.031	−0.011	−0.010	0.0072
	(−1.0)	(−1.0)	(−2.9)	(−0.6)	(1.5)
Log total population (α_1)	0.039	0.093	0.010	−0.036	−0.0014
	(1.89)	(0.94)	(0.65)	(−1.3)	(−0.06)
Log population density (α_2)	−0.020	−0.087	0.035	0.091	0.065
	(−0.92)	(−1.2)	(2.98)	(3.1)	(2.7)
Log % urban population (α_4)	0.0595	−0.073	0.035	0.035	0.0173
	(0.93)	(−1.5)	(1.3)	(3.1)	(1.7)
Log median years of schooling	0.182	1.86	0.44	0.383	0.413
	(0.73)	(4.21)	(3.0)	(2.5)	(4.4)
Log property tax per capita	0.627	0.264	0.17	−0.0004	0.114
	(4.13)	(1.70)	(3.6)	(−0.061)	(2.2)
Log local expenditures per capita	−0.603	0.014	−0.22	0.012	−0.038
	(−3.09)	(0.035)	(−2.9)	(0.13)	(−0.61)
Population over 65	−0.017	−0.031	−0.011	−0.020	−0.020
	(−0.021)	(−0.93)	(−1.9)	(−2.7)	(−4.6)
R^2	0.76	0.91	0.85	0.88	0.87

Source: Nordhaus and Tobin (1972, table A.13, pp. 48–49).
Note: Figures in parentheses are t-statistics.

that *earned income* would be preferable on grounds that those living on transfer payments or wealth, most notably the retired, would choose their place of residence on grounds quite extraneous to any premium that must be paid to attract workers to an environmentally disadvantaged area. To some undetermined extent, of course, variables such as the percent of the population over 65 years of age (which Nordhaus and Tobin use) may control for such influences. Similarly, it is not completely obvious whether wage rate or earned income measures are best. The "rate" measures capture compensation differences per unit of time or effort (and thus perhaps allow for leisure valuations better than total income measures). Income measures, on the other hand, are probably superior in that the total income realized by the family may ultimately count most in determining family economic welfare.

The use of census data for counties introduces an important distortion in the analysis because the census assigns incomes to the place of residence, not to the place of employment. Many labor markets have counties that are the main workplace locations and other counties that are almost exclusively residential. Consequently, high incomes in, say, Fairfield County, Connecticut, can hardly be said to represent the urban disamenities of Fairfield, but may represent "compensation" for the disamenity of commuting to and working in Manhattan.

Other doubts arise from examination of the basic samples used by Nordhaus and Tobin. Most of their coefficient estimates probably depend on differences observed in a large cluster of rural counties (exhibiting very low population densities and levels of urbanization) and a *few* urban "outliers." Regional stratification does have the potential advantage of controlling for the effect of regional price differences on money incomes, but converting observed differences in regional money income into real terms or equivalents for the purposes of interregional comparisons has long been a perplexing and difficult empirical problem. For many years the major source of consumer price indexes for making conversions of money into real income, the Bureau of Labor Statistics (BLS), took an understandably cautious view of all indexes designed for such regional comparisons or conversions. The difficulty, of course, stems from the well-known differences in the market baskets used by consumers residing in different environments. Such considerations probably led Nordhaus and Tobin to a regional, or state-by-state stratification of their samples. However, it is not clear that such a stratification really meets all of the difficulties. There is as much reason to expect that the consumption habits of farm or small-town residents differ from those of large city consumers, even when nearby, as to expect differences in consumption patterns among city dwellers in different regions of the United States, especially since rural dwellers, particularly farmers, realize far more of their income in unmarketed goods.

There are also purely statistical problems in using a cluster of rural counties, on the one hand, and a very few urban counties on the other, to determine the influence of urban disamenities on earnings. Most of the regressions are probably dominated by the particular position of the few outlying urban observations: Milwaukee almost surely represents an extreme value for many of the variables included in the Wisconsin sample, since Wisconsin is otherwise characterized by such medium- or small-sized cities as Madison, Kenosha, Racine, Sheboygan, and Green Bay. The influence of extreme observations may be even more pronounced for the state of New York, whose major city is an outlier among all American cities, let alone for the medium- and small-sized cities that make up the remaining urban population of New York state. New Mexico's urban values or observations are most surely dominated by Albuquerque. The use of the logarithmic forms of some of the variables employed in the Nordhaus and Tobin analysis, while attenuating these difficulties, would not have solved them. Note, for example, in table 1 the remarkable divergence in the results for the different regressions on the different states or regional groupings, and a tendency for the coefficient signs to change inexplicably.

The structural specifications used by Nordhaus and Tobin may also not be adequate. Consider the failure to control certain variables that might be expected to influence "amenities" *independently* of population influences, even within a region or state: significant climatic differences can exist within regions or states; certain kinds of cities, most particularly seats of government or universities, often are deemed to possess amenities lacking in their neighbors. It is simply unrealistic to assume that these other amenity values would be randomly distributed, given what one knows about the special characteristics of, say, a Madison, Wisconsin or a Santa Fe, New Mexico.

The "percentage Negro" and the "over 65" variables also offer some important interpretation problems. Three or four different possible influences of "percentage Negro" on real incomes in a geographic area might be hypothesized. A classic discrimination hypothesis would lead us to expect the coefficient on the "percentage Negro" variable to be positive on the grounds that the "dominant" majority of white workers would need more compensation to work in or near a labor force with many blacks in it. Conversely, if one believes that labor markets are a bit less than perfect and various forms of ologopsony function to the disadvantage of blacks in labor markets, then the coefficients on "percentage Negro" might be expected to be negative (as indeed Nordhaus and Tobin largely find, although their findings may be determined in the main by high incomes in a few "very white" suburban counties in their samples). A negative coefficient might also be justified on "historical" human capital grounds if one accepts that blacks may not have been permitted to participate as extensively in schooling and other opportunities (to develop labor market skills) as whites. If some merit is seen in all of these hypotheses, a coefficient near zero might be expected, on the grounds that the different influences would be largely offsetting.

The percentage of the labor force over 65 years of age poses similar problems of interpretation. The "over 65" variable might be interpreted as measuring the quality of human capital in an area on such diverse grounds as: (1) the possibility that a preponderance of older voters might reduce expenditures, everything else being equal, on schools; or (2) that because of the long-standing trend toward more education, a greater relative number over 65 years of age would reduce the average mix of skills represented in the population; or (3) that a relatively large number of over 65-year-olds might be a proxy for outward migration historically, if not currently, so that an "old region" would be relatively denuded of its younger, better trained, more energetic labor force. Of course, these latter considerations would also suggest that the "over 65-year-old" variable might be a measure of labor market disequilibrium as well as other influences, thereby further confounding its interpretation.

In sum, four major modifications are worth testing to improve the Nordhaus and Tobin empirical measures of the urban disamenity. First, more direct and meaningful measures of real income differences between the particular geographic areas used in the regression sample should be developed. Second, more "continuous" samples would be desirable to make the estimates less sensitive to one cluster of observations at the extreme low end and a few outlying observations at the high end of the expected range. Third, better specifications might be sought, with particular emphasis on controlling for variables that might be expected to influence amenities that are not correlated with urbanization, total population, or population density. Fourth, and finally, more direct measures of any salary or wage inducements necessary to compensate people for accepting locales of lesser amenity might be tested; specifically, various wage or earned income measures might prove to be dependent variables superior to median income for assessing amenity differentials.

3. The Nordhaus–Tobin Functions Reestimated

The basic Nordhaus and Tobin regression equation for estimating urban disamenities can be reestimated using samples or data that at least partially fulfill the four suggestions just outlined. In essence, this permits testing the sensitivity of the Nordhaus and Tobin estimates to alternative samples and functional specifications.

To start, the dependent variable might be converted from money to real values by shifting to a sample that involves Standard Metropolitan Statistical Areas (SMSA's). For these areas, some measures are available, admittedly imperfect, of differences in real costs of living. Both advantages and disadvantages accrue from such a shift in the dependent variable. For example, it is not absolutely certain that the new or "price-deflated" income measure really controls better for living cost differentials than the regional stratification employed by Nordhaus and Tobin, but a "betting man" would probably shade his odds toward asserting that the price-corrected variable would be somewhat better controlled for areal price differences. Nevertheless, there is little empirical evidence, one way or the other, to test the validity of this assertion.[4]

Similarly, the choice of the SMSA instead of the county as the unit of observation does provide a more continuous set of observations over the available range, as evidenced by the 39 SMSA's constituting the BLS labor market sample (appendix). Some of the SMSA's in this list are much larger than the others; New York City is roughly twice the size of the next two largest, Chicago and Los Angeles, which in turn are roughly twice the size of the next largest beneath them. Indeed, some of the SMSA's in the sample are still quite small in size, such as Lancaster, Pennsylvania. It can be argued that by confining the sample to SMSA's, important observations are excluded at the very low end of area population, population density, and urbanization scales. The best guess would be that any such bias tends toward some overestimation of some of the regression coefficients included in the equation since most of the constants in the regression equations, when refitted to the SMSA sample data, are negative.

---

[4] The theoretical importance of the price correction can be readily illustrated. Assume that consumer utility U is a function of local prices P, income Y, and amenities A. Competitive pressures will equate utilities across areas such that, in equilibrium, the utility a consumer realizes in any city would be a constant, U^*: $U(P,Y,A)=U^*$. Incomes are related to wages and wages might vary with the agglomeration of economic activity due to economies of urbanization. For a given amenity level, prices (chiefly land rents) should ultimately capture these labor productivity differences. Since the world is not a frictionless space, sectors other than land might capture some of these differentials, suggesting that a general price deflator, as opposed to merely an index of land prices, might better capture this phenomenon. Unfortunately, the possibilities for substitution within the market basket of goods, due to relative price changes, can create a classic index number problem.

To improve the specification of the Nordhaus and Tobin equation, additional hypothesized measures of amenities can be included. In this connection the most obvious additions on intuitive grounds and from the literature on regional location decisions are (1) various climatic variables such as average temperature or rainfall or location beside a major body of water, (2) measures of public goods that might be expected to create certain kinds of amenities such as the presence of a major university or a state capital in the area, (3) measures of environmental pollution, (4) measures of public safety, for example, crime rates, and (5) certain generalized measures of the state of the local amenity, the local municipal bond rating being one that is sometimes suggested.[5] Needless to say, the directly available measures of such amenities, just as for many concepts included in the original Nordhaus and Tobin specification (e.g., human capital differences), are likely to be limited and less restricted and less precise than one would hope to find; nevertheless, several such variables are available and can be tested for their impact on the basic Nordhaus and Tobin regression estimates (see especially Hansen, 1971).

The fourth modification of the Nordhaus and Tobin estimates, the substitution of salary or wage rate measures for income, raises a host of conceptual and empirical issues well beyond those involved in the other three suggestions. Nor is it clear that this change would represent a real improvement. Accordingly, we have postponed testing, or reporting on tests of such a change, until the next section of this paper. In this section we concentrate strictly on reestimation using the Nordhaus and Tobin dependent variable, median family income, though now price deflated.

The results achieved using the SMSA data, price-deflated median family income as the dependent variable, and employing different specifications of the regression equation, are shown in tables 2, 3, and 4. In addition, a sensitivity test has also been made for the inclusion or exclusion of certain SMSA's from the sample. Table 2 basically pertains to estimates obtained using SMSA instead of county data and exactly the same specification of the underlying regression structure as that employed by Nordhaus and Tobin; the only change is in the dependent variable, which has now been deflated by an SMSA consumer price index derived from BLS data on the cost of a market basket for families with an intermediate level of income. Table 3 extends the Nordhaus and Tobin specification by including certain other variables that might be expected to influence amenities but could also be assumed to be

[5] We quickly add that we harbor uncertainties about the quality of an area's bonds as a measure of its amenities!

Table 2.   Regression Estimates of the Nordhaus-Tobin Specification Estimated
with Real Median Family Income as the Dependent Variable
Using SMSA Data

SMSA data source	All observations	Without D.C.	Without D.C. + N.Y.	Without D.C. + N.Y. + Chi. + L.A.
Migration rate	0.00092	0.00092	0.00091	0.00035
	(0.78)	(0.73)	(0.73)	(0.27)
Population Negro	0.00022	0.00023	0.00023	0.00027
	(3.59)	(2.84)	(2.76)	(2.87)
Log total population (α_1)	0.05	0.06	0.06	0.07
	(3.25)	(3.09)	(2.55)	(3.05)
Log population density (α_2)	0.02	0.02	0.02	0.03
	(1.19)	(1.17)	(1.15)	(1.51)
Log % urban population (α_4)	−0.1	−0.11	−0.11	−0.16
	(−0.68)	(−0.68)	(−0.66)	(−0.94)
Log median years of schooling	0.76	0.82	0.83	1.02
	(1.42)	(1.26)	(1.21)	(1.48)
Log property tax per capita	0.04	0.04	0.04	0.02
	(0.86)	(0.74)	(0.73)	(0.51)
Log local expenditures per capita	−0.007	−0.002	−0.002	0.02
	(−0.13)	(−0.03)	(−0.03)	(0.24)
Population over 65	−0.00058	−0.0006	−0.0006	−0.0009
	(−5.16)	(−3.87)	(−3.11)	(−3.44)
R^2	0.64	0.56	0.53	0.56
$\alpha_1 + \alpha_2$ (independently rounded)	0.07	0.07	0.07	0.10
α_4	−0.1	−0.1	−0.11	−0.16

Note: Figures in parentheses are *t*-statistics.

independent of urbanization or population density or population scale,
the basic urban effect variables included in the original Nordhaus and
Tobin specifications; in short, table 3 reflects an effort to correct for
specification bias that may have been created in the Nordhaus and
Tobin regressions by omission of certain systematic influences on
amenities. Table 4 carries this whole respecification a step further by
including several other amenity measures in addition to those reported
in table 3, including some amenity measures that one might expect to be
correlated with urbanization or population measures, such as the
crime rate or number of newspapers. These three different models
might be characterized or nicknamed as: (1) the Nordhaus and Tobin
specification; (2) the Meyer and Leone specification; and (3) a
"kitchen sink" specification (since it includes almost everything but a
measure of that sanitary facility).

Perhaps the most remarkable aspect of the empirical results is how
little difference the different specifications or changes in the sample seem
to make. If the results using the SMSA data (as shown in tables 2, 3,

Table 3.   Regression Estimates of the "Preferred" Specification of the Basic Urban Amenity Equation with Log Real Median Family Income as the Dependent Variable Using SMSA Data

SMSA data source	All observations	Without D.C.	Without D.C. + N.Y.	Without D.C. + N.Y. + Chi. + L.A.
Migration rate	0.001	0.001	0.002	0.002
	(1.22)	(1.22)	(1.42)	(1.41)
Population Negro	0.00021	0.00026	0.00025	0.00024
	(3.55)	(3.31)	(3.21)	(2.77)
Log total population (α_1)	0.023	0.024	0.008	0.007
	(0.96)	(0.97)	(0.25)	(0.22)
Log population density (α_2)	0.042	0.053	0.06	0.06
	(2.10)	(2.29)	(2.43)	(2.40)
Log % urban population (α_4)	−0.02	−0.08	−0.04	−0.04
	(−0.14)	(−0.49)	(−0.25)	(−0.21)
Log median years of schooling	0.62	0.94	0.82	0.79
	(1.17)	(1.49)	(1.25)	(1.18)
Log property tax per capita	0.02	0.005	0.00002	−0.003
	(0.49)	(0.10)	(−0.01)	(−0.05)
Log local expenditures per capita	0.17	0.05	0.07	0.07
	(0.31)	(0.78)	(0.95)	(0.99)
Population over 65	−0.00054	−0.00063	−0.00054	−0.00054
	(−4.82)	(−4.16)	(−2.91)	(−2.88)
Water dummy	−0.04	−0.05	−0.05	−0.06
	(−1.75)	(−1.98)	(−2.16)	(−2.15)
Log univ. per capita	−0.03	−0.03	−0.04	−0.04
	(−1.46)	(−1.59)	(−1.77)	(−1.77)
Log average temperature	−0.05	−0.04	−0.03	−0.02
	(−0.59)	(−0.41)	(−0.37)	(−0.23)
R^2	0.70	0.64	0.62	0.61
$\alpha_1 + \alpha_2$	0.07	0.08	0.07	0.07
α_4	−0.02	−0.08	−0.04	−0.04

Note: Figures in parentheses are *t*-statistics.

and 4) are compared with the results obtained earlier by Nordhaus and Tobin using county data (shown in table 1), it is quite apparent that the different coefficient estimates are considerably more stable using the SMSA data. This is particularly true if one excludes the results shown in table 4, for the so-called "kitchen sink" specification which, as might be expected, are somewhat idiosyncratic or fluctuating.

Stability in the coefficients is particularly apparent for the population, density, and urbanization variables to be employed in making the urban disamenity estimates. Nordhaus and Tobin sum the population and density coefficients (α_1 and α_2) to make one part of their urban disamenity correction, with the urbanization variable (α_4) used separately. For our preferred specification, shown in table 3, the population

Table 4.   Regression Estimates of an Augmented (Kitchen Sink) Specification of the Urban Amenity Equation with Log Real Median Family Income as the Dependent Variable Using SMSA Data

SMSA data source	All observations	Without D.C.	Without D.C. + N.Y.	Without D.C. + N.Y. + Chi. + L.A.
Migration rate	0.0007	0.0003	0.00035	0.0003
	(0.42)	(0.19)	(0.22)	(0.19)
Population Negro	0.00021	0.0003	0.0003	0.0003
	(0.91)	(3.41)	(3.22)	(2.84)
Log total population (α_1)	0.009	0.002	−0.01	−0.01
	(0.32)	(0.06)	(−0.35)	(−0.34)
Log population density (α_2)	0.04	0.07	0.07	0.07
	(1.88)	(2.60)	(2.65)	(2.57)
Log % urban population (α_4)	0.07	0.01	0.04	0.04
	(0.39)	(0.07)	(0.21)	(0.20)
Log median years of schooling	0.55	1.16	1.06	1.07
	(0.94)	(1.74)	(1.56)	(1.51)
Log property tax per capita	−0.01	−0.07	−0.07	−0.07
	(−0.25)	(−1.11)	(−1.17)	(−1.28)
Log local expenditures per capita	0.04	0.12	0.13	0.13
	(0.56)	(1.50)	(1.59)	(1.54)
Population over 65	−0.00057	−0.0008	−0.0007	−0.0007
	(−4.58)	(−4.47)	(−3.22)	(−3.10)
Water dummy	−0.04	−0.06	−0.07	−0.07
	(−1.65)	(−2.28)	(−2.37)	(−2.30)
Log average temperature	0.004	−0.04	0.04	0.04
	(−0.04)	(−0.41)	(0.41)	(0.39)
Log univ. per capita	−0.03	−0.04	−0.05	−0.05
	(−1.57)	(−2.07)	(−2.16)	(−2.10)
Log particulates	−0.001	−0.002	−0.01	−0.15
	(−0.03)	(−0.04)	(−0.31)	(−0.31)
Log SO$_2$	0.02	0.02	0.02	0.02
	(1.41)	(1.88)	(1.79)	(1.74)
Crime rate	0.0004	0.00057	0.0006	0.0006
	(0.76)	(1.04)	(1.13)	(1.08)
Log bond	0.01	0.03	0.03	0.03
	(0.47)	(1.20)	(1.01)	(0.96)
No. of newspapers	0.01	0.01	0.01	0.01
	(0.53)	(0.67)	(0.74)	(0.69)
R^2	0.73	0.72	0.70	0.69
$\alpha_1 + \alpha_2$	0.05	0.07	0.06	0.06
α_4	0.07	0.01	0.04	0.04

Note: Figures in parentheses are t-statistics.

density and total population coefficient round (as shown in the second to last row in the table) to a remarkably stable sum in the region of 0.07 to 0.08. In the same table, the coefficient for the urbanization variable shows somewhat less stability, varying between −0.02 and

−0.08, but unlike the Nordhaus and Tobin estimates, the signs are always the same and within "hailing" distance of one another. This picture is only slightly changed or modified when one looks at table 2, reporting the results for the original Nordhaus and Tobin specification; again, the sum of the total population density coefficient is 0.07 in three out of four cases and the urbanization coefficient is always negative: at −0.10 more or less in three cases and at −0.16 in the fourth. With the exception of altering the sign on the urbanization variable from negative to positive and reducing the significance of this coefficient to near zero, the results achieved using the "kitchen sink" specification, shown in table 4, are also not too dissimilar. The insignificant coefficient in the "kitchen sink" specification for the urbanization variable, moreover, seems easily explained: the explicit measures of urban amenities or disamenities that might be expected to be related to size are included in this equation, thus obliterating most size effects.

Two of the variables from the original Nordhaus and Tobin specification almost invariably have signs in tables 2, 3, and 4 different from those reported by Nordhaus and Tobin (cf. table 1). Specifically, the Negro population variable invariably enters with a positive, and almost always a quite significant coefficient with the SMSA data while it was generally quite significantly negative in the Nordhaus and Tobin estimates. No easy explanation for this sign reversal is readily apparent, except those tendered earlier. The best guess would be that the Nordhaus and Tobin negative coefficients mainly reflect a few white high-income suburban counties in their samples.

The other sign reversed from the Nordhaus and Tobin results pertains to the urbanization variable. This variable is uniformly negative, although not significantly so, for the results reported in both tables 2 and 3. In table 4 it is positive, but for all practical purposes at a very low or near zero level. A negative coefficient for the urbanization variable may not be all that surprising. Specifically, the results would seem to suggest that while higher incomes are associated with living among a larger population or at a higher density, urbanization as such (with correction for total population and density) is not found to be so associated. A good deal of literature in urban economics is, in fact, built around the presumption that there are many advantages to urbanization or agglomeration for consumers as well as producers; for example, consumers in a large city would have access to a greater variety of private and public goods, among other considerations. A negative coefficient on the urbanization variable might reflect such possibilities.

In sum, the Nordhaus and Tobin results stand up reasonably well when subjected to "sensitivity testing" against other data and other specifications. Only the urbanization variable's interpretation seems to be in question. Specifically, our results using SMSA data, instead of county units, seem to suggest that the fraction urbanized is often associated with some reduction in real income and therefore could be characterized as a measure of amenity rather than disamenity. The other major change from the Nordhaus and Tobin results pertains to the variable measuring the percent of black population where a sign reversal, for reasons noted earlier, may not be totally inexplicable.

4. Real Wage Differentials and Urban Disamenities

In section 2 we suggested that more direct measures of salary or wage inducements necessary to compensate people for accepting locales of lesser amenity should be examined, on the hypothesis that the appropriate *marginal* valuation of urban disamenities might be better found in differentials in the sources of marginal income, principally earnings. Consequently, in this section we examine this possibility using wage information for unskilled workers, skilled laborers, and computer systems analysts. These categories were chosen both for data availability across our sample of SMSA's and because they broadly reflect three different income levels, a characteristic which might make it possible to determine whether the urban disamenity is a reality for all income groups.

The regression results for the original Nordhaus and Tobin specification of the model and our two variants of it are contained in tables 5 through 7. As was the case in the earlier regressions with real median income as the dependent variable, the sums of the coefficients on the population and density variables are quite stable across alternative specifications of the model, while the urbanization coefficient is rather more volatile. In sharp contrast with the earlier results, however, the signs on these variables are systematically reversed; that is, the degree of urbanization enters the disamenity calculation positively, while population and density decrease the measured disamenity.

There are several possible explanations for this. First, the estimated coefficients in the wage regressions are not statistically significant in our preferred specification of the model, although in the Nordhaus and Tobin formulation of the model, density has a statistically significant negative coefficient. With the addition of other amenity measures correlated with but not causally related to urbanization and density as in our preferred specification, the t-statistics on the density coefficients drop. When the District of Columbia and New York SMSA's are deleted from the sample, the standard error increases still more. The exclusion

Table 5. Regression Estimates of the Nordhaus and Tobin Specification with Log Real Wages as the Dependent Variable

SMSA data source	Skilled		Unskilled		Computer analysts	
	All observations	Without D.C. + N.Y.	All observations	Without D.C. + N.Y.	All observations	Without D.C. + N.Y.
Migration rate	0.002 (1.76)	0.002 (1.77)	0.001 (0.97)	0.001 (0.98)	0.00046 (0.25)	0.00046 (0.24)
Population Negro	0.0001 (1.82)	0.00017 (2.26)	0.00013 (2.0)	0.00019 (2.37)	0.00018 (1.87)	0.00023 (1.79)
Log total population (α_1)	-0.003 (-0.22)	0.00043 (-0.02)	0.006 (0.34)	0.01 (0.45)	0.01 (0.39)	0.01 (0.42)
Log population density (α_2)	-0.03 (-2.25)	-0.02 (-1.73)	-0.04 (-2.66)	-0.03 (-2.12)	-0.04 (-1.75)	-0.04 (-1.42)
Log % urban population (α_4)	0.15 (1.13)	0.07 (0.46)	0.07 (0.47)	-0.02 (-0.12)	0.04 (0.17)	-0.03 (-0.11)
Log median years of schooling	-0.59 (-1.22)	-0.18 (-0.30)	-0.20 (-0.36)	0.26 (0.39)	-0.07 (-0.08)	0.29 (0.27)
Log property tax per capita	-0.089 (-2.15)	-0.11 (-2.52)	-0.10 (-2.05)	-0.12 (-2.40)	-0.10 (-1.37)	-0.11 (-1.47)
Log local expenditures per capita	0.07 (1.53)	0.11 (2.07)	0.04 (0.74)	0.08 (1.33)	0.05 (0.65)	0.08 (0.87)
Population over 65	-0.00022 (-2.15)	-0.00032 (-1.88)	-0.00018 (-1.58)	-0.0003 (-1.53)	-0.00018 (-1.02)	-0.00027 (-0.91)
R^2	0.66	0.65	0.57	0.58	0.33	0.33
$\alpha_1 + \alpha_2$ (independently rounded)	-0.03	-0.02	-0.04	-0.02	-0.03	-0.03
α_4	0.15	0.07	0.07	-0.02	0.04	-0.03

Note: Figures in parentheses are t-statistics.

Table 6. Regression Estimates of the "Preferred" Specification of the Basic Amenity Equation with Log Real Wages as the Dependent Variable

SMSA data source	Skilled		Unskilled		Computer analysts	
	All observations	Without D.C. + N.Y.	All observations	Without D.C. + N.Y.	All observations	Without D.C. + N.Y.
Migration rate	0.002 (2.19)	0.003 (2.72)	0.002 (1.58)	0.002 (2.03)	0.00078 (0.42)	0.001 (0.71)
Population Negro	0.0009 (1.82)	0.0002 (2.93)	0.00013 (2.19)	0.00022 (3.12)	0.00015 (1.62)	0.00028 (2.37)
Log total population (α_1)	-0.01 (-0.51)	-0.03 (-1.27)	-0.003 (-0.12)	-0.02 (-0.88)	-0.01 (-0.27)	-0.05 (-0.81)
Log population density (α_2)	-0.02 (-1.21)	0.007 (0.36)	-0.03 (-1.73)	-0.003 (-0.19)	-0.009 (-0.29)	0.03 (0.87)
Log % urban population (α_4)	0.16 (1.22)	0.093 (0.68)	0.08 (0.58)	0.013 (0.09)	0.09 (0.37)	-0.017 (-0.07)
Log median years of schooling	-0.59 (-1.23)	-0.07 (-0.14)	-0.17 (-0.33)	0.35 (0.60)	-0.16 (-0.20)	0.57 (0.58)
Log property tax per capita	-0.09 (-2.31)	-0.14 (-3.41)	-0.10 (-2.35)	-0.15 (-3.45)	-0.10 (-1.48)	-0.16 (-2.23)
Log local expenditures per capita	0.06 (1.22)	0.15 (2.70)	0.02 (0.30)	0.11 (1.78)	0.09 (1.00)	0.21 (2.07)
Population over 65	-0.00019 (-1.85)	-0.00027 (-1.75)	-0.00014 (-1.29)	-0.00022 (-1.32)	-0.00013 (-0.73)	-0.11 (-0.89)
Water dummy	-0.03 (-1.43)	-0.06 (-2.79)	-0.03 (-1.37)	-0.06 (-2.62)	-0.07 (-2.07)	-0.067 (-2.91)
Log univ. per capita	-0.12 (-1.61)	-0.09 (-1.27)	-0.20 (-2.41)	-0.16 (-1.03)	0.152 (2.07)	-0.02 (-0.52)
Log average temperature	-0.003 (-0.18)	-0.02 (-0.96)	-0.006 (-0.29)	-0.02 (-2.13)	-0.002 (-0.08)	-0.00025 (-0.65)
R^2	0.72	0.76	0.68	0.73	0.43	0.51
$\alpha_1 + \alpha_2$	-0.03	-0.02	-0.03	-0.03	-0.02	-0.02
α_4	0.16	0.09	0.08	0.01	0.09	-0.02

Note: Figures in parentheses are t-statistics.

of these same outlying observations from our "kitchen sink" regression has a similar effect. This argument would be a more convincing explanation of the differences if the coefficients were not quite so stable in alternative specifications of the model.

A second explanation of this sign reversal pattern is that our real wage variables may be poor measures of sources of marginal family income. They do not account for differences in number of hours worked or variations in the length of the work year or opportunities for overtime. In this same vein, it might be argued that although wages may be the individual's marginal income source, they may be a poor measure of the family's marginal income earning opportunities. In the case of the family, opportunities for employment of secondary workers or "moonlighting" opportunities for the head of the household might be the relevant sources of additional income earning capability.

Although potentially attributable to measurement errors, observed differences in the median family income and wage regressions may also reflect different work–leisure preferences among different urban populations. To the extent to which a family can augment its total income, whether by added transfer income or higher earnings associated with employment of secondary workers in the household, the observed "urban disamenity" may be overstated.

In our sample of metropolitan areas, the labor force participation rate (total labor force divided by population, aged 18–64) is positively correlated with the fraction of urbanized population. The simple correlation of +0.11 is admittedly low, but is consistent with the hypothesis that urban areas vary in the degree to which they provide individuals with alternative choices of productive activities: this variety of alternative productive activities, coupled with the diversity of consumption alternatives in urban areas, may go a long way toward offsetting much of any urban disamenity. The income elasticity with respect to urbanization varies with income, as we hypothesized it might. In all three specifications of the model, the largest coefficient occurs in the regression for skilled wages and the lowest in the regression for computer systems analysts.

If these two groups have different patterns of intraurban residential location mobility, these results may imply that the urban disamenity is a truly local phenomenon. Specifically, computer analysts may "escape" the disamenities of urbanization by residing in the suburbs. To the extent that suburban locations complement the computer analysts' other consumption decisions and are made independently of disamenities in central areas, little added compensation for higher costs of "escape" is required. In the absence of this kind of intraurban mobility, one might have expected the valuation of the urban disamenity to increase with income on the grounds that there is an increasing distaste for the negative aspects of urbanization with increasing affluence.

The reasonableness of the estimated coefficients on the urban disamenity measures is reinforced by the extent to which the other estimated coefficients on the control variables have the anticipated values. In the various specifications, ten variables have anticipated signs on the coefficients which are unambiguous: migration rate $(+)$, universities per capita $(-)$, average temperature $(-)$, water dummy $(-)$, particulates $(+)$, SO_2 $(+)$, bond rating $(-)$, crime rate $(+)$, and number of newspapers $(-)$. The signs on these variables' coefficients are as expected in 106 out of 127 cases. Two other variables, property tax per capita and public expenditures per capita, have the "wrong" sign in 46 out of 54 cases. Application of two-stage least squares estimation techniques (the results of which are not contained here) usually results in the anticipated signs being observed for these variables as well, without otherwise seriously affecting the estimated relationships.

The remaining control variables have indeterminate signs because they measure both amenity and human capital characteristics. For these variables, sign reversal in alternative specifications is generally limited to the statistically insignificant median education variable. For one other variable, the fraction over age 65, the sign is reversed in the "kitchen sink" equation when the New York SMSA is included in the sample. Otherwise, these control variables are quite stable.

In summary, these real wage regressions do not reduce much our uncertainty regarding either the magnitude or existence of an urban disamenity due to a host of obvious theoretical and statistical limitations. Specifically, the signs on the basic population and urbanization variables remain contradictory or different—though admittedly in a way just opposite to that found when using median income as the dependent variable. In a sense, it seems that what "you lose on the swings, you gain on the roundabouts." In fact, a generous acceptance of these empirical results may raise more questions than are answered, particularly regarding the extent to which a wider range of both production and consumption alternatives in urban areas offsets the negative attributes of urban life.

5. Recalculating the Aggregate Urban and Population Disamenity Corrections

The denouement of the Nordhaus and Tobin urban and demographic analyses was to estimate an adjustment to be made to the national

Table 7. Regression Estimates of the Augmented (Kitchen Sink) Specification of the Urban Amenity Equation with Log Real Wages as the Dependent Variable

SMSA data source	Skilled		Unskilled		Computer analysts	
	All observations	Without D.C. + N.Y.	All observations	Without D.C. + N.Y.	All observations	Without D.C. + N.Y.
Migration rate	0.003 (2.36)	0.003 (2.32)	0.003 (1.73)	0.003 (1.70)	0.006 (2.81)	0.006 (2.63)
Population Negro	0.00013 (2.05)	0.00019 (2.37)	0.00016 (2.35)	0.00024 (2.67)	0.0002 (2.38)	0.00027 (2.15)
Log total population (α_1)	−0.005 (−2.05)	−0.03 (−1.01)	0.004 (0.14)	−0.02 (−0.81)	0.003 (0.08)	−0.01 (−0.25)
Log population density (α_2)	−0.04 (−1.77)	−0.01 (−0.41)	−0.05 (−2.14)	−0.02 (−0.67)	−0.02 (−0.58)	0.003 (0.08)
Log % urban population (α_4)	0.17 (0.98)	0.13 (0.80)	0.09 (0.5)	0.05 (0.30)	0.04 (0.14)	0.00092 (0.004)
Log median years of schooling	−0.64 (−1.24)	−0.26 (−0.44)	−0.19 (−0.34)	0.24 (0.37)	−0.43 (−0.58)	−0.09 (−0.09)
Log property tax per capita	−0.06 (−1.18)	−0.10 (−1.94)	−0.06 (−1.24)	−0.12 (−2.07)	0.02 (0.28)	−0.02 (−0.22)
Log local expenditures per capita	−0.006 (−0.10)	0.08 (1.04)	−0.06 (−0.86)	0.04 (0.50)	−0.07 (−0.79)	−0.005 (−0.04)

Population over 65	−0.00012	−0.00016	−0.00065	−0.0001	0.00057	−0.00019
	(−1.12)	(−0.85)	(−0.55)	(−0.50)	(0.37)	(−0.06)
Water dummy	−0.02	−0.05	−0.02	−0.06	−0.02	−0.04
	(−0.67)	(−1.70)	(−0.80)	(−1.95)	(−0.62)	(−0.98)
Log average temperature	−0.22	−0.18	−0.30	−0.25	−0.17	−0.14
	(−2.24)	(−1.88)	(−2.78)	(−2.44)	(−1.24)	(−0.97)
Log univ. per capita	0.00012	−0.01	−0.001	−0.02	0.004	−0.005
	(0.006)	(−0.63)	(−0.07)	(−0.76)	(0.15)	(−0.16)
Log particulates	0.02	−0.001	0.008	−0.02	0.13	0.12
	(0.57)	(−0.03)	(0.19)	(−0.46)	(2.41)	(1.93)
Log SO₂	−0.006	−0.001	−0.002	0.003	−0.015	−0.01
	(−0.50)	(−0.12)	(−0.15)	(0.25)	(−0.91)	(−0.63)
Crime rate	−0.00032	0.00017	0.00094	0.00033	−0.00095	−0.0008
	(−0.06)	(0.34)	(0.17)	(0.63)	(−1.33)	(−1.08)
Log bond	−0.01	−0.004	−0.01	−0.004	−0.02	−0.01
	(−0.48)	(−0.19)	(−0.43)	(−0.15)	(−0.72)	(−0.42)
No. of newspapers	−0.03	−0.02	−0.03	−0.02	−0.07	−0.07
	(−1.79)	(−1.54)	(−1.76)	(−1.51)	(−3.32)	(−3.05)
R^2	0.79	0.80	0.75	0.78	0.70	0.71
$\alpha_1 + \alpha_2$	−0.04	−0.04	−0.04	−0.04	−0.014	−0.01
α_4	0.17	0.13	0.09	0.05	0.035	0.0009

Note: Figures in parentheses are t-statistics.

income accounts to "correct" for disamenities attached to living in larger or denser populations and urbanized areas. The Nordhaus and Tobin estimates of these aggregates can be recalculated using our SMSA results by substituting a new "best guess" as to the elasticity between income and population change, and by updating the median family income and population figures to correspond to the 1970 SMSA sample rather than to 1960, the relevant year for the county data employed by Nordhaus and Tobin.

The first step in this exercise is to recalculate the disamenity estimates. The results are as shown in table 8 (adapted from table A.14 of Nordhaus and Tobin, 1972, p. 50) which, with its footnotes, is self-explanatory. The Nordhaus and Tobin population effect coefficients are shown in the upper part of the table (as taken from their table A.13 and our table 1) while the new estimates designated as "Meyer–Leone SMSA estimates" are shown in the lower middle of the table. Beneath these elasticity coefficients, the estimates of disamenity per unit change of income in 1958 prices are shown, that is, at the very bottom of the table. As shown in the table, our estimate of the total disamenity attributable to population effects is considerably higher than Nordhaus and Tobin's, being at a level of $2.75 of average household income in 1958 per one million of population, compared with $1.75 for Nordhaus and Tobin. On the other hand, we estimate a substantial *amenity* for urbanization, $4.45 of average household income per percentage point rise in average urbanization, while they estimate a *disamenity* of $3.75. Of course, these estimates are based on the results reported in section 3 using real median family income as the dependent variable. The signs of the corrections would be just reversed, though the net overall effect might not be too different, if the wage rate results of section 4 were used instead. Use of the income estimates, incidentally, also avoids some serious aggregation problems that one encounters with the wage coefficients and data.

The conversion of these disamenity and amenity estimates into corrections to be applied to the national income statistics is shown in table 9 (adapted from table A.15, p. 51, of Nordhaus and Tobin, 1972). On lines six and seven of this table can be found the Nordhaus and Tobin corrections and ours on both a per household and a total basis. We have also extended their estimates to the years 1970 and 1972, whereas the Nordhaus and Tobin estimates end with 1965. Consistent with our finding of a positive urbanization amenity, our estimates are considerably lower than those of Nordhaus and Tobin. Our corrections, though, are still not negligible. Specifically, our corrections start at about

Table 8.   A Comparison of Urban Disamenity Estimates

	Total population effect $(\alpha_1 + \alpha_2)$	Urbanization effect (α_4)
Nordhaus and Tobin county estimates		
Massachusetts, Rhode Island, Connecticut	0.019	0.059
New Mexico	0.006	−0.073
New York	0.045	0.035
Wisconsin	0.055	0.035
Indiana	0.064	0.017
Meyer–Leone SMSA estimates	0.07	−0.04
	Disamenity per unit change of income, 1958 prices	
Nordhaus and Tobin	1.75[a]	3.75[b]
Meyer–Leone	2.75[c]	−4.45[d]

[a] The coefficient is $1.75 of average household income (1958 prices) per one million of population: 1.75 = 0.06 (5,421/180.7) (1.0/1.029), where 5,421 = median family income in the sample states, 180.7 is the population of the United States in millions, 1.0 and 1.029 are consumer deflators for 1958 and 1960, respectively, and 0.06 is the elasticity between income and population change.

[b] The coefficient for urbanization is $3.75 of average household income per percentage point rise in average urbanization: 3.75 = 0.04 (5,421/56.2) (1.0/1.029), where 56.2 is average urbanization, 0.04 is the elasticity between income and the urbanization effect, and all the other figures are as described in note a.

[c] The coefficient is $2.75 of average household income (1958 prices) per 1 million population: 2.75 = 0.07 (10,567.5/208.2) (1.00/1.293), where 10,567.5 = median family income in the sample SMSA's, 208.2 is the population of the United States in millions, 1.0 and 1.293 are consumer deflators for 1958 and 1970 respectively, and 0.07 is the elasticity between income and population change.

[d] The coefficient for urbanization is −$4.45 of average household income per percentage point rise in average urbanization: −4.45 = −0.04 (10,567.5/73.5) (1.0/1.293), where 73.5 is average urbanization, −0.04 is the elasticity between income and the urbanization effect, and all other figures are as described in note c.

one-fifth the level of the Nordhaus and Tobin figures for 1929 and grow to a level just over one-third of their corrections for the years 1958–65. This relatively more rapid growth of our correction than theirs reflects the more rapid increase of population than urbanization effects during this period.

Our calculations also suggest that the total correction for these population and urbanization effects has roughly stabilized in the 1970s and perhaps might even have gone down a bit when calculated on a per household basis. This, clearly, is due to population growth rates slackening while urbanization continued; thus the "amenity" effects of urbanization offset the "disamenities" of continued population growth. A continued decline or a stabilization of presently low birth rates would

Table 9. Corrections for Disamenities of Population and Urbanization, Various Years, 1929–72

	1929	1935	1945	1947	1954	1958	1965	1970	1972
1. Households (millions)	29.5	32.5	38.9	40.3	46.9	51.0	59.0	63.4	66.7
2. Disposable personal income per household (1958 prices)	5,105	4,055	5,904	5,409	5,934	6,251	7,389	9,353	9,491
3. Percent urbanization	56.2	56.3	58.0	58.6	61.4	62.2	65.1	73.5	77.0ᵃ
4. Total population (millions)	121.8	127.3	140.0	144.1	163.0	174.9	194.6	208.2	209.9
5. Population density (persons per square mile)	40.3	42.1	46.5	47.9	53.9	57.8	64.4	68.9	69.4
6. Total correction per household (1958 prices)									
Nordhaus–Tobin	425.1	435.1	464.7	474.4	517.2	541.1	586.6	640.0	656.1
Meyer–Leone	85.0	100.0	126.9	135.5	175.0	204.2	205.5	245.5	234.5
7. Total correction (billions of dollars, 1958 prices)									
Nordhaus–Tobin	12.5	14.1	18.1	19.1	24.3	27.6	34.6	40.6	43.8
Meyer–Leone	2.5	3.2	4.9	5.5	8.2	10.4	14.5	15.6	15.6

ᵃ Estimated.

Line 1. *Historical Statistics* and *Statistical Abstract*, various years. Linear interpolation is used to estimate households in noncensus years.
2. Personal disposable income in 1958 prices (NIP Table 2.1) divided by line 1.
3. Same as line 1.
4. *Economic Report of the President, 1968,* Table B-21.
5. Line 4 divided by 3,022,387 square miles.
6. Equals $1.75 times line 4 plus $3.75 times line 3 for Nordhaus–Tobin. Equals $2.75 times line 4 plus −$4.45 times line 3 for Meyer–Leone.
7. Equals line 6 times line 1 for Nordhaus–Tobin or Meyer–Leone, as the case may be.

thus imply that this population-urbanization correction could or should shrink in aggregate size over the next two decades or so. Indeed, present low population growth extrapolations should make the correction negligible by the end of the century, as the national income totals continue to grow.

The methods that Nordhaus and Tobin used to convert their cross-section coefficients into time series corrections for urban and population disamenities invite several questions: To what extent do cross-section relationships truly measure the forces operative over time, a difficulty endemic to mixing time series and cross-section empirics? How does the particular way in which Nordhaus and Tobin choose to measure population density affect their outcome? As can be seen by studying the calculations in table 9, they essentially do this on an extremely aggregative or national basis. It is doubtful that such a measure truly reflects the "adverse" density increases one might expect to be attached to population growth and urbanization. Density measures are actually quite complex: for example, the peak density that people might experience during their working days, usually at workplace locations, contrasts with the far lower densities experienced at residential locations. In between would be many other densities which could influence most lives, certainly those experienced in commuting and quite possibly in shopping and recreational opportunities as well. In short, there are densities and densities, and exactly which dimensions are pertinent to an exercise such as this is hardly obvious. Nordhaus and Tobin's best defense is that in the absence of more information on these many difficult points, one might just as well proceed with the simplest and most aggregative measure, as they have done. But that is quite clearly a call for further research!

6. Summary and Concluding Observations

In essence, our results suggest that the Nordhaus and Tobin correction for population growth may be sensible, but the reality of the urbanization disamenity is at least doubtful. We find at least as much evidence of an urban amenity as of a disamenity. For the years since 1929, however, the correction for any urban amenity is not enough to fully offset the disamenities attached to population growth; thus the basic hypothesis of Nordhaus and Tobin that some "welfare" correction may be in order on these counts is not refuted. On the other hand, our results, coupled with recent demographic trends, suggest that this correction could well stabilize and become trivial in the near future.

Furthermore, to the extent our findings suggest a lowering of the total level of these corrections, the basic conclusions of Nordhaus and Tobin are only fortified. Nordhaus and Tobin entitled their paper: "Is Growth Obsolete?" Their answer was very much in the negative. Our findings, if correct, would only strengthen that negative response.

At the outset of this paper we were critical of the Nordhaus and Tobin model formulation and suggested several improvements to it. Having tested most of those improvements in our own reestimates, the estimates are, we believe, somewhat improved, but certain basic issues remain even more intriguing. For the most part the analysis remains at the "back-of-the-envelope" level of sophistication. A natural question, therefore, is: Should this wage differential analysis proceed and, if so, in what direction?

Clearly, more geographic detail is needed regarding the level of exposure of individuals to various urban disamenities. Has, for example, the flattening of population densities within urban areas (so-called sprawl) contributed to an urban disamenity or reduced it? Similarly, measures of income more effectively controlled for differences in the human capital stock would be desirable.

Even more troublesome are the efforts to extrapolate cross-section analysis to time series evaluations. On balance, such experiences probably should be discouraged or avoided wherever possible. If price adjustment creates an index number problem in a cross-section analysis, the problem is only compounded over time. Similarly, efforts at aggregation will become more complex as soon as the analysis escapes the simple world of logarithmic specification. Efforts to theoretically and empirically narrow the area of measurement to, say, land rents within urban areas, undoubtedly ought to be pursued, as argued by others in this volume. Such intraurban analysis would be consistent with desired geographic detail and potentially could answer all the questions about urban disamenities with better precision. In general, the alternative approaches to amenity measurement mentioned in the introduction to this paper almost certainly need to be pursued. In fact, wage rate or income studies may be the poorest of the four approaches. When and if these other lines of investigation are completed, an entirely different picture might emerge on the extent and character of any urban disamenity.

Finally, exercises of this type (most emphatically including our own) should not be taken too seriously. The value of the original Nordhaus and Tobin exercise lies in the attention it focused on important questions rather than in its substantive answers. Our paper can be best construed as simply a response to that challenge of unanswered questions.

Appendix

Standard Metropolitan Statistical Area

1	Boston	20	Minneapolis–St. Paul
2	Buffalo	21	St. Louis
3	Hartford	22	Wichita
4	Lancaster, Pa.	23	Atlanta
5	New York, N.E.,	24	Austin
	New Jersey	25	Baltimore
6	Philadelphia	26	Baton Rouge
7	Pittsburgh	27	Dallas
8	Portland, Me.	28	Durham, N.C.
9	Cedar Rapids	29	Houston
10	Champaign–Urbana	30	Nashville
11	Chicago	31	Orlando, Fla.
12	Cincinnati	32	Washington, D.C.
13	Cleveland	33	Bakersfield
14	Dayton	34	Denver
15	Detroit	35	Los Angeles
16	Green Bay	36	San Diego
17	Indianapolis	37	San Francisco
18	Kansas City	38	Seattle
19	Milwaukee	39	Honolulu

References

Hansen, W. Lee, ed. 1970. *Education, Income, and Human Capital.* Studies in Income and Wealth, no. 25 (New York, National Bureau of Economic Research).

Lave, Lester B., and Eugene P. Seskin. 1970. "Air Pollution and Human Health" *Science* (August 21).

Nordhaus, William D., and James Tobin. 1972. "Is Growth Obsolete?" in National Bureau of Economic Research, 50th Anniversary Colloquium, vol. 5, *Economic Growth* (New York, NBER).

Ridker, Ronald G., and John A. Henning. 1967. "The Determinants of Residential Property Values with Special Reference to Air Pollution," *Review of Economics and Statistics* vol. 49, no. 2 (May) pp. 246–257.

4
Problems of Measuring the Quality of City Environments

MICHAEL WHITBREAD

1. Introduction

MEASUREMENT assists with three main types of problem: general acquisition of knowledge, tests of propositions and theories, and the collection of comparative statements. In this paper, the main emphasis of the discussion will be on comparative evaluations of alternative public policies which alter the quality of residential environments. We do not focus on specific policies. The kinds of changes which we have in mind include "comprehensive" area improvement policies, traffic management schemes, developments in high amenity areas, the removal of noxious industries from residential areas, and so on. The task is to measure the welfare consequences of changes like these as precisely as possible for a local community. These changes are assumed to be externally imposed by the authorities.

At a general policy level, demand signals for public goods of the kind envisaged are unlikely to be very clear. Nor are the signals usually expressed in helpful ways as they pass through the political process. But at the local level, once it is known what areas may be affected, members of these communities can find ways to express their individual preferences about possible changes. They may do so through existing political processes or, where the threat is particularly serious, by *ad hoc* community actions.

For individuals to take an active part in collective decisions, the prospective rewards must outweigh the efforts involved. Since both the rewards and the costs of being politically active vary among individuals, not all those affected by the change will participate. For those who do, there is no obvious way in which decision takers can judge the relative merits of conflicts which will invariably arise. Accordingly, there is a possible case at both the local and general policy levels for obtaining independent evidence of gains and losses resulting from alternative options, and hence there is a case for comparative evaluation.

The evidence can be obtained from three broad categories of studies:

a. *Behavioral studies*. Researchers analyze responses of community members to actual or potential environmental changes and use their behavioral responses to make appropriate deductions. Apart from political activity, those groups on the receiving end of some externally imposed environmental change are unable to influence events which affect them except by incurring transaction costs. They can move away, with possible consequences for property prices. They may otherwise take individual steps to exclude a nuisance, for example, by installing sound-proofing in their houses in the case of noise. Or they can try to group together in a private association which attempts to achieve their collective objectives of preserving environmental quality and locally excluding nuisances. Investigations of such behavioral responses to actual and potential environmental changes can provide useful evidence of community preferences. So far, most of this evidence has come from a variety of house price studies. Less extensive material exists from work on exclusion facilities, studies of mobility, and, the least extensive so far, studies of the activities of large leasehold estates, community groups, and other forms of economic clubs. The existence of transaction costs, of either moving or grouping, should influence the interpretation of evidence derived from these behavioral studies. Where transaction costs are large relative to the enviromental change, intramarginal consumers will not provide a behavioral response from which deductions can be made.

b. *Experimental studies*. In these studies, members of the community participate in controlled games. Their reactions to simulated environmental conditions are observed and evidence is obtained by relating the reactions to the objective characteristics of the simulations. Both the simulation itself and the questions which are asked about it are hypothetical. Experimenters have the dual problems of making the situations which are being presented as realistic as possible, and then of constructing a framework of questions which can be used to make judgments about people's preferences and perceptions.

c. *Social surveys*. In such surveys, subjects participate in interviews and express opinions in response to questions, often about their current circumstances and sometimes about hypothetical alternative states. Of the three study categories, this type of attitudinal evidence is the most detached from objective environmental stimuli. The most interesting social survey research exercises have involved some simulation of sorts and hence overlap with the experimental studies. One technique which is often encountered in social survey work is to ask respondents to rate situations, such as their own living conditions, on bipolar "satisfaction" scales (say, on seven points from very poor through to very good). These scores may apply to elements of the scene taken individually and the overall scene; explanations of overall scores are then obtained from the scores on the individual elements.

2. Perception and Relative Valuation

These three categories of research are approaches to measurement. The problem remains of deciding what is to be measured. Before considering in detail some interesting approaches to measurement, we shall first consider some principles. The reduced-form house price model is used as an example.

There are two principal measurement steps in estimating the welfare change; first, the measurement of the environmental change itself in physical units, and second, the valuation of the change over the relevant range by members of the community. When multiplied by the physical measure and summed over all individuals, the relative values give the required measure of welfare gain or loss. The importance of the first stage of this two-step measurement process has been largely glossed over, especially by economists eager to estimate and debate their relative valuation coefficients. Often there is no uncertainty about appropriate physical measures to use. Difficulties come when images are not sharp, as is the case with many environmental phenomena. Here we refer to "perception" as the endeavor to find suitable physical measures of environmental phenomena.

The reduced-form house price model is of the following general structure:

$$P_j = \sum_i \beta_i X_{ij} + \epsilon$$

where:

P_j = price of the jth dwelling
β_i = relative value of the ith characteristic
X_{ij} = quantity of the ith characteristic for the jth dwelling
ϵ = stochastic error term

Simplifying the research process somewhat, with prices observed the researcher's task is to measure the dwelling characteristics, including its environmental characteristics across a range of dwellings, and to undertake a multivariate analysis to obtain β coefficients to fit the model. If all the requirements of statistical scrutiny are met and it is assumed that price is a suitable measure of the value of dwellings in different circumstances (setting aside all problems of interpreting reduced-form price equations), then the model gives the relative values at the margin of the dwelling characteristics. The β coefficients are the marginal values and the X_i's are the measures of the characteristics in physical units. What kind of evidence should be used to obtain these X_i's?

3. Measuring the Environmental Change

The house price model illustrates the measurement problems that exist with the physical indexes of change: the first difficulty is that unambiguous measures can rarely be found for explanatory variables. An example is provided by an extensive house price study of the Bristol housing market by Ball and Kirwan (1975). The authors wished to test the influence of proximate large buildings on dwelling prices. They believed, *a priori*, that "overlooking" would adversely affect perceived dwelling quality and hence, price.

They measured this phenomenon by a dummy variable which took the value of 1 if the "dwelling or site was overlooked by a large building more than seven metres higher than the building containing the dwelling within twenty-five metres radius"; otherwise the value was zero (Ball and Kirwan, 1975, p. 228). The authors did not verify the measure in any way with any other research nor was it obtained from another source. The issue here is not to quarrel with the measure, but rather to point out that it could obviously be replaced by any number of alternative measures of overlooking. Why use a discrete variable? Why 7 meters higher? Why 25 meters radius?

To take a different kind of example, some researchers have used an index of the social composition of the areas in which dwellings are situated as a potential environmental influence on price. Wabe (1971), for example, in his study of house prices in the London region, used as a variable the proportion of occupied and retired males in socioeconomic groups 1, 2, 3, and 4 (mainly professional people and managers), "because it gives a measure of the social character of the boroughs . . . the higher the proportion of these social classes the greater the price of houses, other factors equal" (Wabe, 1971, p. 250). This variable may measure the social character of the boroughs, although some verification of that fact would be welcome. But it may not be the best measure of that characteristic. It would be easy to find other measures which could be used, and other spatial units, apart from the local authority, to employ in the assessment.

So, since not all possible measures of a phenomenon are equally good, some must be superior in some way. The problem of deciding on which *one* to take becomes important as a practical issue where the correlations between different but equally plausible measures are not high. It must be clear from the few examples presented here that the problem of selecting a measure is greater the less precise the concept.

Individuals vary in the way they perceive phenomena because of differences either in their cognitive ability or in their personality traits in relation to the complexity of the phenomena. Extraneous events may also play a part in the interpretation of some environmental factors to produce confusion or distraction. There are often real difficulties of communication which hinder the search for measures. Environmental phenomena present additional difficulties of measurement in that there is a spatial dimension to consider. Views and visual intrusions extend across space. The neighborhood is a spatial unit which has to be defined in conjunction with the neighborhood characteristics which are thought to impinge on the amenities of a particular dwelling.

Poor measurement of environmental variables may produce not only traditional measurement errors but also misspecification of variables. Even if the measures which are used for the environment are the best possible average-value indexes based on perception research, wide variations in perception among individuals imply that there will be econometric difficulties when relative value coefficients are to be estimated. They are analogous to measurement errors of the usual kind since the values as measured will deviate from the values which would apply for people experiencing the phenomenon. This is a complex issue but, in brief, even with the best physical index of an environmental phenomenon, the standard errors of its estimated coefficients in the regression analysis will be large and the coefficients themselves could be biased, probably downward.

So far in this discussion we have implicitly assumed a distinction can be drawn between perception and relative valuation. In the context of the house price model, we are assuming that the β coefficients are independently derived. While this may be the correct analytical procedure, it must be recognized that the greater the subjectivity of the phenomenon in question—and hence the greater the difficulty in measuring it—the greater the confusion between a factual impression of magnitudes and the forming of attitudes toward them.

Experimental research is likely to prove to be the most fruitful in this field where sharply defined stimuli can be carefully prepared for exposure to people. But we have carried out some very simple but wide-ranging tests in a social survey of residents for a variety of less well-defined stimuli. These tests were conducted partly in order to obtain measures, albeit of an unsophisticated kind, for environmental phenomena, but they were also undertaken in order to obtain some insights into how well and how consistently people perceive environmental phenomena in their own residential districts and in what ways selected environmental phenomena are perceived. Respondents were asked questions about features of their neighborhood environment. Their responses were compared with data collected by physical survey and from social variables in the census. For example, one of the questions was about on-street car parking: "Would you either agree or disagree that there are many cars left parked on the streets in this district?" The objective was to test the responses against the actual level of car parking in the streets, for example, as measured at different times and over different spatial extents. We counted vehicles parked on streets per 100 meters in the respondent's area at three different times: during the weekday, during the evening, and on Sunday. The table shows the distribution of values that emerged:

	Number of cars per 100 meters		
Respondents' perception	Weekday	Evening	Sunday
Too many cars ($n = 699$)			
Mean (m_1)	6.7	9.5	8.5
Standard deviation (S_1)	5.1	6.7	6.3
Not too many cars ($n = 283$)			
Mean (m_2)	5.5	7.1	6.6
Standard deviation (S_2)	4.8	4.5	4.0

There are a number of ways of inspecting this data, one of which is a simple index of discrimination (d) between the two groups of respondents, where

$$d = \frac{m_1 - m_2}{S_1 + S_2}$$

Values were as follows: d (weekday) = 0.12, d (evening) = 0.21, d (Sunday) = 0.18.

Accordingly, the evening measure maximally discriminates between them when this index is used and hence, of the three measures tried, it best reflects the environmental item of on-street car parking. This is of some interest since many of the areas where the social survey was conducted had heavy daytime car parking because of nearby factories and shops. Moreover, the correlation coefficients among the three parking measures over all respondents indicate that there is not much association among them:

	(1)	(2)	(3)
Weekday (1)	1.00		
Evening (2)	0.30	1.00	
Sunday (3)	0.34	0.78	1.00

Similar questions were asked about other physical aspects of the urban scene. We also asked about social composition. For example: "Do you think on average people live at much the same social level as you do, or at a lower or higher social level?" A possible reply of "it varies" was allowed. The procedure was then to take the responses of each person interviewed and, using data collected elsewhere in the questionnaire on household characteristics, to compare the response in the context of the respondent's social level with the social composition of the neighborhood. The spatial units were initially the census enumeration districts, and then amalgamations of contiguous census enumeration districts.

Five broad census socioeconomic groups (SEG) were used. Several combinations of groupings were tried, but the most suitable was for "higher" social level to be taken literally as all SEGs of higher rank order and, similarly, "lower" social level was taken as those of lower rank order. Because of the somewhat ambiguous nature of a "same" response, this category was taken to be the same groups plus the next SEG above and below in rank order. Thus, if the respondent was classified as being in SEG II, then:

Higher = SEG I
Lower = SEG III, IV, and V
Same   = SEG I, II, and III

Taking census enumeration districts as the appropriate spatial unit, there were 772 cases for which full data were available, of which as many as 59 percent of responses showed a discrepancy between the response and the characteristics of the enumeration district population. This could be because the census enumeration district is a poor spatial unit for this exercise. However, various amalgamations of enumeration districts showed no improvements. Alternatively, we may have been poor coders of SEG. Perhaps the SEG as traditionally defined is not a very good indicator of social level in people's minds. Whatever the case may be, it does seem that there is some evidence here for supposing that residents do not have a very clear perception of the social composition of their districts, especially given the generous definition of the "same" category.

This evidence does not invalidate the use of the SEG variable in, say, some house price regression studies, since in cases where areas are more socially uniform over wider distances than in our survey areas, no doubt perceptions of social composition would come close to reality. But it does suggest that there are other cases where single measures of environmental phenomena should not be readily based on *a priori* judgments of appropriate measures.

4. Evaluating the Environmental Change

The house price model provided examples of some of the measurement difficulties which are encountered with environmental phenomena. It also provides an example of one approach to the way different characteristics measured in disparate physical units can be converted into units of common relative value. The β coefficients of the linear form of the house price model purport to measure both the willingness of marginal house purchasers to pay for unit increases in their respective characteristics, and their willingness to be compensated for unit decreases in those characteristics, other things being equal.

The relative valuation principle of this example is one of equivalence. When payment is made, the consumer is thereby unable to use that income or wealth in other ways, such as for the purchase of other goods or services, the value of which is assumed to be given by their price. The proposition is that definable and physically measurable changes in a person's well-being are measured by changes in the quantities of other items which are valued at an equivalent rate. Cash has the virtue of convenience in use as a unit of common relative value for the obvious reason that the exchange value of very many consumable goods and services is expressed in those units.

The house price example allows us to inspect the usefulness of this measurement concept. The relative values obtained by it would normally be for small changes in physical characteristics. Few changes which the authorities can make to the environment of dwellings are marginal and many can be very serious, such as the routing of urban motorways through residential areas. Large changes in the environments of dwellings will affect the well-being of existing residents who, after the change, are not then marginal purchasers. Movement costs would have to be zero for the price change to measure the welfare change to these people. They would move out and a new set of marginal purchasers would move in to replace them at the new price. Since transaction costs of changing dwellings are not zero, but are large relative to typical price changes resulting from environmental changes, existing residents may be worse (or better) off as a result of the changed environment by some amount other than the price change. So some alternative principle of relative valuation may be required for large environmental changes.

There are two broadly defined measurement options. Taking the case of a deterioration in quality, we can try to compute either the amount residents would willingly give up to achieve the same amenity levels as before, or the amounts that they would be prepared to just willingly receive and feel themselves no worse off. In the latter case they are assumed to possess an "amenity right" which the authorities must theoretically purchase, while in the former the authorities are assumed to possess the right to remove amenities which the residents must theoretically acquire. Whatever the principle of measurement to be used, the house price model does not provide us with either of these values, given the existence of nontrivial transaction costs. Accordingly, evidence from some other sources would be required to fulfill that task.

There is another problem of a more structuralist nature associated with this use of house price coefficients which should be mentioned in this context. Any changes should apply to only a few dwellings of the total stock available. Widespread changes, such as those discussed by Polinsky and Rubinfeld (chapter 8) in the context of air pollution control, require a general equilibrium model—which those authors discuss—rather than a marginalist model of the reduced-form house price equation.

5. Behavioral Evidence

Despite the difficulties with the use of house prices as a basis for measurements, and the many statistical problems which have been encountered by researchers who have undertaken house price studies, this method supplies the best evidence on relative values of environmental changes that we have to date. Certainly in situations where there is a large, varied, and widely owned housing stock, and given conditions of reasonably free negotiations to exchange property rights, prices are hard behavioral evidence of revealed preference. Unfortunately for those interested in measurement, satisfactory conditions for the free determination of prices do not always exist. Accordingly, it is not always possible to use observed prices as evidence of the gains or losses from environmental change. To illustrate the difficulties involved, we may use the United Kingdom example of a housing sector which is common to many advanced western countries, often referred to as "social" housing. The tenure arrangements and the management of this social housing stock explicitly preclude the free determination of price.

Thus in the United Kingdom about one-third of the housing stock is managed institutionally by local authorities in a manner which is far removed from that of private markets. For this sector, it is impossible to derive satisfactory willingness-to-pay estimates for characteristics of the stock since the rents charged for dwellings, while being loosely related to the dwelling quality, are not intended to allocate households to dwellings. Rather, rents are required only to "pay" for the dwellings; that is, broadly to cover historic costs to the authority.

If we are to obtain behavioral evidence of tenants' preferences for different types and characteristics of housing within this stock, then something other than rent must be found. The precise nature of these demand signals will depend on the institutional arrangements of housing management. Tenants of local authorities in the United Kingdom have a *de facto* right to permanent occupation of their dwelling for nominal obligations. But they cannot sell or in any way negotiate that *de facto* property right. Existing tenants cannot sell up nor can prospective tenants buy into the stock.

There are two main ways for existing tenants to acquire improved housing. The tenant can move out of the public housing sector altogether, thereby incurring the general cost differential between sectors as well as paying the premium for the quality improvement in the private sector. This is a maximum cost of acquiring the improvement and one for which it is possible to obtain estimates of numbers of tenants willing to incur the cost—for whatever reasons—through mobility surveys. Alternatively, tenants can hope to obtain better housing and environmental conditions within their own sector. While this cannot be achieved through financial payments (which are illegal), we do observe queues for the better local authority dwellings. The lengths of time people are prepared to wait for better accommodation in the stock provides another indication of the maximum willingness of tenants to "pay."

We might therefore take a closer look at those tenants who are waiting to move. They are quantity-constrained at the prevailing rents. Categorizing dwellings by type, the net (positive) queue for type (i) is represented by $(Q_b - Q_a)$ in figure 1, where Q_a is the number of those dwellings in the sector and R_a is their rent level. The demand to live in those dwellings by people within the public sector arises from the horizontal summation of demands of existing residents of the dwellings, some of whom want to move out (and hence are *willing* to pay somewhat less than the rent they do pay) and other council tenants who want to move in, of which those who are prepared to pay more than rent will be observable in the queue. These curves are represented in figure 2. Clearly, there are a variety of aggregate benefit measures as expressed

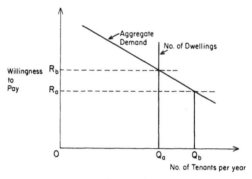

Figure 1

by willingness to pay *(WTP)* to live in these dwellings. Among them are the following:

a. The *WTP* of people who do live in them *(OGCQ_a)*.

a. The *WTP* of people who do live in them $(OGCQ_a)$.

b. The *WTP* of those who would willingly live in them at the prevailing rent if they could $(OGAQ_e + OEDQ_p)$.

c. The *WTP* of those who would willingly live in them at market clearing rents of R_b in figure 1 $(OGZH + OEWI)$.

d. The *WTP* of group c *plus* the willingness (of those who are waiting) to pay to avoid the wait, which depends on the value of their time spent waiting.

There is no obviously superior measure available. But whichever measure is sought, there also is no obvious way of obtaining it without making heroic assumptions about the nature of these demand curves or the costs of having to wait for a better dwelling.

Moreover, apart from the difficulties of estimating a surplus change, any estimates will, at the very least, depend on the persistence of existing institutional arrangements. Any attempt to create and assign negotiable property rights to council dwellings will not only affect their occupants' surplus changes, but will affect them in ways that depend on who receives the benefit from the assignment. The local incidence of the created wealth will affect the surplus values. So, if tenants themselves become the beneficiaries (for example, if they are allowed to freely negotiate their tenancies), they would be wealthier by the value of those rights. This situation can be compared with one in which tenants would first have to purchase negotiation rights from the authorities in the form, say, of buying a conventional freehold interest in their dwelling from the local authority. The willingness to pay for amenities will depend on the wealth of the residents which, in turn, depends on who receives this created wealth.

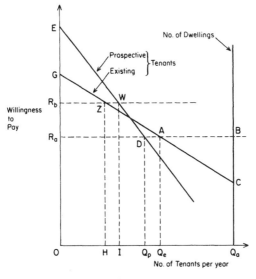

Figure 2

The evidence available suggests that no willingness-to-pay estimates can be derived from observations of tenants' behavior. However, the queuing data are not without usefulness as indicators of the relative weights which tenants attach to attributes of dwellings in their sector. For example, a model can be postulated which is analogous to that of the house price model in free markets:

$$Q_i = f(X_{1i} \ldots X_{ni}, R_i)$$

where Q_i is the queue for dwelling type i, $X_1 \ldots X_n$ are its attributes, and R_i is rent.

Several formulations of queue length are possible; they can be expressed as actual one-way flows into or out of types of dwellings, actual net flows, or as any of these expressed as percentages of the number of dwellings involved. Whichever formulation is adopted, queue length then becomes the dependent variable in cross-sectional analysis of different dwelling types, and price (or rent) is an explanatory variable. Relative values of attributes and rent may then be determined for observed queue variations by regression analysis across different dwelling types. While an exercise of this type may provide us with relative weights for attributes which are *indicative* of tenants' preferences, it is difficult to see how strict economic interpretation can be given to them.

The same conclusion applies to other types of behavioral evidence within the local authority sector, such as actual mobility, which has already been mentioned, or tenants lobbying the authorities for change, or the growth in tenant management and participation arrangements and cooperatives. These events indicate tenant dissatisfaction, but they do not provide very sound evidence of what should be done (if anything) by way of improvements. Accordingly, finding behavioral evidence of sufficient quality may not always be possible because of institutional constraints on behavior, and other factors. Evidence on relative values of environmental changes may have to be obtained by other means.

6. Evidence from Social Survey

Behavioral studies do not always allow us to observe or otherwise assign a monetary value to environmental change, as the preceding section made clear. But they may be based on an analysis of the revelation of preference by a response to alternative environmental conditions. Both the response and the conditions are real, and the problem of the researcher is confined to measuring them within some suitable theoretical framework.

Some social surveys attempt to ask people about their behavior only to provide data for a behavioral study—for example, about a recent move they may have made. Others directly ask people about their preferences. It is this type of social survey which is the subject of this section. Since they are based on *asking* about preferences, they must contrive situations under discussion, and hence they introduce an inevitable amount of artificiality into the research.

At its simplest level, this research can be conducted by asking people to compare stated options by choosing between them, or by ranking. Slightly more complex formulations involve the use of bipolar rating scales from, say, "very poor" through five or seven or so points to "very good." Among his experiments, Troy (1971) asked his respondents to rate their locality in total as a place to live on a five-point scale and also to rate it on the same scale for each of a list of attributes. The essential feature of his subsequent analysis was to use the general rating score as the dependent variable in a linear model, to be explained by the rating scores on each attribute. Hence, the relative contribution or importance of each attribute to overall levels of stated satisfaction could be estimated.

Others have probed preferences using less formal and quantitative approaches, such as adjective checklists and analysis of the semantic differentials in responses to different conditions. In most social surveys of environmental conditions, loadings on responses to structured questions of the general form: "What things do you most like (dislike) about this district?" are analyzed and compared with objective measures of the physical and social characteristics of the places.

These approaches normally use the respondents' own residential area, or ones nearby, as the stimulus. Another way of approaching the question of desirability is for respondents to identify those localities which are broadly comparable on some defined scale of desirability. Mental maps have been used, for example, by Gould and White (1968) and Gould and Ola (1970) at a variety of levels to probe spatial differentials in the desirability of living conditions.

At their most useful level, social surveys can only be used to obtain an idea of relative values of items over a narrow range. They should not be underrated for that. Among recent interesting results emerging from social survey analysis of traffic nuisances, Hedges (1973) found that the popular notion that noise is the primary nuisance was unsubstantiated. Danger from traffic was seen as the main factor. Moreover, noise was found to be no more significant as a nuisance than vehicle fumes.

None of these methods provides us with relative values in units commensurable with other items of cost or benefit. The evaluation of particular nuisances, such as traffic or aircraft noise, has been researched by social survey in order to ascertain money values through direct questions. This approach has been tried by some economists wanting to explore the possibilities of obtaining this evidence. The results have not been wholly successful. In brief, the method relies largely on asking people to stipulate either how much compensation, sometimes expressed as rent changes, they would require for tolerating a given disamenity, or how much they would be prepared to pay to improve a given situation. Hedges (1972), in a comprehensive review paper, points out the many difficulties in interpreting results from this kind of research: the questions are hypothetical and relate to conditions which are difficult to describe; there is a presumption that people have "orderly" minds in nonmarket situations; custom and context may be critical, especially where there is an unwillingness to accept the notion of valuation of social costs (the typical expression from subjects is that it is for the authorities to "do something about it").

Researchers have used ingenuity in varying the manner in which questions are posed. One example is the ping-pong question: the interviewer tries to establish first an upper, then a lower limit to satisfactory compensation payments for the respondent for some defined disamenity, and then tries to narrow the range in successive steps. While this may well produce an answer when otherwise one would not be forthcoming, we do not know if it is anything like the answer we are seeking. If respondents find it difficult to make judgments about an abstraction, bullying them into disclosure will not help.

There is also some evidence to suggest that if a scale of possible values for a disamenity is shown to respondents, similar distributions of responses tend to emerge whatever the scale values. Thus, whether the scale is over the range £0–5 or £0–50 does not much affect the distribution of responses to points on the scale, only the values themselves (by a factor of ten).

The use of a social survey has the obvious advantage over behavioral studies in that more direct and comprehensive information is available to the researcher than is available in the scattered secondary sources. The data collected can be restricted to the problem in hand. But surveys are not inexpensive, and, as indicated here, do not necessarily provide reliable results for ascertaining environmental values.

While improvements may be possible in the way questions are posed, it is more likely that developments in this broad area of social research will come through extending the researchers' control over the nature of the environmental options which are put to people. Some examples of these approaches are discussed in the next section.

7. Experimentation and Preference Revelation

The experiments simulate environmental conditions. This is much easier for some nuisances, such as noise or visual intrusion, than those which are not so spatially specific, such as air pollution. At the level of the simplest technology, the images may be generated by line drawings, photographs, or photoviews of the same scene, but with varying environmental conditions. This was done by Michelson (1966) and by Peterson (1967). Peterson asked respondents to rank options, concentrating on the physical elements and appearance of the scenes, and subjected his results to statistical analysis. Michelson used a content analysis of taped interviews to draw out his conclusions. Social and Community Planning Research in London also has tried a variety of visual aids in experiments, many of them trying to determine relative values by giving respondents a "budget" to allocate across different conditions in display units.

An environmental simulator which has been constructed at the Transport and Road Research Laboratory (TRRL) in England, and which is discussed by Dawson (1974), utilizes a more sophisticated technology. It consists of a simulated living room in which traffic scenes from the "picture window" are shown by means of back projection of sound film. The intention is to associate the traffic flows with sound levels. The sound can be controlled for any level of traffic by "opening or closing" the window. The research method is to have participants in the experiment sitting in the room, a few at a time, and to expose them to the views and traffic noise levels, which can be controlled and varied by the experimenters. A number of short films, each of about five minutes' duration and showing different views and traffic levels, were available. Four films were shown to any one group of respondents in sequence. Respondents then completed a brief questionnaire about them.

One of the ways the experimenters attempted to ascertain relative money values for the disturbances depicted in the different films was to encourage respondents to imagine their own home in the context of each of the views. They were asked to place a value on their home and then to estimate its value to them if it were somehow transferred to each of the sites in the films. Almost all the subjects had great difficulty in making these kinds of judgments and were only able to grope for values, often without much consideration.

A simulator at Berkeley's Institute for Urban and Regional Development takes a different perspective. As might be expected of research based in California, it simulates the view *from* the moving vehicle rather than the view *of* moving vehicles. An accurate scale model of an area of potential development, possibly 5 square miles or so in size, has been constructed in a laboratory. A periscope camera runs around the roads of the model to provide the view from the road, which is projected onto a screen. The view can be altered by the modelers in different runs by moving the developments about from one locality to another. People from the community in question see the resultant films and are able to "vote" on the development possibilities. As far as this writer is aware, no attempt has been made to probe their willingness to pay or to be compensated to accept one scheme rather than another, although electronic voting procedures have been used which might be adapted for this purpose.

Another interesting experiment, worth discussing because it places subjects in a position which is very close to real world environmental degradation, is the "noise machine." One such experiment has been undertaken in the United Kingdom under the guidance of TRRL, but we believe there have been other independent attempts along similar lines elsewhere. The experiment concentrates on one environmental element, noise, rather than a wide range of possible influences which may impinge on subjects' preferences, as in the Berkeley and TRRL simulators. Essentially, it is an indestructible tape recorder which cannot be switched off or disconnected except by the researchers and which continuously relays traffic or aircraft noise. It is installed into the dwellings of willing participants in the experiment (so far, into only one bedroom in each dwelling). The original idea was to have it playing for a short period, say a week, and then for the researchers to go back to the occupants to obtain reactions to the nuisance *and* to offer bribes for permission to continue with the experiment for a much longer period. The researchers have to try to find the minimum acceptable bribe. The nuisance is accurately presented, it is known to those affected and, subject to bargaining margins, something like true compensation values are obtained. Moreover, the experiment can be quite inexpensive since the researchers do not have to pay up; it is sufficient only to know what would have to be paid for the right to create the nuisance. Pilot results of noise machine experiments have provided some money values for disturbance. They have also provided some insights into relative values through subjects' behavioral reactions to the bedroom noise. Sixty percent claimed to have slept through the noise every night, while the remainder moved to another room. One subject moved his visiting mother-in-law into the bedroom.

The noise machine experiment, because of the brilliance of its conception, highlights some of the fundamental problems of experimental research based on simulations. The image to which people are exposed in the experiments must be clear and well-defined; otherwise we cannot be sure that respondents are reacting to those aspects of the simulation which are in the researchers' minds. With the noise machine, the image is precise, but there are very few other disturbances for which this is the case.

The questioning of subjects also requires careful consideration. In the case of the noise machine, there are certain obvious factual data about subjects' reactions during exposure to the nuisance which can be collected. Even so, opinions, especially opinions about the outcome of further exposure to the nuisance, present all the usual interpretational difficulties that exist for social survey evidence. The question of what sum respondents would require as compensation for a continuation of the experiment has to be very carefully handled. Even with genuine bidding, the researchers can never be entirely sure of what has been agreed upon in the transaction. With less straightforward money questions, where respondents have to make some kind of intellectual abstraction and state values on an hypothetical basis without suffering any consequences, the values are easily criticized as worthless.

8. Concluding Remarks

Subtleties of theory regarding the assessment of social gains or losses as a result of public programs which alter urban environments are almost totally academic in the face of the practical measurement problems involved. Margins of error in estimations are likely, in most instances, to swamp any variations in outcomes which would be due to variations in the principles of assessment.

Measurement errors of a special kind exist with the physical representation of phenomena. This is because of the wide variation in subjective responses to comparable objective conditions, especially for those environmental phenomena where it is not possible to isolate sharp images. Nevertheless, there is a real prospect of improving on measures of visual intrusions, townscape quality, and other more nebulous elements of the environment with more intensive research than these topics have received in the past.

Of the three broad kinds of research evidence on relative values, that coming from behavioral studies is clearly the hardest. However, only comparatively rarely does this evidence allow us to obtain direct money values. Conditions which are necessary for us to obtain such values do not always exist, even within housing markets where environmental conditions are consumed. Still, we could use more behavioral evidence even if it is not aimed specifically at the estimation of money values. Some aspects of experimental research have produced useful insights and as long as the experiments can be well constructed (and are cost-effective), there is probably a good case for further encouragement of that line of enquiry. We may, however, have had enough examples of social survey evidence.

All this is not to argue against a rigorous theoretical base for these issues of welfare economics. Nor does it imply that the research efforts to establish empirical values for environmental costs and benefits are futile, even though any one exercise may be open to heavy criticism. On the contrary, it is a case for continuing to explore the topic in a variety of ways and in many different institutional as well as economic and environmental contexts. It is a case for using research to establish a broad base of evidence on environmental values.

References

Ball, Michael, and Richard Kirwan. 1975. *The Economics of an Urban Housing Market, Bristol Area Study, CES RP-15* (London, Centre for Environmental Studies).

Dawson, Ray F. 1974. *Environmental Simulator: Progress Report* (Transport and Road Research Laboratory Report 659).

Gould, P. R., and R. R. White. 1968. "The Mental Maps of British School Leavers," *Regional Studies* vol. 2, pp. 161–182.

———, and D. Ola. 1970. "The Perception of Residential Desirability in the Western Region of Nigeria," *Environment and Planning* vol. 2, pp. 73–87.

Hedges, Barry. 1972. "Attaching Money Values to Environmental Disturbance—A Review Paper" (London, Social and Community Planning Research).

———. 1973. "Road Traffic and the Environment" (London, Social and Community Planning Research).

Michelson, William. 1966. "An Empirical Analysis of Urban Environmental Preference," *Journal of the American Institute of Planners* vol. 32, pp. 355–360.

Peterson, George L. 1967. "A Model of Preference: Quantitative Analysis of the Perception of the Visual Appearance of Residential Neighbourhoods," *Journal of Regional Science* vol. 7, pp. 19–31.

Troy, Patrick M. 1971. "Environmental Quality in Four Sydney Suburban Areas," (Urban Research Unit, Australian National University).

Wabe, J. Stuart. 1971. "A Study of House Prices as a Means of Establishing the Value of Journey Time, the Rate of Time Preference and the Valuation of some Aspects of Environment in the London Metropolitan Region," *Applied Economics* (December).

5

Local Government, the Property Tax, and the Quality of Life: Some Findings on Progressivity

BRUCE W. HAMILTON

1. Introduction

SURELY one of the primary determinants of the quality of life in an urban area is the manner in which wealth is distributed among its citizens. The effects of poverty upon such diverse indexes of human endeavor as birth rate, crime, family structure stability, and physical and mental health, are sufficiently well documented to justify this claim.

Historically, public-sector concern for the distribution of income has been largely the domain of local (city and county) government. Even with the major national redistribution programs instituted in the United States in the 1930s, many observers feel that an important fraction of redistribution still takes place through local governments.[1] These observers point out that local taxes increase with income (though possibly not proportionately), but that the benefits of local expenditure in general do not. Indeed, some programs, such as welfare, public health facilities, and possibly public schools, are used more heavily by the poor than by the rich. So it appears that the poor, paying less and getting roughly the same amount in services, receive a net financial transfer from the workings of local governments.

Recently, the notion that local governments redistribute wealth in the manner outlined above has been challenged by Charles Tiebout (1956) and his followers. They argue that the rich, rather than allow themselves to be taxed in order to fund services for the poor, form

This research was supported by National Science Foundation Grant SOC 74-02255. In addition to contributing data, Peter Mieszkowski made a major intellectual contribution to this work.

[1] See, for example, Gillespie (1965).

exclusive jurisdictions where the fiscal structure can generate no redistribution because there are no low-income residents.

In this paper I am concerned with another aspect of the consequences of income distribution by local governments. In particular, I will present an argument, and some evidence, that the local property tax is much more regressive than is commonly believed, and that as a result the poor are not net financial beneficiaries of the workings of local government.

It is well known that the ultimate burdens of taxes are distributed among the people in a very complicated manner (see Harberger, 1962), and in a manner that sometimes bears little resemblance to the nominal tax structure. For example, a sales tax might reduce the income of consumers, capital owners, or workers, depending upon how the market adjusts to the tax. In the case of the local property tax, I believe it can be demonstrated that the burdens fall more heavily upon the poor than would appear from a casual reading of the statistics. Assume, for example, that every householder spends 20 percent of his income on housing, and that 10 percent of this expense is the property tax. Every householder pays 2 percent of his income in property taxes, and the tax is proportional. But in arriving at this conclusion, we have assumed that the tax structure has not altered any of the prices faced by consumers. I will argue later that the property tax, as it is constituted in many North American cities, tends to increase the price of low-income housing and depress the price of high-income housing. The result, of course, is a fiscal structure much less favorable to the poor than appears from consideration of tax liabilities alone.

I do not intend to offer a full treatment of the incidence of the local property tax, but rather to focus on one force which contributes to the incidence. My concern is with the effect of the local property tax upon the incentive for exclusionary zoning, and the effect of this zoning upon the prices of different types of housing.

The per household tax base of a jurisdiction varies inversely with the number of low-income dwelling units because these units will not generate as much tax revenue as will the more expensive houses. This being the case, it is in the interest of the property owners of a jurisdiction to restrict the number of low-income houses as much as possible. The intent is simply to force the poor to live elsewhere. But the result, if every community pursues the same policy, is to restrict the total supply of low-income housing and to drive up its price. Simultaneously, the price of high-income housing is reduced, because land which would have been devoted to low-income housing is available only for high-income housing. A full analysis of the progressivity of the property tax

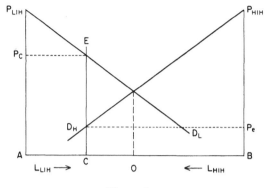

Figure 1

must take into account the effect of this tax on zoning laws and housing price changes.

The framework can perhaps be seen most readily in figure 1. The length of the horizontal axis represents the total amount of land in the urban area (all communities are aggregated here). The left-hand vertical axis represents the price of land if it is devoted to low-income housing (LIH), and the right-hand vertical axis represents the price of land if devoted to high-income housing (HIH).[2] There is a downward-sloping demand curve for LIH, and hence for land devoted to LIH. The latter is depicted, and is labeled D_L. Similarly, there is a demand curve for HIH land, but as the zero point for HIH land is at the right-hand side of the graph, this curve will appear to be upward-sloping.

We can now inquire how the land will be divided between LIH and HIH. In a free market, land would command the same price in both activities, and we would have AO land devoted to LIH and OB to HIH. But if each jurisdiction attempts to exclude LIH, the total amount of land available to this activity will shrink, freeing up land for HIH development. This is indicated by CE and the associated prices P_c and P_e.

2. Taxes and the Price of Housing

Let us define the fiscal surplus as the excess of public-sector benefits over taxes for any housing unit. Since a positive fiscal surplus must be financed by a negative surplus attached to some other house,[3] communities may use zoning to exclude houses with a positive fiscal surplus. The consequence of this restriction is to raise the price of such

[2] For illustration we represent the range of house values by these two classes.

[3] If there is no nonresidential property and no intergovernmental transfer.

housing. Potentially, then, the hypothesis can be tested by observing whether house values are positively correlated with fiscal surplus, after correcting for the physical value of inputs into housing. Or to state the matter in somewhat more traditional terms, we wish to know whether fiscal surplus differentials are capitalized into property values.

If the entire fiscal surplus is capitalized into the value of a house, then any tax advantage to low-income housing is completely offset by the increased price of the house. In such a case, the tax structure is perfectly inelastic with respect to income, making the tax far more regressive than observers have conventionally claimed. But if none of the surplus is capitalized, then traditional demand studies appropriately measure the progressivity of the property tax. So the question of capitalization, or differentials in property values associated with fiscal surplus, is central to understanding the distributional consequences of local fiscal activity. We must specify the conditions under which such capitalization will occur.

3. Theory

In equilibrium, the value of a house, like the value of any market commodity, must be two things at once; it must reflect the present value of the services provided by use, and it must be equal to the reproduction cost, including the opportunity cost of the land.[4] The first (demand) condition indicates that the value of a house must contain the present value of any fiscal surplus, and that any systematic variation in the amount of the fiscal surplus across house-size classes must lead to variations in house value over and above those explainable by differences in the value of inputs. On the other hand, the supply condition specifies that houses must sell at reproduction cost, and this seems to indicate that only variations in building materials and labor may explain variations in house values. Of course, disequilibrium conditions brought about, for instance, by rapid racial turnover or failure of the housing stock to fully adjust to new market conditions might explain house values that exceed or fall short of reproduction costs, but the question is whether such deviations will be maintained.

It is readily apparent that, in the absence of market interference, no capitalization effects may exist; the values of various classes of houses will simply reflect the cost of materials, labor, and land, and the demand for various classes of house will have to accommodate to these

---

[4] In the presence of zoning, it should be noted that the term "opportunity cost" of land must be defined rather carefully, since alternative opportunities are defined by the zoning board and will vary from parcel to parcel.

exogenous prices. Some sort of market interference is required if there is to be capitalization of intrajurisdictional differences in fiscal surpluses. Zoning and other housing and land use controls constitute just such interference. If supplies of various types of houses are controlled by these nonmarket forces, then the price of each class of housing will simply be the intersection of its demand curve with the supply as set by the forces interfering with the market. In such a circumstance, the value of each type of housing may well deviate from its land and construction costs. Or perhaps more correctly, the value of at least some of these resources will vary according to the type of housing to which they are devoted.

It seems clear that land, rather than physical capital or labor, is the resource whose value might vary across housing-type classes. Let us formalize this with a simple model of a jurisdiction containing i house value classes

$$Q_{si} = \bar{Q}_{si} \tag{1}$$

Equation (1) states that the number of units of housing type i supplied,. Q_{si}, is exogenously determined by law.

$$Q_{Di} = [Q_{Di}(V_i + tV_i)] = Q_{Di}[(1 + t)V_i] \tag{2}$$

The number of units of type i demanded is a function of the price of the house, V_i, plus the tax liability tV_i.

$$Q_{si} = Q_{Di} \tag{3}$$

The price of housing must be such that the quantity supplied of each type is equal to the quantity demanded. We wish to solve equations (1)–(3) for V_i, given Q_{si} and the parameters of the demand function. But first we must either take t as given or solve for it. We can solve for it by taking expenditure per house as given, and setting t at that level which will raise just enough revenue to finance local public benefits, X. Thus t becomes a function of house-class mix:

$$t = X/\sum_i b_i V_i \text{ where } \sum_i b_i = 1$$

where b_i is the fraction of houses of type i. So $\sum_i b_i V_i$ is the property tax base for the jurisdiction.[5]

Given b_i, this simple model can be solved for V_i, the value of each type of housing, and for t, the jurisdiction tax rate. Standard progressivity analysis would now inquire how Vt_i varies with income, and draw

---

[5] The relationship between V_i and $\Sigma b_i V_i$ will obviously depend upon the supplies of the housing classes determined by the zoning authorities.

conclusions from the observed functional relationship. I propose, rather, the following procedure. As a first step, examine the relationship between the value of inputs into each class of housing and the sale price of the housing classes:

$$V_i = \sum_j P_j I_{ji} + a(X - tV_i) \tag{4}$$

where P_j is the price of input j and I_{ji} is the amount of input j used in house class i_j, the coefficient a is the rate at which the fiscal surplus $(X - tV_i)$ is capitalized into the value of the property, and X is the value of local public benefits per house. If $a = 0$, then all houses sell at replacement cost. If on the other hand, $a = 10$ and the discount rate is 10 percent, the entire fiscal surplus is capitalized into the property value. I contend that the appropriate way to measure the progressivity of the property tax is to measure the relationship between income and the *sum* of tax liability and capitalization effect (i.e., tax structure-induced deviation of house cost from replacement cost).[6]

As an alternative equivalent statement of the problem, we may consider the value of a house to be equal to the value of its materials, labor, and land, but recognize that the price of one of these, land, can be altered by adjusting its supply, that is, by zoning. We also recognize that the price of land need not be the same for all types of housing. If it is true that low-income housing is higher priced than high-income housing, it must be because land is higher priced when it is devoted to low-income housing. Accordingly, it is useful to recast the relationship between house value and value of inputs as follows:

$$V_i = \sum_{j=2}^{n} P_j I_{ji} + R_i L_i \tag{5}$$

Here we treat the capitalization effect as a determinant of the price of land (L).

Before discussing questions of measurement, it is well to note that capitalization effects and hence the related market interference can only serve to *reduce* (or leave unchanged) our estimates of the progressivity of the property tax, because of the way zoning works in North America. In general, residential zoning classifications set maximum density limits or minimum lot sizes, and lot size is highly correlated with house value. Areas zoned to permit high-density development may be developed to low-density standards, but low-density zoning prohibits high-density development. This characteristic of U.S. and Canadian

[6] Before taking the sum of tax liability and capitalization effect, it will of course be necessary to annualize the capitalization effect or take the present value of the tax liability.

zoning tends to maintain the value of high-density land above that of low-density land: it can restrict the supply of low-income housing, but not high-income housing. Of course there would be no fiscal motivation for encouraging the development of low-income housing at the expense of high-income housing anyway.

We now have two alternative statements of the capitalization hypothesis: (1) the value of housing exceeds or falls short of the value of the inputs in accordance with the magnitude of the fiscal surplus attached to it; (2) the value of land varies according to the fiscal surplus associated with the house to be built upon the land.

These two statements of the hypothesis suggest two different techniques for measuring capitalization effects. First, if capitalization exists, the value of a house is equal to the value of its inputs plus the present value of the excess of public-sector benefits over taxes.[7] So we could examine the values of houses, correct for the value of the physical inputs, and observe whether there is a residual value to be explained by the fiscal surplus.[8]

A potentially simpler approach suggests itself if we assume that any capitalization effects appear in land values. If fiscally motivated zoning makes low-income housing scarce and drives up its price, it must have the same effect upon land which is destined to be developed as low-income housing. This view of the situation is represented in equation (5). If we can observe raw land, some of which is destined for development as high-income housing and some of which is destined for low-income development, and if we can adequately correct for any difference in the parcels (aside from the zoning category) which should influence their prices, we can note whether land values differ because of the type of development permitted, and we can observe the manner in which these differentials are related to the fiscal surplus. This technique is identical to that described in the paragraph above except that observation of raw land rather than developed property enables us to circumvent the problem of correcting for the value of the capital inputs placed upon the land.

4. Land Price Differentials

Several problems must be borne in mind when examining land prices in the manner suggested here. First, within any urban area, land values

---

[7] In this formulation we treat land as having the same value regardless of the type of housing that is built upon it.

[8] The author is attempting to apply this technique in another study. However, as it is not being applied here, I will not discuss it in further detail.

Table 1

(i) Zoning category	Units/acre	(tV_1) Tax rev./unit	(X) Gov't costs/unit	Land price $ acre
R½	½	1800	801	50,000
R3	3	749	801	100,000
R2	2	1210	801	90,000
RM2	12	361	801	150,000

vary significantly for completely nonfiscal reasons such as differences in accessibility or amenity. So any attempt to ascribe land price differentials to differences in fiscal surplus must correct for access-related differences. The second problem is that of accounting for the value of assets attached to the land. We could either use a hedonic price index, or restrict our observations to "raw" land. However, the value of the fiscal surplus is not known until the land is developed, a condition further complicated by the fact that land is occasionally rezoned and developed at a different density than the zoning at the time of observation would indicate. Indeed, if the market anticipates this rezoning, the land value will not represent what we think it does. In addition, land has degrees of "rawness": it increases in value as such infrastructure capital as sewers and sidewalks are attached to it and as government permission to develop it is granted. This is most notable in some cities in the United States and Canada where such items as sewer permits are difficult to obtain.

Bearing in mind these caveats, I will present some rough comparisons between fiscal surpluses and estimated serviced land values per acre for metropolitan Toronto.[9] First we report some fiscal characteristics of various types of zoned land as estimated by the North York (a suburb of Toronto) Planning Department. Table 1 is extracted from the planning department. The next step is to compare fiscal surpluses with land value differentials per acre. The numbers collected by Mieszkowski are reported in the last column of table 1. (See footnote 9.)

The data on 2-acre (R½) lots and R3 lots are both for fairly central locations in downtown Toronto, and thus should be roughly comparable in nonfiscal attributes. And the R2 and RM2 lots are from comparable suburban locations, so I feel fairly safe in treating the nonfiscal attributes of these parcels as similar. Unfortunately, we are not justified in making comparisons across all four classes. Finally,

---

[9] These numbers were assembled by Peter Mieszkowski and have appeared in a somewhat different form in a paper by Hamilton, Mieszkowski, and MacFarlane (1974).

some inaccuracy must result from the fact that the fiscal data are from 1967, whereas the land value data are for 1973, but it seems unlikely that the fiscal variables would have changed very much relative to one another, between 1967 and 1973.

We see that 2-acre lots generate roughly $500 per year in fiscal surplus per acre to the remainder of the city, whereas the R3 lots generate essentially a zero surplus. At a 10 percent discount rate, full capitalization of this differential would lead to a $5,000 per acre land price differential between these two types of land. But the actual price difference is ten times that amount or $50,000 per acre. Or, looking at the same thing strictly in terms of the progressivity of taxes plus capitalization effect, at a 10 percent discount rate, the present value of the taxes on a 2-acre house is $18,010 as against a present value of tax liability of $7,490 for an R3 lot. The fiscal burdens would be identical for the two structures if the land devoted to the 2-acre house sold for $10,520 less than the same amount of land devoted to R3 structures. In this circumstance the income elasticity of the fiscal burden would be zero. But land zoned for R½ sells, not at a $10,000 discount, but at a $100,000 discount per lot ($50,000 per acre times 2 acres per lot). So, within this range it seems clear that the income elasticity of the fiscal burden is negative.[10]

The burden also has a negative income elasticity in the range between R2 (½-acre lot size for detached houses) and RM2 (12 attached units per acre). An R2 occupant pays a present value of $8,490 more in taxes than does an RM2 resident. An R2 lot costs about $45,000, whereas the same land (½ acre) zoned RM2 costs $75,000. So, relative to his $8,490 "excess" tax burden, the R2 resident is more than compensated by the fact that his land costs $30,000 less than if he had to pay RM2 prices. Again, the income elasticity of the burden is negative on the 10 percent discount rate. The burdens are equal if the rate is assumed to be 3 percent.

The above answers are not definitive inasmuch as there is an indeterminacy as to the true opportunity cost of land. In the comparison between R2 and RM2, we stated that R2 is subsidized at the rate of $30,000; this is the amount by which his lot value is depressed below the market or opportunity cost value. But, this is based on the presumption that the opportunity cost of land is $150,000 per acre, or the cost of RM2 land. Suppose instead we take the $90,000 per acre R2 price to be the opportunity cost. We now are led to the conclusion

---

[10] Only if we assume a 1 percent discount rate are the fiscal burdens equal for the two houses. And the rate must be less than 1 percent for the large house to have a greater dollar burden than the small one.

that RM2 occupants pay a $5,000 penalty as a result of the land-market interference. This number, being less than the present value of the tax difference between R2 and RM2, implies that the aggregate burden imposed upon RM2 is less than that imposed on R2. And, this in turn implies, assuming that RM2 residents are less affluent than R2 residents, that the income elasticity of the fiscal burden is greater than zero.

These numbers allow us to obtain some idea of the elasticities involved. We begin by assuming the income elasticity of demand for housing to be +1 (see deLeeuw, 1971) and thus the percent difference in the (assessed) value is equal to the percent difference in income of the two resident groups. On this assumption, the income of R2 residents is 2.4 times that of RM2 residents. The percent difference in fiscal burdens is calculated first under the assumption that the opportunity cost of land is $150,000 per acre, and thus that R2 residents receive a capitalization bonus of $30,000. The total fiscal burden for R2 under this assumption is −$17,900, made up of −$30,000 capitalization effect and +$12,100 present value of tax liability. The fiscal burden imposed on RM2 is $3,600, or the present value of the taxes. There is no capitalization effect here, as this group is required to pay exactly the opportunity cost of land. We find that R2 pays −5.9 times the fiscal burden of RM2, giving an income elasticity of fiscal burden of −2.4. As indicated in footnote 9, the elasticity estimate rises to zero when the discount rate falls to 1 percent and becomes positive at lower rates.

Under the assumption that the true opportunity cost of land is $90,000 per acre, and thus that the capitalization effect appears only in the value of RM2, analogous calculations yield an income elasticity of fiscal burden of +0.169, still a highly regressive tax system.[11] Assuming that the true opportunity cost of land is somewhere between $90,000 and $150,000 per acre, the income elasticity is bounded by the −2.4 and the +0.169 figures. (If we assume a discount rate of 2.5 percent, the +0.169 figure rises to 0.5.)

We have actually calculated, not the income elasticity, but the housing-expenditure elasticity of fiscal burden. This must be multiplied by the income elasticity of housing expenditure—equal to the income elasticity of demand if (1) the price elasticity is −1, or (2) the price of housing is invariant—to find the income elasticity of the fiscal burden. On the assumption that the opportunity cost of land is $150,000 per acre, any positive income elasticity of demand will leave the income

[11] $\Sigma = \dfrac{B_{R2} - B_{RM2}}{B_{RM2}} \Big/ \dfrac{Y_{R2} - Y_{RM2}}{Y_{R2}} = \dfrac{12100 - 5000 - 3610}{5000 + 3610} \Big/ 2.4 = 0.169$

where B_i = net fiscal burden for zoning class i.

elasticity of fiscal burden negative, since higher priced houses have a lower fiscal burden. On the alternative assumption, an income elasticity of demand in excess of unity will raise the estimated elasticity of fiscal burden above the 0.169 figure. Since R2 houses carry a somewhat larger fiscal burden than RM2 houses, a high income elasticity of demand for housing will cause the fiscal burden to grow more rapidly with income. However, it would take a demand elasticity of 6 to make the fiscal burden actually progressive.[12] The highest plausible estimates of the income elasticity of demand for housing are on the order of 2.0, and there seems to be a growing concensus that the true figure is nearer unity (see deLeeuw, 1971). So within this range, the property tax burden appears to be highly regressive, with an income elasticity of no more than 0.2 to 0.4 and possibly as low as −2.

5. Conclusions

These results indicate that the fiscal burden arising from the property tax is distributed much more regressively than, to my knowledge, anybody has ever suggested. Indeed, under one set of assumptions the regressivity is so severe that occupants of R2 housing have a negative fiscal burden! If the land-value data are to be believed (in particular, if we believe that the comparisons are for sites which are identical except for the way in which the land is zoned), and if the fiscal statistics are reasonably accurate, there seems no escaping the fact that burdens are distributed roughly in accordance with the statements made here.

It may, however, be inappropriate to assign this entire distribution of burdens to the local property tax. If restrictive zoning is practiced just as vigorously in the absence of local property taxation as with it, then the price differentials among housing classes should not be counted as a part of the distributive burden of the property tax. This makes little difference if one is interested in the distributive effect of all local government institutions taken together; the burdens exist regardless of the forces which brought them about. But, if one is evaluating the property tax with an eye toward changing it, the distinction becomes of central importance. Then we must know whether restrictions on the supply of low-income housing would be eased if the property tax were replaced with a different revenue instrument.

Finally, even if further research corroborates these estimates for Toronto, it would require an enormous leap of faith to assume that similar patterns of land use restriction exist in cities in general.

---

[12] And, under the other opportunity cost assumption, a demand elasticity of 6 would generate a fiscal-burden elasticity with respect to income of −14.4.

If these findings are, in broad outline, corroborated for other income ranges and for other cities, we can no longer think of local governments as providers of essential services without regard to ability to pay. If our cities are instruments of escape from poverty, it is because of the employment possibilities of the private sector, not the public services and income transfers of the public sector. In the important dimension of redistributing income, the contribution of local government to the quality of life may be negligible or even perverse.

References

deLeeuw, Frank. 1971. "The Demand for Housing: A Review of Cross-Section Evidence," *Review of Economics and Statistics* (February) pp. 1–10.

Gillespie, W. I. 1965. "Effects of Public Expenditures on the Distribution of Income," in R. A. Musgrave, ed., *Essays in Fiscal Federalism* (Washington, Brookings Institution).

Hamilton, B. W., Peter Mieszkowski, and Craig MacFarlane. 1974. "Equity and Efficiency Aspects of Fiscal Zoning," unpublished.

Harberger, A. C. 1962. "The Incidence of the Corporation Income Tax," *Journal of Political Economy* vol. 70 (June) pp. 215–240.

Tiebout, Charles. 1956. "A Pure Theory of Local Public Expenditure," *Journal of Political Economy* vol. 64 (October) pp. 416–424.

PART II

6
Justifiable Government Intervention in Preserving the Quality of Life

DAVID W. PEARCE

1. The Role of Government: A Classification of Views

DESPITE the title of this volume, I find myself in the position of a near-monopolist in that my brief alone appears to encompass the actual role of government in improving the quality of life. While this provides a clear temptation to treat the subject with some abandon, monopolists often have to beware countervailing power, and I have no doubt that this exists in more than adequate supply among my colleagues. I shall therefore try to take care to make my theme clear, since what I have to say will strike some as supporting an authoritarian or nonliberal viewpoint about the role of governmental institutions. Given the enormous scope of the subject matter, I have chosen to take a broad sweep approach to the question of how to determine the function and justifiable extent of government activity in improving the quality of life.

Traditionally, government has been assigned the role of intervening when the market fails. It is then logical to ask what it is that the market fails to achieve, and the conventional answer is that it falls short of securing a Pareto optimum and, on the micro scale, potential Pareto improvements. Already then, this view of government implies an objective function of the Pareto form. It need not do so, of course, because we could equally well establish some other objective function, perhaps incorporating some concept of distributional justice or whatever, and argue that the market fails to achieve this end. The nature of government activity implied by the view that markets fail to achieve Pareto-type ends takes the twofold form of direct provision of public

I am very much indebted to Michael Common of the University of Southampton for comments on the first draft of this paper, and to Lowdon Wingo for his characteristically generous and careful suggestions for improving the expression of ideas in this paper. I remain entirely responsible for errors of fact or argument.

goods which, it is argued, are provided on an insufficient scale by markets, and the regulation of relative prices to reflect otherwise inappropriate or uncompensated externalities.[1] Defense and crime prevention perhaps fit the former category, and developments such as the "polluter pays" principle perhaps fit the latter. The function of government in this view is a secondary one: a successful market is held to be preferable to government as a means of providing the components of the quality of life (QOL). Invariably, the advantages of the market are held to lie in its efficient provision of low-cost information. The justifiable extent of government intervention is then determined by the degree of publicness and the costs (and benefits) of externalities. As long as market failures in these areas are readily identifiable and minor, government activity will be minimized. We might indeed dub this philosophy the "peripheral intervention" view precisely because its advocates invariably appear to believe that the degree of externality constitutes only a minor flaw in the otherwise Pareto-desirable workings of the competitive system.

Even within the confines of this Paretian standpoint, however, the extent of externality may indeed render this view of the minimal role of government untenable. Ayres and Kneese (1969) and Kneese, Ayres, and d'Arge (1970) show that residuals generation in an economy is endemic and pervasive. The first law of thermodynamics requires that whatever is taken from the environment as a resource must reappear as a transformed residual of equal weight discharged from production and consumption processes: retention of resources in physical or biological capital merely alters the temporal phasing of this essential equation. The extent of externality depends on the distribution of residuals in relation to the spatial distribution of environmental assimilative capacity. Such general equilibrium approaches serve at least to remind us that partial approaches are dangerous in fostering "tunnel vision": in this case, the inability to see environmental systems as a whole.

Second, the peripheral intervention view fails to acknowledge that markets do not correct for residuals, which accumulate either because the volume of waste generation exceeds the assimilative capacity of the environment or because some kinds of waste undergo no corresponding short-run degrading process in the environment. The approximate form of government activity in such cases may well have to be coercive rather than regulatory.

---

[1] "Public goods" are here taken to include the provision of "anti-bads"; that is, services, such as pollution abatement, which are designed to ameliorate public bads. See Beckerman and Markandya (1974).

Third, there are forms of externality that accrue unperceived until some threshold is passed. If social learning processes are inadequate, the activities giving rise to such externalities will also require coercive treatment.

The main point is that market failure has to be seen as something that is extensive and endemic to economic systems, not as a peripheral deviation from the ideal. If we accept the government's role of intervention when markets fail, it follows that we have a prescription for widespread government activity. Indeed, Mill's dictum that "the only purpose for which power can be rightfully exercised over any member of a civilised community, against his will, is to prevent harm to others" (Mill, 1859) does not establish the basis for a society with minimum coercion, but for an extensively regulated society.

If the ideology of peripheral intervention cannot be sustained on its own terms, are there other factors which can restore it? First, the mere existence of externalities is not *ipso facto* justification for intervention if the market can in some way be adjusted to cope with them. We contend that in reality the market will not be capable of dealing with significant externalities in the manner suggested by the market bargain literature.

Second, and close to Mill's own view, government intervention is itself an externality. The real merit of this argument lies in the failure of government to identify the preferences of those who are least able to avail themselves of established means of communication and expression. But this failure is also common to markets insofar as they reflect the prevailing distribution of market power. The justification of government activity in this view must then rest on a hazardous comparison of the relative efficiencies of government and market as mechanisms for dealing with the less articulate and less privileged.

2. Markets and the Quality of Life

If indeed, the maximum QOL is characterized by Pareto optimality, can markets be relied upon to achieve it in the presence of apparent market failure without significant modification?[2] There is an apparent paradox in this question, in that it presupposes that they may not be able to do so: if markets really can cope, they will already have done so and any observed externality must be optimal—the so-called Pareto irrelevant externality. Whether we are observing a Pareto relevant or Pareto irrelevant externality, we have little to go on. Indeed, all the pollution and other third-party effects we observe in an economy may, in fact, be

[2] The significant statement on this issue is, of course, that of Coase (1960).

optimal, so that this is, after all, the best of all possible worlds. However, market bargains in externality are conspicuous by their absence—at least, beyond the examples of interdependence that seem to have occupied the literature.

Market advocates will counterargue that bargaining uses real resources, so that the absence of bargains may also be optimal, the welfare gains from any prospective bargain being outweighed by the costs of securing the bargain. More specifically, if bargaining is costless, it will pay both parties to engage in trade to reduce the level of externality. For each unit of externality reduction, that reduction will be justified as long as

$$\Delta TEC > \Delta TB$$

where *TEC* is total external cost and *TB* is total private benefits (net of private costs). This requirement is not altered if we introduce bargaining costs (*TBC*). If property rights are vested in the externality generator, the sufferer will bear the bargaining costs. The condition for trade to take place then becomes

$$\Delta TEC > TBC + \Delta TB$$

If trade does *not* take place, it will be because the sufferer's gains (ΔTEC) are less than the sum required to compensate the externality generator plus bargaining costs. Whatever level of activity is observed then, must be the optimal level: if trade has taken place, we are observing a social optimum and if trade has not taken place, we are also observing a social optimum. But if we cannot say what a *nonoptimal* state would look like, we have no way of testing the validity of the statement that what we observe is a state of optimality.

The issue of bargaining cost is not the only problem with the supposition that the market can cope with externalities.[3] For example, Buchanan (1969) points to the nonapplicability of Pigovian taxes to externality problems in a context of imperfect competition and then uses this defect to substantiate his claim that bargaining, generated by market forces, is superior. His argument can be considered in terms of figure 1, where we have the firm's demand curve $P(X)$, marginal revenue curve $R'(X)$, marginal private cost curve $C'(X)$, and marginal external cost curve $E'(X)$. Marginal social cost is then given by $C'(X) + E'(X)$. Let the starting point be the firm's private equilibrium, (X_p, P_p). Price (P_p) is already in excess of marginal social cost. The imposition of a Pigovian-type externality tax will merely lead the imperfectly competitive firm to equate marginal revenue and marginal social cost

[3] I have looked at the whole array of difficulties elsewhere. See Pearce (1976a).

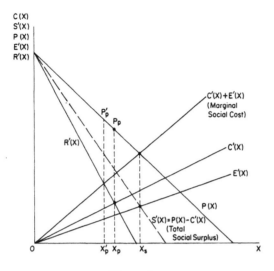

Figure 1

(now that the latter becomes equal to marginal private costs plus tax) at (X'_p, P'_p). This places the firm in an equilibrium position with price (P'_p) above marginal social cost. However, it is simple to demonstrate that a Pareto optimal position will be secured if marginal external cost is equated with what we shall call marginal social surplus—the marginal change in producer's and consumer's surplus combined. The latter can be written as

$$S'(X) = P(X) - C'(X)$$

where $S(X)$ is total social surplus. If marginal external cost $E'(X)$ is set equal to $S'(X)$, we have at X_s

$$E'(X) = P(X) - C'(X)$$
$$\text{i.e., } P(X) = E'(X) + C'(X)$$

which is the condition for a Pareto optimal output (assuming other productive units obey the same rule).

Now, $S'(X) = E'(X)$ could be secured by tripartite bargaining between the generator of the externality, the purchasers of the generator's good, and the sufferers of the externality. Notwithstanding that Buchanan sees this as a vindication of the market bargain analysis, it is, in fact, the opposite, for bargaining is inoperative where bargains have to take place among large groups. Tripartite bargaining takes the bargaining solution further outside the realms of reality (Pearce, 1974c).

The problem of large groups characterizes significant externalities such as air, water, and soil pollution. Furthermore, bargains cannot take place if *ex post* pollution damage is not readily ascribable to identified polluters, as evidenced by the complexities of applying even the current riparian legislation in the United Kingdom. Polluters have every incentive to conceal their activities once they recognize that detection and the ascription of responsibility is difficult. Indeed, distribution of factor rewards could well end up reflecting the distribution of threat-making power rather than marginal productivities (Mumey, 1971).

Finally, it is not clear what relevance market bargains have for the effects of cumulative pollutants. Bargains can be meaningful only if the externality generator has some means of using his *flow* of externality as a bargaining parameter. But where externality is related to non-degenerative and, by and large, noneradicable pollution *stock*, this element is absent (Nobbs and Pearce, 1975). Of course, bargains may take place with respect to the current flow if the stock in existence is already judged Pareto-irrelevant, with the added complexity that the externalities from stock pollutants could occur almost anywhere and at any time. The ingestion and inhalation of cadmium, for example, is, apart from the few dramatic cases, unrelated to spatial proximity to its sources of emission. Equally, since cadmium operates in a cumulative fashion, its ill effects may not be known for decades, by which time it will not be clear who should be bargaining with whom and to what end. And if the argument is extended to such other stock pollutants as certain radioactive wastes, we have the unresolved problem of how future generations can bargain with current and past generations.

We conclude that the market is not capable of coping with significant externalities. We are left in the interim with the conclusion that neither peripheral intervention nor market adaptation defines the function and extent of government regulation. We appear to have support for extensive interference, and all this within the confines of a Pareto optimality framework.[4]

---

[4] Of course, some of the defects of market bargains apply equally to certain forms of governmental regulation. Thus, under imperfectly competitive conditions Pigovian regulatory taxes will not be optimal either unless market failures due to deviation from perfect competition are corrected first. Such taxes may, however, serve non-Paretian ends very well by securing accepted QOL standards at least cost. For this view in the context of environmental pollution, see Baumol and Oates (1971) and for a contrasting view supporting standards without the regulatory support of taxes, see Burrows (1974). In order to limit the scope of this paper, we leave these issues largely undiscussed, treating Pigovian-type regulation and direct control as instances of government control.

3. Government as Externality

The second line of argument designed to reestablish the role of the market in meeting QOL objectives turns to the undesirable aspects of government intervention, that is, government activity itself as a negative externality, as in the reduction in freedom that is inevitably associated with government regulation. Mill epitomizes this liberal tradition when he warns that, even if the state can perform a specific task more efficiently than individuals, assigning that task to government adds to the power of the state and reduces the power of the individual.

Even if government activity does constitute an externality, however, it is far from evident that this externality is more important than the social costs that would otherwise result from the free play of market forces. Because the social benefits of the protective role of government and the social costs of unconstrained activity cannot be quantified, we have little or no chance of ever evaluating the relative merits of intervention and nonintervention in cost–benefit terms alone. The "liberty" argument is indecisive (1) because it fails to recognize the dual role of government as interferer and protector and (2) because we have no quantitative calculus for evaluating the gains and losses of constrained versus unconstrained effects in this context.

Evaluation of the costs of this "government externality" relative to the costs of market failure results in an equivocal outcome. The real dangers in government, however, lie in the tendency of its structure to support social values which systematically exclude the value of individuals who are least capable of adjusting to, confronting, and defeating their own social problems. Government officials all too frequently appear to suffer from "professional deformation"—their behavior reflects what they believe their role to be: the image becomes a reality, and the distance between government and governed becomes unbridgeable. The comportment of government bears little relationship to the problems that people actually face and even less to their expressions of preference about dealing with those problems.

In the United Kingdom, for example, large-scale development and zoning proposals are announced in specially prepared structure plans whose defects are numerous for those individuals whose lives are materially affected. The documents themselves fail to set forth clearly the material of interest to those most affected, they are frequently of great length, and are offered for sale to the public at a forbidding price. Public meetings on such plans tend to be poorly attended and conducted at a level of generality that precludes identification by the ordinary citizen, and the semilegal fashion of such public enquiries acts as an immense disincentive to the individual whose views may be just as pronounced as anyone else's, but who is incapable of articulating them in such an environment. In such an event, those who participate in governmental decisions can articulate their preferences in a particular way, can afford to involve themselves, and can use the established means of communication (Arnstein, 1969; Krause, 1968). Frustration over impotence in affecting the decision-making process generates resignation among individuals who see development plans, motorways, and so on, as being something that "authority" has deemed necessary and that it is useless to resist.

Now, participation in decision making is an integral part of the QOL; if individuals are to have any influence on their own destinies, they must be informed of options and of the consequences of choosing any of them. Further, they must be able to communicate their views to the government institution involved. The absence of any of these conditions disrupts *any* social decision rule purporting to reflect individual preferences. Pareto-type prescriptive rules require that social preference be sensitive to changes in individual preferences. If actual decision making departs significantly from this model, government will be systematically biased in its decisions in favor of certain social groups.[5] Equally, however, market systems function with relative prices that reflect the prevailing distribution of economic power, so that an unmodified market system is also biased. If government mechanisms may be corrected for this bias, in contrast to market systems, maximizing the QOL will entail a configuration of the economy which reflects more and not less government activity, albeit of a form different from current government institutions. If, on the other hand, the institutional structure cannot be so altered, government must remain a major source of externality, and the choice between government and market will be determined by a qualitative comparison of the relevant externalities.

4. The Nonequivalence of Pareto Optimality and Maximum Quality of Life

No *necessary* connection may exist between Pareto optimality and socially desirable policy. Many economists appear to think that Pareto criteria are the *only* relevant criteria for the economist to discuss. Not only can they be selected from a whole set of criteria and judged "best" by some higher order ethical notion, but they identify prescriptive economics with neoclassical welfare economics. However, Paretian eco-

---

[5] For considerable detail on this and other defects of public decision-making processes see Haefele (1973) and chapter 13.

nomics has underlying value judgments which are as much open to disavowal as any others. If this is so, we are at liberty to construct *any* internally consistent welfare economics that we choose, using different sets of value judgments.[6] Choosing between these value sets is then the function of the decision maker, with or without the advice of the economist. What is totally illicit is to assume that Paretian value judgments are more sacred than any others. An even more serious misunderstanding takes Pareto criteria to be value-free, a point of view some recent contributors to the welfare debate have come perilously close to embracing.[7]

Two value propositions underlie Paretian welfare economics: P_1, the decision criterion shall reflect individuals' preferences; P_2, these preferences shall be weighted by market power.[8] It is worth noting that these are the only two value judgments necessary to establish the Paretian system. There is nothing ultimate or sacred about P_1 and P_2 since it is quite meaningful to ask how they are, in turn, justified. P_1, for example, might be founded on some higher order criterion (C_1) that democracy is good. P_2 might be justified by arguing, for example (C_2), that weights distributed according to market power will reflect marginal productivities, which in turn reflect individuals' contributions to social product. Such an argument would be illicit, but the point here is only to show that there exists a hierarchy of value judgments and that there is nothing objective about selecting P_1 and P_2 rather than some set $P_3 \ldots P_N$, the elements of which are sanctioned by other moral notions.[9]

[6] This is perhaps a rather strong statement. It is more likely that there will exist some set of value judgments, established by what is socially permissible, from which to choose, and which is far narrower in range than the conceivable set. Within this socially permissible set, however, there will be room for disagreement over which subset should determine the procedure for socially valuing any change in the status quo. The essential point, that no *unique* subset exists, remains. See Nash, Pearce, and Stanley (1975).

[7] See, for example, Culyer (1973) where Pareto criteria are variously described as being "objective" (p. 6) and "designed to give an unambiguous indicator of improvements in quality of life" (p. 123), and a Pareto optimum is declared to be "a unique level of consumption that is preferred by society" (p. 206). One suspects that others are far worse offenders than Culyer, whose admirable clarity of approach makes it possible for the potential critic to at least understand what it is he believes.

[8] The relationship between value judgments and decision criteria is dealt with at some length in Nash, Pearce, and Stanley (1975).

[9] $P_1 \ldots P_N$ can be thought of as instances of $C_1 \ldots C_N$, in which case there is a sense in which $P_1 \ldots P_N$ describe rather than prescribe. But this does not alter the fact that $C_1 \ldots C_N$ are value judgments. However complex the hierarchy of value judgments and moral notions becomes, there remains no nonmoral justification for selecting one set of P_1 statements rather than another set.

This establishes that replacing a Paretian QOL concept with some other concept in no way imposes an elitist view of the QOL. Nor can there be any real resolution of the indeterminacy which must then surround the choice of the QOL function. Probably the most that can be said is that P_1, the fundamental proposition of democracy, has a higher importance value than the other propositions, but, even then, asserting this does not overcome the problem of how to treat situations in which the application of P_1 leads to conflict.

In light of such indeterminacy, it would seem most sensible to evaluate policy change in such a way that the sensitivity of policy to different value sets can be assessed. Policy analysis should show how the chosen measure of net social benefits responds to changed value assumptions (Nash, Pearce, and Stanley, 1975).[10] This value sensitivity analysis would simply extend the sensitivity analysis that we would expect to see in any QOL calculus, with respect to different discount rates, different engineering data inputs, and so on. Whatever the complexity that such an approach would add to policy evaluation, the relevance for the current discussion is highly important. Quite simply, which QOL objective is chosen determines the extent of government activity. If some just income distribution appears in the QOL objective, the market, unassisted by government regulations, is unlikely to achieve that objective. The possible exception here is a QOL objective that includes distributional factors only insofar as they reflect individuals' philanthropic or altruistic preferences. Hence the extent to which markets fail (and hence the extent to which governments must intervene) is itself variable with the chosen QOL objective. The choice of a Rawlsian objective function would necessitate more intervention than the choice of a Paretian one insofar as income distribution is concerned (Rawls, 1971).

5. Ecological Externality and Consumer Ignorance

One other important dimension of the government's role with respect to the QOL is found in the situation where individuals are unaware of their own potential gains or losses. Rather than consider the familiar examples of merit goods, we concentrate on some bads which have certain im-

---

[10] Various measures are listed in Nash, Pearce, and Stanley (1975) and an empirical application with respect to some value sets can be found in Pearce and Wise (1972). Pearce and Wise (1972) report corrections to an earlier article by Nwaneri (1971) which unfortunately secures wrong results through the misapplication of technique. For example, Nwaneri's application of a relative marginal utility of income weighting produces a result whereby individuals with *higher* income utilities receive *lower* weight, and vice versa.

portant attributes. At least for these bads, the government has a paternalistic function.

Treating all pollution as if it were a straightforward instance of a neoclassical externality phenomenon leaves two problems untreated: first, each of a number of important pollutants exerts its external effects through an accumulated *stock* of the residual rather than via a *flow*: CO_2 might appear in the latter category whereas toxic metals such as lead, mercury, cadmium, and synthetic organic molecules (i.e., chlorinated pesticides and polychlorinated biphenyls), would appear in the former category. Further, to all intents and purposes, the accumulated stock of the residuals is indestructible. Ingestion and inhalation of these stock pollutants occur on a regular and continuing basis without identifiable health effects until some threshold is reached. Cadmium, for example, is certainly implicated in renal failure, and may be implicated in numerous other health defects, including hypertension, cardiovascular disease, and so on.[11] Until these effects are observed, cadmium intake is invisible. Further, the threshold beyond which the effects are observed can be temporally quite distant from the initial intake.

Under these circumstances, do individually expressed preferences have any role to play in forming social policy? Certainly, the individual himself cannot be left to decide because (1) stock pollutants behave as a public bad, (2) the "jurisdiction" of the bad is often extensive, and can well be global, because of the facility of such pollutants to travel through ecosystems, and (3) the individual has no means of personally monitoring his intake.

Cadmium not only travels through ecosystems with air and water currents, but also travels through food chains which, for humans, are extended by geographical trade patterns: populations regarded as safe with respect to atmospheric exposure to cadmium particles need in no way be safe with respect to ingested cadmium. In addition, the externality resulting from such pollutants is irreversible: some of the health effects may be reversible in individuals, but the source of externality is not reducible because of the dissipation of the stock. At the very least, then, government has the role of monitoring such pollutants. Nonetheless, if a monitoring approach is subject to large margins of error (as in the past with mercury), it may be replaced with outright prohibition (Nobbs and Pearce, 1975). If this class of stock pollutant is the proper subject of coercive governmental activity, extensive controls become necessary: witness the extensive uses to which

[11] The current state of knowledge in this respect is summarized in Nobbs and Pearce (1975).

toxic metals and other persistent chemicals such as polychlorinated biphenyls are put.

Now consider pollutants for which the environment has some assimilative capacity. Figure 2 offers one representation of the features of this situation, and follows Pearce (1973, 1974a, b, 1976b).[12] The upper half of figure 2 shows the amount of waste (in physical units) and assimilative capacity on the vertical axis. Assimilative capacity is assumed to be fixed initially at A_0. The horizontal axis shows quantity of economic output. $W(q)$ is then a residuals disposal function relating waste to economic output. If we think of the process of waste degradation as being instantaneous,[13] waste disposed of to the environment cannot generate an externality unless the value of $W(q)$ exceeds A. Consequently, externality cannot appear until at least output $q_{e,0}$ in the lower half of the diagram. Curve E_0' depicts a marginal external cost function (which could, of course, begin to the right of $q_{e,0}$ if physical pollution does not have an economic magnitude because it fails to enter someone's utility function). Curve B' indicates marginal net private benefits to the externality generator, so that a Pareto optimal point is identified as output q_s which is then the optimal level of economic activity, with W_0 as the optimal level of waste generation, and the area $q_{e,0}q_s a$ as the optimal level of externality.

But q_s can be shown to be unstable. For the amount of waste corresponding to economic output $q_{e,0}q_s$ has now accumulated, with the result

[12] More sophisticated models with similar features can be found in d'Arge (1971), Strøm (1972), and Common (1974a, b). D'Arge's model is essentially a Harrod–Domar growth model with waste treatment being incorporated in the form of an investment function, and with biological equilibrium being introduced as a constraint. (In terms of the simplistic model in this paper, biological equilibrium occurs when $W = A$.) The important paper by Strøm extends the d'Arge model by permitting pollution reduction to be a function of the stock of waste treatment capital as well as waste treatment investment. In terms of a Harrod–Domar model, Strøm's conclusions are less doom-laden than d'Arge's, but when Strøm's waste treatment–pollution reduction function is introduced into a Solow–Swan growth model, pessimistic outcomes recur. Common (1974a, b) models the system shown in this paper, with some modifications. While there are many aspects of the workings of ecological systems that could be incorporated into economic models, these papers are, to my knowledge, virtually the only attempts to make such an integration (although, in the same spirit, see Garvey, 1972) as far as ecological stability is concerned. This is all the more unfortunate since this is the type of argument that authentic ecologists have been trying to advance, with apparent disregard by economists, particularly those who appear to hold the strongest opinions.

[13] This is an obvious simplification since the environment can self-purify for many pollutants but will generate external effects (or potential ones) during the actual process. In other words, A really has a time dimension.

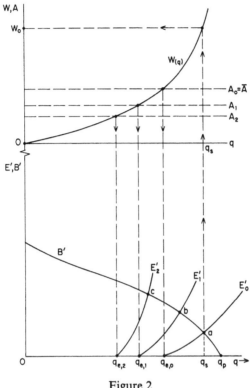

Figure 2

that it inhibits the assimilative functions of the environment.[14] In other words, A_0 shifts down, say to A_1. If sufferers are responsive, E'_0 shifts to E'_1, with E'_1 having a steeper slope now that there is a lower assimilative capacity per unit of waste generated.[15] The Pareto optimum shifts to b, but the system is still unstable in light of the dynamic physical effects of pollution on the receiving environment. The process continues and strictly only converges to a solution at zero output—the so-called "doomsday conclusion." These effects of the presence of dynamic externality can be avoided of course by opting for a point like $q_{e,0}$ at the outset. But such an option is inconsistent with the market mechanism (which gives q_p initially and hence produces more rapid dynamic effects) *and* with Pigovian-type solutions. In short, dynamic externalities provide a rationale for coercive government action rather than regulatory action.

[14] For the direct physical analogy, see Woodwell (1970) and Pearce (1974b).

[15] I am indebted to Jean-Phillippe Barde and Henri Smets of the OECD for pointing out that the slopes of the E' curves will also change—the comparable curves are wrongly drawn in this respect in Pearce (1974b).

Of course, the model presented here is dynamic only with respect to one category of ecosystem effect. Other categories could be introduced at the cost of complicating the model. More important, it is necessary to see what the effects of waste-reduction expenditures (anti-bads) would be on the model. Some of these effects are discussed in Pearce (1974b), where it is concluded that waste-reducing technological change is an ambivalent solution, although it certainly contains the potential for generating stable outcomes. The reason for keeping the discussion limited in the current context is merely to draw attention to a category of side effects which tends to be systematically ignored in arguments about the correct approaches to externality correction.

6. Summary and Conclusions

The broad sweep approach adopted in this paper must clearly be unsatisfactory in that many issues need more detailed discussion. Nonetheless, the framework is, I hope, clear.

It is difficult to see the exact relevance of optimal externality theory to cumulative residuals which have biological effects (glass bottles are also cumulative, but have no biological effects and hence do not fit this category), or to situations in which externality must be extended to include ecosystem instability. While one is always reluctant to infringe the right of individuals to at least meet their end as they choose, there appears to be a strong case for coercive government action in this field.

References

Arnstein, S. L. 1969. "A Ladder of Citizen Participation," *Journal of the American Institute of Planners* (July).

Ayres, Robert, and Allen Kneese. 1969. "Production, Consumption and Externalities," *American Economic Review* LIX (June).

Baumol, William J., and Wallace E. Oates. 1971. "The Use of Standards and Prices for Protection of the Environment," *Swedish Journal of Economics* (March).

Beckerman, Wilfred, and Anil Markandya. 1974. "Pollution Control and Optimal Taxation: A Static Analysis," *Journal of Environmental Economics and Management* vol. 1, no. 1 (May).

Buchanan, James M. 1969. "External Diseconomies, Corrective Taxes, and Market Structure," *American Economic Review* (March).

Burrows, Paul. 1974. "Pricing versus Regulation for Environmental

Protection," in A. J. Culyer, ed., *York Essays in Social Policy* (London, Martin Robertson).

Coase, Ronald. 1960. "The Problem of Social Cost," *The Journal of Law and Economics* (October).

Common, Michael. 1974a. "Pollution, Pareto Optimality and the Ecological Gap," mimeographed (England, University of Southampton.)

————. 1974b. "Pollution: The Dynamic Consequences of Static Externality Correction," mimeographed (England, University of Southampton.)

Culyer, A. J. 1973. *The Economics of Social Policy* (London, Martin Robertson).

d'Arge, Ralph. 1971. "Essay on Economic Growth and Environmental Quality," *Swedish Journal of Economics* (March).

Garvey, Gerald. 1972. *Energy, Ecology, Economy*. Appendix to chapter 10 (New York, Norton).

Haefele, Edwin T. 1973. *Representative Government and Environmental Management* (Baltimore, Johns Hopkins University Press for Resources for the Future).

Kneese, Allen, Robert Ayres, and Ralph d'Arge. 1970. *Economics and the Environment* (Baltimore, Johns Hopkins University Press for Resources for the Future).

Krause, E. A. 1968. "Functions of a Bureaucratic Ideology: Citizen Participation," *Social Problems*.

Mill, John Stuart. 1859. *On Liberty* (London, reprinted by Dent, 1912).

Mumey, G. A. 1971. "The 'Coase Theorem': A Re-examination," *Quarterly Journal of Economics* vol. XVII.

Nash, Christopher, David W. Pearce, and John Stanley. 1975. "Criteria for Evaluating Project Evaluation Techniques," *Journal of the American Institute of Planners* (March).

Nobbs, Christopher, and David Pearce. 1975. "The Economics of Stock Pollutants: The Example of Cadmium," *International Journal of Environmental Studies* (June).

Nwaneri, V. C. 1971. "Equity in Cost–Benefit Analysis: A Case Study of the Third London Airport," *Journal of Transport Economics and Policy* (September).

Pearce, David W., and John Wise. 1972. "Equity in Cost–Benefit Analysis: A Comment," *Journal of Transport Economics and Policy* (September).

————. 1973. "An Incompatibility in Planning for a Steady State and Planning for Maximum Economic Welfare," *Environment and Planning* vol. 5.

————. 1974a. "Economic and Ecological Approaches to the Optimal Level of Pollution," *International Journal of Social Economics* vol. 1, no. 2.

————. 1974b. "Economics and Ecology," *Surrey Papers in Economics* vol. 10 (July).

————. 1974c. "Fiscal Incentives and the Economics of Waste Recycling: Problems and Limitations," in Institute of Fiscal Studies, *Fiscal Policy and the Environment* (London, IFS).

————. 1976a. *Environmental Economics* (London, Longman).

————. 1976b. "The Limits of Cost–Benefit Analysis as a Guide to Environmental Policy," *Kyklos* Fasc. 1.

Rawls, John. 1971. *A Theory of Justice* (Cambridge, Harvard University Press).

Strøm, Steiner. 1972. "Dynamics of Pollution and Waste Treatment Activities," *Memorandum*, University of Oslo, Institute of Economics (May).

Woodwell, Graham. 1970. "Effects of Pollution on the Structure and Physiology of Ecosystems," *Science* (April 24).

7
The Quality of Life and the Limits
of Cost–Benefit Analysis

A. J. CULYER

1. Introduction

THIS paper deals with some features of nonmarket choice processes in which economic imperialists have recently been active and in which some rather subtle but by no means unimportant threats to the quality of life have arisen which have tended to be glossed over by economists. I conjecture that the two reasons for this have been on the one hand the blindness characteristic of all proselytizers, which makes them dismiss, sometimes contemptuously, the criticisms of the uninitiated, and, on the other, the pathetic reliance of the uninitiated upon ordinary English rather than the jargon used by the imperialists (which is often the only language in which the latter can communicate).

Lest my remarks be taken in the wrong spirit, I should confess that I am an incorrigible jargon-user and spend much of my time in proselytizing, in nurturing young proselytizers, and in encouraging fellow proselytizers. In this paper, however, I shall argue that there should be and, indeed, logically are, limits to the applicability of applied welfare economics in the design of social policy. There should also be constraints on the role and methodology of applied welfare *economists*, but in this case, there are unfortunately no logically compelling reasons why these constraints should be binding.

In the major part of the paper (section 2) I wish to focus upon a fundamental problem that arises in applying efficiency analysis to social service areas. The analysis I have in mind includes all applied welfare

Acknowledgment is made to members of the Public Sector Studies Programme Research Group at the University of York and to the Social Science Research Council for a program research grant in Public Sector Studies at the Department of Economics and the Institute of Social and Economic Research in the University of York.

141

economics: from the design of allocatory "institutions" (e.g., ration coupons, education vouchers, subsidized health insurance) to cost–benefit analyses of specific alternative ways of doing things in the welfare state. The kinds of areas of social policy in which such analysis is increasingly applied include health care, education, poverty relief, crime prevention, and the administration of law. The fundamental problem concerns an aspect of the familiar equity/efficiency dichotomy, and I shall illustrate the problem as it arises in the use of cost–benefit analysis in social policy.

The second problem, which unfortunately receives rather shorter shrift here, concerns the proper role of specialists and experts at all levels of the decision-making machinery of supposedly democratic governments. Casual empiricism suggests that this influence is steadily increasing. I shall not try to prove the existence of such a trend toward an elite technocracy. Indeed, it does not matter whether it exists or not, so long as people believe that it does, for the mere belief implies a decline in the quality of life as the sense of personal autonomy fails and as cynicism about contemporary political processes spreads. Society is seen as divided into "them" and "us," the governors and the governed, the decision "makers" and the decision "takers." The belief is engendered that one has been effectively disenfranchised. In this context I shall examine the function of cost–benefit analysis and the role of cost–benefit analysts, who claim to operate in the social interest.

2. Limits of Efficiency Analysis

One of the most persistent British critics of economists in general was the late Richard Titmuss (1970) who believed that both eastern and western, rich and poor, countries had become dominated by economic and material-maximizing values and that many economists increasingly, "after taking strong oaths of ethical neutrality, perform as missionaries in the social welfare field and often give the impression of possessively owning a hot line to God."[1] Although Titmuss's critique made no major impression on economists because of his incorrect understanding of such notions as "externality," and because of imprecision in his argument, the feeling persists that somewhere in his polemic there lurks a profound truth that relates to a principal objective of social policy: the creation and sustenance of institutions which foster integration and discourage

---

[1] Titmuss (1970, p. 199). This book, despite being poorly argued and wrong in many of its arguments, contains the passionately felt essence of a real problem for social scientists in general and economists in particular. In this paper I am trying to deal with two aspects of the problem as I interpret it.

alienation in society—a goal that may conflict with efficiency objectives, no matter how widely they are construed.

The issues have been confronted more frankly—though they have not been very satisfactorily resolved—in the economic analysis of law enforcement. Lester Thurow (1970) has argued, for example, that if efficiency is couched in terms of minimizing the seriousness of total criminal activity, a characteristic of an efficient allocation of police resources may mean fewer arrests for minor offenses and thus the neglect of the most frequent violations of individuals' security.[2] Health economists have frequently encountered the view that too literal application of the economic calculus might substantially reduce the social costs of sickness but also deny some individuals—hopeless cases, for example—medical care. Even though medical intervention may have zero productivity in social terms, there is surely something substantial in the view that a society operating its medical services on so strictly a "rational" basis would be rather horrifying. Some critics, Titmuss, again, for example, have argued that the good, "medical care," is so fundamentally different from other goods that an entirely different kind of economics is required to analyze it. This, of course, is an overreaction and diverts attention away from the object of real concern and toward what are often only pedagogic and semantic confusions.[3]

Although there are many criticisms from "outside" that do little damage to the proselytizers' case, there remains a serious criticism to be answered.[4] Perhaps the most comprehensive recent treatment of the issue is that of Abraham Tarasovsky (1976), which is far from being the kind of argument that any self-respecting applied welfare economist has become adept at parrying. The essence of Tarasovsky's argument is that when individuals in the community know of certain apparently rational procedures being adopted in public decision making, "Cherished Illusions" become eroded, if not totally destroyed. This represents a cost which, though never quantified, may considerably outweigh the net benefits suggested by the cost–benefit analysis. Cherished Illusions (as opposed to "articles of faith" which relate to supernatural or transcendental beliefs) include the beliefs that firemen will protect and

[2] See also Shoup (1964), and for a survey of economic approaches to crime and punishment, see Anderson (1974).

[3] See, for example, Titmuss (1966) reprinted in chapter 12 in his *Commitment to Welfare* (London, Allen and Unwin, 1968) and for a rebuttal of the specific criticisms of economics but not, perhaps, of what lay at the core of Titmuss's position, see Culyer (1971), more extensively discussed in chapters 6 and 7 of the *Economics of Social Policy* (London, Martin Robertson, 1973).

[4] For some criticisms and a no-nonsense rejoinder, see Self (1972) and Williams (1972).

serve everyone's interests with equal zeal; that magistrates and judges will deal with everyone with equal objectivity and thoroughness; that the police will rush to everyone's assistance with equal alacrity; that doctors will care for their patients with all their power and all the resources at their command. More precisely, while allowing for human weakness and error in practice, the Cherished Illusions relate to beliefs about the moral and professional values held by such public function-aries as policemen, firemen, judges, and doctors. Cherished Illusions may be entertained by both the providers of the final service and their clients. Clients cherish the illusion that the providers have a professional ideology that makes them behave with scrupulous fairness and the providers cherish the illusion that they try as hard as they can to be fair and "total" in their commitment. Thus, patients believe that doctors do everything possible to preserve life and doctors usually do try to keep patients alive, no matter how old, poor, or unemployable they may be. The retention of the Cherished Illusion in the minds of the providers is an incentive for them not to slack in the performance of their duties, while its retention in the minds of clients helps to prevent aliena-tion and reassures them that with a common commitment to certain basic values, everyone (client and professional) will act in a respon-sible and fair manner.

Cherished Illusions, argues Tarasovsky, are a principal human but-tress against fear and anxiety. In particular, they are a major defense against what psychologists refer to as "characterological anxiety." "Anxiety differs from fear, introspectively and presumably physiologi-cally, by being a response to precursory signals of perception of the true fear object. It is a tentative alerting by cues and signals rather than by concrete, present danger. Consequently, it has the associated qualities of uncertainty and of lasting longer. . . . The level of characterological anxiety does not necessarily have any relation to immediately present, objectively observable danger. That is, although internal dynamic con-flict, or characterological anxiety, is traceable in the last resort to external experience, this experience may be historical, remote, and long embedded in the sentiments and complexes of the individual so that he is reacting to signals of danger as he has known it rather than to a fresh and realistic appraisal of possible danger in the present situation. . . ."[5]

While, at least in principle, it would be possible to incorporate fear responses into a cost–benefit appraisal by using the theory of risk, so far as I am aware, we do not have the principles by which the costs of anxiety could be incorporated. In any case, as we shall see, it is not at all clear that such costs *ought* to be included in an appraisal.

[5] Quoted by Tarasovsky from Cattell and Scheier (1961).

Tarasovsky's solution to this problem is to derive the cost of maintaining the Cherished Illusion in question. This will be, according to Tarasovsky, mainly a function of the quantity and character of the information available to the individual: how decisions are made and how services actually get allocated. It would not, however, in principle, seem correct to infer that the cost–benefit analysis should be conducted in secret, since that would undermine a major advantage of doing the analysis in the first place. What character could the information, whether about decision processes or performance, have other than being designed fundamentally to support these illusions by deception? If, for example, it is a fact that decision makers are imputing values to human lives in making decisions about roads and building intensive-care units, then to sustain the illusion that they are not is to sustain a lie, to destroy the opportunity that any intelligent citizen should have to question whether the values being imputed are the right ones, and to entrench the position of the economic experts in the decision-making apparatus of the state. As I shall argue later, this is bad for economists as well as for the rest of society. Or, if it is a fact that the police are being deployed mainly to protect the night clubs of the wealthy rather than Working Men's clubs on the grounds that, *ceteris paribus*, their productivity in preventing crime is higher in the former than the latter, then to sustain the illusion that every kind of club gets equal protection is again to sustain a lie and to limit the effectiveness of the governed in controlling the governors through democratic institutions. Such an illusion is, of course, hard to sustain among those who deliver such services even if they are not party to the decisions and have not been given work rules since they will usually be able plainly to see how in practice services actually do get allocated.

Alternatively, it can be asserted that cost–benefit analysis is designed *not* to undermine Cherished Illusions but rather *to define the circumstances* in which the agent supplying services is able to supply it. The object of cost–benefit analysis in health care is not to tell the doctor which patients to treat, nor to tell the lifeboat crew which sailors to rescue, but to suggest what the appropriate number of doctors in a particular specialty is and what equipment and manpower they may in total deploy, or what the appropriate distribution of lifeboats is around the coast, and so on.

This seems to be a far more defensible response, yet it begs the crucial question of where to draw the line between those resource allocation decisions that are to be made on the principle of efficiency (potential Pareto improvements) and those that are to be made on the principles of equal service for equal need and maximum useful service for any recognized need. The latter sustain Cherished Illusions and mask the unpleasant facts of economic life by apparently denying the existence of scarcity.

A third response has been made by Thurow (1970). He argues, in the case of efficient deployment of police forces, that geographic equity, for example, requires the equalization of the incidence of crime among areas (weighted according to severity) whereas efficiency requires the equalization of the effectiveness of marginal police resources in reducing crime in different areas. Consequently, since the difficulty of detection varies from area to area, some areas where crime detection or prevention is difficult or impossible may, on efficiency grounds, be denied protection altogether. His suggestion to cope with the resulting inequity is to make compensatory payments to the victims of crime.[6] One could also argue anyway that market transactions will effect compensations: house prices would, for example, be lower (*ceteris paribus*) in high crime areas. Even within the field of criminal justice, however, this solution is at best a partial one, it being not at all clear what compensation is appropriate for persons suffering severe injuries (let alone death) from criminal assault. It is altogether unthinkable, surely, to imagine compensation for those "trivial" cases which the courts deem it inefficient to try, or those "hopeless" cases the doctors judge it unprofitable (in social terms, naturally) to treat, or those "too distant" homes that the firemen cannot risk visiting lest a more important fire begin closer to the station.

A fourth response could be the elevation of rationality and efficiency to a level at which they dominate all other moral considerations.[7] Doubtless some cost–benefit analysts would adopt this position, deliberately shattering every Cherished Illusion in the cause of rational and explicit decision-making, and applying the method (at least in principle) to every decision about resource allocation. The outcome, of course, to the extent that Cherished Illusions do fend off anxiety-promoting events, could well lead to a substantial shift away from a Pareto-preferred position. So much the worse for the Pareto criterion, these analysts might say. So much also the worse I would guess, for society, if Titmuss's argument about integration is to be taken as seriously as it should be, and so much also the worse for democracy.

If, then, we accept none of these defenses of orthodoxy as satisfactory, it becomes necessary to ask the question that each of them studiously avoids: What are the appropriate limits to the application of cost–benefit analysis? To answer this we need a criterion of "appro-

---

[6] Thurow also suggests weighting monetary losses from crime according to the victim's marginal income tax rate, an argument that is criticized in Anderson (1974).

[7] Efficiency is itself, of course, a moral notion.

priateness" that transcends the moral content of cost–benefit methodology, and that criterion is provided, I suggest, by an extension of the Paretian apparatus.

Decisions concerning appropriate applications of cost–benefit analysis may be usefully seen as constitutional devices, since they ultimately concern the selection of a rule or set of rules to govern the way in which society is to make decisions.[8] Utilizing modern contract theory, we might ask what decision an individual would make behind John Rawls's (1972) "veil of ignorance" concerning the application of cost–benefit decision rules in subsequent choice situations where, of course, the veil of ignorance no longer exists. Thus we might discover where the line should be drawn.

Now, in a Rawlsian "original position," I do not believe that we would choose a rule for resource allocation that stipulated, for example, that doctors should rank patients according to their social productivity in deciding who should receive priority in care. The reason is obvious. Any one of us will, in the original position, consider that we may later have a low "social productivity" (assuming that this term has some relevant economic content), yet we are likely to consider ourselves as having as much of a right to live, or to live in good health, as the next man. Such a rule would indeed offend our natural sense of justice and, it seems reasonable to suppose, would also offend everyone who conducted the conceptual experiment of putting himself in the "original position" of contract theory. This judgment is likely to be reached because it is hard to see how the difference principle can be utilized to moderate the strong egalitarianism of Rawls's two principles of justice in the distribution of primary goods.

Recalling Rawls, the principles which concern us are that each person should have an equal right to the most extensive total system of equal basic liberties compatible with a similar system of liberty for all, and that social and economic inequalities are to be arranged so that they are to the greatest benefit of the least advantaged (Rawls, 1972, p. 250). It is precisely to the distribution of certain crucial primary goods that welfare economists have increasingly been applying their analysis, that is, to the distribution of those goods necessary to any normal individual's ability to plan his life in society, whatever that plan may be: health, the legal enforcement of his rights, protection of whatever property is his, opportunities for the development of his intellect, and so on. It is in the use of efficiency criterion to allocate these goods that concern has reasonably been expressed.[9] It is possible to imagine special cases where

---

[8] In the sense used by Buchanan and Tullock (1962).

[9] One interpretation of Titmuss's argument about blood could be that it, too, is a primary good, but I do not find this interpretation persuasive.

particular people ought to get priority in, say, their medical care, over others with identical conditions because of beneficial side effects upon the more disadvantaged, but in general this does not seem a plausible argument. Similarly, for the rich (say) to receive more fire or police protection, or more favorable treatment in the courts, or better education for their children, would not appear to be justified by the difference principle.[10]

The related aspect of every Cherished Illusion that "all possible will be done," must necessarily be qualified by "given the resources available," and would, on closer inspection, appear to be less a moral precept than a method of indoctrinating those whose task it is to provide primary goods and services so that they perform their tasks as diligently —and equally diligently for each person they serve—as they can. From the social point of view, these illusions are a desirable part of professional ideologies, though they may rarely be sufficient to ensure that public servants discharge their duties to the full.

From this we infer that the quantity of *resources* at the disposal of such public servants or, indeed, the number of public servants, is not itself subject to the principles of justice, but is a proper subject for efficiency analysis. The allocation of *primary goods*, however, is not. They are, or should be, beyond efficiency considerations.

Tarasovsky's term Cherished Illusion, while suggestive, is somewhat misleading, for it is not necessary to assume that anyone has any illusions about anything. Instead, they have an idea about morality (equality before the law, socialism in health care)[11] and an idea about the proper attitude of public providers of services ("always do your best"). Cost-benefit analysts, therefore, should have an eye open for the limits of efficiency analysis. Nor is it the case that the ethical "losses" from shattered Cherished Illusions can be incorporated into the cost-benefit calculus. For, if I am right, no illusions at all will be shattered, but what may well be shattered is a relatively just organization of society. These things cannot be made commensurable *within an efficiency appraisal:* as far as the economist is concerned, the arrangements chosen may be efficient and just, or inefficient and just, or efficient but unjust, or both inefficient and unjust, but they cannot be merely efficient or inefficient. In asserting this I do not have to hold that justice has a lexicographic

[10] Education may readily be conceded to be a primary good to which all should have equal access. Equality of educational quality, however, is an elusive goal, since there are many conceptions about what good education consists in. Any social policy that ignores this diversity of opinion probably violates the first principle of justice.

[11] I believe this neat encapsulation of social attitudes toward health is due to J. M. Buchanan.

priority over efficiency, but merely that the professional economist is in no way qualified to make the utilitarian tradeoff between them. He can, of course, apply his own intuition and seek to persuade decision makers that his intuition is to be preferred to other people's intuitions. But he has no special professional competence in this regard, and it is therefore unjust that his intuition should receive more weight than that of others. On the other hand, people who have been fairly appointed to a position in which they must make decisions about justice and efficiency—and for which decisions they, unlike economists, are publicly responsible—may legitimately trade off justice and efficiency, but economists should resist any attempt to assist them in that task.

3. Limits on Efficiency Analysts

As I hope to show, it is unfortunate that the modesty imposed upon professional economists by the Paretian rubric has been frequently dismissed as "emasculating" and has led many with an influence on the outcome of policy questions to reject the Pareto criterion as a basis for identifying social improvements. One set of dangers inherent in this rejection has been discussed above: the neglect of the principles of justice. Some are even more extreme. Ralph Turvey (1963, p. 96), for example, in an extraordinary burst of professional arrogance has declared "My feeling is that the value-judgments made by economists are, by and large, better than those made by non-economists. . . . The point is simply that those who are experienced in systematic thinking about a problem are usually those who make the best judgments about it. Thus, whatever their theory of aesthetics, most people are prepared to accept the judgment of an art critic about the merits of a painting." Perhaps less extremely and much more frequently, the economists' inability to resist the temptation to "say something" about the fairness of distributions of income and to incorporate distributional considerations into efficiency analyses, is a more characteristic manifestation of professional arrogance as well as inconsistency. For, if economists professionally submit to the Paretian admonition against making interpersonal comparisons of utility since they cannot do so with sufficient accuracy to be useful for policy advice, then to do so is either to play games (which would probably serve only to confuse clients of policy advice) or to lend a spurious scientific authority to purely personal prejudices.[12] If

[12] There has been, for example, much economic discussion of the dependence of the distribution of health services on income distribution and of the appropriate income weights to apply in cost–benefit analysis of health problems. In a normative context this amounts to an utter trivialization of ethical issues in health care

we cannot, *as economists,* say much about the relative acceptability of income distributions, then perhaps we should not say anything at all. If we have private beliefs about income distributions, then we should not say more than other private people are able to say. To do more is elitist—it is also, on the difference principle, unjust.

The only available mechanism by which it seems possible for individuals to express a view about the propriety of the income distribution is political, and it is the job of professional *politicians,* not professional economists, to interpret the public's preferences in this regard. Alternatively, from considerations of justice in income distribution and efficiency in resource allocation, states of society may be ordered only in terms of their justice *and* their efficiency (two orderings): attempts to "weight" values other than according to actual or predicted income distributions are attempts to combine what cannot be legitimately combined by economists. If the analyst, consequently, believes that according to the principles of justice the prevailing income distribution is unjust, he is at liberty to demonstrate as much, but he is not at liberty to attempt to alter the existing weights supplied by the existing income distribution. If he demonstrates by cost–benefit analysis that a particular course of action would increase efficiency, he is also at liberty to demonstrate that it may lead to less justice by causing a deterioration in the state of the income distribution. In each case he may either comment on efficiency, or on efficiency and justice, but he may never subsume justice under the efficiency criterion: to do so is to presume without warrant the supremacy of utilitarian ethics.

Now, the careful follower of the Paretian rules is likely to adopt neither the arrogant presumption that he is specially qualified to interpret the wishes of the community regarding income distribution nor the even more arrogant presumption that his own values are in some way worthy of special consideration. He will either remain silent on such matters, or he may adopt the thoroughly Paretian conceptual experiment of trying to identify just distributions by asking himself what principles of justice would gain a consensus in Rawls's "original position." Contrary to the views of those who fret against the restraints of Paretian methodology, we should make a virtue of necessity and not

---

and, to the extent that economists are taken seriously, a dangerous trivialization. The real difficulty with health care is that its just distribution, according to our argument, should be *completely independent* of income levels but related to a whole complex of personal, family, and social characteristics which the unsophisticated have had the nerve to call "need." The injection of various weights in a cost–benefit exercise can satisfy only the least sensitive of social consciences. Much better is Paretian agnosticism which, it turns out, can form a useful basis for a much richer investigation of "need" than is customary even among noneconomists. For a fuller discussion, see Culyer (1976).

invite the well-deserved contempt of noneconomists who can easily see through metascience, even though they cannot always articulate the criticism as precisely as is needed to teach us that our influence in policy should be restricted to those analyses in which we have a genuine comparative advantage.

Most of us would agree that the costs relevant to any individual's choice are those that he himself perceives, not those that "objectively" exist after the choice has been made, nor necessarily those that ought, according to the cost–benefit analyst, to be taken into account.[13] Indeed, one of the strongest arguments for cost–benefit analysis has been that by ensuring that the basis for making any particular decision is as explicit as possible, it reduces the opportunities for public decision makers to allow their personal costs to influence decisions. Viewed in this way, cost–benefit analysis is an institution promoting efficiency by modifying the behavior of decision makers and not merely the range of their intellectual considerations.[14] It could also become an institution for the promotion of justice if cost–benefit analysis were to include commentaries upon the justice of the likely shifts in income distributions that would follow from implementation of the policies suggested by the efficiency analysis.

Obfuscation of the separateness of efficiency and justice, and injection of arbitrary additional personal value judgments about distributions reduce the effectiveness of cost–benefit analysis as an efficiency-promoting institution and also preclude a proper consideration of what is just. If the basic virtue of the Paretian system is that it adopts as value judgments only certain commonly shared presumptions about what is acceptable, even if they appear trivial, and argues to specific conclusions from these weak premises, then the inclusion of justice as an additional, but separate, set of (contractarian) considerations in the evaluation is perfectly consistent.[15] The introduction of *ad hoc* judgments plucked from among one's own values is, of course, wholly inconsistent with this conventional method of tackling philosophical and scientific problems. Thus, while I do not think that economists should feel that they

---

[13] For example, Wiseman (1973).

[14] A view argued cogently by Roland McKean (1972).

[15] It is also possible to interpret cost–benefit analysis as an attempt to predict what is preferred, rather than what is preferable, that is, as a *positive* exercise. See Buchanan (1959). For a thoroughly Paretian interpretation of the basis of cost–benefit analysis, see Mishan (1971). My impression is that some users (and critics) of the Paretian method present the basic value assumptions more strongly than is necessary. For example, it is not necessary to assume that the individual is the best judge of his own welfare. It would seem to follow from modern conceptions of the meaning of utility that the individual is the *only* judge of his own welfare/utility. Even this is not as strong as it may appear, for there is

may not comment on issues of social justice as well as social efficiency, I do think that there are particular ways in which they should do it and they are not ways in which many cost–benefit experts appear to be leading us.

To return to the starting point of this paper, the rise of the technocracy presents, it seems to me, a serious threat to some primary goods that are essential to the integrity of society. Since economists are plainly part of that technocracy and play a currently fashionable part in the organs of government, the case for a self-denying ordinance, which sets limits to what kind of advice we may offer as professionals, seems overwhelming. The appropriate rubric is at hand. We may call it P-R (Pareto-Rawls).

4. Conclusions

I have attempted to show that a too thorough-going application of the principles of efficiency has within it the potential for doing vast damage to the quality of life in so-called free societies. Attempts to incorporate equity considerations into efficiency analysis may be logically inconsistent and, as often practiced by economists, professionally arrogant.[16] They would give better advice, especially in areas of social concern, if they kept the categories of justice and efficiency entirely separate. And I do not believe that they would be as tightly constrained from making interesting and important contributions to policy making as is sometimes supposed to be a corollary of using the Pareto criterion. I suspect that they may get on with sociologists, social administrators, moral philosophers, doctors, and teachers a little better than they do at the moment. They would also probably become the most modest of social scientists—and they could take pride in that!

References

Anderson, Robert W. 1974. "Towards a Cost–Benefit Analysis of Police Activity," *Public Finance* vol. 29, no. 1, pp. 1–18.

nothing at all in the Paretian rubric (apart, perhaps, from sloppy usage) that specifies *which individuals* are to "count" in society (and thence the social welfare function) or *which arguments* in individuals' utility functions are to "count." Both of these seem to be proper matters for constitutional choice at which level it is highly likely that we would all agree to exclude certain individuals (e.g., the mentally subnormal, whose welfare would be that *perceived by others*) and certain arguments (e.g., the fact that A. K. Sen may not like *my* bedroom walls pink). Thus, it may be possible for Paretians and (moderate) paternalists to share the same bed.

[16] Though not, of course, in a scheme of utilitarian ethics.

Buchanan, James M. 1959. "Positive Economics, Welfare Economics and Political Economy," *Journal of Law and Economics* vol 2.

————, and Gordon Tullock. 1962. *The Calculus of Consent* (Ann Arbor, University of Michigan Press).

Cattell, Raymond, and Ivan H. Scheier. 1961. *The Meaning and Measurement of Neuroticism and Anxiety* (New York, Ronald Press).

Culyer, A. J. 1971. "The Nature of the Commodity 'Health Care' and Its Efficient Allocation," *Oxford Economic Papers* vol. 23.

————. 1976. *Need and the National Health Service: Economics and Social Choice* (London, Martin Robertson).

McKean, Roland. 1972. "Property Rights within Government, and Devices to Increase Governmental Efficiency," *Southern Economic Journal* vol. 39.

Mishan, E. J. 1971. *Cost–Benefit Analysis: An Informal Introduction* (London, Allen and Unwin).

Rawls, John. 1972. *A Theory of Justice* (London, Oxford University Press).

Self, Peter. 1970. "Nonsense on Stilts: The Futility of Roskill," *New Society* (July).

Shoup, Carl S. 1964. "Standards for Distributing a Free Governmental Service: Crime Prevention," *Public Finance* vol. 19, no. 4, pp. 383–394.

Tarasovsky, Abraham. 1976. "Cost–Benefit Analysis, Cherished Illusions and Anxiety: An Aspect of the Hickey Effect," in Gordon Tullock, ed., *Frontiers in Economics, 1976.*

Thurow, Lester G. 1970. "Equity versus Efficiency in Law Enforcement," *Public Policy* vol. XVIII, no. 4 (Summer) pp. 451–462.

Titmuss, R. M. 1966. *Choice and the "Welfare State"* (London, Fabian Society).

————. 1970. *The Gift Relationship: From Human Blood to Social Policy* (London, Allen and Unwin).

Turvey, Ralph. 1963. "Present Value versus Internal Rate of Return: An Essay in the Theory of Third Best," *Economic Journal* vol. 73, pp. 93–98.

Williams, Alan. 1972. "Cost–Benefit Analysis: Bastard Science? And/or Insidious Poison in the Body Politick," *Journal of Public Economics* vol. 1, no. 2.

Wiseman, Jack. 1973. "The Theory of Public Utility Price—An Empty Box," reprinted in J. M. Buchanan and G. F. Thirlby, eds., *L.S.E. Essays on Cost* (London, London School of Economics and Weidenfeld and Nicolson).

8
Property Values and the Benefits of Environmental Improvements: Theory and Measurement

A. MITCHELL POLINSKY AND DANIEL L. RUBINFELD

1. Introduction

ATTEMPTS to measure the benefits of environmental improvements encounter a problem common in economics: the difficulty of determining the values of goods and services not directly traded in markets. Although consumers are thought to value the environment highly (a term used generically to include air, water, land, visual aesthetics, and so on),[1] there are no directly observable market prices which can conveniently be interpreted as the consumer's marginal willingness to pay for environmental attributes. Four approaches have been employed to overcome this problem:

> *Health studies*, which seek to determine the relationship between improvements in the environment and human health and then place a dollar value on these health improvements;[2]

This paper was circulated as Discussion Paper 404, Harvard Institute of Economic Research, March 1975. It is a synthesis and extension of previous work undertaken by the authors and Steven Shavell; see Polinsky and Rubinfeld (forthcoming) and Polinsky and Shavell (1975, 1976). Research on the present paper was supported by the National Bureau of Economic Research under contract with the National Academy of Sciences, in conjunction with a report on air quality and automobile emission control prepared for the Committee on Public Works of the United States Senate. Valuable research assistance was received from David Ellwood and Robert N. McDonald, and helpful comments were provided by Herbert Mohring and Steven Shavell.

[1] See, for example, Nordhaus and Tobin (1972, p. 13) who estimate that environmental degradation reduces GNP by 5 percent. However, Meyer and Leone (this volume) question these results.

[2] The best-known example of this approach is Lave and Seskin (1970).

154

Cost studies, which seek to ascertain the extra costs created by environmental disamenities, such as the physical damage to buildings caused by polluted air;[3]

Wage rate studies, which seek to determine the wage differences among urban areas that are necessary to compensate a given quality of labor for urban disamenities;[4] and

Property value studies, which seek to determine the relationship between property values and environmental amenities in order to predict the change in aggregate property values (interpreted as willingness to pay) resulting from an environmental improvement.[5]

This paper is limited to a discussion of what can be learned about the benefits of environmental improvements from property value studies. The question of whether the benefit measures derived from this approach should be added in part or in whole to the benefits derived from the other approaches is left unanswered.[6] In section 2 the essential issues involved in property value studies are explored in detail. Section 3 presents a nontechnical version of a model that can be used to determine property values in an urban area. In section 4 the model is used to analyze and at least partially answer the questions raised in section 2. In the process, a new procedure is suggested for measuring the benefits of environmental improvements. In section 5 a numerical illustration using this procedure is undertaken for St. Louis and compared with the estimates obtained by other methods.

2. An Overview of the Issues

Economists employing the property value approach to determine willingness to pay for environmental attributes first estimate the parameters of an equation explaining urban residential property values.[7] Although

---

[3] See, for example, Salmon (1970).

[4] See, for example, Nordhaus and Tobin (1972, pp. 12–13, 49–54).

[5] The best-known example of this approach is Ridker and Henning (1967).

[6] The relationships among these approaches are not well understood. Health and cost studies can be justified on the grounds that consumers do not fully perceive the damaging effects of dirty air, and therefore would not receive complete compensation through higher wages or lower property values. See, for example, Lave (1972, pp. 213–214, 234–236). On the other hand, wage rate and property value studies can be justified because they reflect in part aesthetic benefits which would be missed by the health and cost studies.

[7] For some representative examples, see Anderson and Crocker (1971), Kain and Quigley (1970), and Ridker and Henning (1967).

variables and functional forms differ somewhat from author to author, the equation can be represented by:[8]

$$v_j = \beta_0 + \beta_1 y_j + \beta_2 a_j + \beta_3 s_j + \beta_4 n_j \tag{1}$$

where v_j = residential property value (i.e., value of land and improvements)[9] of site j

y_j = income of household at site j[10]

a_j = index (or indices) of environmental amenities at site j

s_j = structural characteristics of site j

n_j = neighborhood characteristics associated with site j

A number of generally recognized assumptions underlie equation (1). The equation must be correctly specified. The relevant markets are assumed to be competitive and in or near equilibrium (which implies at least that the cost of moving among residential locations is low). If the markets are not, the estimated regression coefficients may not reflect the extent to which amenity variations over space are capitalized in property values. Perfect information about amenities and other relevant data is assumed. If consumers do not have perfect information, then low coefficients with respect to the amenities may reflect imperfect knowledge rather than a lack of consumer concern for environmental quality. Finally, it must be assumed that there are no serious measurement problems with respect to amenities. If, for example, the level of air pollution at any point in space fluctuates over time, it is not easily summarized by a single number.[11]

Granting these assumptions, the next step usually taken is to use equation (1) to predict the change in residential property values associated with a specified improvement in amenities.[12] Let b_2 equal an estimate of β_2, and a_j' equal the index of environmental amenities at site j after the hypothesized improvement. Then the predicted change in residential property values at site j is $b_2(a_j' - a_j)$, and the predicted change in aggregate

[8] Usually the unit of observation is a census tract, as in Ridker and Henning (1967), although in Kain and Quigley (1970) individual dwelling units are used.

[9] Property (land) values are the present discounted value of the stream of annual housing (land) expenditures.

[10] There is some disagreement about whether income should be included as an explanatory variable. See, for example, Ridker and Henning (1967, p. 247), Anderson and Crocker (1971, p. 173), and Small (1975).

[11] These and related issues have been discussed at length elsewhere. See, for example, Edel (1971, pp. 9–12), Lave (1972, pp. 213–215, 234–236), Ridker (1969, pp. 87–89, 97–98), Crocker (1969, pp. 192–193), Weiand (1973; 1974), Mullet (1974), Small (1975), Pollakowski (1973, pp. 994–1000), and Anderson and Crocker (1971, pp. 171–173).

[12] See, for example, Kain and Quigley (1970, p. 31) and Ridker and Henning (1967, p. 254).

residential property values in the urban area, APV, is the sum of these property value changes at all residential sites:

$$APV = \sum_j b_2(a'_j - a_j) \tag{2}$$

A number of questions have been raised about the validity of this procedure. The first question arises because the property value prediction for each location presupposes that everything else, including environmental amenities throughout the rest of the urban area, is held constant.[13] To see why the procedure described in (2) may be wrong, consider an urban area with a fixed population and fixed boundary in which air quality improves with distance from the center. If air quality were then raised throughout the area to a uniform level, say to the level at the boundary, this would induce an excess demand for land in the inner part of the urban area, bidding up property values there, but it would also induce an excess supply of land in the outer area, lowering property values there (even though air quality also improved). This could not be predicted by the procedure in equation (2). Thus, it appears that the estimated coefficients of the equation cannot be used in this way to predict the pattern of property value changes throughout the urban area.[14]

Even if the change in aggregate residential property values is correctly predicted, whether this change corresponds to the benefits of environmental improvements is still questionable. Unless this correspondence exists, there is little consolation in the ability to predict property values correctly. In general, the change in aggregate property values will measure benefits only when all surpluses (consumer surplus and producer profits) are eliminated by property value adjustments. When this condition does not hold, as is likely in practice, the change in aggregate property values may be either an underestimate or an overestimate of the benefits.[15] For example, under certain conditions it is possible to show that the sum of the absolute values of the changes in

[13] This was initially raised by Freeman (1971) and Edel (1971, pp. 8–12), and elaborated on by Capozza (1972, pp. 16–23).

[14] Freeman (1971, p. 415) concluded that "the regression equation cannot be used to predict the general pattern of property values or changes in the value of any given property when the pattern of air quality over the whole urban area has changed." Anderson and Crocker (1972) have suggested an alternative procedure employing equation (1) to predict property values. This procedure is based on an assignment model of the type developed by Lind (1973). However, Polinsky and Shavell (1975) and Pines (1974, pp. 1–2) have raised doubts about the validity of such a procedure.

[15] Much of this theoretical discussion has evolved in the context of an assign-

property values is a lower bound for aggregate benefits.[16] Thus, the change in aggregate property values is also a lower bound for benefits. Under different conditions, when factor substitution in housing production is present, property value changes will exceed land value changes. Since the change in aggregate land values will correctly measure benefits in the long run with perfect migration (to be demonstrated in section 4), the change in aggregate property values will then overstate benefits.

The apparent inability to predict property values correctly and to relate changes in aggregate property values to benefits has encouraged alternative uses of the property value equation (1). Interest has centered on attempts to identify the underlying demand curve for amenities, from which willingness to pay for environmental improvements can be deduced. Unfortunately, the property value equation (1) almost certainly reflects both demand and supply influences, making identification of the demand curve difficult.[17] Nonetheless, several authors concluded that the derivative of the property value equation with respect to an environmental attribute does identify the marginal rate of substitution between that attribute and all other goods, evaluated at the existing equilibrium.[18] Thus, for *marginal* changes in amenities, the procedure described in (2) correctly estimates benefits even though it incorrectly estimates the change in aggregate property values.[19] Although this approach provides estimates of the benefits of marginal changes in amenities, it may not be very helpful in evaluating nonmarginal changes. Thus, the applicability of the analysis to the substantial environmental improvements actually proposed in many public programs is limited.

The amenity and property value literature raises three conceptually distinct sets of issues:

---

ment model of land markets. For a description and critical evaluation of the applicability of the assignment model to the present question, see Lind (1973), Freeman (1975), and Pines (1974).

[16] This result was presented initially by Strotz (1968) and generalized recently by Lind (1973). Under a different set of conditions, it is possible for air quality to rise everywhere and for the aggregate change in property values to be negative. See Oron, Pines, and Sheshinski (1974, pp. 391–393) and Pines and Weiss (1976).

[17] See, for example, Freeman (1971, 1974b, pp. 74–79) and Small (1975).

[18] See Freeman (1974a), Small (1975), and Pines and Weiss (1976, pp. 9–10). Small's argument presupposes that income is not an explanatory variable in the equation.

[19] See, for example, Freeman (1974b) and Small (1975). Pines and Weiss (1976, p. 10) were thus led to conclude that "using quite general assumptions ... observable data can be used to obtain an unbiased estimate of the benefit." Note that β_2 is the derivative of property value with respect to an environmental attribute only in certain functional forms. In any case, the derivative is easy to calculate.

Can the property value equation be used to predict correctly the new residential equilibrium property value schedule (and therefore the change in aggregate property values) resulting from a change in the amenity schedule?

Does the *actual* change in aggregate residential property values equal willingness to pay for improved amenities?

Are there alternative interpretations or procedures by which willingness to pay for both marginal and nonmarginal environmental improvements can be identified (regardless of the answers to the first two questions)?

The next two sections of this paper develop detailed responses to these questions. In general, the first two questions must be answered negatively. However, the third question can be answered positively under certain conditions. Specifically, if the forms of the utility functions of different consumer groups are known and if the consumption of amenities within each group varies, it may be possible to make inferences about willingness to pay for both marginal and nonmarginal environmental improvements.

3. A Long-Run Model of an Urban Area with Environmental Amenities

The following model of an urban area is admittedly unrealistic, but captures the features which are important for describing the impact of environmental amenities.[20] Assume that there are three types of land use—business, residential, and agricultural. The use of any one plot of land is determined by competitive market forces. To simplify matters, also assume that plots having the same use are contiguous and that the business area is surrounded by the residential area, which in turn is surrounded by the agricultural area. Wherever land is used for business purposes, a private consumption good is produced according to a technology of constant returns to scale from land, labor, and capital.[21] Wherever land is in residential use, housing services are produced according to a technology of constant returns to scale from land and capital. Wherever land is not used for business or residential purposes, it is employed in agriculture "outside" the urban area. The agricultural sector determines a minimum price for land, below which farmers will

[20] The model presented in this section is a less technical and more general version of ones described in Polinsky and Rubinfeld (forthcoming) and Polinsky and Shavell (1976). A number of fine points discussed in those papers will be ignored here for expositional clarity.

[21] Capital should be thought of as any mobile factor of production other than labor.

outbid other users of land. Otherwise, this sector is exogenous to the rest of the model.

It is useful, although artificial, to associate each set of activities with separate actors. For example, occupants of housing rent their dwelling units from housing producers, who in turn rent land from landowners and capital from capital owners. Another simplifying device is to treat everyone but the occupants of the residential sector as "absent" from the urban area. Thus the analysis can focus on the effects of amenities on utility and on factor and product prices, while avoiding the complexities which arise if capital gains are a source of nonwage income to consumers and producers.

The residential portion of the urban area is of primary importance. It is inhabited by one or more groups of individuals, the members of each group having identical tastes and endowments of labor services. There is a sufficiently large number of consumers in each class to generate competitive behavior within and among groups. Within any given class, each consumer works a fixed period of time and makes a fixed number of trips to his workplace. This guarantees an identical income for all individuals in that class, although per capita incomes will vary among classes.[22] Each individual maximizes his utility by choosing a residential location and by allocating his remaining income (net of transportation costs) between housing services and a private composite good. Since environmental amenities enter positively into each individual's utility function (and may affect the desirability of consuming housing and the private good, everything else equal), the schedule of amenities[23] over space will affect the individual's decision about where to live and how to allocate his budget. The amenity schedule is assumed to be exogenous to the urban area,[24] and not to *directly* affect the location and production decisions of the producers of the private good and housing.

The remaining economic actors play a less visible role in the model. Producers of the private good maximize their profits subject to their

[22] It will simplify the exposition to think of the wage rate as measuring the payment for a unit of labor input of a standard quality. Then all workers are paid at the same wage rate, and variations in income arise because of differential endowments of labor services.

[23] For simplicity the amenity index will be treated as a scalar. However, nothing in the analysis prohibits treating the index as a vector.

[24] This simplifies the exposition at the cost of leaving out the potential effects on amenities of population, land use, and traffic density. This type of model could be expanded to allow for endogenous shifts in the amenity schedule, as in Oron, Pines, and Sheshinski (1974). Since the present focus is on whether the benefits resulting from any specified improvement in amenities can be inferred from market data, this is not a serious assumption.

technology, the product and factor prices they face, and the exogenous cost of shipping each unit of the good to a central distribution point. This determines where they locate within the urban area (or whether they relocate in another area), and their demands for factors of production. From the central distribution point it is costless to transport the private good to any residential location. In addition, the output of the good in any one urban area is a small fraction of total output. Therefore, the price of the good is exogenous to any one urban area. Like private good producers, housing producers maximize their profits subject to their technology, the price of capital, and the schedule of land prices. Owners of land maximize their profits by supplying their land to the highest bidder. Owners of capital also seek the highest possible return, but have more flexibility than landowners since capital is, by assumption, perfectly mobile within and among urban areas. It is also assumed that the amount of capital supplied by any capital owner or demanded by producers in any one urban area is small relative to the total amount available, so that the price of capital is exogenous to any one owner or user of capital.

There are four important equilibrium conditions which connect the various economic actors within the urban area. First, in the private good market, constant returns to scale and competitive behavior imply that producers make zero profits in equilibrium. Wherever a producer locates, his production costs plus shipping costs per unit just equal the exogenous price at the shipping point. Since the price of capital is exogenous and the transport cost schedule is fixed, only the wage rate and the price of land are left to adjust to bring about zero profits. Thus, equilibrium in the private product market determines an implicit relationship between land prices in the business sector and the wage rate paid to consumers. For example, a higher wage is only consistent with equilibrium if the price of land in the business sector falls. Otherwise, private good producers would make negative profits and would leave the urban area.

Second, in the land market, the demand for land must equal the supply of land at each location, whether it is used to produce the private good or housing. In either case, the demand for land is derived from the factor mix and output decisions of the producers. Third, in the labor market, equilibrium occurs when the total supply of labor equals the total demand. The demand for labor at each location in the business sector is derived from the factor mix and output decisions of private good producers at that location. Aggregate demand is the sum of the labor demands at all locations. The aggregate supply of labor is equal to the sum, over all classes, of the labor services supplied by individuals in each class.

The final and most important condition is the locational equilibrium for consumers. Two polar cases will be considered with regard to the locational options available to consumers. The first, referred to as the *open model*, assumes that consumers are perfectly mobile (that is, can move at no cost and have complete knowledge of all opportunities) both within and among urban areas. The second, referred to as the *closed model*, assumes that they are perfectly mobile within the urban area but immobile among urban areas. Because individuals (and producers) are free to move from one location to another within the urban area, the equilibrium pattern of land prices must be such that, given the amenity and transport cost schedules, no individual could increase his welfare (or firm increase its profits) by moving. For example, for a given wage rate and transport cost schedule, if one location is more attractive to consumers than another because of better air quality, then land prices rise at the first site and fall at the second until both locations are equally desirable. Locational equilibrium implies that, within each class of consumers, members of that class achieve the same level of utility regardless of their location. Whether the urban area is open (and small) or closed determines whether these levels of utility are exogenous or endogenous to the area's equilibrium. If the urban area is both open and small, there are in effect limitless opportunities else-where. Thus in the equilibrium of the system of urban areas, there is a level of utility associated with each class of individuals which is exogenous to any one area. A change in any one urban area—for example, an improvement in the environment—cannot affect these levels of utility.[25] It may merely lead to in-migration, bidding up the price of land and lowering the wage rate. On the other hand, if the urban area is closed, there are no opportunities elsewhere and in-migration is nonexistent. Consequently, structural changes in this urban area affect only the utility levels of its residents. For example, environ-mental improvements in a closed urban area generally lead to higher levels of utility (although not all classes of consumers may be better off in the new equilibrium).

For a more explicit account of the locational equilibrium condition, consider a consumer from class i who lives at location x, earns w_i dollars per year, spends $j(x)$ dollars per year on transportation, and spends the remaining $w_i - j(x)$ dollars per year on the private good

---

[25] Although the urban area is small, a shift in its amenity schedule may lead to a small change in the equilibrium levels of utility in the system. The general equilibrium effects are difficult to predict because of the resulting changes in wages and land prices throughout the system. As an approximation the utility changes are assumed to be zero.

and housing. His utility depends positively on his income net of transportation outlays $w_i - j(x)$, and on amenities at his location $a(x)$. It depends negatively on the rental price of housing services per year $p(x)$ (which in turn depends on the rental price of land per year $r(x)$, and the rental price of capital per year s), $\bar{p}[r(x),s] \equiv p(x)$. It also depends negatively on the price of the private good, which is fixed and arbitrarily chosen to be unity (since this good is used as the numeraire). The functional relationship relating the level of utility to these variables can be written as $\tilde{V}_i\{\bar{p}[r(x),s], [w_i - j(x)], a(x)\} \equiv V_i(x)$. The function $\tilde{V}_i\{\ \}$ is called the indirect utility function and can often be derived explicitly, given the form of the utility function.

If V_i^* is the equilibrium level of utility for members of class i (whether determined exogenously or endogenously), then in equilibrium

$$V_i^* = \tilde{V}_i\{\bar{p}[r(x),s],[w_i - j(x)],a(x)\} \tag{3}$$

for all locations x at which members of class i reside. Implicit in equation (3) is the equilibrium relationship between housing (and land) prices on the one hand, and the level of utility, transport costs, net income, and environmental amenities on the other. This relationship is written explicitly as

$$p(x) \equiv \bar{p}[r(x),s] = f_i\{V_i^*,[w_i - j(x)],a(x)\} \tag{4}$$

for all locations x at which members of class i reside in equilibrium.[26] The demand function for housing, $\bar{h}_i\{p(x), [w_i - j(x)], a(x)\} \equiv h_i(x)$, together with (4), imply the equilibrium relationship between housing expenditures and the same variables:

$$p(x)h_i(x) = g_i\{V_i^*,[w_i - j(x)],a(x)\} \tag{5}$$

Solving the locational equilibrium condition (3) to obtain an explicit relationship for housing prices—as in (4)—is a complex procedure in general. However, it is useful to do this for the special simplified case of one class of consumers with the Cobb–Douglas utility function:

$$U[c(x),h(x),a(x)] = Ac(x)^\alpha h(x)^\beta a(x)^\gamma \tag{6}$$

where c represents the private good, h represents housing services, A is a positive constant, and α, β, and γ are positive constants and less than one. Without loss of generality assume that $\alpha + \beta = 1$.[27] The individual's

---

[26] Equation (4) could be solved for $r(x)$ as a function of the arguments of $f_i(\ )$.

[27] Since only the ordinal properties of the utility function matter, the sum of the exponents (or any subset) is irrelevant.

demand functions for the private good and housing can be derived from (6). Substituting the demand functions into (6) yields

$$V(x) = C[w - j(x)]p(x)^{-\beta}a(x)^{\gamma} \tag{7}$$

where $C = A\alpha^{\alpha}\beta^{\beta}$

Setting $V(x)$ equal to the equilibrium level of utility V^* and solving for $p(x)$ leads to

$$p(x) = \left(\frac{C}{V^*}\right)^{1/\beta}[w - j(x)]^{1/\beta}a(x)^{\gamma/\beta} \tag{8}$$

For the case of a Cobb–Douglas utility function and one consumer group, (8) illustrates the dependence of housing prices on the equilibrium level of utility, net income, and environmental amenities.

4. Implications of the Model

The model just outlined can be used to answer the three questions raised in section 2. The important variables in the following analysis are the wage rate, the price of land at each location (residential and business), and the level of utility attained by each class of individuals.

1. *Can the property value equation be used to predict correctly the new equilibrium residential property value schedule resulting from a change in the amenity schedule?*

First consider a small and open urban area when all individuals are identical. In order to predict changes in property values at *residential locations*, equation (5) is directly relevant since property values are proportional to housing expenditures.[28] In equilibrium, (5) may be interpreted as a cross-section regression in which all parameters can be estimated. For a specified improvement in the amenity schedule, the new schedule of property values can be predicted using (5), provided there are no general equilibrium effects on the wage rate and transportation costs. The level of utility will not change since the area is open and small. In general, however, both the wage rate and the transportation cost schedule will be affected by a change in the amenity schedule. For example, an improvement in air quality would probably attract more residents to the urban area. This increases the supply of labor and, everything else being equal, lowers the wage rate. Another possibility is that improved air quality would be so complementary with housing that per capita demand for land would increase substantially. This

---

[28] This result follows from the implicit assumption of a steady stream of housing expenditures.

would result in a decline in population and labor supply and thus an increase in the wage rate, *ceteris paribus*. Furthermore, changes in workplaces and residential locations alter the pattern of commuter traffic, which may affect the transportation cost schedule.[29] Therefore, even if equation (5) were properly estimated, property value changes could not be predicted correctly merely by calculating the *ceteris paribus* effect of the change in amenities. *Ex ante* forecasts of changes in property values can be made only if separate predictions are made for changes in all of the "explanatory" variables in the equation which are endogenous to the general equilibrium of the urban area.

The prediction of property values in an open urban area is even more difficult when there are two or more classes of individuals in the area. Property value changes must then be predicted using a separate version of (5) for each consumer class. In order to make correct predictions, it is therefore necessary to know *ex ante* what class of individuals will live at each location in the new equilibrium.[30] This seems a rather hopeless task empirically. As an approximation, one might predict property values assuming that in the new equilibrium each location is inhabited by a member of the same class of consumers that lived at that location originally. However, the problems for prediction caused by the endogeneity of the wage rate and the transportation cost schedule remain.

Next consider the prediction of property value changes in the closed model with a single class of consumers. The discussion of the open model is applicable, with one further caveat. When the urban area is closed, an improvement in amenities generally leads to a change in the level of utility for every individual. Prediction becomes even more difficult because the level of utility appears in the housing expenditure equation. It is impossible to predict property values correctly without solving a general equilibrium model of the urban area in which the equilibrium level of utility is calculated endogenously. If the predictions are made on the assumption that utility is unchanged, the change in property values may be overestimated or underestimated, depending on the actual change in utility.

Finally, if there are two or more classes of consumers, prediction is even more difficult because utility could rise for some classes of consumers and fall for others as a result of an improvement in the environment. Thus, predictions made on the assumption that utility has

---

[29] Of course, the adjustments in location and population density may also affect air quality, making the analysis more complex.

[30] The extent to which amenity changes alter the mix among residential, business, and agricultural land uses must also be known.

not changed may overstate the change in property values for some groups and understate it for others.

2. *Does the actual change in aggregate residential property values equal willingness to pay for improved amenities?*

Each economic actor's willingness to pay is defined as the maximum amount of money which could be taken from him after the environmental improvement and leave him no worse off than before.[31] For producers and the owners of factors other than labor, this is the change in profits which occurs as a result of the improvement. Note that the change in profits of landowners is the change in aggregate land values. For consumers (suppliers of labor), willingness to pay is that amount of money which could be subtracted from (or must be added to) the consumer's budget to return him to the level of utility attained prior to the improvement. Given the assumptions of competitive behavior and constant returns in the production of the private good and housing, the willingness to pay of producers is zero, since their profits are always zero. Similarly, given the assumption of a perfectly elastic supply of capital, the willingness to pay of owners of capital is zero.[32] Thus, it is necessary to determine the willingness to pay of only two sets of actors, consumers and landowners.

In a small, open, urban area, an improvement in the environment will not change each consumer's utility, so that consumers' willingness to pay is zero. This result holds regardless of the number of classes of consumers in the urban area before and after the improvement. Since willingness to pay is zero for all parties except landowners in a small, open, urban area, the change in aggregate land values equals total willingness to pay. Business as well as residential land values must be included, since environmental improvements in the residential sector will affect land prices (and land values) in the business sector. For example, an improvement in amenities may attract a larger population, leading to a decline in the wage rate. Unless land prices in the business sector rise, private good producers would make positive profits.[33]

---

[31] This measure of willingness to pay is not the only one possible, but it is plausible and convenient.

[32] The supply of capital to any one urban area may not be *perfectly* elastic. Even though a change in environmental amentities may have only a small effect on the price of capital, it may have a substantial effect on the total willingness to pay of owners of capital in all urban areas.

[33] The importance of including land price (value) changes throughout the urban area is illustrated by the apparent possibility that land prices could fall everywhere in the residential area when amenities improve (if housing and amenities are highly substitutable). Willingness to pay is not necessarily negative, since the

In a closed urban area, an additional complication arises because changes in aggregate land values do not fully reflect the willingness to pay for amenity improvements. By definition, the change in aggregate land values equals the willingness to pay of the landowners. However, the willingness to pay of consumers is no longer zero. Some groups may be better off and others worse off due to amenity improvements. The willingness to pay of each class of consumers must be added to the willingness to pay of landowners. To the extent that net willingness to pay among consumers is positive, the change in aggregate land values will understate total willingness to pay.

The discussion in this subsection has three implications for conventional property value studies. First, willingness to pay depends on residential land values rather than on residential property values. Because of factor substitution and a fixed price of capital, the absolute change in aggregate property values exceeds the absolute change in aggregate land values. Second, determination of willingness to pay within the residential sector must also allow for changes in the utility of consumers. Finally, willingness to pay includes business land values as well as residential land values. Thus, focusing on the prediction and interpretation of property value changes in the residential sector may omit important effects.

3. *Are there alternative interpretations or procedures by which willingness to pay for both marginal and nonmarginal environmental improvements can be identified?*

An alternative method of determining willingness to pay might begin by measuring the immediate impact on consumers of a marginal or nonmarginal environmental improvement before the urban area adjusts to a new equilibrium. This requires the identification (up to a positive monotonic transformation) of the utility function for each class of consumers. In general, it is possible to identify each utility function only if the form of the utility function is specified, and if the level of amenities consumed varies within each consumer class. Given the specific forms of the utility functions, data on housing prices, the levels of amenities and net incomes, housing price equations of the form represented by (4) can in principle be estimated since (4) is derived from the individual's utility function.[34] It may then be possible to interpret the estimated regression coefficients in terms of parameters of the utility function for that consumer class. Since individuals with the same

decline in residential land prices is associated with a lower wage rate (for otherwise the individual's utility increases), and therefore higher business land prices.

utility function and income obtain the same level of utility in equilibrium regardless of whether the urban area is closed or open, the fact that utility may be different in the new equilibrium after an amenity improvement presents no difficulties for this approach.[35]

The conceptual issues involved in this approach may be illustrated with the Cobb–Douglas example of section 3. Equation (8) can be rewritten in linear form by taking logarithms of both sides:

$$P(x) = \psi_0 + \psi_1 W(x) + \psi_2 A(x) \qquad (9)$$

$$\text{where } P(x) = \log p(x)$$
$$W(x) = \log [w - j(x)]$$
$$A(x) = \log a(x)$$
$$\psi_0 = \log (C/V^*)^{1/\beta}$$
$$\psi_1 = 1/\beta$$
$$\psi_2 = \gamma/\beta$$

Estimates of α, β, and γ can be obtained from the regression coefficients in (9) (since $\beta = 1/\psi_1$, $\alpha = 1 - \beta$, and $\gamma = \psi_2/\psi_1$). In other words, if sufficient variation in net income and amenities exists within the set of locations inhabited by each class of consumers, the utility function may be identified. This may appear surprising because there is no actual market for amenities. However, after housing prices are adjusted for transportation cost, the remaining differences among prices per unit of housing at alternative locations can be imputed to differences in amenities.

The estimated utility function may now be used to calculate how much each consumer would be willing to pay (in terms of forgone income) for a change in amenities, assuming that everything else (including location, prices of all commodities, and net income) is held constant. Summing this figure over all individuals gives an estimate of aggregate willingness to pay, *WTP*. Formally, the procedure involves the following steps:

1. Estimate $p(x) = f_i\{V_i^*, [w_i - j(x)], a(x)\}$ using observations from all locations occupied by consumers in class i.
2. Use the estimated parameters from step 1 to identify the utility function for consumer class i.

[34] Recall that equation (4) is the locational equilibrium condition (3) solved for the price of housing, and that the right-hand side of (3) is the indirect utility function.

[35] For a discussion of the conditions under which the structure of demand is identified in a similar context, see Rosen (1974). He argues (p. 51) that "If buyers are identical, but sellers differ, ... single cross-sectional observations trace out compensated demand functions."

3. Given an amenity change from $a(x)$ to $a'(x)$, find the wage rate $w_i^*(x)$ which satisfies the equation $V_i^* = \tilde{V}_i\{p(x), [w_i^*(x) - j(x)], a'(x)\}$ for all locations occupied by consumers in class i.
4. Estimate willingness to pay of each individual at location x as $w_i - w_i^*(x)$.
5. Sum willingness to pay over all locations and over all consumer classes i,

$$WTP = \sum_i \sum_{z \in I_i} m_i(x)[w_i - w_i^*(x)],$$

where $m_i(x)$ is the number of individuals in class i at location x and I_i is the set of locations inhabited by individuals in class i.

The estimate of willingness to pay, WTP, is not an exact measure since no economic actor is allowed to adjust to the changes in the environment. As a result, WTP is likely to be a better approximation for marginal than nonmarginal changes.

5. The Benefits of an Improvement in Air Quality—A Numerical Illustration

This section compares empirical estimates of willingness to pay, using the procedure developed in section 4, part 3, with estimates obtained using other procedures. Air pollution and socioeconomic data for census tracts in the St. Louis metropolitan area are used to estimate separate housing expenditure equations for renters and owners.[36] The data are described in the Anderson and Crocker (1971) air pollution study.[37]

---

[36] Although the appropriate unit of observation is the individual household, the use of grouped data does not in itself bias the estimated parameters. See, for example, the references in Theil (1971, p. 249).

[37] We wish to thank A. Myrick Freeman III and Thomas D. Crocker for providing us with the data. The type I and type II equations of Anderson and Crocker (1971, p. 175) were reestimated using the same functional form and variables. However, to make the results more compatible with the present model, the sample was limited to those census tracts where median family income is greater than $4,000 and less than $8,500. High and low income census tracts were eliminated because the assumption of identical utility functions is least likely to hold for these groups. The exact cutoff points were determined by a direct examination of the distribution of median family income across census tracts. Fifteen low income tracts and eighteen high income tracts were eliminated from the owner equation, and fifteen low income and six high income tracts were eliminated from the renter equation. Because the purpose of this exercise is purely illustrative, a number of econometric issues are not addressed. (The possibility of simultaneous equation bias is especially troubling.)

To illustrate the calculation of *WTP*, consumer groups are assumed to have identical Cobb–Douglas utility functions but different incomes. Since income varies, it is also necessary to allow the level of utility to vary. In terms of the housing price equation derived in the Cobb–Douglas example (9), this is accomplished by including a dummy variable in the regression for each class of consumers (except one). The validity of such a procedure can be seen by rewriting equation (9):

$$\log [p(x)] = (1/\beta) \log (C/V^*) + (1/\beta) \log [w - j(x)] + (\gamma/\beta) \log [a(x)] \qquad (10)$$

Only the intercept in (10) varies with utility. Since it varies inversely, the estimated dummy coefficients should be such that the intercept in the regression falls as income rises.

An important problem arises because the dependent variable is median gross rent in the renter equation and median property value in the homeowner equation, rather than the price of housing. Since property values and gross rents are the product of a price of housing and a quantity of housing, some adjustment should be made for the fact that the quantity of housing consumed varies across observations. The consequences of not making any adjustment may be seen by adding the logarithm of housing quantity, $\log [h(x)]$, to each side of (10):

$$\log [p(x)h(x)] = (1/\beta) \log (C/V^*) + (1/\beta) \log [w - j(x)] \qquad (11)$$
$$+ (\gamma/\beta) \log [a(x)] + \log [h(x)]$$

Viewing (11) as a correctly specified regression equation, the omission of $\log [h(x)]$ on the right-hand side will in general bias the estimated coefficients of the included variables. The expected biases of the coefficients with respect to $\log [w - j(x)]$ and $\log [a(x)]$ are θ_1 and θ_2 respectively in the auxiliary regression of $\log [h(x)]$ on the included variables:[38]

$$\log [h(x)] = \theta_0 + \theta_1 \log [w - j(x)] + \theta_2 \log [a(x)] \qquad (12)$$

A priori, one would expect the sign of θ_1 to be negative and θ_2 to be indeterminate.[39] Thus, β will tend to be overestimated (and therefore α

[38] This result is a straightforward application of specification error analysis; see, for example, Theil (1971, pp. 548–551).

[39] Recall that the constant term in equation (11) [and therefore in (12)] is allowed to vary by consumer classes since the level of utility varies. Thus θ_1 is interpreted as the elasticity of housing demand with respect to net income, holding air quality and utility constant. Consider the indifference surface in three-space (private consumption good, housing and air quality) corresponding to this fixed level of utility, and the indifference curve in two-space (private consumption good and housing) corresponding to this fixed level of air quality. As net income

Table 1. Summary of Regression Results

Variable	(I) Homeowner equation	(II) Renter equation	(III) Homeowner equation	(IV) Renter equation
PSN	−0.062[a]	−0.006	−0.062[a]	0.006
	(0.033)	(0.026)	(0.033)	(0.025)
PPT	−0.132[b]	−0.137[b]	−0.140[b]	−0.149[b]
	(0.044)	(0.034)	(0.045)	(0.033)
MFI	1.580[b]	1.226[b]	1.188[b]	0.727[b]
	(0.468)	(0.342)	(0.117)	(0.085)
DLP	−0.066[b]	−0.038[b]	−0.072[b]	−0.038[b]
	(0.008)	(0.006)	(0.008)	(0.006)
OLD	0.040[b]	−0.053[b]	0.009	−0.063[b]
	(0.018)	(0.020)	(0.016)	(0.019)
NWT	0.030[b]	0.020[b]	0.038[b]	0.022[b]
	(0.006)	(0.004)	(0.006)	(0.004)
DIS	−0.111[b]	0.011	−0.120[b]	0.009
	(0.035)	(0.026)	(0.035)	(0.025)
C45	−0.160[b]	−0.087		
	(0.080)	(0.055)		
C50	−0.132[a]	−0.029		
	(0.069)	(0.049)		
C55	−0.054	−0.076[a]		
	(0.062)	(0.044)		
C60	0.010	−0.058		
	(0.053)	(0.038)		
C65	−0.001	−0.007		
	(0.050)	(0.036)		
C70	0.013	−0.021		
	(0.050)	(0.037)		
C75	0.011	−0.013		
	(0.051)	(0.047)		
C80	0.013	−0.036		
	(0.071)	(0.084)		
Intercept	−3.464	−5.294	−0.150	−1.056
	(3.94)	(2.88)	(1.03)	(0.752)
R^2	0.76	0.80	0.73	0.79
Size of sample	203	153	203	153
S.E.R.	0.150	0.097	0.156	0.097

Note: Standard errors are listed in parentheses.
[a] Significant at the 10% level.
[b] Significant at the 5% level.
S.E.R.—Standard error of the regression.

rises, holding utility and air quality constant, the price of land (and therefore of housing) must rise (otherwise utility would rise). Along a given indifference curve, an increase in the relative price of housing implies a decrease in the demand for housing. Similarly, θ_2 is interpreted as the elasticity of housing demand with respect to air quality, holding net income and utility constant. The consumption of either or both the private good and housing must decrease (otherwise utility would increase). The demand for housing may increase or decrease depending on the degree of "complementarity" or "substitutability" between air quality and housing consumption.

will be underestimated). Although the direction of the bias of the estimate of γ cannot be determined *a priori*, it will tend to be positive due to the bias of the coefficient with respect to $\log[w - j(x)]$. In practice the problem of specification bias is partially resolved by the inclusion of the logarithms of two proxies for housing quantity as explanatory variables in the regression.[40]

The regression results are summarized in table 1. The following variables are used in logarithmic form (except for the dummy variables):

Dependent variables: MPV = median property value [regressions (I) and (III)]

MGR = median gross rent [regressions (II) and (IV)]

Independent variables: PSN = annual arithmetic mean ambient air concentration of sulfur oxides[41]

PPT = annual arithmetic mean ambient air concentration of suspended particulates

MFI = median family income[42]

DLP = percentage of housing units classified as dilapidated

OLD = percentage of housing units more than twenty years old

NWT = percentage of occupied housing inhabited by nonwhites

DIS = distance of census tract from central business district (miles)

[40] The proxies are the percentage of housing units classified as dilapidated and the percentage of housing units more than twenty years old.

[41] We assume that each air quality index is proportional to the inverse of the corresponding air pollution index. Given the logarithmic form of (11), the coefficients of the air pollution indices differ only in sign from the coefficients of the air quality indices.

[42] Since the specification adopted here follows that of Anderson and Crocker (1971), no adjustment is made for transportation cost, although a variable representing distance from the CBD is included separately. The inclusion of the separate income and distance variables can be viewed as an approximation to the correct specification (which includes net income as a variable), since the wage and transport cost appear in the first term of the Taylor series expansion of the logarithm of net income.

$$C45 = \text{dummy variable equal to 1 if MFI is}$$
$$. \qquad \text{greater than or equal to \$4,500; equal}$$
$$. \qquad \text{to 0 otherwise}$$
$$.$$
$$C80 = \text{dummy variable equal to 1 if MFI is}$$
$$\text{greater than or equal to \$8,000; equal}$$
$$\text{to 0 otherwise.}$$

Regressions (I) and (II) are the homeowner and renter equations in which the dummy variables are included to allow for variations in income, and therefore utility, across consumer groups.[43] The coefficients estimated in these regressions are then used to identify the utility function and to estimate the willingness-to-pay measure, WTP (as described in section 4, part 3) for various percentage reductions in the air pollution indices at all locations in the urban area. Regressions (III) and (IV) are the same as (I) and (II) except that the dummy variables are not included in order to make the regressions comparable to conventional property value equations. The coefficients from (III) and (IV) are used to estimate two alternative measures of the benefits of environmental improvements. The first measure, MRS, interprets the derivative of property values or gross rents with respect to air pollution as the marginal rate of substitution between air pollution and all other goods, and implicitly assumes that this rate is constant (see section 2). The second measure, APV, estimates the change in aggregate property values (see section 2). The details of each measure are presented in the appendix and the results for the three measures are summarized in table 2.

Several points are worth noting about the results in table 2. First, MRS and APV are similar, especially for small improvements. This is not surprising, however, since MRS and APV would be identical if a linear rather than a logarithmic form of the equation were estimated. When the logarithmic form is used, the two measures are still close because MRS is a linear approximation of APV for small values of k.[44] Second, there is a substantial discrepancy between WTP and both MRS and the conventional measure of benefits, APV. The predicted benefits of improving air quality using the approach developed here are two to three times larger than the predicted change in aggregate property values.[45] However, these discrepancies are accounted for in part by the

[43] The dummy coefficients in equations (I) and (II) are generally consistent with the expected pattern of declining intercepts.

[44] For a proof see the appendix. k is the fractional reduction in air pollution.

[45] Some intuition as to why WTP is large can be gained by interpreting the estimated parameters of the Cobb–Douglas utility function. The results from

Table 2.   Summary of the Benefit Measures for Various Air Pollution
Reductions in St. Louis, Missouri

(*millions of dollars*)

k	WTP	MRS	APV
0.05	147	53	55
0.10	300	107	114
0.15	461	160	176
0.20	631	213	243
0.25	811	266	315
0.30	1001	320	394
0.35	1203	373	479
0.40	1420	427	572
0.45	1653	480	676
0.50	1905	533	791

Note: For details, see the appendix.
WTP = aggregate willingness to pay (see section 4, part 3).
MRS = aggregate benefits of improvement of air quality assuming a constant marginal rate of substitution between air quality and other goods (see section 2).
APV = predicted change in aggregate property values (see section 2).
k = fractional reduction in level of PSN and PPT at all locations.

specification biases.[46] Third, equal percentage reductions in pollution levels imply *increasing* percentage improvements in air quality. Thus, despite the appearance of the results for WTP and APV, the numbers are consistent with a *diminishing* marginal willingness to pay for air quality as air quality improves. Fourth, because of the enormous simplifications involved in constructing the example in this section, the focus should be on the divergence between the estimates rather than on their absolute magnitude. Most importantly, the results show the need for careful specification and interpretation of property value studies.

6. Concluding Remarks

The difficulties encountered in measuring the benefits of nonmarginal environmental improvements are due primarily to the inherent general

---

regressions (I) and (II) in table 1 imply that if individuals could purchase improved air quality, they would spend roughly 11 percent of their income if homeowners and 10 percent if renters. Since other environmental attributes, such as noise pollution, may be correlated with air quality but are omitted from the equation, these figures perhaps should be interpreted as how much would be spent on a number of environmental attributes. They should also be interpreted with caution since the assumption of a Cobb–Douglas utility function is very restrictive.

[46] All three measures are biased in the same direction due to the bias of the coefficient with respect to log $[a(x)]$. However, the bias with respect to log $[w - j(x)]$ only affects the WTP measure. As noted above, this leads to an estimate of γ, and therefore of WTP.

equilibrium nature of the problem. Such improvements will have important effects on the pattern of residential location, on the structure of the central business district, and on other features of the urban area. As a result of these adjustments, economic actors besides consumers living in the residential sector will be affected. Ideally, one would measure aggregate willingness to pay for an improvement in the environment by examining the utility or profits of each actor in the new general equilibrium. The purpose here has been to describe the complexities of this task and to propose a method of benefit measurement which is derived from a structural model of the equilibrium of an urban area. While this procedure is not demonstrably superior to other procedures when nonmarginal changes are involved, the process of estimating benefits in this way does generate useful information about individuals' tastes for amenities.

Appendix

Notes for Table 2

1. The benefit measure WTP (defined in section 4, part 3) is determined as follows:

   (a) Determine $\log V_1^o$ and $\log V_i^r$ in each census tract, where

   $$\log V_i^o = \log C^o + \log MFI_i + (c_1^o/b^o) \log PSN_i \\ + (c_2^o/b^o) \log PPT_i - (1/b^o) \log MPV_i$$

   $$\log V_i^r = \log C^r + \log MFI_i + (c_1^r/b^r) \log PSN_i \\ + (c_2^r/b^r) \log PPT_i - (1/b^r) \log MGR_i$$

   where
   V_i^o = utility achieved by homeowners in census tract i
   V_i^r = utility achieved by renters in census tract i
   c_1^o, c_2^o = estimated air pollution coefficients in homeowner equation
   c_1^r, c_2^r = estimated air pollution coefficients in renter equation
   b^o, b^r = estimated income coefficients in homeowner and renter equations, respectively

   (b) Find MFI_i^o and MFI_i^r (the new income levels that will leave individuals equally well off after pollution abatement) such that:

   $$\log MFI_i^o = \log V_i^o - (c_1^o/b^o) \log PSN_i' - (c_2^o/b^o) \log PPT_i'$$
   $$\log MFI_i^r = \log V_i^r - (c_1^r/b^r) \log PSN_i' - (c_2^r/b^r) \log PPT_i'$$

   where PSN_i' and PPT_i' are the new pollution levels in each tract.

(c) Calculate

$$WTP' = \sum_i (MFI_i - MFI_i^o)NH_i + \sum_i (MFI_i - MFI_i^r)NR_i$$

where NH_i = number of owner-occupied housing units in census tract i and NR_i = number of rental housing units in census tract i.

(d) $WTP = 0.848\ WTP'$

This involves a crude adjustment to allow for the fact that housing units are not the most desirable weighting units in the formula for WTP'. We would rather have used the number of families who own homes and who rent. Since such a breakdown is unavailable by census tract, we choose to adjust WTP' by multiplying it by the ratio of the number of families in the SMSA to the number of all housing units (using 1960 Census data).

(e) If we assume that air pollution is reduced by a fraction k, $0 < k < 1$, in every census tract, the formula for WTP' becomes the following:

$$WTP' = [1 - (1 - k)^{-(c_1^o + c_2^o)/b^o}] \sum_i MFI_iNH_i$$
$$+ [1 - (1 - k)^{-(c_1^r + c_2^r)/b^r}] \sum_i MFI_iNR_i$$

2. The benefit measure MRS is determined directly from the air pollution parameters as estimated in regressions (III) and (IV) of table 1 as follows:

(a) $d_1^o \simeq \dfrac{\partial MPV_i^o}{\partial PSN_i}\dfrac{PSN_i}{MPV_i^o}$ $d_2^o \simeq \dfrac{\partial MPV_i^o}{\partial PPT_i}\dfrac{PPT_i}{MPV_i^o}$

$d_1^r \simeq \dfrac{\partial MGR_i^r}{\partial PSN_i}\dfrac{PSN_i}{MGR_i^r}$ $d_2^r \simeq \dfrac{\partial MGR_i^r}{\partial PPT_i}\dfrac{PPT_i}{MGR_i^r}$

where d_1^o, d_2^o are the estimated air pollution coefficients in the home-owner equation and d_1^r, d_2^r are the estimated air pollution coefficients in the renter equation.

Equality will hold in the above equations when all variables lie on the estimated regression line.

(b) $B_i^o = \dfrac{\partial MPV_i^o}{\partial PSN_i}(PSN_i' - PSN_i) + \dfrac{\partial MPV_i^o}{\partial PPT_i}(PPT_i' - PPT_i)$

$B_i^r = 100\left[\dfrac{\partial MGR_i^r}{\partial PSN_i}(PSN_i' - PSN_i) + \dfrac{\partial MGR_i^r}{\partial PPT_i}(PPT_i' - PPT_i)\right]$

where 100 is an arbitrarily chosen gross rent multiplier.

(c) $MRS = \sum B_i^o NH_i + \sum B_i^r NR_i$

$$= d_1^o \sum MPV_i^o \left(\frac{PSN_i' - PSN_i}{PSN_i} \right) NH_i$$

$$+ d_2^o \sum MPV_i^o \left(\frac{PPT_i' - PPT_i}{PPT_i} \right) NH_i$$

$$+ 100 \left[d_1^r \sum MGR_i^r \left(\frac{PSN_i' - PSN_i}{PSN_i} \right) NH_i \right.$$

$$\left. + d_2^r \sum MGR_i^r \left(\frac{PPT_i' - PPT_i}{PPT_i} \right) NR_i \right]$$

(d) If we reduce air pollution by a fraction k in every census tract, the formula for MRS reduces to:

$$MRS = -k(d_1^o + d_2^o) \sum MPV_i^o NH_i - 100k(d_1^r + d_2^r) \sum MGR_i^r NR_i$$

(e) The measures of benefits were calculated in terms of reductions in the air pollution indices, rather than improvements in the air quality indices (see footnote 41). If MRS were measured in terms of air quality (rather than air pollution) changes, a different measure of benefits, MRS^*, would have been obtained, where $MRS^* = MRS/(1 - k)$. However, WTP and APV would be unchanged.

3. The benefit measure APV is determined from regressions (III) and (IV) of table 1 as follows:

(a) $\log MPV_i' - \log MPV_i = d_1^o(\log PSN_i' - \log PSN_i)$
$$+ d_2^o(\log PPT_i' - \log PPT_i)$$

$\log MGR_i' - \log MGR_i = d_1^r(\log PSN_i' - \log PSN_i)$
$$+ d_2^r(\log PPT_i' - \log PPT_i)$$

(b) $MPV_i' = MPV_i \left[\left(\frac{PSN_i'}{PSN_i} \right)^{d_1^o} \left(\frac{PPT_i'}{PPT_i} \right)^{d_2^o} \right]$

$MGR_i' = MGR_i \left[\left(\frac{PSN_i'}{PSN_i} \right)^{d_1^r} \left(\frac{PPT_i'}{PPT_i} \right)^{d_2^r} \right]$

(c) $APV = \sum_i (MPV_i' - MPV_i)NH_i + 100 \sum_i (MGR_i' - MGR_i)NR_i$

(d) If we reduce air pollution by a fraction k in every census tract, the formula for APV reduces to:

$$APV = [(1 - k)^{(d_1^o + d_2^o)} - 1] \sum_i MPV_i NH_i$$

$$+ 100[(1 - k)^{(d_1^r + d_2^r)} - 1] \sum MGR_i NR_i$$

(e) For small k, *APV* will closely approximate *MRS*. This follows directly by applying the result that $(1 - k)^{(d_1+d_2)} \simeq 1 - k(d_1 + d_2)$ for small k.

4. All benefit measures are summed over all census tracts available on the data tape, which does not include approximately 20 percent of the tracts for the St. Louis SMSA.

5. Since aggregate willingness to pay is measured in dollars per year, a discount factor must be applied to make it comparable to the *MRS* and *APV* measures. We have arbitrarily chosen to apply a multiplier of 8.33 to obtain the present discounted value of willingness to pay. This is consistent with the value of 100 chosen for the gross rent multiplier.

References

Anderson, Robert J., Jr., and Thomas D. Crocker. 1971. "Air Pollution and Residential Property Values," *Urban Studies* vol. 8, no. 3 (October) pp. 171–180.

————, and ————. 1972. "Air Pollution and Property Values: A Reply," *Review of Economics and Statistics* vol. 54, no. 4 (November) pp. 470–473.

Capozza, Dennis R. 1972. "Measuring the Benefits of Urban Improvements." Paper presented at the 1972 Winter Meetings of the Econometric Society (Toronto, December 28–30).

Crocker, Thomas D. 1969. "The Measurement of Economic Losses from Uncompensated Externalities," in William R. Walker, ed., *Economics of Air and Water Pollution* (Springfield, Va., National Technical Information Service) pp. 180–194.

Edel, Matthew. 1971. "Land Values and the Costs of Urban Congestion: Measurement and Distribution," *Social Science Information* vol. 10, no. 6, pp. 7–36.

Freeman, A. Myrick, III. 1971. "Air Pollution and Property Values: A Methodological Comment," *Review of Economics and Statistics* vol. 53, no. 4 (November) pp. 415–416.

————. 1974a. "Air Pollution and Property Values: A Further Comment," *Review of Economics and Statistics* vol. 56, no. 4 (November) pp. 554–556.

————. 1974b. "On Estimating Air Pollution Control Benefits from Land Value Studies," *Journal of Environmental Economics and Management* vol. 1, pp. 74–83.

————. 1975. "Spatial Equilibrium, the Theory of Rents, and the

Measurement of Benefits from Public Programs: A Comment," *Quarterly Journal of Economics* vol. 89, no. 3 (August) pp. 470–473.

Kain, John F., and John M. Quigley. 1970. "Evaluating the Quality of the Residential Environment," *Environment and Planning* vol. 2, pp. 23–32.

Lave, Lester B. 1972. "Air Pollution Damage: Some Difficulties in Estimating the Value of Abatement," in Allen V. Kneese and Blair T. Bower, eds., *Environmental Quality Analysis* (Baltimore, Johns Hopkins University Press for Resources for the Future) pp. 213–242.

————, and Eugene Seskin. 1970. "Air Pollution and Human Health: The Quantitative Effect of Air Pollution on Human Health and an Estimate of the Dollar Benefit of Pollution Abatement," *Science* vol. 169 (August 21) pp. 723–733.

Lind, Robert C. 1973. "Spatial Equilibrium, the Theory of Rents, and the Measurement of Benefits from Public Programs," *Quarterly Journal of Economics* vol. 87, no. 2 (May) pp. 188–207.

Mullet, Gary M. 1974. "A Comment on Air Pollution and Property Values: A Study of the St. Louis Area," *Journal of Regional Science* vol. 14, no. 1 (April) pp. 137–138.

Nordhaus, William D., and James Tobin. 1972. "Is Growth Obsolete?," in National Bureau of Economic Research, 50th Anniversary Colloquium, vol. 5, *Economic Growth* (New York, NBER).

Oron, Yitzhak, David Pines, and Eytan Sheshinski. 1974. "The Effect of Nuisances Associated with Urban Traffic on Suburbanization and Land Values," *Journal of Urban Economics* vol. 1, no. 4 (October) pp. 382–394.

Pines, David. 1974. "A Note on the Relationship Between Public Program Benefits and its Effect on Equilibrium Rent." Unpublished manuscript.

————, and Yoram Weiss. 1976. "Land Improvement Projects and Land Values," *Journal of Urban Economics* vol. 3, no. 1 (January) pp. 1–13.

Polinsky, A. Mitchell, and Daniel L. Rubinfeld. "The Long-Run Effects of a Residential Property Tax and Local Public Services," *Journal of Urban Economics*. Forthcoming.

————, and Steven Shavell. 1975. "The Air Pollution and Property Value Debate," *Review of Economics and Statistics* vol. 57, no. 1 (February) pp. 100–104.

————, and ————. 1976. "Amenities and Property Values in a Model of an Urban Area," *Journal of Public Economics* vol. 5, no. 1, 2 (January/February) pp. 119–129.

Pollakowski, Henry O. 1973. "The Effects of Property Taxes and Local Public Spending on Property Values: A Comment and Further Results," *Journal of Political Economy* vol. 81, no. 4 (July/August) pp. 994–1003.

Ridker, Ronald G. 1969. "Strategies for Measuring the Cost of Air Pollution," in Harold Wolozin, ed., *The Economics of Air Pollution* (New York, W. W. Norton) pp. 87–101.

——, and John A. Henning. 1967. "The Determinants of Residential Property Values with Special Reference to Air Pollution," *Review of Economics and Statistics* vol. 49, no. 2 (May) pp. 246–257.

Rosen, Sherwin. 1974. "Hedonic Prices and Implicit Markets: Product Differentiation in Pure Competition," *Journal of Political Economy* vol. 82, no. 1 (January/February) pp. 34–55.

Salmon, Richard L. 1970. *Systems Analysis of the Effects of Air Pollution on Materials* (Kansas City, Midwest Research Institute, January).

Small, Kenneth A. 1975. "Air Pollution and Property Values: Further Comment," *Review of Economics and Statistics* vol. 57, no. 1 (February) pp. 105–107.

Strotz, Robert H. 1968. "The Use of Land Rent Changes to Measure the Welfare Benefits of Land Improvement," in Joseph E. Haring, ed., *The New Economics of Regulated Industries: Rate-Making in a Dynamic Economy* (Los Angeles, Economics Research Center, Occidental College) pp. 174–186.

Theil, Henri. 1971. *Principles of Econometrics* (New York, Wiley).

Wieand, Kenneth F. 1973. "Air Pollution and Property Values: A Study of the St. Louis Area," *Journal of Regional Science* vol. 13, no. 1 (April) pp. 91–95.

——. 1974. "More on Air Pollution: A Reply to Mullet," *Journal of Regional Science* vol. 14, no. 1 (April) pp. 139–142.

9
Estimating Access Values

PETER BOHM

LIFE has many qualities for which there are no markets. Sometimes this is fortunate, sometimes not. For example, most qualities of the physical environment are administered by government without any reference to the preferences of those who are affected; such a reference could be provided if these commodities were of the so-called private-good type and hence were traded on a market. In the absence of markets, output may fall short of an optimum, in some sense. In the age of a return to nature ideology, even the opposite may become true, of course.

Information about consumer preferences is in fact required not only for access to public goods, but also for access to markets for private goods produced under decreasing costs and sold at marginal cost prices, as may be the case for public transportation, for example. Information about consumer "access values" is desirable first of all as a basis for investment decisions. But it is also required for effective income redistribution policy. Moreover, it may in some cases enable the government to select an efficient financing method from a set of feasible financing alternatives. This wider relevance of information about access values will be elaborated on in section 1.

The remainder of the paper is devoted to a discussion of possible techniques for estimating access values. In section 2, an overview of some possible alternatives is presented and their relative merits and shortcomings are discussed briefly. In section 3, one special technique is suggested and developed in some detail. This concerns an approach by which a sufficiently narrow interval for access values of different consumer groups could be determined.

1. The Policy Relevance of Estimating Access Values

The importance of information about demand for public goods is straightforward. Knowing the consumers' aggregate willingness to pay (WTP) for such goods, it can be determined whether total benefits

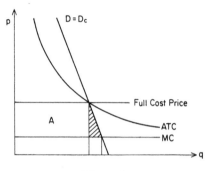

Figure 1

exceed total investment costs. Knowing the benefits accruing to individual consumers or consumer groups would make it possible to make an investment and finance it without violating the Pareto criterion. Moreover, such information would reveal the effects of different output levels and different financing devices on the distribution of real income and so make public goods projects more precise instruments for real income redistribution.

For excludable commodities produced under decreasing costs, we know that in principle optimal output and price would imply a financial deficit. Information on how much consumers would be willing to pay for access to markets for such commodities sold at a marginal-cost price would help to determine whether aggregate WTP (or aggregate access value) exceeds costs not covered by the user charges, whether fixed charges could be designed to meet the Pareto criterion, and how differentiated fixed charges could be used as a redistributive device. In the real world, however, governments often use (or accept) full-cost pricing for this kind of commodity. The reason seems to be that governments want to avoid tax financing or want beneficiaries to pay all costs of production, or both. Information about access values may allow a more efficient solution than the full-cost pricing scheme, taking such political constraints as given. Since these possible benefits from estimating access values do not seem to have been observed in the literature, this latter point will be developed in some detail here.

Assume for simplicity that marginal costs (MC) are constant and that demand (D) equals compensated demand (D_c). If prices were set equal to average total costs, an approach often used by governments to avoid tax financing and to make only beneficiaries pay, we would end up with an efficiency loss equal to the shaded area in figure 1 (assuming individual consumer's surpluses could be meaningfully added).[1] A marginal-cost price would make it possible to avoid this efficiency loss. And by introducing fixed charges in the total amount of A in figure 1, all costs would again be covered by payments from the beneficiaries. Thus, as is well known, a two-part tariff could make efficiency compatible with a self-liquidation constraint.

It would be simple to adopt this solution if individual demand were fairly uniform or if there were just a few easily separable consumer groups with similar preferences in each group; in the latter case, a differentiated fixed fee may be required to cover costs and to achieve efficiency.[2] But when demand is heterogeneous and/or when differentiation of fixed charges is impracticable, a straightforward application of the two-part tariff solution is ruled out. In such cases it may be possible and "locally" efficient to reduce the number of fixed charge categories below what would otherwise have been called for. This reduction, however, creates a new efficiency problem in the sense that certain consumers would have to face too high a fixed charge to be willing to pay the entrance fee and stay on as consumers of the commodity. We shall illustrate this problem for the simple case where there are three consumer groups with different levels of demand, but only one level for the fixed charge.

For a consumer i belonging to a group with a small demand for the commodity (group 1), we may have a situation as shown in figure 2. To simplify the exposition we have assumed that marginal cost equals zero and hence that the user charge should equal zero. (We could equally well have assumed that the horizontal axis is moved up to the level of a positive marginal cost.) The fixed charge $\bar{F}$ is indicated by the hyperbola $\bar{F} = pq$; thus, the fixed charge can be represented by the area corresponding to any point on this hyperbola, for example, the rectangle $p_u f\, q_u 0$. For consumer i the fixed charge obviously exceeds his WTP for being able to buy the commodity at the marginal-cost price, as $\bar{F}$ exceeds the consumer's surplus given by the area under the (compensated) demand curve. Hence, this consumer and the others in the group

---

[1] The consumer's surplus at a certain price is obviously the same thing as the WTP for access to a market with this price and also the same thing as our term access value. Thus, these three terms are used interchangeably throughout this paper.

[2] It should be noted that the commodities of main interest in this context concern (public) services, for which two-part tariffs as well as differentiated tariffs are feasible much more often than for goods that may be resold among consumers. It should also be pointed out that the use of two-part tariffs does not presuppose that consumers know their future demand with certainty. In cases of substantial uncertainty, consumers could be given the option to pay the fixed charge beforehand or to get the advantages of the two-part tariff when they can document at a later date that they have in fact paid an amount equal to the fixed charge but in the form of ordinary prices.

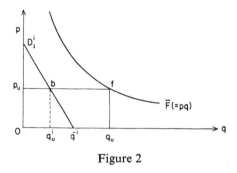

Figure 2

will abstain from consuming the commodity. Since this means also that the two-part tariff will imply a welfare loss (for simplicity, the sum of consumers' surpluses in group 1), it is no longer certain that a two-part tariff will be superior to a uniform full-cost price (disregarding the implementation costs of the two schemes). Specifically, if this welfare loss exceeds that of the full-cost price (see the shaded area in figure 1), a two-part tariff would no longer be desirable.

It can be shown, however, that both of these alternatives are inferior to a third scheme. This is a combination of the first two schemes, where there exists a two-part tariff $(\bar{F}, p = MC)$ along with an alternative uniform price, $p_u > MC$. (Mixed pricing schemes like this exist, for example, in public transportation where single tickets can be bought at p_u or, if an annual or monthly fee of $\bar{F}$ has been paid, at some fraction of p_u or at zero.)

Under the mixed pricing scheme, consumers in group 1 may buy at least part $(q_u{}^i)$ of their "first-best optimum" quantity $(\bar{q}^i)$ as shown in figure 2. Thus, consumers in a situation such as that of group 1 would be better off than under the two-part tariff alone. This, however, is not enough to prove that the mixed scheme is superior to the two-part tariff alone. The reason is that the introduction of p_u may cause other consumers (say, those in consumer group 2) to shift from the two-part tariff to the single price, p_u. This is shown in figure 3 for a member j of this consumer group.

As WTP at $p = MC(=0)$ exceeds the fixed charge, $\bar{F}$, consumer j would have chosen to pay $\bar{F}$ if only the two-part tariff existed. Now, he can choose p_u instead, which means that he would consume $q_u{}^j$ instead of $\bar{q}^j$ and would pay a smaller amount than in the two-part tariff case. Thus, from figure 3 we can see that he loses $E + C$ and gains $E + B$. Consequently, if B exceeds C, he would prefer p_u to $(\bar{F}, p)$. The rest of the economy, however, would incur a loss from this shift by consumers in group 2, as the amount $E + B$ would no longer be paid by the

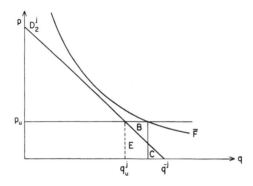

Figure 3

members of this group and would thus have to be paid by others. In other words, there will be a net loss for the economy as a whole equal to $E + B - (B - C) = E + C$.

Now, p_u is a parameter whose optimal value has to be determined. In principle, it is clear that p_u reaches a locally optimal level if p_u is increased up to the minimum level of p_u at which consumer j would find it worthwhile to choose the two-part tariff. Let us call this locally optimal value p_u^1 (figure 4). Obviously, this local optimum of the mixed system must be preferable to the two-part tariff as long as consumers in group 1 benefit from p_u^1, given that there is no change for the worse in other groups.[3] In fact, other groups will benefit as well once we observe that the addition of revenue from consumer group 1 means that the fixed charge (and consequently, p_u^1) can be reduced without violating the budget constraint.

It may be noted in passing that p_u^1 may not represent the optimal version of the mixed system. Introducing a third consumer group with a still higher demand (see D_3^k in figure 4 for consumer k), we can envisage a minimum level of p_u, p_u^2, at which this group still chooses the two-part tariff. In the transition from p_u^1 to p_u^2, where $p_u^1 > p_u^2$, we have that, *ceteris paribus*, groups 1 and 2 make gains and group 3 is indifferent. However, as group 2 pays less than before and group 1 pays more or less than before, depending on its demand elasticity, the total contribution to fixed costs from these two groups may increase or decrease. Consequently, group 3 will become worse off if the fixed charge has to be increased (which of course affects p_u^2) to meet the budget constraint. Given a compensatory mechanism or a political

---

[3] If there were no consumers in group 1, that is, no consumers with a WTP below F and yet a positive demand at p_u^1 (see D_o in figure 4) the mixed system would cease to be superior to the pure two-part tariff.

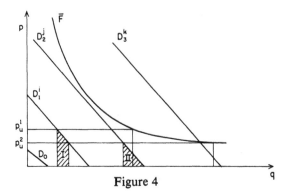

Figure 4

weighting of marginal income among groups so that marginal dollars are given the same weight in all groups within relevant intervals, the criterion for selecting $p_u{}^2$ instead of $p_u{}^1$ can be summarized as follows. The sum of additions to social surplus with respect to group 1 (area I in figure 4 for the individual consumer i) should exceed the sum of reductions in social surplus with respect to group 2 (see area II for the individual consumer j).

Given now that the optimal version of a mixed system is preferable to (or at least as efficient as) a uniform two-part tariff, it remains to be shown that the mixed system is superior also to the second alternative, full-cost pricing. Let p_{fc} in figure 5 be the full-cost price and introduce a two-part tariff so designed that it will appeal only to people who have a high demand for the commodity, that is, group 3. Moreover, let the fixed charge equal F^*, so determined that the revenue from this group will be the same as it would have been with the full-cost price alone. This means, of course, that group 3 will be better off (see the shaded area in figure 5) and no one worse off. Hence, the mixed system is clearly superior to a full-cost pricing system.

To make practical use of all the results derived so far, we would certainly need a discouragingly large amount of information about (future) consumer demand. To calculate a full-cost price *ex ante*, we need to know the aggregate demand curve (or the relevant portion of it). To calculate a differentiated two-part tariff, we need to know the consumer's surplus of the different consumer groups at the marginal-cost price (hopefully, fairly constant). And to calculate optimal prices and fixed charges in a mixed system, we need to know the demand curves of the different consumer groups (or relevant portions of them). However, information about access values, that is, about consumer's surplus at a marginal-cost price, could also be useful for the mixed system and the full-cost pricing solution. With such information we

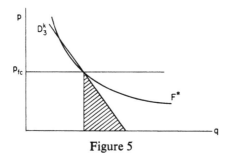

Figure 5

would at least know the integral of the aggregate (compensated) demand curve and of the (compensated) demand curve for different consumer groups, if such groups could be discerned, which would lend itself to better "informed guesses" about these curves (e.g., assuming a certain constant elasticity or linearity with a certain slope). In addition, it should be noted that knowing access values at the marginal-cost price would enable us to calculate the optimal version of a two-part tariff with a uniform fixed charge, provided such a system could meet the budget constraint. We would then know how many people would abstain from being consumers of the commodity at each level of the fixed charge. But more important perhaps, information about access values would in certain cases make it possible to design an *efficient* financing system where no one would abstain from being a consumer. This would be the case when access values do not differ very much among individuals or when the aggregate access value is so much higher than fixed costs that the fixed charge could be set at such a low level that "hardly anyone" would abstain from paying this amount. Moreover, in some cases it would be possible to determine a sufficiently fine structure of differentiated fixed charges to accomplish the same end. Thus, in these situations information about access values would make it possible to locate an efficient financing method.

To sum up, information about access values would not only help in guiding investment decisions and distribution policy with respect to public goods and decreasing-cost private goods, but also serve as a basis for avoiding inefficient financial solutions and inefficient pricing formulas. It is with this background in mind that we now turn to the question of how to estimate access values in practice.

2. An Evaluation of Some Existing Proposals for Estimating Access Values

For a long time it has been regarded as a fact that consumers would not reveal their true preferences for access to public goods. The same argument would of course apply to the other kinds of access values we have mentioned above. However, some attempts have been made to find strategies which could be used to avoid or counteract the existing incentives to misrepresent preferences. We shall comment on four such proposals. The first two concern divisible goods and require repeated referenda of some sort; the last two concern given (indivisible) projects to be rejected or accepted.

In his now-classical article from 1943, Bowen suggested that each consumer should pay the same percentage of project costs. By assuming that median demand equals mean demand, repeated referenda where people voted yes or no with respect to an increase in the public good would eventually reveal a Pareto optimal point where 50 percent voted yes and 50 percent no. Aside from the practical difficulties or repeated referenda, the usefulness of this proposal is restricted by the special assumption about the demand distribution. This is something we cannot regard as given without prior knowledge of individual demand. Moreover, several arguments can be raised which make it likely that the demand distribution in fact is highly asymmetrical, for example, when mean demand is "close" to zero. Under such circumstances, the Bowen method would lead us astray.

Recently, several proposals have been made with essentially one and the same idea in common (cf. Malinvaud, 1971; Drèze and de la Vallée Poussin, 1971; and Tideman, 1972). The basic principle may be summarized as follows: If a hypothetical level of the public good output is found which consumers cannot say is obviously too small or obviously too large relative to an optimum level, people would reveal their true preferences, provided they behave according to a minimax strategy. More specifically, we may imagine a sample of consumers being asked to state their (marginal) WTP for a small change Δq in output away from a given (hypothetical) output level $\bar{q}$. The individual consumer is thus hypothetically placed at a point $(\bar{c}, \bar{q})$ where $\bar{c}$ represents his net consumption of other commodities, given $\bar{q}$ and given how the financing of $\bar{q}$ affects him. If he had believed that optimal output (where aggregate marginal WTP equals marginal cost of the public good output) is higher than $\bar{q}$, he might have tried to misrepresent his preferences. This is indicated by $\tilde{\Delta}c$ and the dotted indifference curve in figure 6, I_1 and I_2 being his true preferences. In other words, he would have tried to move to a better position than would otherwise be possible. But given the assumption that he finds a reduction from $\bar{q}$ to be possible as well, a response indicating $\tilde{\Delta}c$ would make him worse off than if he had told the truth, should output in fact be reduced and given that consumers are then compensated in line with their WTP statements (see the shift to a

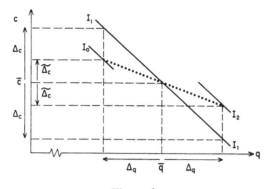

Figure 6

point on I_0). Assuming that he wants to maximize the worst possible outcome, he would in fact state his marginal WTP as equal to Δc. In that case he obviously would end up on the same indifference curve I_1, regardless of what happens to output.

Several problems are involved in an approach of this kind. First, it is doubtful whether the required uncertainty about the direction of output change can be created—especially after some referenda have been carried out; for example, if some people believe that $\bar{q}$ is below the optimal level, the incentive to misrepresent preferences will reappear. Second, there is hardly any empirical basis for the assumption that consumers will react according to a minimax strategy; it is particularly doubtful when the likelihood of a change in one direction is judged to be much larger than a change in the opposite direction.[4] Third, this approach does not work at all for the great many cases of indivisible (quasi) public goods or public goods where marginal changes in size make no sense to consumers (such as a bridge, purification of a lake, and so on).

Among the proposals that deal explicitly with given projects (although, in principle, they are applicable to different levels of divisible projects as well), some suggest that misrepresentations of preferences could be avoided by a two-stage approach. Kurz (1973) has suggested a solution of this kind (see also Arvidson, 1974), where in a first stage a sample of consumers is asked about their views on the probability that the project will be adopted (i.e., that aggregate WTP will turn out to be larger than project costs). The stated probability, p^j for individual j, is

---

[4] If people behaved more according to a maximum expected payoff rule, they would misrepresent preferences in such cases. If, for example, the subjective probability of an increase in q was ¾, the expected payoff from bluffing ($\tilde{\Delta}c < \Delta c$) would be ¾ $(\Delta c - \tilde{\Delta}c) + ¼ (\tilde{\Delta}c - \Delta c) = ½ (\Delta c - \tilde{\Delta}c)$, i.e., positive.

used in a second stage, where each person is asked about his *true* willingness to pay, F^j, given that he will have to pay an amount equal to his *stated* WTP, f^j, if the project is adopted and will be paid an amount equal to

$$f^j \cdot \frac{p^j}{1 - p^j}$$

if the project is rejected. Thus, his expected payoff would be

$$p^j[F^j - f^j] + (1 - p^j) \frac{p^j}{1 - p^j} f^j = p^j F^j$$

which can be seen to be independent of his stated WTP, f^j. It is assumed that he will not try to bluff, when he finds out that it is not worth doing so in terms of expected payoff.

This approach, however, would hardly work for several reasons. First, it is doubtful whether people actually behave as if they maximized expected payoff or can be convinced to do so. Second, it is· unlikely that people would agree to respond at all to the question in the first stage, as they often would not have any idea whatsoever about the probability of the project being accepted. Third, the design of the method can hardly be such that the individual is allowed to state p^j equal to one, as this means that he would get an *infinite* amount of money should his subjective probability prove to be wrong.

But more important, this approach cannot even in principle fulfill what it promises to do, that is, avoid misrepresentation of preferences. If people know what their stated probabilities will be used for (which they presumably will require and which they would know anyway after the first time this approach has been used in practice), incentives for misrepresentation will appear in both stages. Denoting true probability by P^j and stated probability by p^j, expected payoff becomes

$$P^j[F^j - f^j] - (1 - P^j) \frac{p^j}{1 - p^j} f^j = P^j F^j + f^j \left[(1 - P^j) \frac{p^j}{1 - p^j} - P^j \right]$$

As the expected payoff can be seen to be an increasing function of stated probability p^j, it pays the respondent to exaggerate the probability that the project will be adopted, where maximum expected payoff is achieved at $p^j = 1$. Moreover, if probabilities are misrepresented, it follows from the expression given that it would also pay the respondent to overstate his WTP for the project.

Finally, it has been suggested (see Bohm, 1971) that uncertainty about payment consequences could be constructed so as to make it impossible for the individual to know whether overstating or understating would be the best strategy; if so, it is possible that the respondent would prefer to tell the truth. The political background for this approach is a situation where the government finds that it cannot decide which financial solution to use until it is known what the project benefits mean to different people. Once this is known, income distribution aspects and practical aspects with respect to collection costs will be taken into account. However, it may be stated explicitly what the set of possible payment alternatives is, including alternatives which, if certain, would have provided incentives for overstatements as well as alternatives that, if certain, would have provided incentives for understatements of WTP (such as no payment at all and payments according to stated WTP, respectively). If people cannot form probabilities with respect to the different payment alternatives, or if they do not try to minimize expected payments, or if the maximum payments involved typically are so small that the complicated calculation of expected payment is not attempted, people would simply not know if there is any strategy superior to that of stating their true WTP.

Of course, problems are encountered in this approach as well. For example, people may simply not believe government officials when they assert that they do not know which payment alternative will eventually hold, if the project is accepted. Consequently, people may respond as if, for example, one payment alternative was certain; this would of course make incentives to misrepresent WTP reappear. Furthermore, people may in fact try to minimize expected payment, thereby giving all alternatives the same probability; and this might also make it seem profitable to bluff. Moreover, although this proposal is advanced as one that should be tried in practice (along with other methods) before it can be evaluated, possible success by some definition could not guarantee that the method suggested would continue to reveal true preferences in future applications.

To sum up, so far no proposed method for estimating access values can guarantee the performance desired; indeed, few even look promising enough to support practical experimentation. Thus, we must approach the problem from the starting point that no single method works and that the possibility of misrepresentation must be built into a realistic attempt to estimate access values. In the next section we suggest a procedure in line with this view.

3. A Technique for Estimating a Narrow Interval for Access Values

Since no single approach meets all the requirements of accuracy and political realism, a less ambitious perspective is called for. An essential property of the method to be suggested here is that it is useful when it works and harmless when it doesn't. To illustrate this approach, assume that two large representative samples are drawn from the population of possible beneficiaries of a certain project. The samples are assumed to be stratified with respect to consumer groups of various kinds, deemed relevant for this project. Individuals in both samples are asked to state their WTP, where payment consequences differ between the two groups. Thus, in the first sample people are informed that they will have to pay an amount equal to their stated WTP if the project is adopted. In the second sample people are told they will have to pay a given fee, equal for all. This fee is determined so that it would clearly fall short of the maximum individual WTP of a vast majority of the population. (If such a fee is found to be difficult to specify, there is always the alternative that people in the second sample need not pay at all.)

People in the first sample are obviously exposed to an incentive to understate their preferences. Those in the second sample will have an incentive to overstate their WTP; specifically, all those who have a WTP above the given fee (≥ 0) will be in this situation. To the extent that people have a WTP below the level of this fee, the incentive would be the opposite, as these individuals might do what they can to make it less likely that the project would be adopted. Therefore, any individual statement of WTP below the level of the given fee could be raised to this level before it was added to the statements from others. This would ensure that the responses from the second sample would be an upper bound to the true WTP.

Given then that we have a lower bound to the average WTP in different consumer groups from the first sample and an upper bound from the second sample, we are supplied with an interval for the aggregate WTP as well as intervals for the WTP of different consumer groups. If respondents turn out to have reacted strongly to the existing incentives to misrepresent preferences, these intervals would be wide. In this case we may find that the costs of the project appear inside the interval of the aggregate WTP. Thus, the result of the inquiry would be inconclusive, and we would be back where we started with no guidelines for decision making and with money spent on useless information. But as long as wide intervals for WTP are not *proved* to result from inquiries of this kind, such money would not be wasted. Indeed, there is ground for optimism with respect to the outcome of such experiments.

In an experiment some time ago (see Bohm, 1972), it turned out that there were no significant differences among the responses to the two different modes of inquiry outlined above for the two samples. In fact, there were no significant differences for the five different methods analyzed in this experiment. Although the test involved actual payments (when relevant) and actual collective decision making with respect to a public good (a program shown on closed-circuit TV, provided aggregate WTP exceeded costs of showing it), the test cannot be said to prove that people do not react to incentives to misrepresent preferences. But what it does indicate, I think, is that further experimentation is worthwhile—with larger sample sizes and more valuable public goods. In the meantime, some arguments may be advanced in support of the possible condition that people do not react strongly to incentives to misrepresent preferences.

In the test, people were informed about the possible benefits as well as the possible disadvantages of bluffing (e.g., that the good would not be produced if many people understated their WTP). People were subjected to moral arguments (they would help the administration find out about true preferences in order to perform better in the public interest); these arguments were very much like those advanced for getting people to come to the ballot boxes in general elections, although there are often strong incentives to abstain in terms of time, transportation costs, and so on, combined with virtually a zero effect of the individual vote on election results. People had to sign their statements; thus, they were not anonymous and their statements could be checked by anyone, "friend or foe," interested in seeing them and perhaps questioning them.

Then, if it turned out that the distance between the upper and the lower bound to true WTP were in fact narrow, we would for all practical purposes have the same information as if we had a single direct method for estimating true WTP. First of all, the likelihood that the aggregate WTP interval would coincide with project costs would be small. Second, if this still occurred, the interpretation would be that the consumers were "indifferent" to realization of the project. Moreover, we would have estimates for different consumer groups that would help in finding the desired financial structure for the majority of consumers (outside the two samples), in the context of which both distribution and efficiency aspects would be taken into account as outlined in section 1.

4. Practical and Theoretical Problems of the Method Suggested

I would like to end by enumerating some possible problems of the method suggested, without making any attempt to resolve them.

1. Would people and politicians accept the fact that some individuals, those included in the samples, pay amounts different from those of the rest of the consumers? They would perhaps not even accept having

people in the two samples pay different amounts. Or will future possibilities for different people to participate in different referenda help make these temporary injustices acceptable?

2. Rejecting a procedure by which people are forced to respond (which, if nothing else, would probably be counterproductive), how can we make sure that a sufficient number of people would show up? And in using the same procedure as in the experiment described above, that is, paying people for showing up, how does this "windfall" income or compensation affect stated WTP?[5] Could people effectively be asked to regard the sum paid to them as a compensation for time spent, pure and simple, and thus to respond without regard for this additional and very special income item? If not, are there reasons to believe that the stated *intervals* will be significantly higher due to these payments or only that the upper bound, if any, would be affected?

3. Given that the method should be used for estimating only a limited set of access values (e.g., where the government feels that information is most badly needed), what is the effect on determination of the output level of commodities for which such inquiries are made in relation to output levels for other public goods?

4. Should inquiries be conducted with respect to several issues at the same time or should a sequential procedure be used?

5. Are systematic adjustments in responses to inquiries of this type to be expected as experience from them starts to accumulate?

6. When people are asked to state their maximum WTP, do they actually think in terms of an amount which, if paid, would mean that they were as well off as before or would their perception of this concept mean that they would be better off than before? Maximum WTP could, of course, be conceived of as something like a maximum offer at an auction where people are expected to benefit if their highest bid is accepted.

7. Do people conceive of their *true* WTP as invariant with respect to the case where all consumers pay the same "price" for the same rights compared with the case where they pay different amounts, for example, in some relation to stated WTP?

It should be noted that the problems presented here—with the exception, perhaps, of the first one—appear relevant to all approaches aimed at estimating access values and not only to the technique suggested here.

---

[5] The objective of this experiment was to compare different approaches; thus, no particular interest was attached to absolute levels of WTP *per se*. In other words, it was assumed that the effect, if any, on responses from the payments for participation was the same for all the methods tested.

References

Arvidsson, G. 1974. "A Note on Estimating the Demand for Public Goods," *Swedish Journal of Economics* vol. 76 (September).

Bohm, Peter. 1971. "An Approach to Estimating Demand for Public Goods," *Swedish Journal of Economics* vol. 73 (March) pp. 55–66.

————. 1972. "Estimating Demand for Public Goods: An Experiment," *European Economic Review* vol. 3.

Bowen, H. R. 1943. "The Interpretation of Voting in the Allocation of Economic Resources," *Quarterly Journal of Economics* vol. 58.

Drèze, J. H., and D. de la Vallée Poussin. 1971. "A Tatonnement Process for Public Goods," *Review of Economic Studies* vol. 38 (April) pp. 133–150.

Kurz, Mordecai. 1973. "Experimental Approach to the Determination of the Demand for Public Goods," mimeograph (Stanford).

Malinvaud, Edmund. 1971. "A Planning Approach to the Public Good Problem," *Swedish Journal of Economics* vol. 73 (March) pp. 96–117.

Tideman, Nicolaus. 1972. "The Efficient Provision of Public Goods," in Selma J. Mushkin, ed., *Public Prices for Public Products* (Washington, D.C., The Urban Institute).

10
Neighborhood Externalities, Economic Clubs, and the Environment

ALAN EVANS

THE concept of an economic club was first formulated explicitly by Buchanan in a paper published in 1965. Since then, a few other papers on the subject have been published, notably those of Pauly (1968, 1970), McGuire (1972, 1974), and Ng (1973, 1974). Following Buchanan's initial development, however, the tendency has been to assume that access to the club good can be controlled, and to compare the competitive solution with the Pareto optimal solution. In general, it has been found that Pareto optimality can be achieved, but that market failure may occur if (1) the club is controlled by its members (the consumers of the good), who maximize the benefit per capita and not the total benefit (Ng, 1974); it may be noted here that Ng implicitly assumes that the club good, although expandable, is not reproducible, so that it is not possible for rival clubs to be set up by the persons wishing to enter the club but excluded from it; (2) the club good is provided by a local government elected by its consumers, who fail to reveal their preferences (McGuire, 1974); (3) the number of members cannot be allocated to the desired club membership without having some left over (Pauly, 1970).

In this paper I wish to show that market failure in a "club" situation may have consequences more drastic than those resulting from these conditions and may arise because access to the club good is not, or cannot be, controlled by a single organization, whether it be a government, firm, or the club membership. In this event, the theory of clubs is analogous to the theory of the common property resource, and many of the conclusions which can be derived from the one theory can be applied, with the necessary changes, to the other. In doing so we provide some justification for Mishan's pessimistic view in *The Cost of*

Economic Growth (1969) that increases in population and improvements in mobility can cause the quality of life to deteriorate. Moreover, we demonstrate that Mishan is in fact too optimistic, for in a footnote (1969, p. 137) he states that

> Rising economic rent in response to increasing population is one way of coping with, or correcting, the incidence of an external diseconomy caused by increasing numbers of people seeking to settle within a given area. *Though a well-functioning market promotes optimal adjustment in respect of this particular form of external diseconomy*, regressive distributional effects can be a source of conflict [my italics].

In fact, if the ownership of land in the area is fragmented and there are no controls, or taxes, on the density of the development, this density will be too high, and even if the market is "well-functioning" it does not promote optimal adjustment for this particular form of external diseconomy.

1. Clubs and Common Property Resources

To demonstrate the relationship between the analysis of economic clubs and common property resources, we apply Worcester's (1969) method of analyzing technological diseconomies to the analysis of consumption diseconomies. To do so we assume cardinal utility. Suppose then that the utility surface of a representative consumer is as shown in figure 1. The quantity of the club good of which he is one of the consumers is indicated on the vertical axis, and the number of people with whom he jointly consumes it (the membership of the club) is indicated on the horizontal axis. In general, consumers move to higher utility levels if more of the club good is provided and to lower utility levels if there is an increase in the number of people with whom they have to share the good. Thus U_2U_2 indicates a higher indifference curve than U_1U_1. In figure 1 we also assume, though this is not necessary to the analysis, that the representative consumer prefers some company in the consumption of the good but not too much, so that when the membership is very small, increases in the membership will actually be welcomed by the existing members as making them better off.

Suppose now that we consider the total utility produced by the club good, that is, the sum of the cardinal utilities of the members of the club. When the club has only one member, the total utility at any level of provision of the club good is indicated by the utility of that single consumer; when there are two members, the total utility produced is

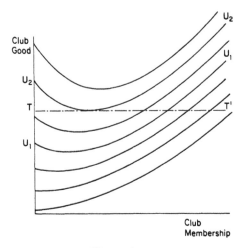

Figure 1

the sum of the utilities of the two consumers, and so on. A possible set of isoquants showing the total utility derived from the joint consumption of the club good as the membership is varied in size is shown in panel A of figure 2. Let us now assume that the quantity of the club good is fixed. It is, for example, an American national park or national monument such as Yellowstone, or the Arches, and this fixed size is indicated as $\bar{T}$ in panel A. What happens as the number of members of the club increases in this situation? Curve OZ in panel B shows the result of a cross section through the total utility surface of panel A along the line $\bar{T}\bar{T}'$. As the membership of the club is increased from zero, the total utility produced increases initially at an increasing rate. This is because of our assumption that when the membership is very small people prefer more members, more companionship, to less. Therefore the average utility per member increases as the membership increases. The marginal benefit per (existing) member steadily diminishes, however, as membership increases so that at some membership (the inflection point a on OZ in panel B) the total utility, while still increasing, starts to increase at a diminishing rate, though the average utility per member still increases. At some, still greater membership, however, the average utility per member starts to decrease; new entrants cease to be companionship and become congestion. This membership is indicated by the point b on OZ at which a line from the origin is tangential to the total utility curve in panel B of figure 2. The total utility produced still increases, however, as indicated by the upward slope of the total utility

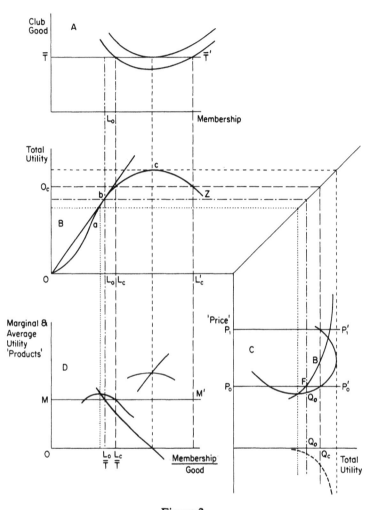

Figure 2

curve of panel B, because the utility accruing to the additional member outweighs the total reduction in the utility levels of the existing members due to the increase in congestion. Yet there will probably, but not necessarily, be some membership, at point *c* on *OZ* in panel B which will be so large that the total utility produced will reach a maximum and start to decline with any increase in membership, because the reduction in the total utility of the existing members due to the increase in congestion will equal, and then dominate the utility attributable to the person admitted.

To complete the parallels with the analysis of technological diseconomies, we can go on to derive panels C and D, though this is not necessary for the rest of the analysis. Suppose that it costs m per person in travel expenses to visit this national park. We can use this to derive panel C. In that diagram, total utility produced is indicated on the horizontal axis and the average and marginal cost per util are indicated on the vertical axis.[1] Note that we obtain in this way the precise equivalent of the backward-bending average cost curve which has been observed in the analysis of road congestion (see for example, Walters, 1961), and a road, it may be noted here, is both a club good, for consumers, and a common property resource, for producers.

If the price per util which the consumer has to pay at other sites is P_1, and this price is not affected by the number of people visiting this national park, then the demand curve for the product of park is shown by the line P_1P_1' in panel C, and the equilibrium output (of utility) is Q_c with a club membership derived from panel B, of L_c'. Note that because of the backward-bending average cost curve, if the price fell to P_0 the same total utility would still be produced.

In panel D the marginal and average products in utils are shown on the vertical axis, for both the membership and the club good, and the membership, as a ratio of the quantity of the club good (i.e., L/T), is shown on the horizontal axis. If the marginal utility of money is taken as a constant, λ, then λm, indicated by M on the vertical axis, is the cost of visiting the park in utils. Equilibrium with free access to the park is shown by the intersection of the horizontal line MM' with the average utility level at a ratio of members to land of $L_c/\bar{T}$.

If the cost per util produced elsewhere is at the price indicated by the line P_1P_1 in panel C, the total utility produced will be Q_c in panels B and C, and the marginal utility per additional member is shown in panel D to be negative at the membership of L_c'. If the cost per util is at the lower price indicated by the line P_0P_0', then the total utility produced will still be Q_c, though with a lower membership of L_c. The difference between the two situations is that with the higher price considerable resource costs are used in transporting people to the national park with no gain in welfare.

Even at the lower price, however, the use of resources is not efficient. This can be seen from panel C. The marginal cost per util at a total

---

[1] The marginal cost curve is shown by Worcester to slope backward, and be positive in a fashion similar to the average cost curve. In fact, as Tangri (1966) shows, the section of the marginal cost curve relating to the backward-sloping section of the average cost curve, as shown in panel C, is negative, though still backward sloping.

utility level of Q_c is indicated by the point B when the price per util is P_0. The marginal cost at this park is thus greater than the price (equal to marginal cost, by assumption) at all other locations. Hence, resources could be saved by charging admission to the park equal to a cost per util of FC_0, thus fixing the total utility output at Q_0 and the number of people entering the park at L_0 (in panels A, B, and D). As panel D shows, when the membership of the club is L_0, the marginal utility per additional member is just equal to the marginal utility of the costs of reaching the park.

2. A System of Clubs

In the preceding section we presented an analysis of the situation in which there is a single club. The analysis can also be applied to the situation when there is a system of club goods. To do so, we borrow the analysis of alternative systems of managing common property resources proposed by Weitzman (1974). Given then, cardinal utility and the applicability of the analysis of common property resources to the analysis of clubs (with some alteration in terminology), Weitzman's mathematics leads to several conclusions if it is applied to the theory of clubs and to free access and private ownership (or controlled access) as alternative systems of managing the clubs.[2]

1. Private ownership is an efficient system for managing clubs while free access is not.
2. Free access will mean that more people will consume the club goods than would do so if they were privately owned, that is, crowding will be general.
3. The "best" club goods, the individual pieces of better quality property, will be more overcrowded with free access than if access is controlled.
4. The "worst" club goods, the individual pieces of the lowest quality property, *may* be more crowded if access is controlled than if access is free.
5. The persons who visit the club goods when access is free will be worse off if access is controlled unless, as Weitzman (1974, p. 234) puts it, "they get a specific kickback in one form or another." Thus, with no redistribution, if the admission charges are siphoned off to some other people in the economy, the visitors to the clubs will be made worse off by controlled access. "The distribution effect is always stronger than the efficiency effect."

[2] For mathematical proof, see the appendix.

3. Tourist Attractions

Now that the analysis of common property resources has been shown to be applicable to the analysis of clubs or "joint consumption goods with congestion," we can set out some examples of economic clubs and the implications of the theory.

1. Systems of Recreational Areas, for example, National Parks. The analyses suggest that the best, most beautiful, most interesting areas are likely to be overcrowded and that the worst areas may be underutilized. Is this so? Certainly increasing disquiet has been expressed at the number of people visiting the best known of the American and British national parks and at the possibility that these parks may be swamped by crowds. It has also been remarked that increases in the numbers of people visiting the parks may cause environmental damage, both temporary and permanent. The analysis of common property resources could also be applied to this problem, since recent analyses have tended to concentrate on the problem of resource depletion when the resources are either replenishable (e.g., a fishing ground) or nonreplenishable (e.g., an oil field).[3] Damage to the environment in a national park would fall into one or the other of these categories insofar as it is reversible (e.g., destruction of vegetation) or irreversible (e.g., removal of fossilized rocks). In the second case, an optimal rate of depletion or extinction has to be found. The first case is more complicated. Since the number of people entering the park will depend upon the quality of the environment (after deterioration by other visitors), and the rate of deterioration depends upon the number of visitors and the compensating effect of natural replenishment, it has to be ascertained whether there is some ecological balance (if possible, optimal) at which the number of visitors is constant and the rate of deterioration is nil.

2. Historic Sites. Over the past few years there has been concern over the overcrowding of the better known British tourist attractions by foreign visitors. These historic sites, in central London, Oxford, Cambridge, Stratford-upon-Avon, and Edinburgh, almost by definition cannot be improved, enlarged, or extended so that these, together with the other less well-known historical buildings and sites, form a system which fits exactly the model presented in the preceding section. Thus we would expect that the best, or best-known areas will be overcrowded, while attempts to persuade people to visit less well-known areas will be unsuccessful.[4] It has been suggested that there should be a tourist tax or

---

[3] See, for example, Smith (1968).

[4] We equate best with best-known here. It may be that a trip to Britain would not be undertaken if the major sites became too expensive because these sites *are* Britain as far as the tourist is concerned. In that case there might be a balance-of-payments argument for not imposing taxes.

room tax on visitors to London; the theory provides some justification for this proposal, and suggests that some sort of tax system covering all the major tourist attractions would even be preferable.

4. Residential Density

In the preceding analysis we assumed that the club goods were consumed jointly and that the only way to control access was by imposing admission charges. Mishan (1967, p. 137) suggests that when the club good consists of the characteristics of the environment at a particular location, "rising economic rent in response to increasing population is one way of coping with, or correcting, the incidence of an external diseconomy caused by increasing numbers of people seeking to settle within a given area." Before going on to consider examples of this kind of external diseconomy, I have to show that this is not so if land ownership is fragmented. To prove it, we analyze a general rather than a specific problem, assuming merely that people generally prefer fewer people to live in the same area as themselves; that is, people prefer lower residential densities. We have analyzed the problem diagrammatically elsewhere (Evans, 1974) but analyze it mathematically here using a variation of the method adopted by McGuire (1974) in his analyses of the theory of clubs.[5]

First we set out the conditions for a competitive equilibrium in the housing market in an area which is to be developed by a single firm. As far as the developer is concerned, P, the rent he can obtain for each house, is a function of the size of the dwelling or the amount of space provided denoted by x, and n the number of households the area is to be shared by. Thus n, divided by the area A is the residential density. Obviously $\partial P / \partial x = P_x$ is positive, and, by assumption, P_n is negative. Of course the rent P is also dependent upon the location of the area relative to the rest of the economy and upon the characteristics of the surrounding environment, but these are not under the control of the developer.

The costs to the developer are the cost of land GA where G is the ground rent per unit of area, and the building costs $b(d)$ which are a function of the total space provided ($d = nx$). The profits of the developer are then:

$$\Pi = nP(x,n) - GA - b(d) \tag{1}$$

[5] I have always been worried about the correctness of the diagrammatic analysis. McGuire's method gives me the opportunity to prove the result. However, he assumes that all the effects of variations in the number of people sharing the club can be allowed for by variations in the cost of use of the good to the individual, a purely technical relationship. This is in fact incorrect, since the variations in

The first-order conditions for profit maximization are then

$$\Pi_n = P(x,n) + nP_n - b'(d)x = 0 \tag{2}$$

and

$$\Pi_z = nP_z - b'(d)n = 0 \tag{3}$$

Equation (2) can be rewritten as

$$P(x,n) = xb'(d) - nP_n \tag{4}$$

Thus to maximize profits, the area should be developed at the density at which the rent for one additional house is just equal to the cost of building that house, $xb'(d)$, plus the cost of the fall in the rents received from all the other occupants of the development, nP_n, due to the increases in density.

Is this density optimal? To find the optimality conditions, we take a representative household which we assume to have a utility function $U(x,z,N)$ and an income y. Utility depends upon x, the household's consumption of housing space, z, its consumption of other goods, and N, the number of households within the area surrounding it. This area is not the same as A above; it is simply the area which contains households, the density of which affects the representative household. I apologize for the circularity of this definition!

The total cost of housing in this area is $C(x,N)$ so that the cost per household is $C(x,N)/N$. Substituting for z, the utility function can be written

$$U = U\left\{x, \left[y - \frac{C(x,N)}{N}\right], N\right\} \tag{5}$$

The necessary conditions for an optimum are

$$U_z - U_y \frac{C_z}{N} = 0 \quad \text{or} \quad N\frac{U_z}{U_y} = C_z \tag{6}$$

and

$$U_N - U_y\left[\frac{C_N - C/N}{N}\right] = 0 \quad \text{or} \quad N\frac{U_N}{U_y} = C_N - C/N \tag{7}$$

Equation (7) can be rewritten in the form

$$\frac{C}{N} = C_N - N\frac{U_N}{U_y} \tag{8}$$

and in this form it is equivalent to equation (4) if n is equal to N.

---

number of members of the club will affect the member's utility schedule, not only through the variation in cost but also through his taste for sharing.

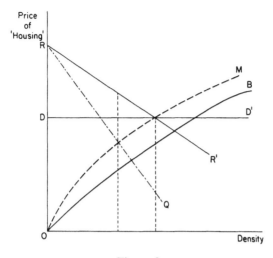

Figure 3

It follows that if n, the population of the area developed by a single firm, is equal to N (or, of course, greater than N), the density will be Pareto optimal; the density of development outside the area developed by the single firm will then be immaterial to the welfare of those living within that area. If n is less than N, however, the developer will fix the density of development, taking into account the effects of any increase in this density of development on the price of space outside the area, and so the density of development will be too high.

The problem can also be analyzed diagrammatically. In figure 3 the curve OB indicates the average building cost of space (on an annual basis), and OM is then the marginal cost curve. The developer faces an average revenue curve for the development he is about to undertake in a particular area. This will be the "true" average revenue curve if the area he is about to develop extends to the limit of the interest of the possible residents, that is, if $n = N$. This is unlikely and so the curve he faces is likely to slope less steeply. If the site he is to develop is small, he can take the price of space as given because the density of development of his particular site does not affect the price he can obtain; this price is dependent only on the density of the surrounding area.

Suppose that RR' is the "true" average revenue curve, but that each development is carried out piecemeal so that each developer faces a horizontal average revenue curve. Equilibrium would occur when the density and rent were indicated by the intersection of RR' and OM. The horizontal average revenue curve DD' would then pass through this point. This is because the profit maximizing rent and density for each

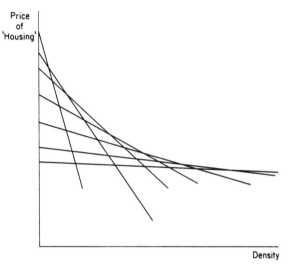

Figure 4

developer is indicated by the intersection of his marginal revenue curve, in this case, *DD'*, and the marginal cost curve *OM*, but the rent and density in an area must be indicated by a point on the "true" average revenue curve *RR'*. Hence, although disequilibrium situations are almost inevitable, the only long-run equilibrium is indicated by the intersection of *RR'* and *OM*. The optimal position, however, is indicated by the point on *RR'* lying above the intersection of the "true" marginal revenue curve *RQ* and the marginal cost curve *OM*, for only at that point will the social cost of increases in density (the vertical distance between *RR'* and *RQ* in the diagram) be taken into account and social costs (plus private costs) be equated with social benefits.

From the analysis, it can clearly be seen that rents do rise with increases in density, but that if this increase in density is itself disliked, and if land ownership is fragmented, then, even if the land market is well functioning, optimal adjustment to this particular form of external diseconomy will not be promoted.

The diagram can be used to clarify the process of club formation, in a partial equilibrium context, at least. For each set of households who might live in an area, there will be an average revenue curve, relating density to the rent they would be willing to pay. The slope of any curve will depend upon the price the households are willing to pay for low residential density; its position, and to a lesser extent, its slope, will depend upon the alternative locations which are available. Some of these average revenue curves are shown in figure 4. What we have called above the "true" average revenue curve for an area is the upper envelope of all the curves, that is, the curve linking together the prices which would be paid by the highest bidders at each density. This analysis suggests that if through either monopoly, taxes, or zoning restrictions the density in an area is kept to the optimal level (and the rents therefore kept up), households occupying the area will have characteristics different from those of the households who would occupy the area if land ownership was fragmented and development uncontrolled. One would expect of course that the occupants would be wealthier if development were controlled than if it were uncontrolled and piecemeal. Thus Dyos (1961), for example, in his study of the nineteenth-century development of the London suburb of Camberwell attributes some of the differences between development in the north and south of the suburb to differences in the pattern of land ownership, and Rudé (1971) in his volume on the history of London also attributes some of the differences in the development of the East and West Ends of Hanoverian London to the fact that in the East End land ownership was fragmented, while in the West End land was owned in large estates, the best-known examples being the Bedford, Portman, and Grosvenor estates. Each of these estates is famous for its squares, a pattern of development which would be impossible if land were not owned by a single landlord.

5. Congestion and Other Diseconomies

In the preceding sections of the paper we tended to speak as if congestion is the only external diseconomy to which the analysis is relevant. In fact, it is relevant to all cases in which the external diseconomies are inflicted on the occupants of an area, generally by the occupants themselves. Strictly, the club–common property analysis is applicable to all external diseconomies which are functions of the mass or density of the population, for example, pollution, crime, and congestion of one form or another. To cite one example of an analysis of pollution which could as well have been described as a problem in the theory of clubs, Seskin (1973) analyzes the welfare economics of an economy in which there are two cities in one of which steel is produced and in the other bread. What makes the problem clearly one of economic clubs is that he assumes that pollution in the steel city is a linear function of the number of persons in that city. His purpose was to discover whether the concentration of all polluting activities in a single city would be an optimal policy. His finding that the equilibrium (competitive) population of steel city would be too great is in accord with our analysis.

Having established in section 4 that a well-functioning land market will not lead to optimality, and that our analysis is applicable to external diseconomies other than congestion, we can present other examples of the applicability of the analysis.

1. In holiday areas, such as the Mediterranean holiday resorts, the set of areas open to a tourist constitutes a system of clubs; one would therefore expect that there would be general overcrowding, and that the best areas would be very crowded. Mishan (1967) has pointed out that the tourist trade is rapidly destroying places of scenic beauty or historic interest. In some areas, notably the Algarve region of Portugal, strict control has been exercised over the amount, location, and type of development—no skyscraper hotels, no ribbon development, and a high proportion of villas; as a result, and as we could expect from the theoretical analysis, Portugal has been more expensive as a holiday area than Spain and has attracted different people. Indeed, Mishan suggests an alternative policy of increasing the time costs of holidaying in some or all areas, instead of increasing the money costs.

2. The set of areas within a country (or a region or the world) which have natural environments of different qualities can also be considered in terms of a set of clubs. Once again, it would follow that areas with the best environments would tend to be the focus of migration and would become overcrowded or despoiled until the environments of the area were degraded to some average level. Thus in Britain, in view of people's preferences for locations in the south of England to those in north Britain (see Gould and White, 1968), there would be a tendency to move southward, in the absence of controls, until the over-development of the south eliminated its advantages. This is what seemed to be happening before 1939, the result being the ribbon development along the south coast. If effective controls are imposed, as they have been since 1945, the price of existing development tends to increase, and the net advantages of different areas are then equalized by price rather than congestion. In the United States, of course, the preferred locations would be in the Southwest and on the Pacific coast and one would expect unchecked in-migration to lead to a gradual deterioration of the environment in these areas.

Although it is true that the theory of clubs shows that a more efficient allocation of environmental resources could be obtained, and that this would entail less congestion in the favored areas, the final result which we derived using Weitzman's analysis must be borne in mind; that is, unless those who are excluded receive some compensation, they will be worse off. Moreover, controls on entry may be the worst possible remedy, since they make those who wish to enter the area no better off, and benefit (some of) the landowners by causing rents and property values to rise in the favored areas. Taxation of those wishing to enter an area would seem to be much more equitable, though this solution would be difficult to apply. Moreover, the situation is made more complex by the fact that migration, whether seasonal or permanent, is often across national or state boundaries and thus its consequences are not easily internalized.

3. I have argued elsewhere that the theory of clubs is applicable to the theory of city size (Evans, 1972). The above analysis would suggest that in general the largest cities, being those in the most favorable locations, will be too large and too crowded, and this view is argued by Tisdell (1975) who cites the theory of common property resources as theoretical support. Whether existing small towns are too small or new small towns should be brought into existence is a question left open by the analysis. The problem with city size, however, is that although we can all agree that there are external diseconomies of city size due to pollution, congestion, and so on, there are also external economies resulting from the increased scale of provision of services. This means that it is unclear which effect is dominant, since the problem is so complex.

Moreover, in the case of city size, there is one other relevant result which can be derived from an analysis of common property resources. We have assumed throughout that each person generates identical external effects, and we have assumed that taxes or prices to restrict admission to a club good would do just that. Schall (1971) shows, however, in the case of the common property resource, that a tax or price may in fact increase use of the resource if users do not generate identical external effects. This will occur if those generating high externalities are deterred more than those generating low externalities. To give an example of a club where this could happen, suppose that two classes of users visit a park, the one to play football, the other to admire wildlife; a charge for admission might deter the footballers enough to encourage more wildlife and hence more people to visit the park. The charge would be more effective if it was related to the "strength" of the external effect.[6] Thus Henderson (1974) constructs a model showing that taxes on the pollution caused by some industries in a city may cause the size of the city to increase because the improvement in the urban environment caused by the reduction in pollution attracts people to the city to

[6] For an analysis of the situation when it is not, see Diamond (1973).

work in other industries. Obviously, this type of model is implicit in many of the proposals for cleaning up the older industrial areas of Britain.

6. Conclusions

The argument in this paper is relevant to three areas of interest. First, for those concerned with the quality of life, it has been shown that where congestion of some kind can occur in the consumption of some club good, the number of people sharing in the consumption of the good will be excessive, and the situation will not be Pareto optimal. The enjoyment (or consumption) of the environment at a particular location has been shown to be particularly susceptible to this form of market failure. Congestion may thus prevent the optimal enjoyment of holiday areas, parks, residential neighborhoods, and particular cities and regions, since the quality of any more favorable environment, in the absence of controls on access, will be leveled down by in-migration, whether temporary or permanent, and the consequent increase in congestion at these sites. Second, from the point of view of the applied economist, it has been shown that it may be difficult to estimate the value of environmental differences between areas from differences in property values since migration and the consequent variations in congestion levels will always tend to minimize the differences in property values. Finally, from the point of view of the economic theorist, the theory of clubs has been shown to be formally analogous to the theory of common property resources.

Appendix

Assumptions

Let there be n club goods called parks, each being fixed in size and having the property that visitors derive pleasure from it. This pleasure is assumed to be cardinally measurable, and the number of utils of pleasure derived by each of the visitors to any park at the same time are assumed to be the same.

The utility, u_i, derived by any visitor to the ith park, is assumed to be a decreasing function of the number of visitors to the park, x_i, so that

$$0 < x \leq x' \rightarrow u_i(x) \geq u_i(x') \tag{1}$$

The total utility produced by the ith park is given by

$$y_i = f_i(x_i) \equiv x_i u_i(x_i)$$

For convenience we assume throughout that for all $i, x_i > 0$. Let $w_i \geq 0$ be the net utility derived from visits to a park; for obvious reasons the net benefits will be equalized so that $w_i = w$ for all i. The number of people visiting the parks S will be a function of the net benefit w, and

$$S(w) = \Sigma x_i$$

where the summation sign indicates here and elsewhere that the numbers indexed over $i = 1, \ldots, n$ are summed. The number of people visiting the parks is an increasing function of the net benefit, so that

$$w \leq w' \rightarrow S(w) \leq S(w') \tag{2}$$

Free Access

Where access to each of the parks is free, and there are no controls on access, visitors will allocate themselves among the parks until the net benefits from a visit to any park are the same. We denote this system as *FA*, and *FA* equilibrium values of variables are capped by a tilde. Then, in equilibrium

$$\tilde{w} = u_i(\tilde{x}_i) = \frac{f_i(\tilde{x}_i)}{\tilde{x}_i} \tag{3}$$

and

$$S(\tilde{w}) = \Sigma \tilde{x}_i$$

Private Ownership

Each of the parks is owned by a rentier who charges the admission fee which maximizes his profits. We denote this system as *PO*, and *PO* equilibrium values of variables are capped by a circumflex. In *PO* equilibrium, the admission charge to the ith park is τ_i and the profits from the ith park are equal to $\tau_i \hat{x}_i$. The marginal utility of money to each visitor is assumed to be a constant λ, so that $\hat{w} = u_i(\hat{x}_i) - \lambda \tau_i$ and the rental R_i is equal to

$$\hat{x}_i \tau_i = f_i(\hat{x}_i) \lambda^{-1} - \hat{w} \hat{x}_i \lambda^{-1} \tag{4}$$

Since profits are maximized, in equilibrium, for all i,

$$f_i(\hat{x}_i) \lambda^{-1} - \hat{w} \hat{x}_i \lambda^{-1} = \max_{x \geq 0} f_i(x) \lambda^{-1} - \hat{w} x \lambda^{-1} \tag{5}$$

and

$$S(\hat{w}) = \Sigma \hat{x}_i$$

A solution of these equations is assumed to exist. Note that in *PO*, $\hat{w}$, the "marginal benefits" in utils accruing to the visitors to a park, is tangent to $f_i(x_i)$ at $x_i = \hat{x}_i$.

Efficiency

PO must constitute an efficient economic system. If it were not, for some set of x_i' with

$$\Sigma x_i' \leq \Sigma \hat{x}_i$$

we would have

$$\Sigma f_i(x_i') > \Sigma f_i(\hat{x}_i)$$

This would mean that for some j

$$f_j(x_j') - \hat{w}x_j' > f_j(\hat{x}_j) - \hat{w}\hat{x}_j$$

which contradicts (5).

Efficiency and Distribution

We wish to prove that $\tilde{w} \geq \hat{w}$. Suppose by contradiction that $\tilde{w} < \hat{w}$, it would follow from (2) that $S(\tilde{w}) < S(\hat{w})$ and so it would also follow that

$$\Sigma \tilde{x}_i < \Sigma \hat{x}_i$$

Since $\Sigma \tilde{x}_i > 0$, it would follow that there must be at least one $\tilde{x}_j > 0$ with $\tilde{x}_j \leq \hat{x}_j$. Because $\tau_j \geq 0$, from (5),

$$\hat{w} \leq \frac{f(\hat{x}_j)}{\hat{x}_j} = U_j(\hat{x}_j)$$

But it would then follow from (1) and (4) that

$$\hat{w} \leq U_j(\hat{x}_j) \leq U_j(\tilde{x}_j) = \tilde{w}$$

which is a contradiction. Therefore, the net benefit to each visitor from admission to the park with free access is greater than with private ownership, and visitors have good reason to oppose efficiency-improving moves toward marginalism, such as the introduction of property rights or tolls, unless they get specific compensation in one form or another.

Overcrowding Under Free Access

Since it has been shown above that $\tilde{w} \geq \hat{w}$, it follows from (2) that

$$\Sigma \hat{x}_i \leq \Sigma \tilde{x}_i \tag{6}$$

It follows that there will be general overcrowding with *FA* since more people visit the system of parks than with *PO*. Moreover, being more specific, it can be shown that the better quality parks will be overcrowded.

Suppose that the average toll charged in PO is $\bar{\tau}$ so that

$$\bar{\tau} \equiv \Sigma \tau_i \hat{x}_i / \Sigma \hat{x}_i$$

then we have to show that the number of people visiting the parks will be greater with FA than PO when the toll is greater than $\bar{\tau}$.

If $\tau_j > \bar{\tau}$, then $\tau_j > 0$ and it follows that $\hat{x}_j > 0$. But

$$\frac{f_j(\hat{x}_j)}{\hat{x}_j} = \lambda \tau_j + \hat{w} > \hat{w} + \lambda \bar{\tau}_j = \hat{w} + \lambda \frac{\Sigma \tau_i \hat{x}_i}{\Sigma \hat{x}_i}$$

$$= \frac{\hat{w} \Sigma \hat{x}_i + \Sigma \tau_i \hat{x}_i}{\Sigma \hat{x}_i} = \frac{\Sigma f_i(\hat{x}_i)}{\Sigma \hat{x}_i}$$

or

$$f_j(\hat{x}_j)/\hat{x}_j > \Sigma f_i(\hat{x}_i)/\Sigma \hat{x}_i \tag{7}$$

From (5), summing over all properties (parks),

$$\Sigma f_i(\hat{x}_i) - \hat{w} \Sigma \hat{x}_i \geq \Sigma f_i(\tilde{x}_i) - \hat{w} \Sigma \tilde{x}_i$$

By dividing the (nonnegative) left-hand side of the above inequality by (positive) $\Sigma \hat{x}_i$ and the right-hand side by $\Sigma \tilde{x}_i$ and simplifying, because of (6) we obtain

$$\Sigma f_i(\hat{x}_i)/\Sigma \hat{x}_i \geq \Sigma f_i(\tilde{x}_i)/\Sigma \tilde{x}_i \tag{8}$$

Substituting from (4) into the right-hand side of (8)

$$\Sigma f_i(\hat{x}_i)/\Sigma \hat{x}_i \geq w = u_j(\tilde{x}_j)$$

So from (7) $f_j(\hat{x}_j)/\hat{x}_j > u_j(\tilde{x}_j)$ and since it follows from (4) that $u_j(\hat{x}_j) > u_j(\tilde{x}_j)$ it follows from (1) that $\tilde{x}_j > \hat{x}_j$ so that there is specific overcrowding of the better quality parks.

Greater Utilization with Private Ownership

The sections above are a mere transposition with a few amendments of Weitzman's analysis of the economics of common property resources. It seems pertinent to ask, however, whether if there is overcrowding of the better quality parks with FA, the lower quality parks are underutilized. The answer is that this is in general possible. To prove this, first write $\tilde{w} \geq \hat{w}$ in the form

$$u_k(\tilde{x}_k) = \tilde{w} = \hat{w} + \epsilon \tag{9}$$

where $\epsilon \geq 0$. We know that, in PO equilibrium,

$$u_k(\hat{x}_k) = \frac{f_k(\hat{x}_k)}{\hat{x}_k} = \hat{w} + \lambda \tau_k$$

Therefore if τ_k is small and $\lambda_\tau < \epsilon$, it would follow that $u_k(\hat{x}_k) < u_k(\bar{x}_k)$ and, from (1), $\hat{x}_k > \bar{x}_k$ so that poor quality properties, where the toll is low, may be used more if access is controlled.

References

Buchanan, J. M. 1965. "An Economic Theory of Clubs," *Economica* vol. 32, no. 1 (February).

Diamond, P. A. 1973. "Consumption Externalities and Imperfect Corrective Pricing," *Bell Journal of Economics and Management Sciences* vol. 4, no. 2 (Autumn).

Dyos, H. J. 1961. *Victorian Suburb* (Leicester, England, Leicester University Press.)

Evans, Alan W. 1972. "The Pure Theory of City Size in an Industrial Economy," *Urban Studies* vol. 9, no. 1 (February).

———. 1974. *The Economics of Residential Location* (New York, St. Martin's Press).

Gould, P. R., and R. R. White. 1968. "The Mental Maps of British School Leavers," *Regional Studies* vol. 2, no. 2 (November).

Henderson, J. V. 1974. "Optimum City Size: The External Diseconomy Question," *Journal of Political Economy* vol. 82, no. 2, part 1 (March/April).

Kuhn, T. S. 1970. *The Structure of Scientific Revolutions* (Chicago, University of Chicago Press, 2nd ed.).

McGuire, M. C. 1972. "Private Good Clubs and Public Good Clubs: Economic Models of Group Formation," *Swedish Journal of Economics* vol. 74, no. 1 (March).

———. 1974. "Group Segregation and Optimal Jurisdictions," *Journal of Political Economy* vol. 82, no. 1 (January/February).

Mishan, E. J. 1967. *The Costs of Economic Growth* (London, Staples Press; 1969, Harmondsworth, Penguin Books).

Ng, Y. K. 1973. "The Economic Theory of Clubs: Pareto Optimality Conditions," *Economica* vol. 40, no. 3 (August).

———. 1974. "The Economic Theory of Clubs: Optimal Tax/Subsidy," *Economica* vol. 41, no. 3 (August).

Pauly, M. V. 1968. "Clubs, Commonality, and the Core," *Economica* vol. 35, no. 3 (August).

———. 1970. "Cores and Clubs," *Public Choice* vol. 9.

Rudé, George. 1971. *Hanoverian London 1714–1808.* (London, Secker and Warburg).

Schall, L. D. 1971. "Technological Externalities and Resource Allocation," *Journal of Political Economy* vol. 79, no. 5 (September/October).

Seskin, E. P. 1973. "Residential Choice and Air Pollution: A General Equilibrium Model," *American Economic Review* vol. 63, no. 5 (December).

Smith, V. L. 1968. "Economics of Production from Natural Resources," *American Economic Review* vol. 58, no. 3 (June).

Tangri, O. P. 1966. "Omissions in the Treatment of the Law of Variable Proportions," *American Economic Review* vol. 56, no. 3 (June).

Tisdell, Clement A. 1975. "The Theory of Optimal City Sizes," *Urban Studies* vol. 12, no. 1 (February).

Walters, A. A. 1961. "The Theory and Measurement of Private and Social Cost of Highway Congestion," *Econometrica* vol. 29, no. 4 (October).

Weitzman. M. L. 1974. "Free Access vs. Private Ownership as Alternative Systems for Managing Common Property," *Journal of Economic Theory* vol. 8, no. 2 (June).

Worcester, D. A. 1969. "Pecuniary and Technological Externality, Factor Rents, and Social Costs," *American Economic Review* vol. 59, no. 5 (December).

PART III

11

The Treatment of Externalities
in National Income Statistics

MANCUR OLSON

1. Introduction

THERE may be no change in beliefs in recent times more striking than
the change in attitude toward economic growth. Only a few years ago,
right and left, old and young, rich and poor agreed that economic
growth, as measured by rising per capita incomes, was altogether
desirable; the great ideologies differed about what policies would best
attain growth and on how its fruits should be shared. Economic growth
remains a widely accepted goal, of course, but to many, a growth of
national or per capita income has become an ambiguous blessing, and to
a few a noisome evil. Legions of undergraduates have called the GNP a
measure of "Gross National Pollution," ecologists of all ages have
denounced its side effects, and a journalistic book, *The Limits to
Growth*, has made headlines (Meadows and coauthors, 1972).

This change in popular opinion has drawn some support, and even
some inspiration, from the work of professional economists. E. J.
Mishan, the distinguished welfare economist, argued, in what may have
been the first serious and extended discussion of the subject, that "the
continual pursuit of economic growth by Western societies is more likely
on balance to reduce rather than increase social welfare" (Mishan, 1967,
p. 171). It is a rare economist who agrees with Mishan that when per
capita income corrected for changes in the price level rises, welfare

Most of the ideas in this essay were first set out in my paper in the *1970
Business and Economics Statistics Section Proceedings of the American Statistical
Association*, but that publication is not available even in most research-oriented
libraries. Substantial portions of this chapter will also appear in my forthcoming
book, tentatively entitled "Beyond the Measuring Rod of Money."

I am most grateful to the National Science Foundation, Resources for the
Future, and the Woodrow Wilson International Center for Scholars for supporting
my research on this topic.

probably declines, but there are many economists who think that economic growth as it is defined in the official statistics has become a mixed blessing. They conclude that welfare in the United States at least is not increasing (if it is increasing) nearly as fast as the measured growth in real per capita incomes would suggest. Even so respectable and orthodox an economist as Paul Samuelson (1969) has endorsed this latter view:

> most of us are poorer than we realize. Hidden costs are accruing all the time; and because we tend to ignore them, we overstate our incomes . . . costs are accruing in our advanced economy that no traditional accounting methods can measure. Thomas Hobbes said that in the state of nature the life of man was nasty, brutish, and short. In the state of modern civilization it has become nasty, brutish, and long.[1]

Kenneth Boulding has expressed similar reservations about whether recent increases in measured income represent genuine increases in welfare (Helferich, 1970).

On another side, William Nordhaus and James Tobin, in an interesting paper entitled "Is Growth Obsolete?" have constructed a "measure of economic welfare" (MEW) more comprehensive than the Net National Product (NNP), and offered alternative estimates of it, some of which suggest that welfare may have been increasing faster in recent decades in the United States than the official statistics would lead one to expect.[2] Many other leading economists have shared Nordhaus's and Tobin's judgment that economic growth, far from being obsolete, might have been fully as advantageous as the national income statistics made it out to be.

Some people are inclined to dismiss the issues raised in this widening debate because they believe that one side or the other is obviously wrong. But the issue cannot be dismissed: societies inevitably face a

---

[1] Samuelson was obviously writing here for a wide and diverse audience, and may understandably have allowed himself some journalistic license. For a more sedate statement of Samuelson's views, see the latest edition of his elementary textbook. See also Lekachman (1970).

[2] A first draft of Nordhaus's and Tobin's paper was presented at a conference commemorating the 50th anniversary of the National Bureau of Economic Research. This draft concluded that MEW had probably increased faster than official real per capita income. A later draft the authors kindly sent me makes a range of estimates, based on alternative assumptions, some of which show MEW increasing more slowly than the figures in the national accounts suggest. A paper presented by Nordhaus at a session of the American Association for the Advancement of Science meetings in December 1971, estimated that MEW was increasing about two-fifths as fast as conventional income statistics would suggest. For their later views, and the final form of the paper, see Nordhaus and Tobin (1972).

tradeoff between those goods that are measured in the national accounts and those that are not, and must choose how much of one type of goods they want at the expense of the other. Even extreme positions cannot be dismissed, if at all, until the matter is understood better than it has been. The disagreements, it is true, are partly about what relative values, or marginal rates of substitution, most people do (or should) place upon various market and nonmarket goods, and such disagreements cannot be completely resolved. But the disagreements, and the choices societies make, are in part the result of the lack of the conceptual tools and relevant data that are needed. Thus there is no alternative but to ask how the arguments of the different sides should be assessed and how a society could make informed and rational decisions about how much "economic growth" (defined here as real per capita NNP), if any, it ought to trade off for other goods.

2. Accounting for the Direct Effects of Externalities

One fundamental problem that has to be dealt with before the relationship of the national income and the "quality of life" can be properly discussed is that of the relationship between externalities and the national income accounts. Many people, including some very skillful economists, have been confused about this matter, and even the technical literature is incomplete and at times misleading.

There have been particularly serious misunderstandings about externalities that affect the welfare of consumers or citizens directly, rather than through producers' costs. The extent of these misunderstandings, and the inadequacy of the explanations in the literature, became clear as a result of criticisms of an argument that this writer made some time ago, so it will be necessary now to quote brief passages from an article I wrote for a lay audience and published in *The Public Interest* (1969):

> Yet, for all their virtues, the national income statistics don't tell us what we need to know about the condition of American society. . . .
>
> They even misconstrue or neglect many values that can readily be measured in monetary terms. When the criminal buys a gun, or the honest citizen buys a lock, the national income rises. When a smoke-spewing factory is constructed near a residential area, the expenditures on that factory add to the national income, but so do the expenses of additional housepainting and cleaning forced on the nearby householders by the soot from the factory.

Several highly qualified economists have argued that the foregoing passages are technically incorrect. The have specifically denied the contention that the externalities that occur when a smoke-spewing factory is set up in a residential area, and induces additional housepainting or cleaning expenses, make the NNP or other national income statistics a misleading source of information about whether or not a society is coming to be "better off." Characteristically, the objection to the foregoing argument has emerged in seminars and conversations, but one very distinguished economist put the usual objection in writing in the form of a letter (which he later withdrew) to the editors of *The Public Interest:*

> If I were to build a factory and spend $1,000 to eliminate smoke from its chimneys, no one could doubt that this $1,000 (of resources) was a legitimate part of the input (= output, in value terms) of the economy, and a proper inclusion in the costs of production of the item. If instead, neighbors can eliminate the effects of soot for $1,000, it is a matter of indifference which method is used—preventing soot, or removing it from clothes. (The costs to neighbors will be reflected in land values, and hence rents, and hence national income.) Whether the most efficient problem [method] of dealing with soot is or is not being used, the national income is an appropriate measure.

It will be useful to consider the most elemental part of the problem first—those external diseconomies that reduce the welfare of consumers directly, but do not lead to what I call "defensive expenditures." There is "defensive expenditure" whenever the victims of an external diseconomy (or their governments) buy goods or services designed to help them elude or combat the external diseconomy or in any other way reduce their loss from it. In many cases, there will be no economical way for the victim of an external diseconomy to spend money to protect himself against it, in which case it will simply reduce his well-being or welfare (i.e., what is sometimes loosely called his "psychic income"). There will virtually always be at least some direct loss of welfare or psychic income from external diseconomies: even when an economical technology to combat the external diseconomy exists, the rational consumer will cease buying more of this technology when the marginal rate of substitution between "protection from the diseconomy" and "other goods" equals the price ratio of these alternatives;[3] at this point some of the diseconomy will remain.[4] Thus this aspect of the problem

---

[3] My critic probably overlooked this when he referred to a situation in which "neighbors can *eliminate* [italics mine] the effects of soot."

[4] I am thankful to my colleague Martin McGuire for reminding me of this point.

Table 1. Period 1

Expenditure		Income	
Value of marketed output to final consumers	$1,000,000	Earnings of factors	$1,000,000
Value (positive or negative) of externalities to final consumers	00	Value (positive or negative) of externalities	00
Ideal NNP	$1,000,000	Ideal NI	$1,000,000

must be considered, even if it may not have been the aspect that the critic had primarily in mind.

The essence of this particularly simple part of the problem can be seen by constructing a hypothetical set of national income and products accounts for a simple economy and then introducing external diseconomies. In table 1, which depicts an economy that has not yet been affected by externalities, the total expenditures on *final* goods are listed on the left side of the accounts. Since every dollar spent must of course go to some wage earner, profit taker, interest receiver, or other factor supplier, that is, provide income to someone, the sum of expenditures on final products naturally equals the earnings of factors listed on the right side. Government, foreign trade, and other complications will be ignored here, since they have nothing to do with the point at issue. With no government, the National Income here equals the NNP rather than falling short of it by the amount of indirect taxes as it does in the U.S. government accounts. Depreciation of the capital stock is for now assumed away, so we have the Net rather than the Gross National Product. To preserve the double entry character of the accounts, externalities are added (if economies) or subtracted (if diseconomies) from both sides of the accounts.

Now suppose that the absurdly simple economy that has been depicted produces more market output, and this brings external diseconomies that reduce the well-being of consumers but do not provoke defensive expenditures. In this case, it is immediately obvious that externalities that directly affect consumers make the NNP a misleading source of information on welfare: the value of the extra market goods produced is added to the NNP and its companion measures of social output, but loss of "psychic income"—what the people would have been willing to pay to be rid of the diseconomy—is not subtracted. Thus the NNP as it is conventionally measured by the Bureau of Economic Analysis and corresponding institutions in other countries shows the value of the increase in market output alone, whereas true NNP or

Table 2.   Period 2

Expenditure		Income	
Value of marketed goods to consumers	$1,500,000	Earnings of factors	$1,500,000
Value (here negative and "psychic") of externalities	− $250,000	Value of externalities	− $250,000
Measured NNP	$1,500,000	Measured NI	$1,500,000
True NNP	$1,250,000	True NI	$1,250,000

National Income would have changed by this amount minus what the people in the society would have been willing to pay to have avoided the diseconomy. This point is so obvious there is no need for a numerical illustration, but table 2, depicting the situation in the second period, is included to facilitate a comparison that will be needed later.

3. Externalities and Defensive Expenditures

We are now in a position to tackle the general case, where externalities not only reduce the psychic incomes of consumers but also induce them to undertake defensive expenditures, and to get at the essence of the matter. My critic pointed out that if the expenditures to eliminate smoke were borne by the factory owner, no one could doubt that these expenditures were "a legitimate part of the input . . . of the economy," and rightly indicated that the value of inputs (i.e., total factor earnings) had to equal "output, in value terms." Similarly, he argued, if the residents near the factory have to bear this cost of the factory's output, by paying laundries to wash out the soot, it makes no difference so far as the national income accounts are concerned.

In fact, it makes a great deal of difference who pays the costs. If the costs are external diseconomies and thus borne by the people living near the factory, the generator of the diseconomies will have no incentive to limit these costs.[5] He will indeed have an incentive to continue his emissions or other side effects to the point where they add at the margin nothing at all to his profits; if the emission or the nuisance is truly an external economy, his profits will be greatest if he spends nothing at all to reduce the emission. The right to dump wastes without

[5] If only a few parties are involved, bargaining may give the generator an incentive to limit these costs, but only because the bargaining to some degree makes them costly to the generator and thus to some degree internalizes them.

charge into the environment or to create other side effects is equivalent to having a free factor of production. If the factory owner were charged for the trouble and expense he causes others, he might locate his factory in a remote area where transportation costs are greater, or use a less polluting but for him more costly method of production, or buy smoke inhibitors; he would, in other words, have lower costs and normally[6] a higher level of output than if he had been charged for his side effects.

Just as the rational consumer equates his marginal rate of substitution between any pair of goods he consumes to the price ratio of these two goods, so a profit-maximizing producer also uses any pair of factors of production up to the point where the ratio of their marginal productivities is equal to their price ratio. This means that if there is no charge or prohibition against external diseconomies, firms will produce these diseconomies until their marginal productivity becomes zero. This is particularly obvious when, as is usually the case, side effects vary with a firm's market output; the profit-maximizing firm produces until marginal cost equals marginal revenue, and thus it could normally reduce output (and its side effects) by one unit at no loss at all and to a modest degree at negligible cost.

The externalities that a firm, if it maximizes profits, will necessarily continue emitting until the marginal productivity of doing so falls to zero, normally entail, as they increase, ever greater losses of utility or higher defensive expenditures for the victims. Though external diseconomies sometimes bring only minor difficulties to their victims, in other cases they can bring losses that are enormous, and that (at least at the margin) greatly exceed the profits the generating firm gains from them. The intense resistance to the enforcement of many environmental standards, and the concern that the taxes or regulations needed to achieve desired levels of environmental quality would prove "ruinous" to many businesses or industries, suggest that some diseconomies are very large in relation to the total profits from the activities that generate them. There is nothing in the working of a *laissez-faire* economy that would rule out external diseconomies with damages that are tens or even hundreds of times greater than the savings the generator of the externalities derives from them. This is obviously possible in cases where

---

[6] Normally but not invariably. The reason for this is that the side effect or emission that was internalized, and thereby made costly to the firm that had generated the diseconomy, in special cases could be an "inferior factor of production," analogous to an inferior good. If imposing side effects on the environment happens to be profitable *only* with the technology used at a low level of output, an optimal tax on, or any internalization of the costs of the side effects could induce the firm to switch to a higher level of output.

a large unorganized group that cannot bargain with the generator of the diseconomy is the victim.

The situation in equilibrium in a purely competitive *laissez-faire* economy with external diseconomies is therefore as follows: businessmen produce to the point where the extra cost to them (marginal private cost) of an additional unit of output equals the price they receive for that unit of output, and generate diseconomies whenever this makes a positive contribution, however small, to the profits of the firm. But the generation of the external diseconomy may entail substantial losses for victims. This means that the firm's production cost plus the cost to the victim of the diseconomy of at least the last unit of output must exceed the price, or what people are willing to pay for the good.

The foregoing paragraph shows only that external diseconomies lead to a supraoptimal output of the goods with the external diseconomies and thus to inefficiency, which my critic would never have denied. I have yet to show that the national income is not an appropriate measure of output.

This becomes immediately evident if we assume that the soot-spewing factory, or the whole sector of enterprises that trouble consumers with diseconomies, is limited in its emission of diseconomies by regulation or taxation. The regulation or taxation will reduce the use of the physical and social environment as a factor of production in the production of market goods; it will constrain firms in their choices about waste disposal, plant location, and methods of production, so that in at least some cases they will have to choose options which involve higher costs for them than they had before the regulation or taxation. But a limitation on the external diseconomies that can be imposed on the neighboring householders or other consumers[7] will not lower costs for those firms that had no external diseconomies to begin with, so the production of every type of marketed good will require at least as much privately purchased resources per unit of output for its production as before, and some types of output will require more such resources. (This can be seen by examining the "market goods opportunity frontier"—a production possibility frontier for marketed output alone—in figure 1. The production of sector X is assumed to generate diseconomies affecting consumers, whereas the production sector Y by assumption does not. If sector X is constrained in the extent of its emissions, the opportunity frontier for market goods is generally inside the market goods opportunity frontier for these goods that would have prevailed under *laissez-faire*, so society must find that the private costs of both X and Y are

---

[7] The case in which producers are victims will be considered shortly.

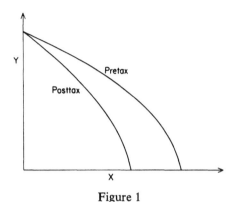

Figure 1

greater with the constraint on diseconomies than without it, except in the special case where only Y outputs have been produced and thus no diseconomies are generated.[8])

Now the answer to my critic has become clear: *any limitation or inhibition on the amount of diseconomies affecting consumers will raise costs per unit and marginal costs[9] to producers of market output. With higher marginal costs, firms will reduce outputs of marketed goods. But, with qualifications that have no relevance here, the NNP measures only the output of final goods sold in markets, so NNP as conventionally measured will fall.* The higher quality of the environment that was obtained by the regulation or taxation of diseconomies is purchased at the expense of a lower level of market output and thus of NNP and National Income as they are conventionally measured (as shown[10] in figure 2). If monetary and fiscal authorities maintain a constant price level, both the money value of NNP and measured real NNP will fall; if they do not curtail aggregate effective demand as the output of market goods drops, prices will rise and nominal NNP need not fall, but price-

[8] Note that a third good, Z, the "quality of life," is not depicted, to avoid the need for a third dimension. It is the diversion of resources (that is, not using air or water for waste disposal) to the production of this good that makes the posttax opportunity frontier for market goods fall inside the pretax frontier. See also figure 2.

[9] In certain very special cases, switching to a more costly method of production can lower *marginal* costs in the relevant range even as total costs are increased. (See Olson and Zeckhauser, 1970.) That possibility does not, however, vitiate the conclusion here; if after the limitation on diseconomies, one good is produced at higher total but lower marginal costs, the higher total costs will require additional factors that will limit the output of other goods.

[10] Goods X and Y, or all market goods, are considered together on the N axis, and the "quality of life" is measured on the Z axis.

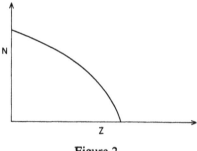

Figure 2

corrected measured NNP, some index number problems notwithstanding, necessarily will.

The fact that measured real NNP falls does *not* mean that true income
or welfare falls; the value of the loss in the output of marketed goods
may very well be less than the value to consumers of the greater satisfaction they get from a more congenial environment plus the gain that
arises because at least some of the defensive expenditures can be diverted
without loss to the purchase of goods that bring additional satisfactions.
Indeed, if we assume that the diseconomies are subjected to an optimal
tax (one that is equal to the damages victims suffer[11]), that there are
no other distortions in the economy (so we can avoid possible "second
best" problems[12]), and that all the losers from the changes brought
about by the tax are compensated by "lump sum" subsidies[13] (so that
there will be no change in the distribution of income to complicate our

---

[11] That is, the damages victims suffer if they are *not* compensated for their
losses and therefore have an incentive to keep their losses to a minimum. See
Olson and Zeckhauser (1970, pp. 516–517).

[12] If, for example, there is monopoly as well as external diseconomies, the
curtailment of output resulting from the monopoly might conceivably already
have brought the emission down to or below an optimal level, and a tax on the
remaining emissions might reduce output still further, and make the loss from
the monopolistic restriction of output exceed the gains from the diminution of the
emissions. In general, there can be no assurance that the piecemeal application of
the marginal rules that must *all* be met to achieve a Pareto optimal allocation of
resources, will increase efficiency.

[13] A "lump sum" subsidy is one that changes income without introducing a new
inefficiency by changing incentives. In principle, the firms that are faced with an
optimal tax on their emissions of the diseconomies, which optimal tax would
increase their tax liability as their emissions increased, could be compensated by
a "lump sum" payment which would not vary with their emissions or other
behavior, and therefore have no incentive effects. In practice, of course, the lump
sum subsidy or lump sum tax can only be approximated; in one way or another
any real tax or subsidy is likely to have some effect on incentives.

assessment), we can say for certain that welfare or true income has increased. The true worth or utility value of the aggregate of both market and nonmarket output in these conditions must necessarily be greater after the tax on diseconomies than it was before. Before the tax, each good was produced to the point where marginal private cost equaled price ($MPC = P$) but marginal social cost, by the definition of the external diseconomy, must have exceeded marginal private cost, so $MSC > P$, that is, the last unit, at least, of the good with diseconomies costs society more to produce than people are willing to pay for it, and (because, as we know, the ratio of marginal utilities equals the price ratio) more than the utility people obtain from this last unit. Since the size of an optimal tax on the diseconomy is equal to the loss suffered by the victims, it will make marginal private cost exactly equal to marginal social cost. This means that when $MPC = P$, then $MSC = P$. This means in turn that production of the good with the undesirable side effect ceases just at the point where the damage done by the side effect of an additional unit of output, plus the value of the other resources used in producing the unit of the good, just equals the worth to society of the last unit of output. If all goods are produced under conditions of increasing cost,[14] this will mean that with the optimal tax, every unit of the good that brought more utility than would have been obtained with any other use of the same resources will be produced, but no units of the good beyond these will be produced, and under the postulated conditions this entails an increase of true income or welfare. When an optimal tax is imposed on external diseconomies affecting consumers, then, true income or welfare will increase, but real measured NNP will fall. My critic's assertion that "the national income is an appropriate measure" in the presence of an external diseconomy that affects houses near a factory is therefore demonstrably false.

4. Defensive Expenditures

Another aspect of the matter emerges when we look at hypothetical national accounts that reveal the accounting process that occurs when there are external diseconomies with consumer victims. If we assume that the simple hypothetical economy depicted in tables 1 and 2 experienced a growth of market output and an increase in external dis-

[14] If the average cost to the society of producing a good decreases as more of this good is produced, the production possibility frontier will be concave from the top, and it might then be more efficient to concentrate on the production of one good, that is, to have a "corner solution," than to satisfy the marginal rule that is being adumbrated in the text.

Table 3.   Period 3

Expenditure		Income	
Value of marketed goods to consumers ($200,000 def. exp., $1,800,000 other goods)	$2,000,000	Earnings of factors	$2,000,000
Externalities ($200,000 def. exp., $300,000 psychic loss)	− $500,000	Externalities	− $500,000
Measured NNP	$2,000,000	Measured NI	$2,000,000
True NNP	$1,500,000	True NI	$1,500,000

economies which led consumers to undertake defensive expenditures, then we would have a result in the next period such as that shown in table 3. By this time, the value of marketed final output is assumed to be worth $2,000,000 and external diseconomies have risen to half a million, of which $200,000 consists of defensive expenditure. (If there were no technology on which defensive expenditures could economically be used, the loss of externalities would have been greater than half a million; we know that the $200,000 of defensive expenditures would not have been undertaken unless they were expected to reduce the psychic loss from the diseconomies by more than that.) Since the defensive expenditures count as final output in the measured NNP and National Income, they must be subtracted out again, along with the psychic loss, to get true income or welfare; if the growth of market output had not had adverse side effects, consumers would not have had to use some of their income to countervail these effects. Thus it is again clear that externalities with an impact on consumers lead to error in the national accounts; measured NNP and National Income exceed the true figures by half a million in this case.

The reason why the laundry, housepainting, or other defensive expenditures are added to measured NNP, whereas they must be subtracted to arrive at true NNP, is that they are treated as a final good in the measured NNP, but are in fact only an intermediate good that is purchased to help obtain the unmeasured final good of a clean environment. The situation is akin to that which would prevail if food output was not measured in the national accounts, but farmers' fertilizer usage was, and this rose over time in relation to food output because (say) firms found it advantageous to emit air pollutants which lowered agricultural yields.

Table 4.   After Hypothetical Optimal Tax on External Diseconomies
Has Been Imposed

Expenditure		Income	
Value of marketed goods to consumers	$1,700,000	Earnings of factors	$1,700,000
Externalities	00	Externalities	00
Measured NNP	$1,700,000	Measured NI	$1,700,000
True NNP	$1,700,000	True NNP	$1,700,000

The effect of the imposition of an optimal tax on the diseconomy is shown in table 4. As has been shown, marketed output and measured income would fall; let us assume in this case from $2,000,000 to $1,700,000. Since the tax is assumed to be optimal, true income must rise; let us assume in this case from $1,500,000 to $1,700,000. The assumption that the tax on the external diseconomy is optimal requires that the external diseconomies fall to zero. But *emissions* need not have disappeared; there will usually be some types of emissions that are so profitable that it will be advantageous for those who generate them to have them take place at some level, even when they are charged for the full cost of the damage these emissions do to the victims; to say that factors of production such as the generation of noise or pollution have a positive price after the imposition of the optimal tax is not to say that they will no longer be used. Though some (an optimal amount of) noise, pollution, and the like will probably remain, there are no *external* costs: all of the costs of production are now borne by those who sell the good, and are reflected in its market price.

After the optimal tax has been imposed, and external diseconomies have disappeared, it becomes true, as my critic said, that the value of inputs measured in the national accounts equals the value of outputs. Such emissions as still occur are not only a cost of production, they now are also a cost that enters into the accounts in just the way other costs do, so that the total cost of *all* factors of production will just equal the value of output. When there are externalities affecting consumers, on the other hand, my critic's assertion was incorrect; the accounting identity assured that what was spent on what was deemed (sometimes incorrectly) to be final output would equal the costs of production that were borne by those who sold the products. But when there are external diseconomies, there are also other costs of production, in excess of the market value of output, borne by the consumers who were victims of the diseconomies, which are neglected or misstated in the national accounts.

The only aspect of the dispute that remains to be dealt with is my critic's parenthetical assertion that "the costs to neighbors will be reflected in land values, and hence rents, and hence national income." It is, to be sure, likely that land values and rents in the area next to the factory will fall. But nothing in this process will subtract an amount that measures the loss due to the external diseconomy from the NNP or National Income. There is no assurance that the fall in rents will equal the psychic loss from the external diseconomy plus the defensive expenditures against it. This is partly because some of the damage done by diseconomies occurs in streets, sidewalks, parks, and other public facilities for which no rent is charged. But the more important point is that, even if rents did fall by just the amount of the loss from the diseconomies, and the asset value fell by an amount equal to the capitalized value of the diseconomy,[15] that would not reduce the NNP by the amount of the diseconomy, or necessarily reduce it at all. Unless there was an accidental contraction in monetary or fiscal policy, or in the propensity to consume, or in business investment, the reduction in rents would be offset by greater spending on other goods, or perhaps housing outside of the catchment area of the diseconomy. Only if the diseconomy drove victims out of the country whose national income was at issue, or somehow impaired their capacity to produce and earn income,[16] would the national income tend to fall. It does not follow that because external diseconomies will reduce the relative prices of those assets the relative desirability of which is lessened by the diseconomy, that the diseconomy will reduce the level of aggregate effective demand in the economy, or the measured quantity of marketed output,[17] or the amount of resources devoted to production for sale in the market, or any other variable that influences the level of either real or money NNP.

5. Externalities with Producers as Victims

The principal conclusion of the argument in this paper should not be confused with a superficially similar conclusion that occasionally appears in discussions of the subject. The contention that the national income statistics are misleading if there are externalities or "social costs" is sometimes supported by an examination of the relationship between two

---

[15] Since the present national accounts do not measure the stock of capital, the change in the capital value of owner-occupied housing would not be captured in any case.

[16] This case will be considered later in the paper.

[17] If corrections for quality changes made when price indexes are calculated took pollution fully into account, the diseconomy would be reflected in price-corrected NNP figures.

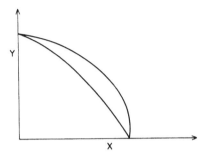

Figure 3

firms, one of which imposes an external diseconomy on the other. Suppose, the argument runs, that a chemical factory is constructed next to a river, into which it dumps a pollutant. The output (actually, value added) in this factory will increase real national income. Suppose also that the effluent of this factory forces a preexisting factory downstream, which uses the water in its productive processes, to use a more expensive method of production. The growth of the national income that results from the new upstream factory is then misleading, according to this argument, because it ignores the social cost imposed on the downstream firms.

In fact, if the effluent of the new factory has no effects other than that costs of the downstream firm rise whenever it is being issued, the *NNP and National Income will take full and correct account of the external diseconomy.* Just as the capacity to dump wastes into the river tends to lower costs, and raise market output, in the upstream firm, so the higher costs for the downstream firm that uses the water will lower its market output. If the market output of both firms is measured in the national accounts, both the higher output in the upstream firm and the lower output in the downstream firm will be properly accounted for in the NNP and National Income statistics.

In general, whenever external diseconomies affect only current producers' costs, they cause no problems for the national accounts. If sector X has a side effect that raises the cost of producing the output of firms in sector Y, then the total output of the economy is diminished, but this diminution in output is correctly measured in the national income statistics. If an optimal tax is imposed on the external diseconomy of sector X, efficiency and total output will increase (because MSC is made equal to MPC and P), and this increase will be correctly reflected in an increase of *measured* income, which in the absence of other problems is the same as true income. (As figure 3 shows, it is only when only X

or only Y is produced that the production opportunity frontier is the same whether or not the external diseconomy is internalized. For every mix of output involving both X and Y, more of both X and Y can be had if the diseconomy is internalized through an opitimal tax, merger, interfirm bargaining, or whatever, so that society can get to the outer opportunity set or production possibility frontier. It can be shown that, at least with convexity, even index number problems cannot obscure the fact that measured NNP must be greater after the internalization of the diseconomy: every point on the opportunity set reflecting the diseconomy is dominated by one or more points on the outer set.)

The distinction between "producers" and "consumers" must not be made in purely institutional or conventional terms. If an individual breathes air pollution at home in his leisure hours, but because of this falls ill and loses efficiency as a worker, the output of market goods will be reduced and NNP diminished. External diseconomies in city centers have presumably induced some workers with jobs in the central city to move to distant suburbs, and if the long commute reduces the supply of labor to producers, the NNP is affected.[18] Thus a great many diseconomies must have some effect, however slight, on the level of marketed output.

Similarly, it isn't easy to think of very many diseconomies that would affect producers but have no direct effect on consumers. When the air is filled with noise or pollution, or the water with effluents, this affects the individual as a consumer at least as much as it affects firms or the productivity of workers. Thus it is useful to think of external diseconomies on a continuum, with those that affect only consumers as consumers at one pole and those that affect only producers as producers at the other pole. The most important point to remember is that, at every point along the continuum except the latter pole, there will be some loss to consumers not reflected in any change in their production of market goods, and in almost all cases where there are externalities the NNP will accordingly be to a greater or lesser extent misleading.

Even when *only* producers' costs are affected by externalities, the NNP will still be a misleading measure if the damage done by the diseconomy does not pass away directly, but affects future as well as present production. If the ecology of a river system, or the productivity of agricultural land, or the potential of fishing grounds is damaged, future market output will be less than it would otherwise have been, and the NNP will be misleading as a welfare measure. The reason is that

---

[18] I am thankful to Clopper Almon and Julius Margolis for emphasizing the effects external diseconomies ostensibly affecting only consumers could have on producers' oosts and market output.

the national accounts do not measure the depreciation in the value of unowned assets; if a natural asset in the public domain is made less useful for some future years, the NNP in the year that damage was done ought in principle to be reduced by the resulting loss output in all of the future years, discounted by an appropriate interest rate. But in the United States as well as in at least most other countries, only the depreciation of assets that are privately owned is taken into account in calculating the NNP.

6. Distinguishing Defensive Expenditures

If externalities are not usually properly taken into account in the national income statistics, what should be done about it? One part of the answer is clear: there is a need for separate measures of externalities and other collective goods. These "social indicator" measures of social performance should be made available initially without a price being attached, because individuals and groups with different values or conceptions of what the "social welfare function" ought to be can then draw their own informed conclusions about how true income or social welfare is changing.

These separate measures could not, however, be sufficient by themselves to deal with the problems of externalities, since some part of the loss from an external diseconomy is of course often in the form of defensive expenditures. These defensive or offsetting expenditures will eliminate or neutralize some part of the damage done by external diseconomies, and this part of the loss would not or should not be captured by the social indicator—the appropriate measure of loss is instead the money values of the resources that would otherwise be used to obtain desirable goods but which are instead diverted to combating the external diseconomy. When the defensive expenditures of the government and the business sectors are added to those of the consumer sector, it becomes clear that the magnitude of the expenditures at issue is rather large. As we shall soon argue, a large part of the government budget falls in this category, and recent changes in environmental legislation and regulation are forcing business firms to devote increasing amounts of resources to facilities designed to limit the damages they can do to consumers, to commonly owned resources, and to other firms.

Important as they are, defensive expenditures and the way they must fit into the national accounts and any coherent system of social evaluation are not usually understood, again probably because of the lack of an adequate explanation in the specialized literature. Part of the difficulty seems to stem from the misunderstanding described earlier in this paper, but most of the problems we shall discuss involve far different issues.

A variety of writers have for many many years suggested, as did my *Public Interest* article, that defensive expenditures against external diseconomies in principle ought not to be included in the NNP, though the practical difficulties of distinguishing such expenditures and other *ad hoc* considerations might argue for reluctantly leaving things as they are. This suggestion has also brought forth intense disagreement from many distinguished students of national income accounting. If defensive expenditures against noise or pollution are to be subtracted from the NNP, it is widely and sometimes eloquently argued, why not also subtract out food expenditures because they are a defense against hunger, or clothing expenditures because they are a defense against the cold, or religious expenditures because they are a defense against the fires of hell? So the litany goes on—if all defensive expenditures are subtracted out of the NNP, there will be little if anything left in it. One of the most entertaining statements of this widely held opposition to the principle that defensive or externality offsetting expenditures ought ideally to be separated out of the NNP, has come from the critical letter to *The Public Interest* referred to earlier:

> The fact that one can find expenditures that can be viewed as offsetting other expenditures holds far beyond these examples [of smoking factories and other external diseconomies]. Gymnasiums combat restaurants in the fight over obesity; policemen combat strong automobiles in the fight over speed; the salaries of Bell and Olson, while writing erroneous economics, are included in the national income—along with mine in replying.

Though the critic has since changed his position, his letter nonetheless leads on to some more substantial and practical issues that have not been properly handled, even in the specialized literature. In discussing these issues, we shall deal first with the logical principles involved and turn only later to the difficulty of making estimates and other practical difficulties.

The most basic aspect of the problem is already clear from table 3. As earlier sections of this paper (and other writers) have made clear, defensive expenditures, though they really purchase an intermediate good, are treated as a final good in the accounts. If the negative side effects of the production of market output increase over time, any defensive expenditures against these negative side effects will also tend to increase. Some part of the market output would be diverted to

Table 5. Externalities with Defensive Expenditures

Expenditure		Income	
Value of marketed goods to consumers ($600,000 def. exp., $2,100,000 other goods)	$2,500,000	Earnings of factors	$2,500,000
Externalities ($600,000 def. exp., $300,000 psychic loss)	− $900,000	Externalities	− $900,000
Measured NNP	$2,500,000	Measured NI	$2,500,000
True NNP	$1,600,000	True NI	$1,600,000

offsetting the adverse externalities resulting from economic growth. But in the national accounts of the present day, these expenditures are treated as though something new and desirable had been added—that is, as expenditures on a final good. If market output grew $500,000 from period three, depicted in table 3 to $2,500,000 in the next period (shown in table 5), but defensive expenditures rose by $400,000, it would clearly be wrong to count all of the $500,000 increase in market output as income; all but $100,000 of it had to be used to offset the adverse side effects of the growth. Thus, whether or not we take account of the psychic loss, the NNP provides a better measure of true income or welfare when we subtract out (or never enter) the defensive expenditures.

But if we should subtract defensive expenditures against external diseconomies that damage consumers, wouldn't consistency require, as many of the experts say, that we subtract gymnasium expenditures because they offset expenditures on food, or clothing expenditures because they are a defense against the cold? Not at all. When the rational consumer values both good food and a trim figure, he can rationally seek to attain both by a combination of restaurant and gymnasium expenditures. Since there are by assumption no external diseconomies in this case, his consumption of food creates no problems for anyone else. Since the food the consumer can buy is relatively unchanged over time, as are the slimming effects of gymnasiums, it follows that if increasing productivity makes it possible for a person to buy both more good meals and more gymnasium facilities with the wages of a day's work, he has (if other things are equal) a higher true income. If, on the other hand, a consumer's food consumption made *other* people fat, greater productivity and higher food consumption would mean that the need for gymnasiums increased over time; in this fantastic example, food consumption would have an external diseconomy, and there would be an increasing need for gymnasiums to offset the fact that it was becoming progressively more expensive in real terms to stay slim. The defensive expenditure against a side effect of economic growth affecting consumers (and their psychic losses) should in principle be subtracted from the NNP, then, because the growth brings with it an increased need for another good; there is usually some such systematic change in needs when external diseconomies are involved.

In a few cases, the need for expenditure on a good can vary from one situation to another for reasons that have nothing to do with the side effects of market activity. The need for clothing, for other forms of shelter, and for fuel to heat houses, will tend to be greater in cold climates than in warm ones. (Though an adverse climate is not usually a by-product of economic activity, it should be regarded as a "collective bad," since it inevitably impinges, often more or less uniformly, on everyone in some area.) When the need for defensive expenditure for shelter against the cold varies greatly, it is sometimes taken into account in estimates of the cost of living in different regions, and then affects estimates of true income. There can be no doubt that this is right in principle. In sum, all defensive expenditures to protect consumers against external diseconomies, and all other expenditures that merely compensate for some greater need, should in principle be subtracted from the NNP, whereas other so-called defensive expenditures should not be.

One form of defensive expenditure that is very important in the budget of modern national governments, but which presumably does not often involve the side effects of market activity, is of course expenditure for defense against military attack.[19] The relatively high military budgets of recent decades have diverted resources from the production of other goods. Even if it is true that these expenditures have always been efficiently used to attain greater military capability, and that greater military capacity for an individual nation always markedly increases its national security, these expenditures should in principle still be subtracted from the NNP. The reason is that we presumably have no more of any final good. The citizens of the United States, at least, are probably no more secure against military attack today than in the late nineteenth century. But a larger amount (and even proportion) of resources are

---

[19] If military forces are built up for aggressive purposes, they should not be considered defensive expenditures in the sense in which that term is used here; they would rather, for the aggressive nation, be an investment undertaken for the future spoils they were expected to bring.

used for defense now than then, and this increase in defense spending ought to be subtracted in any comparison of living standards then and now.

When military and related expenditures are added to those the government undertakes to protect the consumers against external diseconomies, a large part of the government budget is accounted for. Those defensive expenditures that consumers make in their own behalf can also be significant, as when people who work in large cities commute to homes in rural areas to avoid external diseconomies. This is clearly a quantitatively important phenomenon.

There is another view about defensive expenditures and some related costs that is far more subtle than the one that has just been attacked, yet it is very much in need of qualification.[20] This view, which initially came to my attention through informal discussions with some specialists in national income accounting, is despite its flaws very instructive. Since to my knowledge it has not yet been stated in print, no exact quotation or citation is possible, but the view at issue can be stated approximately as follows:

"What Olson has said is true for the special case in which what he calls defensive expenditures occur because pollution or other side effects have increased, but is not true when defensive expenditures have increased because new technologies for combating adverse conditions have developed, or because tastes have changed in such a way that people now give a higher priority than before to combating the adverse conditions. In these cases true income will never tend to fall, and with the technological advance it will rise, but this gain in welfare will not be captured if defensive expenditures are subtracted from the accounts. The best course on balance is to leave defensive expenditures made by consumers or governments as they are in the national accounts. But another and quite different change probably is needed; those higher costs of production for business firms which have been brought about by government regulations and taxation designed to improve the environment ought to be distinguished from other business costs and added to the total of final output, because these higher costs reduce market output and measured NNP, but if justified produce an environmental improvement. The extra business costs brought about by regulation and taxation

[20] I am very thankful to Edward Denison, Edgar Dunn, Orris Herfindahl, George Jaszi, Allen Kneese, and Thomas Juster for helpful discussions relating to the rest of this chapter at a seminar on this subject in the Spring of 1971 sponsored by Resources for the Future. The ideas in this chapter were set out in my paper on "The National Accounts and the Level of Welfare," which was prepared and circulated in mimeographed form in June 1971.

can be taken as a measure of the value of the additional amount of the final good of environmental quality that has been purchased. If the treatment of defensive expenditures is left as it is, but the extra costs to business resulting from environmental regulation and taxation are distinguished and added to final product, the tendency for measured NNP to grow more slowly because of the concern about the environment will be corrected."

The view that has just been described is entitled to a great deal of respect, but it also invites some obvious questions. If a change in tastes is assumed, how can anyone say what really ought to be done? Welfare measurement requires a stable set of wants or criteria in terms of which different bundles of goods can be compared. If an improvement in technology takes place, the resulting gain in welfare ought to be captured, but it is noteworthy that the gain in welfare from technological advances that lead to new consumer goods is not in general captured now in the accounts.[21]

More importantly, why should we want to doctor the national accounts in such a way as to make them show a higher rate of growth, and at a time when so many people have come to believe that the NNP overstates any increase in true income or welfare? The implicit assumption behind the view described is that there has been no real or significant growth of adverse side effects in recent times, at least because of market activity; the recent spate of concern about the physical environment, and the probable growth of discontent with government and the social order, reflect an arbitrary change of tastes. To the extent that increases in defensive expenditures by consumers or governments acting for them reflect increased emissions and congestion resulting from the growth of the market economy and the population, it makes no sense at all to deny that these defensive expenditures should be subtracted. Similarly, if the rate of measured growth of NNP slows as regulation and taxation to limit side effects raise private costs to business, that is beyond question what ought to happen if the environment is getting worse; any other result could create a false impression of progress.

Though there is unquestionably much that is false and faddish about the current concern about the environment (Brubaker, 1972) and several areas in which the physical environment is better now than it has been, there are some fundamental reasons why we should expect the cost of protecting the environment to rise with the growth of population and market output. The external diseconomies arising out of congestion surely tend to rise with population growth. And, as Robert Ayres's and Allen Kneese's "materials balance" theory makes clear (Kneese, Ayres,

[21] This is discussed in my forthcoming book.

and d'Arge, 1970), the wastes or residuals equal the weight of materials used by the economy, minus any increase in materials recycled, because of the law of conservation of matter; if matter is neither created nor destroyed, and recycling does not increase, economic growth will tend to bring a steady increase in diseconomies. The losses from emissions will normally vary strikingly with the spatial distribution, type, and processing of emissions; pollution-intensive production can move to less settled areas, incinerators can be closed down (albeit at the expense of more solid wastes), etc. But it is difficult to imagine that any such changes in recent generations have entirely compensated for the many-fold increase in residuals, especially given the simultaneous increase in the use of throwaway containers, nondegradable materials, and pesticides. As far as the future is concerned, it is difficult to see how the economy can keep growing exponentially forever in a finite world without an increase in environmental problems. This matter is much too large to settle in a paragraph, but it does already seem safe to question the implicit assumption that side effects have not been increasing, at any event enough to explain most of defensive expenditures and costs of environmental protection imposed on business.

Thus the view at issue—that defensive expenditures should be left as they are, but the costs to business of environmental protection should be added to the total of final output—has some weaknesses. Yet it might, because of its obvious advantages, on balance be the best alternative, except for one more serious consideration that has not been properly understood. It is to this consideration, and the hypothetical national income accounts that help to elucidate it, that we now turn.

7. How to Avoid Double Counting

To deal appropriately with this consideration, it is necessary to deal first with the "psychic" loss from external diseconomies, and to break this down into two different variables: first, the level or amount of the side effect, which is measured by a social indicator, and second, the weight or value attached to each unit change in the social indicator. The social indicator will be in different units, depending on the phenomenon at issue; in one case it will be parts per million of a pollutant, in another in decibels of noise, and so on. Since we are considering side effects in general rather than any particular situation, we shall here suppose that the side effect is divided into "arbs," a shorthand expression for arbitrary units in general.

The price to be attached to the social indicator will, for reasons already pointed out, vary from group to group or individual to individual. Since this variation does not, however, affect the principle at issue at the moment, we shall accept a hypothetical observer's conception of the proper social price, or (what in this operation amounts to the same thing) assume that there is complete consensus and that the value of a unit change in the social indicator to any individual, multiplied by the number of people in the population, gives its social price. We shall also assume that only one external diseconomy is at issue (to avoid an irrelevant complication involving consumer surpluses[22]), in which case the appropriate price per arb is given by dividing the total value of whatever change in the level of the diseconomy takes place by the number arbs of change.

---

[22] When large changes in many social indicators are at issue, the question of what price to put on each of these large changes becomes difficult to determine. The problem arises from the fact that what people are willing to pay if confronted with the alternative of buying large changes in the quantity of many side effects, or else getting no change at all, is more than what they would pay if they paid a marginal cost price for each unit of change in each social indicator: in the former case they would pay for some "consumer's surplus," in the latter they would not. The problem is to determine when and to what extent this consumer's surplus should be included in the price of the side effect in the social accounts. Even when the change in the social indicator is very large, there is no problem if there is a change in only one social indicator. The significance of any one social indicator will probably be so small in relation to the output of the entire economy that the "income effect" of all-or-nothing or discriminatory pricing arrangements would be small, so the demand curve would not shift appreciably as one price or another was assumed. When this is the case, the total amount people would pay for the change—the total area under the relevant portion of the demand curve—is what should be used to determine the welfare loss or gain from a given change: this is what the change is worth to the affected parties. If, on the other hand, there are large changes in important social indicators throughout the society, so that in the aggregate they have a significance that is large in relation to NNP, then we come up against the fact that "consumer's surplus" is a partial equilibrium concept that is misleading when naively applied to a large proportion of the economy. If people in fact had to pay out the amounts given by the area under the demand curves for large changes in many cases, the income effect of this would lead to a downward shift of most or all of their demand curves. So the values of the changes taken one at a time would not in fact be the same as what people would pay for the changes in the aggregate.

One possibility worth considering would involve multiplying each estimate of total value of a large change in a social indicator (with each change looked at as though it were the only one) by one minus fraction the total of all such changes were to the NNP. Thus if the sum of all changes taken singly were valued at one fourth of NNP, each of these changes would be multiplied by three fourths. This would provide an adjustment that would approximately allow for the degree to which the partial equilibrium estimates on consumer's surplus are inevitably overestimates when aggregated into a total that is substantial in relation to the entire economy.

Table 6.   Preinvention

Expenditure		Income	
Value of marketed final goods ($100,000 def. exp., $1,900,000 other goods)	$2,000,000	Earnings of factors	$2,000,000
Social indicator of diseconomy	2,000 arbs		
Proper social price	− $275 ea. arb		
Negative value of psychic loss from side effects	$550,000		
Defensive expenditures	$100,000		
External diseconomy	− $650,000	External diseconomy	− $650,000
Measured NNP	$2,000,000	Measured NI	$2,000,000
True NNP	$1,350,000	True NI	$1,350,000

The question of whether defensive expenditures, when they arise because of the invention of a new and superior technology for combating the diseconomy, ought to be subtracted from the NNP, can be examined in terms of the two hypothetical accounts below. Table 6 presents a situation before the invention of such a new technology, table 7 the situation after the invention has led to an increase in defensive expenditures.

In the period before the new invention, there are 2,000 arbs of the pollutant or other diseconomy, each of which has a negative value of −$275. There is also $100,000 in defensive expenditures which were advantageous even under the old technology. When the new technology is discovered, the old technology is no longer used, but it pays to spend, say, twice as much on defense against externalities with the new technology than with the old, so a further $100,000 or a total of $200,000 is now diverted from consumption of other goods to combating the external diseconomy. The increase of defensive expenditures under the new technology must reduce the loss of psychic income by more than the $100,000 increase in these expenditures or it would not have taken place. In this case, to make the increase in welfare from the defensive expenditure under the new technology relatively striking, we assume that the psychic loss from side effects falls from $550,000 to only $50,000; the $100,000 of additional defensive expenditure has brought an increase in psychic income five times as great as itself, and a $400,000 net

Table 7. Postinvention

Expenditure		Income	
Value of marketed final goods ($200,000 def. exp., $1,800,000 other goods)	$2,000,000	Earnings of factors	$2,000,000
Social indicator of pollution	500 arbs		
Observer's conception of proper social price	− $100 ea. arb		
Negative value of psychic loss from side effects	$50,000		
Defensive expenditures	$200,000		
External diseconomy	− $250,000	External diseconomy	− $250,000
Measured NNP	$2,000,000	Measured NI	$2,000,000
True NNP	$1,750,000	True NI	$1,750,000

increase in welfare. This has happened because the number of arbs of the side effect has fallen from 2,000 to 500 and with a lower level of the side effect it becomes less onerous per arb, so that the price per arb falls from $275 to $100. Though the hypothetical example is particularly favorable to the view of those who oppose the subtraction of defensive expenditures, it is clear that there is a serious error if these expenditures are not subtracted; if they are not, true income would be overstated by $200,000.

A comparison of tables 7 and 8 shows what happens if government regulation or taxation of business in the interest of reducing side effects on consumers also reduces external diseconomies still further. As the item next to the "Earnings of Factors" entry in table 8 points out, it is assumed that businessmen are required to use $100,000 in factors of production to diminish their external diseconomies. These resources will not, of course, usually be easy to distinguish from other business costs; though the costs of additional waste treatment may be readily segregated, the extra transportation costs of using remote locations, or the costs of reducing the noise from airplanes, may be harder to distinguish. In any event, if the value of the extra resources used to produce marketed output with fewer externalities was $100,000, marketed output of final goods would have to fall by that amount, because these resources are now producing environmental protection rather than

Table 8.   Postregulation

Expenditure		Income	
Value of marketed final goods ($40,000 def. exp., $1,860,000 other goods)	$1,900,000	Earnings of factors ($100,000 of factor earnings result from measures to reduce external diseconomies)	$1,900,000
Social indicator of pollution	200 arbs		
Observer's conception of proper social price	$50 ea. arb		
Negative value of psychic loss from side effects	$10,000		
Defensive expenditures	$40,000		
External diseconomy	− $50,000	External diseconomy	− $50,000
Measured NNP	$1,900,000	Measured NI	$1,900,000
True NNP	$1,850,000	True NI	$1,850,000

market output. The increase in true income from the regulation or taxation of the external diseconomies would clearly be overstated if the $100,000 in business costs were added to the final output. The final goods that result from these expenditures are the further reduction in arbs of pollution, the diminished damage done by each such arb, and the desired final market goods that can be purchased by consumers now that their need for defensive expenditure has diminished. These business expenses are a cost of production of marketed output, which should be treated in the same way as other costs of production.

The conclusions are therefore as follows: in any comprehensive system of national income statistics or social accounting, defensive expenditures by consumers or governments acting on their behalf, whether there is a new technology or a change of tastes or not, *must show up in the level of a social indicator, or in the damage each arb of it does and therefore its appropriate price, or in both; similarly, all of the benefits of government regulation or taxation of business in the interest of consumers must show up in the same way, or in a reduction of defensive expenditures, or in both.* The impacts of the defense expenditures by consumers and government will therefore be double counted if they are not subtracted out of the accounts, since these expenditures represent intermediate goods (though they have been wrongly treated as final goods in the accounts). If the extra business expenses growing out of government regulation or taxation are, as some have suggested, added to final product, there will again be double counting, for these expenses are also intermediate goods (which have by contrast traditionally been rightly so classified in the accounts).

It may be said that my argument assumes we already have social indicators covering goods the national accounts exclude, whereas we often do not, or that the NNP is being revised with monetary estimates of the damage done by external diseconomies, whereas at least in the official statistics this is not being done. In fact, the argument requires no such assumption: it assumes only that people have eyes to see, or other senses to discern, the external diseconomies that have an impact on their welfare. And if these side effects do in fact have an impact on consumer welfare which would induce defensive expenditures, or lead to government regulation of business, it follows that consumers must have the senses needed to perceive them. Thus so long as consumers take account of the side effects that they must perceive in their judgments about the overall performance of society, it follows that there is double counting if defensive expenditures are not subtracted out of the NNP, or if the cost to business of environmental protection is.

Whatever may be thought about defensive expenditures or costs incurred on behalf of people as consumers, the situation is different when the impact of external diseconomies is on producer costs. When there are external diseconomies from firms (or for that matter from governments or individual consumers) that increase the costs of firms, the inefficiency reduces marketed output and therefore measured NNP. Similarly, any defensive expenditure the business sector makes on its own behalf affects its costs and outputs, and therefore NNP again. The national accounts as they stand accordingly measure externalities among firms rather well. There is no need, where such externalities are concerned, for either social indicators or any change in the treatment of defensive expenditures. If governments or consumers, on the other hand, were to undertake expenditures designed to spare or protect the business sector form external diseconomies, those expenditures would incorrectly be considered part of final output: their contribution to output is in the form of greater output by firms, which is already counted, so there would be double counting if they were included again.

8. Reforming the National Accounts: Is It Desirable?

The economist or other social scientist should not jump directly from a theoretical argument, however valid, to a practical policy judgment. Other considerations, which a theory can leave out without invalidating the insight or instruction it contains, may have decisive significance in a particular real world situation. Thus, to repeat a caveat for emphasis, it does not follow from the argument of this paper that defensive expenditures which consumers make on their own behalf, individually or through government, should be handled differently in the National Income and Product Accounts than they now are. There are two types of considerations, outside the framework of the arguments that have been discussed here, that might argue for leaving the treatment of defensive expenditures as it is, and lead *a fortiori* to the conclusion that there should be no change in the treatment of the business costs of environmental regulation.

One of these is the difficulty of distinguishing defensive expenditures and the costs due to environmental regulation from other spending and costs. Though a large part of the government budget can easily be distinguished as defensive, some defensive expenditures by consumers and costs of regulation or taxation to business are difficult to distinguish. If estimates of defensive expenditures or costs of regulation and taxation are subject to such an extraordinary margin of error that they cannot be on a par with any other figures in the accounts, there is much to be said for leaving the accounts unchanged.

The other consideration grows out of the importance of social inertia. As Simon Kuznets has argued,[23] there is by now a social consensus about the NNP and its companion measures that argues against making even many changes that are on all other grounds desirable; the national product figures are generally accepted and are of use despite their faults, whereas any new measures or estimates that replace them might not be generally understood and used for a long while. This argues, said Kuznets, for leaving the National Income and Product Accounts as they are, and dealing with the need for new estimates and measures of welfare separately, even in new institutions or agencies of government. Though Kuznets did not refer in any event explicitly to social indicators, his argument clearly strengthens the case for them as well as for other efforts to measure welfare that are distinguished from the official national income accounts that most countries have.

Even if the arguments in this paper should not be deemed sufficient to justify a change in existing procedures for calculating the NNP, that does not mean they are without practical relevance. They argue, first, for additional breakdowns and separate estimates designed to distinguish defensive expenditures from other expenditures, and to separate defensive expenditures in terms of whether they are mainly expected to

[23] At the meeting of the Conference on Income and Wealth of the National Bureau of Economic Research at Princeton, New Jersey, in November 1971.

protect consumers or to lower costs for producers, and also in terms of the sector of society which made the expenditure. If these estimates do not dilute some aggregate whose other components are known with greater accuracy, they will be useful so long as they are more accurate than alternative estimates or judgments of the same magnitudes, even if they are subject to a considerable margin of error. If appropriate breakdowns and estimates give those who use national accounts a better basis for understanding them, they will be quite useful, even apart from the other purposes these breakdowns and estimates might serve.[24]

Second, the argument of this paper, even if it should not lead to any change in official estimates, must be taken into account when the NNP figures are interpreted. Whatever else may continue to be disputed, there can be no question that the logical implications of the existing treatment of different kinds of defensive expenditures need to be understood when discussing the effect changes in real NNP will have on welfare.

References

Brubaker, Sterling. 1972. *To Live on Earth* (Baltimore, Johns Hopkins University Press for Resources for the Future).

Helferich, Otto. 1970. "Fun and Games with the GNP," in Otto Helferich, ed., *The Environmental Crisis* (New Haven, Yale University Press).

Kneese, Allen, Robert Ayres, and Ralph d'Arge. 1970. *Economics and the Environment: A Materials Balance Approach* (Washington, Resources for the Future).

Lekachman, Robert. 1970. "The Poverty of Affluence," *Commentary* (March) pp. 39–44.

Meadows, Donella L., Denis L. Meadows, Jorgen Randers, and William Behrens III. 1972. *The Limits to Growth* (New York, Universe Books).

Moss, Milton, ed. 1973. *The Measurement of Economic and Social Performance.* (New York, National Bureau of Economic Research).

Mishan, E. J. 1967. *The Costs of Economic Growth* (New York, Praeger).

Nordhaus, William D., and James Tobin. 1972. "Is Growth Obsolete?" in National Bureau of Economic Research, 50th Anniversary Colloquium, vol. 5, *Economic Growth* (New York, NBER). Also published in Milton Moss, ed., *The Measurement of Economic and Social Performance.* Conference on Income and Wealth, National

---

[24] Orris Herfindahl and Allen Kneese persuasively argued for separate breakdowns and estimates of defensive expenditures in their paper in Moss (1973).

Bureau of Economic Research (New York, NBER, 1963) pp. 509–532.

Olson, Mancur. 1969. "The Plan and Purpose of a Social Report," *Public Interest* (Spring) p. 86.

————, and Richard Zeckhauser. 1970. "The Efficient Production of External Economies," *American Economic Review* vol. LX (June) p. 515.

Samuelson, Paul. 1969. "True Income," *Newsweek* (October 6) p. 108.

12
Conceptions of the Quality of Life in Theory and Practice

DAVID DONNISON

1. Introduction

EACH of us, said John Stuart Mill, "is the person most interested in his own well-being . . ." and "with respect to his own feelings and circumstances, the most ordinary man or woman has means of knowledge immeasurably surpassing those that can be possessed by anyone else."[1]

I revere this intellectual tradition and its libertarian conviction that, without strong evidence to the contrary, each man must be assumed to be the best judge of his own interests. But applied in its simpler forms to problems of collective decision, this principle has three major defects. It is *unhistorical* because it takes too little account of the way in which preferences are shaped (and could thus in time be reshaped) by influences extending backward and forward over long periods of time. It is *unsociological* because it tends to treat people as atomistic individuals, each deciding only for themselves, rather than as members of families, classes, and social groups of many kinds which support and constrain them (and which could influence them in different ways if the social structure changed). And it is "*unurban*," intellectually speaking, because it pays too little attention to the links between the different sectors of an urban economy—its power structure and value systems, its markets for labor, housing, education, and so on—which together make it so difficult to change one sector unless consistent adjustments are made in many other sectors of the economy.

These intellectual defects are powerfully reinforced by many features of the institutions through which collective action usually has to be taken. A good deal has been written about the tendency of monopolies in the private sector of the economy—its "taste makers"—to distort or constrain demand. But some features of the public sector should be

[1] *On Liberty* (Everyman edition), p. 133.

250

noted lest academics too readily assume that the politicians will be more successful than the entrepreneurs at solving these problems for us. If possibilities of collective action are in question, we should not rest content with asking "What do people want—now and for themselves— and how badly do they want it?" (although that alone would often be an advance on current practice). We should ask "*Why* do they want what they want?" We should also ask hypothetical questions of the form "What *might* they want if they lived in a different world?" and more speculative questions such as "How should we change the world?"

These questions are successively less and less popular with the academics, who often regard them as falling outside their scope. But collective decision makers do not like them much either, because the answers and the action they imply can rarely be confined within the territory of one public service program or profession. To enable the more deprived children to realize higher educational aspirations, for example, may call for changes in the labor market, in industrial processes and the wage system, in the housing market, and in many other sectors of urban society besides the schools—changes made on a scale which is perceived to affect the position of whole classes in society. Even then we cannot be sure (Jencks would remind us) of any results. Likewise, many other things may have to be done before the people in a polluted neighborhood will give high priority to the reduction of pollution. But collective decision makers normally have to take a less synoptic view.[2] They usually have a law which empowers them to do specific things, a budget, a program, and a department staffed by people trained in particular skills. They want to run the "best" schools, or the "best" pollution control program. Thus, children who do not want to go to school and citizens who do not care about pollution are in three ways unwelcome to them: (1) they perform badly (they fail examinations and burn discarded linoleum in their back yards), (2) they do not contribute to public applause for the program (they may even vote against it), and (3) anyone seriously concerned with their needs is obliged to seek action from other branches of government or even to create new ones (which provokes discord in neighboring departments and professions that do not like being told how to manage their affairs, and which will, if successful, capture resources that might otherwise have gone to those who make such proposals). Thus a determined attempt to identify deprived "target groups" in the population and gain them whatever help

2 "Pluralist" political economists have long stressed and even applauded this aspect of democratic government. For an early and vivid example, see Lindblom (1959).

seems most fitting may not win promotion for its advocates—except, perhaps, to very distant places.

To preserve the rigor of their disciplines and the scientific authority of the counsel they offer, economists and other intellectually trained advisors may eschew such questions. If so, they must not comfort themselves with the thought that practicing administrators and politicians will deal with them instead, for they have even more pressing reasons for evading them.

The dilemma which concerns me can be summarized briefly. If we care about liberty, and are disposed to believe that other people's preferences, perceived from their own viewpoint, will generally be as rational as our own and much better informed, then how do we decide what collective action to take (and how do we preserve the legitimacy of government, and manage change without too destructive conflicts) in a world where people's preferences are the product of many influences, some of which can be changed by collective action itself? To rely on preferences *ex ante* is to adopt a relatively conservative stance. But preferences *ex post* cannot be forecast because they will depend partly on the collective action to be taken (and even when that has been decided, such forecasts are notoriously unreliable). Let us start by recalling the standard approaches to this problem.

2. Some Procedures for Assessing Preferences for Public Goods

When assessing the supply and demand for public goods, it is usually the demands, and the potential benefits of action, which present the most difficulty: the resources required for action, their opportunity costs, and the supply side in general are a little easier to handle. Thus I will concentrate on the demand side of the analysis and briefly list some of the main aproaches to the task of measuring and aggregating preferences in situations where ordinary market behavior cannot be observed. All of them, I believe, are valuable, but each is an attempt to answer different questions and none are foolproof or capable of furnishing complete and authoritative answers.

1. Ideally, most would agree, the task should be approached by looking for market behavior which is sufficiently comparable to the demands to be studied to throw light on the preferences motivating those demands. Most of the householders living in an area which is to be improved or exposed to the intrusion of a new motorway, for example, will not be in the market for housing; but the prices at which comparable houses in comparable neighborhoods change hands can provide relevant evidence about the value of their property and the impact which improvement or motorways may have on it.

Familiar problems arise. Householders actually in the market are at the margins where people are most responsive to the signals given by current prices. Their behavior provides inadequate evidence about the consumer surpluses and preferences of intramarginal households—the nonmovers who may claim that the right to stay undisturbed in their homes has an infinite value to them. Moreover, the supply and demand equated at current prices reflect the current level and distribution of incomes—a pattern which gives greater weight to the preferences of some people than to those of others. The greater preference that rich people have, for instance, to economize in travel time, at the expense of other things if need be, will be overweighted if their contribution to "effective" demand is read without correction as an indication of human needs or the preferences of the majority of citizens.

2. In situations where there is no comparable market to be observed (as in Britain's largely free National Health Service to which about 95 percent of the population turn for their medical care, or in the public housing of a city like Glasgow, where more than half the houses belong to the City Council), it may be possible to observe other relevant, "quasi-market," behavior, such as the queues which form for different kinds of medical service, or different kinds of Council housing, and the requests which patients and tenants make for transfers from one kind to another.

Although such behavior can provide useful evidence about preferences, it is subject to exactly the same limitations as the previous kind of evidence, and to a few more of its own. The volume and distribution of observed demand will be shaped to an unknown extent by administrative procedures, local folklore, and other influences unrelated to preferences. There is no point, the customers may believe, in applying for transfer to a particularly popular doctor or Council estate because "they never have any vacancies there." If no "reading" appears for some options, it may be hard to tell whether that means they are the most or the least preferred. Even if reliable evidence can be assembled, there is no common currency in which to compare preferences within different markets—no means of assessing, for example, whether people would prefer a better house to a better doctor, if the choice had to be made.

3. Faced with these complex problems, some people have fallen back on cruder rules of thumb: asking, for instance, about the choices made by those who have the maximum opportunities for choosing (the rich). They then try to bring others closer to this standard when opportunities arise. Applied with caution, this simple procedure might have forestalled a good deal of unnecessarily expensive social research (directed to such questions as whether municipal tenants prefer balcony or internal access to their apartments, and whether parents prefer their

children to be taught in large or small classes), but it has its dangers too: it will, for example, conceal the fact that preferences tend to be directed, not by individuals to one thing at a time, but by groups of people to a whole package of related goods, services, and conditions, among which the presence of other members of the group may be a crucial element. (They may care less about the design of the apartment block or the size of the class than about the other tenants or children who will be in it.)

4. Partly because they are aware of these problems, some researchers have tried to "get behind" specific preferences and identify the more general or "basic" attainments which people want to maximize, in the hope that these will provide a short-hand summary of a whole package of preferences in particular fields. Research has repeatedly shown, for example, that within the range of conditions found in countries like Britain, children in the smaller classes of a school are no more successful academically than those in the larger classes. (Indeed, for good but complicated reasons, the smaller classes are generally *less* successful.[3]) Thus it might be better and it would at least provide a useful cross-check on other evidence to measure educational *attainment*, which is presumably what the parents are seeking. Unfortunately this kind of attainment is peculiarly difficult to measure in any way which commands general assent.

5. It is time to turn from the option of "exit" to the option of "voice," to use Albert Hirschman's (1970) terms. We can give people a voice by asking them what they want. Survey researchers now use techniques of increasingly sophisticated kinds to reveal the intensity as well as the direction of preferences, and to make relevant comparisons among preferences—showing (for example) not only that people want privacy, traffic-free streets, and public open space, but also how much of each of these good things they believe they would sacrifice for ready access to work, shops, entertainment, and other good things. "Intensity" means little unless it can be expressed at least approximately in the form of relevant opportunity costs. Some useful games have been invented to simulate such options and to compare preferences in money terms.[4] These approaches have the advantage of stripping away the mask of an unequally distributed medium of exchange, focusing attention on people, and encouraging comparisons among the preferences of different kinds of person and household. But we cannot be sure how realistically they assess actual preferences, even when the respondents are discussing

---

[3] See Central Advisory Council for Education (England) (1967), paragraphs 781–784 for a clarification of this issue.

[4] See, for example, Berthoud and Jowell (1973).

familiar options, and the whole technique is as weak as those previously listed when it comes to assessing preferences for the unfamiliar and remote; that is, for nonmarginal changes.

6. Democratic government itself is the most ambitious attempt to assess and aggregate preferences. Unfortunately its institutions and their decision-making rules are often poorly adapted to the task. Anthony Downs (1957) and others have shown that the political marketplace will often select and distort demand signals as badly as the economic marketplace because (among other reasons) we all tend to specialize as producers and generalize as consumers, and it is exceedingly time-consuming to secure and maintain the up-to-date contextual knowledge required for effective participation in politics. Procedures for collective decision are costly, and the externalities of collective action may be negative as well as positive—governments, that is to say, may do things we do not like. The more threatening the potential externalities, the more costly the decision-making procedures required to protect us. Building on those observations, Buchanan and Tullock (1965) have shown that much could be done to improve the political process as an aggregator and communicator of demand signals, but that to perfect it would call for freer use of log-rolling, pork barrel legislation, and bribery—practices now generally disapproved or outlawed.

Although Buchanan and Tullock are more explicit than most writers, and far more enlightening, the proponents of all six of the approaches I have so briefly outlined generally assume that once individual preferences have been determined, aggregated, and communicated, the rest of the job can be left to decision makers: the academics at this stage hand over to (or become) politicians.

Any government which could get as far as Buchanan and Tullock suggest they should go, would have achieved great and liberating things. Critics who have dismissed this school of thought as if it were merely a form of conservative apologetics for the defense of the status quo can have little understanding of the ways in which governments—even reforming ones—normally work. Nevertheless, this approach leaves a lot of problems unsolved and it is to them I now turn.

3. The Formation and Meaning of Preferences

People's preferences and the distribution of life chances among the people concerned may appear to be entirely separate phenomena, but they are in fact closely linked. The meaning of the question "What do you want?", indeed, the meaning of any choice, depends on the situation of the person choosing and the scope of the options open to him, and hence on his position in various distributional hierarchies.

In Britain, repeated studies have shown that parents, even the least skilled and poorest of them, have high aspirations for the education of their children when those children are in primary school.[5] But they and their children, particularly among the least skilled and poorest families, tend to abandon these aspirations, and a large proportion of the youngsters leave school, unqualified, at the age of sixteen, although many of them have the ability to take their education much further. Later, many of the early school leavers regret their decision to give up so soon (Schools Council Enquiry, 1968). Teachers and "educationists" often assume that such decisions are based on ignorant, casually formed tastes which could be changed if education were (in effect) better advertised and more carefully matched to the customers' demands. But closer examination of the students' risks of failure, the job opportunities likely to be available, the pay offered for each, the economic and social costs of moving to other places for training and work, and so on, suggests that many of these youngsters are making perfectly rational decisions. Many other things must be changed before they can be expected to take their education much further.

Suppose (to take another example) a population consisting predominantly of rather ill-paid manual workers shows no enthusiasm for action which would reduce the air pollution caused by nearby factories where many of them work. Their preferences, too, may be attributed to ignorance (they do not know how serious or how dangerous to their health the pollution is), or to tastes arising from their limited experience (many of them work all day in environments far more polluted and unpleasant and they do not mind too much about the air they find when they get home). But, as in the case we have already considered, these preferences may be the product of rational calculation: people may with good reason fear that aggressive measures to reduce pollution will bankrupt their employers or drive them away, and that since they cannot afford to travel far each day, there will then be no equally good jobs within reach of their homes.

The recurring finding that the least skilled and the lowest paid people get less help from social services than more fortunate people,[6]

---

[5] For example, Central Advisory Council for Education (1967), vol. 2, appendix 3, p. 121.

[6] There are many sources of this kind of evidence. A brief one can be found in Donnison (1972) which shows that in a representative sample of 16,000 British children born in 1958, those whose parents held unskilled manual jobs were less likely than other children to be immunized or vaccinated, to attend clinics or visit the dentist, or to have had physiotherapy, and more likely to have parents

even from services designed particularly for them, can often be explained, I believe, in similarly rational ways. Some people are ignorant of their rights and some lack the taste for them: these are the conventional explanations of what is often described by social administrators as a "problem of non-take-up." But many potential users of these services calculate that it is not worth their while to use the nursery schools, to seek dental treatment, the protection which the Rent Acts can give them,[7] or the help of other services intended for them, and, considered from their own point of view, they may be right.

For the purposes of this paper, there is no point in arguing how often such rational calculations are made, provided it is accepted that they do occur from time to time. It then follows that analyses which look no further than the current, short-run preferences of the individual as the basic criteria for action must accept many of the social arrangements, the distributional patterns, and the general culture of the society concerned, for all these are built into the preferences which they have helped to form. This presents no problem in conventional economic analysis operating in contexts where the current structure of society is not in question. (A consultant advising a maker of widgets about the demand for his products and the optimal mix of factors for producing them is not expected to worry about all that: widget makers have to accept the social structure as "given.") But in analyses of the case for collective action of various kinds, whether the action be taken by governments or voluntary associations, the structure of society will repeatedly be in question. The case for collective action itself rests largely on the opportunities it may provide for changing things which must be accepted as "given" under a regime of purely individualistic behavior. Thus the advisors of collective decision makers are apt to find themselves telling their clients what kind of world they should create: the one which validates, and is validated by, present preferences, or a world which validates, and is validated by, new preferences. Most economists are aware of this problem—it is discussed in first-year teaching these days—but once it has been recognized, they tend to press on regardless.

4. An Alternative Strategy

The account which follows briefly summarizes a strategy for dealing with some of the innumerable questions which might be posed under the

who do not consult their teachers (all of them free services) and more likely to have homes which are overcrowded or ill-equipped with baths, etc. (p. 7).

[7] In a revealing little study in London, Michael Zander (1968) showed, not only that the poorer and more exploited kinds of tenants whom the Rent Acts were intended to protect knew little about their rights under this legislation, but that the great majority took no action when offered help in gaining these rights.

"quality of life" heading. I do not present it as a model for others to copy—its weaknesses are obvious—but for the purpose of this paper it has the merit of being a real and recent attempt to tackle the kinds of questions which concern us, and since it has been published in full elsewhere (National Economic and Social Council, 1975), I need only summarize the essential logic of the strategy without conveying the content of the document.

My Report on Social Policies was written for the National Economic and Social Council (NESC) of Ireland, a body appointed by the Irish government and similar in many ways to the British National Economic Development Council, but with more extensive responsibilities for social and regional planning. The NESC asked me for: (1) advice about the meaning and character of "social" policies, (2) a critical review of current Irish social policies, and (3) some preliminary recommendations about the action the NESC itself should take in this field. My clients readily agreed (for me these were essential features of the plan) that I should circulate a first draft of my report for comment and get it critically discussed at a day-long seminar of experts drawn from many quarters (including the trade unions, the universities, industry, agriculture, and the church, besides official and professional bodies concerned with social policies) and that a final report should be published over the author's name along with the NESC's recommendations.

In Ireland, where relevant data on these questions are even scarcer than in many other countries, the analyst at least has the advantage of dealing with a society which differs strikingly from its neighbors in various respects. (What *can* be said, can thus be said with greater confidence.) Table 1 presents a few social indicators for Ireland and other European Community countries. It suggests that the Irish eat better (or more?) than their neighbors and have had for fourteen years a faster increase in real wages. They also have more hospital beds. Other evidence, not given here, shows that in comparison with many neighboring countries, the Irish also have more plentiful housing space, but larger families, more unemployment, and fewer people in the working age groups, cleaner air and water, but more people living in sparsely populated areas, a more honest civil service and lower crime rates but, of late, a higher incidence of politically motivated violence. They have a trade union movement which is unusually militant in industrial matters (strikes are common and notoriously long), but the unions have played little part in formulating social policies. The two main political parties are coalitions based on alignments forged during the civil war which occurred shortly after the present state was founded: they do not represent the interests of distinctively different social classes. The third party,

Table 1. A Comparison of Some Social Indicators for the European Community Countries

Indicators	Ireland	Belgium	Germany	France	Italy	Luxem-bourg	Nether-lands	U.K.	Denmark
GNP in $ per capita, 1972	1,760	3,351	3,840	3,489	2,008	3,255[a]	3,193	2,641	3,889
Increases in wages and salaries (1958 = 100) 1972	215	191	215	197	244[a]	170[a]	211	163	n.a.[b]
Consumption in kg per unit of consumption, 1970–71									
Meat	83.6	82.7	87.2	96.0	57.3	n.a.	65.7	72.3	62.5
Eggs	13.3	12.8	16.3	12.6	10.9	n.a.	11.8	15.0	11.0
Butter	10.2	8.5	7.0	7.3	1.6	n.a.	2.2	18.5	7.5
Fresh milk (liters)	213	78	77	71	66	n.a.	107	140	113
Per 1,000 inhabitants, 1972									
Private cars	140	219	253	256	207	291	220	222	228
TV sets	164	216[c]	299	227	191	209[c]	243	298	277
Telephones	109	224	249	185	188	346	280	289	356
Per 100,000, 1970									
Doctors	102	154	163	133	180	106	119	127	145
Hospital beds	1,308	820	1,123	885[d]	1,055	1,174	526	974	881

Source: Report on the Development of the Social Situation in the Community in 1973, Brussels, 1974; pp. 211 and 228.
ᵃ Provisional.   ᵇ Not available.   ᶜ 1971.   ᵈ 1969.

the Labour Party, which is the only one that does claim to do so, has been very unsuccessful until recently. I turn now to the argument of my own report.

I had first to define the meaning and describe the character of "social" policies, and concluded after discussing this field that although they are usually described as the concern of particular departments of government, particular programs, or particular clients, it is more useful to regard social policies as being concerned with the distributional effects of all government actions—actions which include the provision of public services, subsidies and grants, the levying of taxes, the legal regulation and inspection of the citizens' property and activities, and the statements and behavior of governments which help to set the "tone" or shape the values of society. Thus there are social aspects to the work of *all* departments of government, and the questions of equity and conflicting preferences which might have been treated as qualifications or marginal complications of my main analysis are, on the contrary, the central problems to examine.

In the second section of my report I tried to show that: many of the problems to which social policies are supposed to be addressed are, in effect, the living conditions, needs, and behavior of the poorest people; the Republic (like its neighbors) is in many respects a grossly unequal society; government actions often exacerbate rather than remedy this situation; and Irish political parties, trade unions, church authorities, and other opinion leaders are now more publicly committed to achieving greater equality than they have been for many years past. This led to the conclusion that social policies should be increasingly organized for this purpose, particularly by raising the standards of the poorest. That, I pointed out, was a major value judgment based on empirical assumptions. (Emphasizing the distributional character of social policies does not necessarily lead to the conclusion that they should be designed to equalize, and equalization will not necessarily improve the living conditions of the poorest—all might grow more equal, *and* poorer, together.) The exposure of these assumptions to the widest possible criticism was one of the main purposes of the circulation of drafts and the discussion at the seminar already mentioned. If this phase of the argument had not been widely endorsed in these discussions, the rest of the project would have had to proceed differently.

Third, so far as inadequate data and understanding permitted, the main patterns of inequality in Ireland were analyzed and the overlapping social groups benefiting or suffering from each were identified. These patterns were: (1) a lifetime cycle of incomes producing, for all social classes, alternating periods of relative poverty and affluence during child-hood, early adulthood, early parenthood, middle age, and retirement; (2) inequalities due to the differing inheritances (material, cultural, and personal) and the differing bargaining strengths of the social classes in an urban, industrial, bureaucratic society; (3) "spatial" inequalities due to (a) interregional, (b) urban–rural, and (more doubtfully) (c) intraurban differences in living standards (Ireland, it must be remem-bered, is a sparsely populated economy on the periphery of Europe, heavily dependent on agriculture, and suffering the aftermath of 130 years of massive emigration); and (4) the effects of discrimination against particular groups, of which the most numerous current victims are women, and the most severely deprived are itinerants (tinkers or gypsies). These are not four distinct patterns: they are overlapping influences. Those suffering from the most severe deprivations or en-joying the greatest affluence are those who suffer, or enjoy, the com-bined effects of several of these patterns of inequality. To form a clearer judgment about their relative importance, it would in future be necessary not only to compare the severity of each, but also to make similar comparisons with these patterns in other European Community countries.

Fourth, with data even more inadequate to the task, an attempt was made to identify the main actions of government bearing deliberately or accidentally upon these inequalities, leading to the conclusions that policies for the elimination of each pattern of inequality will: often have positive-sum effects in time; but because their costs tend to come sooner than their benefits, the initial balance is likely to be zero-sum at best; and these policies will frequently tend to conflict with each other. Thus, to take one of many examples: more equal opportunities for women in the labor market will tend, if no other action is taken, to exacerbate inequalities that are caused by the lifetime cycle of incomes (for benefits will go to households at the peaks of the cycle), inequalities resulting from the class system (because the best-qualified women are likely to gain most), and inequalities resulting from inter-regional and urban–rural disparities in living standards (because benefits will be concentrated mainly in industrialized, urban areas).[8] The essen-tial point made at this stage of the argument was that to advocate equality, unqualified, is to pose questions, not to answer them. There are different patterns of inequality which vary in intensity in different coun-tries and at different stages of economic development, and the policies which ameliorate one may exacerbate others.

[8] For an excellent analysis of some of these questions, See Commission on the Status of Women (1972).

Fifth, by examining the history and prospects of the Republic, an attempt was made to estimate ("guess" may be more appropriate) which kinds of inequality are currently most severe (in relation to each other and to the patterns of other countries) and how these patterns are likely to change in future. This led to various tentative conclusions, of which the most important were that patterns (1) and (3)—the lifetime cycle of incomes and the effects of interregional and urban–rural differences—have long been specially severe in the Republic and deserve high priority for some time to come, but that the country's growing pace of economic development means that pattern (2)—the effects of social stratification in urban, industrial, bureaucratic societies—will in time become the dominant one and demand increasing attention. Meanwhile pattern (4)—the problems of discrimination—should be tackled in ways which do not exacerbate other patterns of inequality, and which help to build constitutional arrangements that make it easier to identify and remedy new forms of discrimination which constantly tend to arise (and might well arise, for example, if large numbers of Irishmen resident in Ulster or in Britain were driven by political violence to seek refuge in the Republic). The major, and crippling, omission at this stage of the analysis was the lack of data (within the time available) for any systematic comparisons of the costs (in real resources and in transfers) of programs likely to ameliorate different patterns of inequality.

Sixth, decision-making procedures, and public knowledge and attitudes were briefly examined. Among the most important conclusions reached from this phase of the discussion were: (1) the need for better, regularly published and critically interpreted information about living conditions, patterns of inequality, the resources devoted to the principal social policies and their distributional effects; (2) the obligation of political leadership to start from current public opinion (which in the Republic is much more sympathetic, for example, to elderly farmers in remote areas than to unemployed men in cities) *and* to educate and develop that opinion in ways which will create an evolving consensus more closely attuned to reality and to the vision which leaders have of their country's future; and (3) the need to find ways of giving the more vulnerable clients of specific social policies a voice in the development of these policies, stressing the importance of ensuring that innovations in policy are actually welcomed by those whom they are supposed to benefit as well as by staff of the services concerned.

Seventh, and finally, it was a matter of principle, already espoused by my clients, that supposedly expert argument and advice about these matters should be published as widely as possible (with help from the mass media) and exposed to the critical attention of all.

5. Conclusions

The conclusions to be drawn from this paper are not very exciting, but that is apt to be the outcome of pragmatic attempts to walk down the middle of a political road. They can be summarized in nine points.

1. Economists (like other scholars and scientists) can only provide rigorously authoritative solutions to problems defined in a restricted and precisely specified fashion. Such specifications are likely to include an assumption or instruction that any individual preferences which are to furnish criteria for action should be the current, short-term responses of people whose aspirations may already have been confined to a restricted selection of those which could potentially be open to them in the longer term. In some cases the rigor attainable from precise speci- fications of this sort will be well worth any restrictions such a strategy imposes. (People's willingness to express such preferences in money terms makes it easier, for example, to compare the intensity of preferences for different goods.) But when larger issues are at stake, the economist who confines himself to problems and criteria of this sort will repeatedly find that he has come on the scene at the end of a story, as it were, at a point which affords him less choice about the outcomes than he and his clients might otherwise have had.

2. In such cases it will often be more helpful to decision makers, and bring to bear the deeper understanding of society which a well-trained mind will have acquired, if the economist secures broader terms of reference, treats his clients' formulation of the problem seriously, but refuses to confine his thought only to that formulation: the power holders' perceptions of their problems are not the only ones worth examining. Economists adopting these wider terms of reference should be as concerned as ever about current preferences, but prepared also to consider what people might want in future circumstances which collec- tive action could bring into being. That calls for speculative thought and judgment, which means the economist can no longer rely on his scientific authority. Hence he must adhere, not less, but more carefully to the conventional scholarly virtues (laying bare his sources, data, and methods, clarifying the confidence limits of his assertions, and generally enabling his readers to check whether they would rely on the same evidence or reach the same conclusions from it).

When he engages in controversy, the analyst will dispute sometimes on empirical grounds ("you've got your facts wrong"), sometimes on analytical grounds ("you're being inconsistent"), and occasionally in hortatory style ("you ought to be ashamed of yourself"). Scientific rigor consists, not in avoiding all exhortation, but in distinguishing clearly between these different kinds of argument, and using them in appro- priate ways. To exclude moral valuations on the ground that scholars should divorce reason from passion does not necessarily make people dispassionately rational. It may, on the contrary, make them irrationally passionate.

3. The analyst's task is first to learn, and then to teach others, about the problems he is working on—their character and causes, and the potential priorities for action. He must study people's preferences carefully because they tell him a great deal about the meaning and intensity of the problems to be dealt with and the impulsions and constraints to which politicians are likely to be exposed. But current preferences alone cannot be his guide.

Before he discusses action, the analyst will do well to identify the people or groups most urgently in need of help. That may call for preliminary consideration of various options for action and an approximate comparison of the resources each may require. It will certainly demand a frank explanation of the essentially moral and political character of the choices to be made. (In my Irish example, extensive and critical discussion of different patterns of deprivation in the light of the stage of social and economic development this country had attained was an essential part of the inquiry.) The purpose of this phase of the work is to formulate, and help others formulate, clearer ideas about social priorities *expressed in terms of target groups rather than programs.*

4. If the first phase is handled well, the main options for action will often flow naturally from it without any need for exhortation. At this stage the analyst is trying to envisage a program—possibly several alternative programs—of mutually consistent actions which will create or sustain patterns of social development which benefit particular groups. No one can pursue that sort of prognostication far with much confidence —there are too many unpredictable or imponderable factors to be considered—but the analyst should not lose sight of the fact that he is trying to imagine, and help people realize, feasible new worlds. It is important to focus attention on the groups to be helped and the reasons for choosing them before discussing in any detail the action to be taken. If anything important is expected to happen, there will be powerful "program" interests waiting in the wings—ministers, committees, departments, public service professions and their client groups among the public—each anxious to capture the issue as "their" problem, suitable for treatment at the taxpayers' expense. Meanwhile, interests which fear the issue may be captured by other branches of government, and their clients will be unenthusiastic or outright hostile about proposals for action. It will be easier to keep these natural tendencies under control and to tackle the issue rationally if decision makers and the public at large focus first on the people to be helped and the human

needs at stake, and if all concerned are reminded about these realities from time to time thereafter.

5. In such cases, decision makers and the electorates to which they are accountable are being asked to consider and select scenarios, or sequences of consistent actions, which will ultimately satisfy the large groups of people exposed to them. The evolving general pattern of opportunities, attainments, and living conditions among the "target" groups chosen for attention will often be a more important guide to action than the current preferences of these people. No good will be done (Buchanan and Tullock are right about this) by calling the analyst's chosen priorities "the *public* interest." That is usually a fraudulent attempt to claim authoritative rectitude for one of several potential courses of action—an attempt which conceals the essentially moral choice that has to be made.

But although current preferences of the majority often cannot be the only, or even the main, criterion for action in situations of this kind, the preferences of the target groups expected to benefit from the action should certainly be a constraint on policy makers. If the groups which are supposed to benefit from the policies chosen are consistently hostile to them, that is a warning that decision makers and their advisors have probably misunderstood the circumstances of the people they wanted to help.

If this kind of strategy threatens to take a long time and to call for the collaboration of many different departments of government, that is what the social problems of an urban society are apt to be like: it would show, I have argued, little understanding of history, sociology, or "urban" studies to expect otherwise.

6. Priorities for collective action will change over time, not only as political fashions come and go, but because evolving demographic, economic, and social trends exacerbate some problems and ameliorate others. The advisor of governments should try to place his analysis in an historical context which helps decision makers foresee some of the issues which are likely to grow more important before long, and thus prepare the way for future policies when opportunities arise (or at least avoid placing too many obstructions in their path).

7. In a democracy it is the government's job to keep in touch with public opinion and not to move too far ahead of it, no matter how worthy the cause. Thus, it is also their job to envisage and advocate happier futures in which present conflicts may be resolved, and the nation's arrangements will be fairer and more consistent with changing social realities. Analysts and advisors have a special responsibility to contribute to the general program of public education which all this implies by ensuring that the country's social and economic structure is

better understood, that the attainments, living conditions, and resources of its main social groups are monitored year by year and compared with each other and with similar data for countries at comparable stages of development, and that the allocation of resources to programs benefiting different groups and the costs of new proposals for action are more widely known. Advisors who communicate only with governments and never with a wider public are not doing the job for which they were trained (largely at public expense).

8. I close with two more general comments on the approach adopted in this paper. In my Irish example, and in the wording of these conclusions, the "economist," "analyst," or "advisor" is described as working through "government," "decision makers," or "power holders" (although he is not confined to their definition of the problem or to communicating only with them). The assumption implied is that progress can often be made in this way. But this rational-liberal strategy is not necessarily the most effective way of bringing about changes; neither are governments necessarily the most effective institutions to work through. In all countries there will be some issues which can be more effectively dealt with through pressure and conflict rather than rational analysis. Meanwhile, there may be issues on which action (political or analytical) is best originated outside government. In some countries, moreover, government may be an inappropriate institution for *any* analyst of integrity to work through. The first and inescapable value judgments every analyst has to make before he can start are about which issues to work on and which institutions to work through.

9. Running through my Irish example and much else in this paper is an egalitarian bias characteristic of what a recent American Vice President described as "the Radical-Liberal Establishment." I tried to make it clear to my Irish clients, and again in the report they published, that this preference is a value judgment which can be fruitfully argued about (indeed, it would do the "Rad-Libs" good if it was more often argued about) but which ultimately remains a matter of personal choice. I explained, too, that it is not as simple a bias as might at first appear: there are so many different problems of equity in a complex urban society that to call for more "equality," *tout court*, amounts to little more than a general appeal for thought about interpersonal comparisons and social justice.

Of all people, however, economists should recognize that an egalitarian bias is much more than a personal taste. It is a value judgment which was built into their discipline from the start by those who insisted that the criteria for collective action must be the action's consequences for individuals as perceived by those individuals themselves. When in doubt about the competing utilities of different individuals, we must try, said John Stuart Mill, to follow Bentham's dictum, "everybody to count for one, and nobody for more than one." Utilitarianism, he said, "is a mere form of words without rational signification, unless one person's happiness . . . is counted for exactly as much as another's."[9]

It would not have occurred to Mill that there could, or should, be "nothing moral or ethical about an analytical assumption."[10] If some economists choose to espouse the utilitarians' individualism and turn it into the first principle of their analytical technique while simultaneously draining it of any practical, human content (so that while each individual must be regarded as equal "methodologically," no implication follows for the incomes, housing, status, and life chances of real people), then they have emasculated their discipline and their own intellects.

References

Berthoud, Richard, and Roger Jowell. 1973. "Creating a Community: A Study of Runcorn New Town," *Social and Community Planning Research* (December).

Buchanan, James M., and Gordon Tullock. 1965. *The Calculus of Consent. Logical Foundations of Constitutional Democracy* (Ann Arbor, Mich., University of Michigan Press).

Central Advisory Council for Education (England). 1967. *Children and their Primary Schools* (London, Her Majesty's Stationery Office).

Commission on the Status of Women. 1972. *Report to the Minister of Finance.* Prl. 2760 (Dublin, Stationery Office).

Donnison, David, ed. 1972. *A Pattern of Disadvantage* (London, National Foundation for Educational Research).

Downs, Anthony. 1957. *An Economic Theory of Democracy* (New York, Harper & Row).

Hirschman, Albert O. 1970. *Exit, Voice and Loyalty* (Cambridge, Mass., Harvard University Press).

Lindblom, Charles E. 1959. "The Science of Muddling Through," *Public Administration Review* vol. 19, pp. 79–88.

National Economic and Social Council. 1975. *An Approach to Social Policy.* Prl. 4438 (Dublin, Stationery Office).

Schools Council Enquiry. 1968. *Young School Leavers* (London, Her Majesty's Stationery Office).

Zander, Michael. 1968. "The Unused Rent Acts," *New Society* (September 12).

[9] *On Liberty*, p. 68.
[10] *The Calculus of Consent*, p. 266.

13
Toward a New Civic Calculus

EDWIN T. HAEFELE

1. Introduction

EVERY so often in Anglo-American history, the question of "who decides" has been resoundingly answered by citizens who say "we do!" During the 1960s this cry was heard again in the United States. Reacting against bureaucratic indifference, corporate arrogance, and legislative irresponsibility, citizen groups were formed to stop freeways, dams, subdivisions, and unsafe toys. In California, citizens used a ballot initiative to force upon their reluctant legislature a coastal zoning measure designed to protect the coast, from border to border, from unrestricted private development. In Oregon the referendum was used to enact, over frantic industry lobbying, a ban on nonreturnable bottles. In New Hampshire the citizens of one town voted in special referendum to refuse an oil refinery a site within their town. A few miles away, another set of citizens voted 2 to 1 to allow an oil refinery site in their town.

Bracing as such examples of the voice of the people may be, we still must ask: "Who designs the questions we are to vote upon?" "How do we know when to vote?" and "What is the relation of what we act on today to what will come tomorrow?" In considering these questions, we should remember James Madison's reflection in Federalist paper no. 55. "Had every Athenian citizen been a Socrates, every Athenian assembly would still have been a mob." Certainly, the failure of the Interregnum in England and of our own instructed delegates under the Articles of Confederation should cast a long shadow over the apparent simplicities of direct citizen decisions on an issue-by-issue basis.

Nevertheless, present U.S. law requires that maximum citizens participation be allowed, indeed *generated*, at every stage of proposed federal expenditures. The result of such laws has been, undoubtedly, to open up the decision process to a larger and more diverse set of interests. There are many examples of good that has resulted from such a process. But, when everyone has a lever, or a veto power, governments can become transfixed with equal pressure from all sides.

268

The bureaucrat assumes all these pressures are merely advisory, and that when all voices have been heard, he may choose a course of action. However, in the United States, the system is not working like this and it will not work like this in the future. The question of who decides has been asked in earnest and will not be answered either by a return to technocratic rule or by submission to a new interest group that purports to represent the public. This is because we live under a system of government that has imbedded in it processes designed to stop action when no consensus is present. And at present we have no consensus, nor can economic reasoning, legal precedent, or the processes of citizen participation substitute for it in our system.

It should be clear that present structures of local and state decision making might suffice, that is, that solutions might be arrived at through our present processes of argument, were it not that the boundaries of our problems and our powers are so porous. Financial interests can range over the entire nation (and indeed farther), changing preferences and upsetting any equilibrium. The nation, speaking through a federal law, can decree that a certain river is a "national resource"; that a certain harbor has national importance. A state government can decide to build a major recreational facility near a locality, totally changing its future development. Likewise, both industry and government can close facilities or disinvest, or both, creating local havoc by changing the economic base on which most local decisions, public and private, had been calculated. Interdependence is more than a word, both for economic health and for choices affecting the quality of life. Any new civic calculus must be designed to cope with interdependence as well as with the claims of economics, the law, and citizen participation.

Rules for Choice

It is inevitable that we begin, in any Anglo-American context, with individual preferences and their aggregation. Economists have, with trivial exceptions, always taken preferences as given and concentrated on the aggregation problem. Politicians have, with trivial exceptions, always taken preference formation (political leadership is their name for it) as the essence of the problem and accepted the aggregation rules as given. The new civic calculus must deal with both preference formation and aggregation.

Economists who theorize about social choice generally assume a given agenda and focus on the rules necessary to choose within it. Politicians generally assume a given set of rules for choice and focus on devising an agenda which, when operated on by that set of rules, will give the result they seek. These distinctions, deliberately overdrawn for emphasis, are crucial. The inability to understand them, or to make the understanding explicit, is responsible for real confusion and even, at times, the unwillingness of each party to take the others' insights seriously.

The economists' concern with the rules for choice was shared by politicians of the seventeenth century both in England and in the American colonies. On both sides of the Atlantic such men were intoxicated by the vision of a perfected constitution—a set of rules by which men could govern themselves and make social choices. The history of the unfolding of that vision is, it must be stressed, a history that started at the top of society and moved down. Thus, what the barons won at Runnymede, the gentry won at Marston Moor and Naseby. What ordinary folk were denied at Putney, they later won at Yorktown.

The construction of the perfected U.S. constitution has never been, therefore, an overturning of society in the French or Russian tradition, but rather the gradual (though often bloody) broadening of a set of liberties of choice to encompass more and more classes of people. Preference aggregation has never been, and is not now, the total social choice mechanism, but only a part.

Preference aggregation was provided for in two areas: (1) the election of representatives (mayors, city councilmen, governors, legislators, and presidents) and (2) the passing of laws by legislative bodies using simple or extraordinary majorities. The latter system was used, along with a provision for requiring majority vote by two different bodies (concurrent majorities by representatives of different constituencies) or by the same body at two different times to ensure an enduring consensus on matters of great moment.

2. Elements of a New Civic Calculus: The Representation of Place

Equal voting power for each citizen in the selection of representatives, and equal numbers of citizens for each representative is a recent development on both sides of the Atlantic. Before the great electoral reform in England, some citizens, for example, those in universities or who dwelt in the Cinque Ports, had greater representation in Commons. Before *Baker* v. *Carr* and its aftermath in the United States, some citizens, for example, those in less populated rural areas or towns, had greater representation in state legislatures, particularly in state senates.

This fact is recalled to emphasize that such overrepresentation sometimes, not always, had a point. In an earlier time, the towns making up the Cinque Ports, facing the English Channel, would bear the brunt of an invasion from the Continent. It was a simple act of statecraft to give their voices more weight than their numbers would otherwise warrant. In the United States, at a time when our cities were composed overwhelmingly of still unassimilated immigrants, it was an act of prudence to weigh the earlier immigrants' preferences more heavily.

A more subtle, and for our purposes, more important inequality also existed traditionally in England and the United States. It was the historic rule in both that fictive persons, that is, municipal corporations and boroughs, could be considered equal for purposes of representation because they were, and still are, equal in legal terms. In many state senates, each town, no matter how small, was entitled to a seat simply because it was a town. With the coming of one-man, one-vote representation in the United States, it is unusual for any *town* to be represented in a legislative body. Instead, districts of equal population are devised, most often covering a part of a town or a part of one town and a part of another. Moreover, with every census the district shifts and a different set of individuals, and a different geographical area, is represented. In such a case, which is the rule rather than the exception, the question, "Who speaks for this place?" must be answered: "Nobody."

In our pursuit of equality, we have totally disconnected local governmental power, which must be exercised through one or another municipality (a corporate entity that can enact ordinances through a social choice mechanism), from power at the state level, that is, the state legislature. An electoral district, no matter how perfect its equality with other electoral districts, has *no* mechanism for legislating within its borders. It has, in fact, no legal existence at all beyond its selection of a representative at the next higher level of government. Congressional districts likewise have only an electoral function. Neither district has any governmental or corporate existence. No one, least of all the elected representative, has any governmental powers within its borders.

All this is, of course, well known. What has not been recognized is that a traditional and heretofore useful part of the social choice mechanism has been dismantled and nothing put in its place. I am not saying that the dismantling was inadvertent; those who advocated a majority composed of citizens did so because they did not like the policies enacted by a majority composed of towns.

It is, however, a dangerous business to change social choice rules to produce certain outcomes. Some of those who decried rural domination of their legislatures now are trying to reestablish some kind of local option to keep from being overwhelmed by the voting power of a majority elsewhere who wish to push problems away from them. If such majority decisions did not have crucial "place" consequences, that is, consequences crucial for the quality of life in particular places *where the majority does not live,* then no one would question the right of the majority to make them. But, since these decisions *can* adversely affect the quality of life in particular places, it is not so clear that the simplistic one-man, one-vote doctrine of the courts is sufficient.

In the new civic calculus, corporate *places* as well as people would be represented, either by allowing the corporate collectivities to sit as equals in one house of the legislature or by allowing each such collectivity a veto power over actions taken by others that primarily affect it and only it.

Place should also be represented when decisions to invest or disinvest are made by corporate or governmental bodies. It may have been the case, in Lord Bryce's time, when one could propose with justice as he did, that local governments which make stupid decisions should be allowed to suffer for them. Nowadays most local governments are no match, legally or technically, for private industry or higher level government bureaucrats who choose a particular place to bestow or withdraw their favors.

No one could argue, however, that every local government should have a veto power over economic activity or higher level government action. What is required, as a part of a new civic calculus, is that such actions be contractually made with the locality, for precise dates and times, and that withdrawal or changes be penalized to the extent that social costs must be borne by the citizenry affected. For example, a town may have an overexpanded school infrastructure as a result of military expansion and then sudden withdrawal. The local citizens, with a reduced tax base, bear the total burden of retiring the debt on that infrastructure. Any correct civic calculus would have levied *both* the capital and operating costs of the expansion on the federal government as a part of the initial contract. Calculating those costs in advance would have given the military a needed dimension in comparing the cost of locating at one site rather than another. Such calculations should become routine for all public and private investments of any consequence.

Before leaving this discussion of the representation of place, it is important that two caveats be offered. First, if municipal corporate entities are to receive enhanced powers, then some attention must be given to minimum size. In the particulars of each case, this will be complicated, but the principle is clear. Enclaves of privilege that are economically dependent on neighboring activity will not hold up against the legal strictures of equal protection of the law. I am not advocating the Balkanization of the countryside or the breaking up of traditional cities that remain economic units.

Second, if municipal corporations are to be given enhanced powers, then boundary conditions to deal with inevitable externalities must be imposed. If one New Hampshire town accepts a refinery that its neighbor did not want, then we must ensure that the second action does not negate the first. This can be accomplished by establishing boundary conditions such that no municipality can export, or discharge from its boundaries, lower quality (more degraded) air or water than it receives from outside its own boundaries. States could be covered by similar boundary conditions. Exceptions could, of course, be contractually negotiated among municipalities or states. Other kinds of degradation, such as traffic congestion, could be included once the question of minimum size had been dealt with. (The domino effect would also need specific handling in the initial setting-up period.)

3. Elements of a New Civic Calculus: Preference Aggregation by Representative Bodies

If municipalities and states are to perform in this manner, and if preference aggregation is taken to be the normative basis of collective action, then changes will have to be made in legislative bodies to enable them to function as preference aggregation mechanisms. Two matters are at issue: (1) the rules of legislative process; and (2) the information by which legislative preferences are informed. Each must, unfortunately, be discussed at some length.

Legislatures have been so long among us, and their appalling weaknesses so long apparent, that we mostly neglect to remember their strengths and their subtleties as preference aggregation devices. Their history and procedures contain most of our as-yet unrecorded knowledge about social choice. Measured against that knowledge, our formal theory of social choice, beginning with Duncan Black (1963) in England and Kenneth Arrow in the United States, is still in an early stage of development. Modern theory has concerned itself almost exclusively with the problem of choosing among or ordering a set of mutually exclusive alternatives (social states or candidates). From this concern came Arrow's (1951) famous possibility theorem, a generalization of Condorcet's paradox of voting in which it is possible that no majority winner emerges from pairwise choices over three alternatives, given certain preference orderings by each of the voters. The paradox and the theorem have been widely misinterpreted as "proving" the impossibility of democratic preference aggregation.

The root of the problem can be traced, I believe, to the almost exclusive focus on social states and to an inadequate examination of what is contained in a social state, which we may define as a bundle of policies in effect at one time. For example, the sum total of federal, state, and local laws in force at one time can be thought of as one social state. In every social state there must exist a set of policies and within each policy, a set of elements. The set of policies resulting from a congressional session, for example, all laws that were passed by the first session of the 91st Congress, could be considered as having moved us from one social state (what we had before the 91st Congress) to another social state (what we have after the 91st Congress's first session). Each set of policy elements will be composed of two subelements: a preference about the substance of the policy chosen and a preference about the amount of money that should be spent in pursuit of this policy.

While the social states are mutually exclusive (only one can exist in any one time period), the various policies are independent and so can be combined and/or traded off or compromised. This is also true for the elements within the policy and for the subelement that is the preference for the substance of the policy chosen. However, the preferences about the money spent in pursuit of the policy are mutually exclusive, that is, one amount of money must be decided upon. See appendix A for a symbolic representation of this procedure.

In Jefferson's day, only friends of a bill were appointed to the committee charged with drafting it. In the new civic calculus, standing committees charged with functional areas of responsibility would be abolished and replaced by special committees appointed from among those "friendly" to each bill before the house. Following Jefferson, "the bill now being as perfect as its friends can make it, this is the proper stage for those fundamentally opposed to make their first attack."

Two lines of attack are possible when the bill is reported back. If the coalition building has been unsuccessful, that is, no majority has been achieved, bill A can simply be called to a vote and rejected. If, as is more likely, a majority has been attracted, then bills B, C, D, and so on come into play as rivals for passage. The rivalry can be caused by a budget constraint that makes all bills rivals for a limited sum of money, or it may be that some supporters of bill A may be willing to trade off their support of A in order to ensure the passage of B, which they favor more strongly. The preference intensity calculus is shown symbolically in appendix B.

There remains the case of the noncooperative legislature in which three groups confront each other, causing an impasse either at the bill formation stage or at the policy (bill) passage stage. As Walter Bagehot (1905) observed nearly 100 years ago, about the House of Commons, "If everybody does what he thinks right, there will be 657 amendments to every motion, and none of them will carry or the motion either."

The English have already achieved the solution for this case: dissolve and have a new election. In the new civic calculus, dissolution of legislative bodies should be provided for either by a confidence vote in the body itself or by recall provisions initiated by the electorate affected. In early America, all legislative bodies were elected for short periods. The practice has something to recommend it for towns undergoing much stress.

4. Information and Preference Aggregation

If we expect to use preferences as the lodestar of our decisions, we must do something about two situations that can only be described as desperate. The first involves preference formation and the second relates to foreseeing the consequences, in particular the distributional consequences, of alternative courses of action.

James Coleman (1974) has recently traced the growth of the power of that other fictive person—the private corporation—in relation to the individual, and alluded to the impact of this new power on preferences. Corporations have preferences and means to promote them far beyond those available to individuals, acting singly or through special interest groups. Corporations are undying, single-minded, and can use your money and mine to instruct us in our civic duties and views. A recent example is the attempt to correct our opinions about the energy crisis; we have been told by newspaper and television ads how the energy industry has not been at fault in energy use and conservation, and how almost every one else, including governments, has been.

The power of modern corporations to set the public agenda, to generate options, and to control information on which preferences must be based, has grown so much that we must look back to the medieval power of the Roman church to find an historical analogue. It is no use pretending otherwise: the contest between highly paid full-time narrow corporate interests and unpaid, part-time broad individual interests is unfair and growing daily more so. Whether in legislative actions, electoral competition, or legal battles, the scales are badly tilted against the personal preferences we take as primary. Any new civic calculus must take care to redress the balance in favor of personal over corporate preferences.

I hope not to be misunderstood on the point. I argue no conspiracy theory of wicked capitalists plotting against the people, but only the inevitability of interested parties acting in their self-interest. If some gain inordinate power, their actions begin to be a threat to the body politic. It should be remembered in this connection that not long ago in every community the industrialist could be introduced, amid wide acclaim, as *the* public benefactor. This was the same period in which the universal symbol for urban well-being was a skyline of smoking chimneys. The smoke has vanished from the symbol now, and the acclaim no longer surrounds the industrialist. We have not learned how to reflect that shift in our public processes of choice, although a start has been made in controls on advertising, public funding of political campaigns, consumer advocacy, and similar developments. Using governmental power to counter corporate power has its own dangers, however. We may find ourselves ground between two giant bureaucracies, one private, the other public. One of the roads to 1984 starts on that battleground.

In an earlier era, that of the robber barons in the United States, the weapon of citizen referendum was used to slow the debasement of the public fisc by private companies in league with venal politicians. It may be that a new civic calculus must again turn to that crude instrument to guard against corporate actions that despoil for profit. Perhaps more sophisticated devices can be invented. One such device, desperately needed, is the ability to foresee consequences of alternative actions. If consequences, particularly distributional consequences, can be foreseen in advance, and publicized in advance, much of the corporate hold on information can be broken.

At Resources for the Future we have been developing more sophisticated techniques for generating regional economic and environmental management information. A number of technical papers have appeared which detail our approach.[1] I shall not, therefore, rehearse these papers, but will simply put that effort into the context of a new civic calculus. It is, in my judgment, the linchpin of such a calculus.

The effort involves combining economic optimization models with models of environmental consequences (showing resulting ambient conditions, geographic area by geographic area) and making the results of both available for use by legislative bodies made up of representatives of the area affected. This last link comes through a vote-trading mechanism which, when supplied with the individual legislators' ordinal preference vectors, shows each legislator what he may achieve environmentally and what it will cost (in taxes, unemployment, and higher user charges). The mechanism shows what coalitions can be formed through

[1] For an overview, see Russell, Spofford, and Haefele (1974).

vote trading, consistent with given preferences, and thus whether any "solution" exists. By a solution we mean whether or not the preferences of legislators can be met. If so, can they *all* be met? If not, which preferences can be met, and on what issues? Sometimes no "solution" exists, that is, the preferences of some legislators are either inconsistent or are technically impossible to achieve.

The procedure used is an iterative one, that is, the optimization models are solved, the results shown to the legislators, their reactions impose new constraints, and the models are solved again. This process is repeated until the socially preferred solution is reached, that is, the solution that is preferred to any other by the choice rule in effect. Various choice rules, such as simple majority vote or a constraint such that no area falls below minimum conditions, can be exogenously imposed. The combined models are, therefore, not simply black boxes that grind out "the answer," but are tools that can be used by elected officials to assess the consequences of particular courses of action.

We have applied the models to a large, complex, industrial area (the Delaware Valley from Trenton to the Bay) having steel mills, oil refineries, petrochemical, and paper industries. The results of that application made us confident that it is technically and financially feasible for regions to use this model. I consider such models, suitably altered to fit particular circumstances, a major component of any new civic calculus.

5. Conclusions

I have fallen far short of constructing, in all particulars, a new civic calculus. However, let me suggest some applications of the new calculus that I have suggested.

First, present decision structures composed of planning boards, zoning boards, sewer districts, city councils at the local level, and a multitude of state agencies, including coastal resources boards and economic development corporations in addition to the state legislature, would be replaced for policy purposes by two bodies—a local council and a state legislature. No other board or agency would be empowered to make decisions.

This would have one "bad" effect. It would focus all attention and political pressures on elected representatives who would have to choose and be seen to be choosing. (No politician could imagine a worse fate!)

Second, each council, state and local, would have procedural rules designed to perform the complete accounting of all member preferences and intensities of preference.

Third, each council would be subject to dissolution or recall when an impasse occurred.

Fourth, one house of the state legislature would be composed of representatives of towns (which is, of course, an element in a very old civic calculus).

Fifth, a town would have the right to contract with, or refuse to contract with, private industry or other governments. An element of such contracts would be the calculation of social costs likely to be borne by the town through initiation or withdrawal of activity.

Sixth, all towns in the state would have boundary conditions imposed on them to ensure attention to externalities.

Seventh, the citizens of the town and the state would have certain referendum rights concerning any proposal of such scale or consequence as to have irreversible effects on land use, air or water quality, or life style.

Eighth, both local and state councils would have available to them economic and environmental tools to assess the distributional consequences of alternative proposals. The results of such assessments would be public knowledge. (The application of these tools would, no doubt, provide employment for all bureaucrats I have so far thrown out of work.)

In general, the changes I propose would greatly simplify a decision process that has grown Byzantine in its complexity over the years. The complexity favors politicians, bureaucrats, and special interest groups who can afford to master its mysteries. The complexity acts as a barrier to public understanding, accountability, and preference aggregation.

As citizen conflicts mount in an attempt to impose a certain quality of life on particular places, some such calculus of decision making will, perforce, be imposed. That calculus should be worthy of a free people, a people possessed of all the tools of self-government, including that of individual protection against majority tyranny. Those tools must be mastered, however, by the living generation and freed from the thoughtless incrustations we have allowed to accumulate on them during the past several decades.

What it comes down to is this: choices made by citizens collectively determine the quality of life all have to endure or enjoy. Collective choices can never be left to an automatic process, be it an economic, legal, or simple one man-one vote process. Self-government was not given to us as an *easy* answer; it was proposed as the *only* answer.

Appendix A

In a legislative setting the following possibilities are present:

(1) $\left.\begin{cases} a_i \cup a_j \\ a_i \cap a_j \\ a_i \odot a_j \end{cases}\right.$ $\quad\quad\quad \forall\ a \in A$ $= a_i \bigcirc a_j$, where $\bigcirc$ is the operator signifying $\cup$, $\cap$, or $\odot$, and $\odot$ indicates some mutual accommodation other than $\cup$ or $\cap$.

$$\left.\begin{array}{l} i = 1 \text{ to } n \\ j = 1 \text{ to } n \\ i \neq j \end{array}\right\} \text{where } n \text{ is the number of legislators}$$

The union of a_i and a_j indicates a log-roll (you support my preference and I'll support yours); the intersection of a_i and a_j means we have agreed to support a bill A combining the common element of our preferences, while $\odot$ represents the situation in which both of us have agreed to change our original positions to support a transformed A differing from a_i or a_j, considered separately or jointly.

All three operations can and do go on routinely in legislative bodies. The notational conceit is simply to make clear the logical distinctions of each operation.

The operations $\{a_i \bigcirc a_j\}$ represent coalition formation over A and will continue so long as the gains to be made by the addition of new members of the coalition outweigh the losses felt by the initial members as the resulting A gets farther and farther away from their original preferences. This is the stage of legislative development Jefferson referred to in his Manual as the process by which the bill is perfected by its friends. The object is, of course, to so perfect it that it can attract majority support when it comes up for a vote.

Appendix B

Intensity of preference on the part of every legislator may be expressed by a vector of ordinal ranking of issues, thus

$$\begin{bmatrix} A & Y_3 \\ B & N_1 \\ C & Y_2 \\ D & N_4 \end{bmatrix}$$

where Y indicates support, N indicates disapproval, and the subscripts give the ordinal ranking made by the legislator.

When A is considered in the legislative area, we have, again, these possibilities:

$$\left.\begin{array}{l} \{A_i \cup B_j\} \\ \{A_i \cap B_j\} \\ \{A_i \odot B_j\} \end{array}\right\}$$
$A \And B \epsilon S, \quad i \neq j$

$= A \bigcirc B$ as in (1) except that $\{A \cap B\}$ is now the null set ϕ_{AB} indicating a cooperative arrangement to kill off both bills.

We may generalize (2) to the set $\{A, B, \ldots N\}$ of bills making up a legislative session and consider the total output of the session as the choice of a social state S. In the general case the fate of any bill *may* be settled by trades involving other bills. This fact has been widely interpreted in the literature as a violation of Arrow's condition 3—the independence of irrelevant alternatives (Sen's condition I) (Sen, 1970). That such is not the case can be seen by noting that such trades are "bargains" which Arrow assumes to be implicit in making up any one social state (in his refutation of an early Tullock attack) (Arrow, 1963, p. 109).

Moreover, to interpret trades as a violation of Arrow's condition 3 is to contradict the condition of unrestricted domain (Sen condition U) (Sen, 1970). Thus, if any subset $\{A \bigcirc B \bigcirc C\}$, V, A, B, $C \epsilon S$, is condition U violated. The independence of irrelevant alternatives applies only to the mutually exclusive Ss and not to the elements a, b, c ... nor to the policies (bills) A, B, C. ... Otherwise, the two conditions are in logical contradiction and one must give way.

A further argument has been made that even though we allow vote trading, a cyclical majority may still occur, given the following situation.

Member 1 prefers $\{A_1 \bigcirc B_2\}$
Member 2 prefers $\{B_2 \bigcirc C_3\}$ subscripts refer to members' bills
Member 3 prefers $\{C_3 \bigcirc A_1\}$

But, since each of the above subsets involves a cooperative arrangement, these subsets cannot occur. Member 1 will not allow $\{C_3 \bigcirc A_1\}$ to arise, 2 will not allow $\{A_1 \bigcirc B_2\}$, and 3 will not allow $\{B_2 \bigcirc C_3\}$ since each prefers a different subset. Hence, over the set $\{A, B, C\}$ the null set ϕ_{ABC} will result, and nothing will be passed.

It must be emphasized that present legislative rules which prevent legislator preferences from being expressed (committee dominance, for example) may allow such situations as depicted above to occur. The fault, in that case, is with the present rules and not in the theory.

References

Arrow, Kenneth. 1951. *Social Choice and Individual Values*. 1963 ed. (New York, Wiley) pp. 46–60.

Bagehot, Walter. 1905. *The English Constitution* (London, Kegan Paul, Trench, Trübner) p. 141.

Black, Duncan. 1963. *The Theory of Committees and Elections* (New York, Cambridge University Press).

Coleman, James S. 1974. *Power and the Structure of Society* (New York, Norton).

Russell, C. S., W. O. Spofford, Jr., and E. T. Haefele. 1974. "The Management of the Quality of the Environment," in J. Rothenberg and Ian Heggie, eds., *The Management of Water Quality and the Environment* (New York, Macmillan).

Sen, A. K. 1970. *Collective Choice and Social Welfare* (San Francisco, Holden-Day) p. 41.

14
Measuring the Quality of Life of the Elderly

ALAN WILLIAMS

1. Introduction

THE characteristic approach of economists to the valuation of social goods is to try to find some private good which is systematically related to it, and by measuring the values people place on the latter, make some inferences about the implicit (upper or lower bounds of) values they place on the former. Much of the work reported elsewhere in this collection falls within this fruitful and valuable field of endeavor.

On occasions, however, social policy confronts problems where the community has explicitly rejected one or another of the basic assumptions on which this approach rests. Among these basic assumptions, two are especially important: (1) people are the best (or even sometimes the sole) judges of their own welfare; and (2) the preferences of different individuals are to be weighted according to the prevailing distribution of income and wealth.

In some areas of social policy (e.g., mental illness and physical handicap), the first assumption is challenged, and over a much wider range of social concerns the second one is considered ethically unacceptable as the basis for public policy valuations. Put another way, the market is considered to be an inefficient "signaling system" for these social priorities, because the distribution of "signaling power" is inappropriate. The market is therefore replaced by a political signaling system, based on the prevailing distribution of political signaling power, which then has to

In this paper I have drawn heavily on the work of colleagues cited herein. Because the paper draws on such a wide range of research activity, the sponsors who deserve credit are also numerous, and, since their help is not acknowledged elsewhere, should be mentioned here, namely, the Chartered Institute of Public Finance and Accountancy, the Department of Health and Social Security, the Nuffield Provincial Hospitals Trust, and the Social Science Research Council (Public Sector Studies Programme at the University of York).

cope with the job of establishing social valuations in an operational (as opposed to a rhetorical) manner.

The economist's role in this system is perceived very differently by different people. At one extreme stand those who say that once we abandon the potential Pareto improvement, and the equivalent and compensating variation concepts associated with it, the economist has no claim to expertise and hence no professional role. At the other extreme stand those economists who would take over political science and simulate the political valuation system as if it were a market valuation system, but with a different notion of currency, income, and wealth. On the sidelines stand those who seek common criteria by which both "economic" and "political" valuation systems can be appraised in relation to some higher order principles of efficiency, justice, or fairness.

My position is to say that all valuation processes must face the same kinds of problems, and I am anxious to see how far the concepts and practices of sociologists, doctors, administrators, and policy makers can be elucidated in the valuation process and made intelligible to economists. This involves casting them within an economist's conceptual framework and making them more explicit than they typically are when using the jargon of their own discipline.

At a more mundane level, this paper is concerned with the substantive issues that arise when applying these rather grand notions to the measurement of the quality of life of the elderly. With this task in mind, the paper has been divided into seven parts, each of which tackles a different aspect of measuring this quality. They are: (1) the elderly as a peculiarly vulnerable group, (2) the public policy issues involved, (3) the relevant costs, (4) assessing the "needs" of the elderly, (5) social indicators as a quality of life concept, (6) assessment of client state as a quality of life indicator, and (7) the valuation process.

In considering the problems of measuring the quality of life for the elderly, I concentrate mainly on the health aspect, though this is interpreted in a fairly broad way. But it does mean that I give no systematic consideration to material living standards (income and wealth levels) as such, nor to aspects of the physical environment which are not likely to show up in improved health, nor themselves constitute measures consciously applied for that purpose. I would, however, argue that the elements I concentrate on are fundamental in an important sense, whereas income, wealth, better housing, cleaner air, more pleasant surroundings, are all instrumental; so that I only feel *mildly*, not *abjectly* apologetic, for having placed the emphasis where I have.

The paper will also inevitably be biased by my own preoccupation with the problems of caring for the elderly in a British setting, and this may lead to some selection/rejection or emphasis/deemphasis judgments which seem strange to others. Worse still, I have been at this problem for some years now, and I may have taken for granted things which cause the reader puzzlement. I rely on readers' reactions to identify and clarify these points, though I do not necessarily hold out any hope that I will be converted to an alternative formulation or standpoint. My ignorance is, however, remediable, even though my stupidity is not, so within the limits set by the latter, the former may yet be dispelled.

Briefly, the message of this paper is that we are likely to make more progress in this field by building on, systematizing, and, if necessary, reformulating the work of medical scientists, sociologists, and social workers regarding the assessment of their clients, than by taking as our starting point the traditional concerns of economics (incomes, prices, costs). I do not believe the two to be wholly incompatible, but I do consider some economists to be so heavy-footedly aggressive in this field that many sensitive and intelligent people have come to believe so.

2. The Elderly as a Peculiarly Vulnerable Group

The peculiar problems of the elderly arise from the following combination of circumstances: (1) Declining physical and mental capabilities. (2) Withdrawal (sometimes enforced) from employment, so that they are largely dependent on nonlabor income (e.g., past savings, social security benefits, etc.). (3) Greater geographical mobility of population, that breaks up the extended family system as a source of economic, social, and emotional support; those in large urban areas are particularly vulnerable in this respect. (4) All the above plus a high incidence of deaths of contemporaries (especially spouse) leads to strong sense of isolation, desolation, and general feeling of uselessness and unwantedness.

From a more general economic viewpoint, a further problem is that the elderly form an increasing proportion of the population, and although they are living longer, these extra years are not necessarily spent *in good health and spirits*. One important asset they do have, however, is that they have a vote, have organized pressure groups working on their behalf, and have some able and resourceful contemporaries to put forward their views in the political process.

3. Public Policy Issues

The most fundamental public policy issue is, of course, the dividing line between individual, familial, and social responsibility in this area. A subordinate question, within the area of social responsibility, concerns the appropriate nature and field of jurisdiction of the public agencies to be given the task of discharging any such social responsibilities. Should they be all-purpose, client-centered organizations dealing with all old people in a local community, or should they be functional organizations with a nationwide remit not exclusively (or even primarily) concerned with old people?

The list of all the governmental activities potentially relevant to these problems is enormous, and encompasses practically the whole realm of collective activity. Apart from some rather obvious key activities such as the provision of medical and personal social services, income support through social security schemes, and special tax concessions, there are important areas such as housing, urban renewal, public transport, fuel policy, and so on, which can play a significant role in influencing the quality of life for the elderly. The community also has the option of supporting the elderly by governmental support for voluntary bodies or other private welfare agencies, or by stimulating such effort by providing certain infrastructure support.

Thus the general public policy issue could be formulated broadly as being to determine which mix of these various activities and mechanisms is the most cost effective in sustaining the quality of life for the elderly.

4. Relevant Costs

Although most of this paper is about the measurement of effectiveness, something must be said first about the measurement of costs. In this field I see three broad problems, which in my experience tend to have major repercussions in practice, all leading to rather misguided decisions.

The first of these harks back to the multiplicity of agencies having some kind of interest or responsibility, or both, for the quality of life of the elderly. This creates many problems about the collection, processing, and dissemination of information, generates both overlap and hiatus, and makes it extremely difficult for anyone to form a general view of the situation of a particular client or group of clients, actual or potential. This fragmentation may or may not be justifiable on some other grounds, but it has one very unfortunate consequence, and that is that each party operates within a very partial framework, with no incentive (apart from satisfying his own high sense of social responsibility . . . which itself is a very scarce resource) to take into account the repercussions of his own activities upon the problems the others are dealing with.

Focusing those general statements on the problem of costs, I would draw attention to the lack of systematic consideration given to the costs borne by the other parties when moving patients between hospital/ residential home/family house (in either direction), the treatment of voluntary labor as a free good by many public bodies (and vice versa), the differential rules of access to local authority homes according to whether the person occupies a council house or is an owner-occupier, and so on. It has many manifestations, the crudest (and commonest) of which is embodied in the thought-stopping phrase: "it's not on my budget."

As if this inadequate consideration of interdependency and externalities were not enough, a second problem accentuates it, namely obsession with cash accounting and cash flows. This is not only so in the notoriously cash-conscious U.S. medical field, but, in a quite different context and with quite different motives, in most British agencies, too. In Britain it is all the fault of accountants and accounting principles, with which the whole bureaucratic structure is heavily infused. As a tribute to the probity and public responsibility of the administration it is commendable, but as a stumbling block to the perception of real resource costs it is execrable. On balance, I therefore execrate it! I do so because I believe that our cash-based, input-oriented budgetary systems have now become major obstacles to greater efficiency, instead of the vehicles by which efficiency is promoted, and this will not change until the economists' notion of opportunity cost (in real resource terms) becomes dominant in everyone's thinking, and a major source of control over their performance.

Finally, there is the problem of time horizons. These tend to be short anyway, but the system of cash accounting, based on an annual cycle, more relevant to an agrarian than an urban community, shortens planning horizons to a quite unnecessary extent. In many cases this is not even moderated by effective arrangements for intertemporal transfer of current resources, for, in Britain at least, the tyranny of annual accounting is not moderated by permitting funds to be brought forward or deferred, even at the 10 percent (real) rate of discount promulgated for use in making real investment decisions. The situation is not much better regarding virement between current and capital allocations, where it is usual to permit only limited movement, and then only in one direction (current to capital). Finally, it is rarely that any intertemporal redistribution of capital budgets is permitted, and, stranger still, the 10 percent real rate of discount plays no role in this tradeoff.

All in all, cost matters are not in a happy state, so that every costing exercise tends to be a major piece of analysis, cutting against the grain of the system. Small wonder, then, that those concerned primarily with "effectiveness" rely uncritically on the "cost" data given to them by the accountants, for to do anything else would require a large intellectual endeavor for which very few of them have either the training or the inclination. Better to get on with helping the old folks as best one can.

5. Assessing the "Needs" of the Elderly

A characteristic approach to the problem of sustaining a tolerable quality of life for the elderly is to define certain "needs," then estimate the prevalence of such needs, and finally (though less frequently) to set about testing effectiveness by seeing how far the provision of various forms of governmental support has actually reduced such needs.

It sounds a sensible procedure, but as everyone knows who has ever looked at it closely, it is fraught with such ambiguity at the level of principle that it becomes rather misleading as an operational tool. The problems are manifold, and I will only outline them briefly here.[1]

1. A person's "needs" can be assessed by a variety of parties—himself, his friends and relatives, experts of one kind or another, or the community at large, and there is no guarantee that these will coincide, and plenty of evidence of cases where they definitely do not.
2. Discussion in terms of "need" is antithetical to notions of priority in tradeoff terms, for it strongly suggests lexicographic orderings, and is even used by some participants in the advocacy process to stifle all debate about priorities by insisting that needs *must* be met, no matter what the cost.
3. "Needs" are in fact conditioned, albeit implicitly and vaguely, by existing (or believed) resource constraints, and as these constraints become more or less stringent, notions of need vary similarly. Hence the well-known impossibility of eliminating poverty, or the existence of waiting lists for services rationed by professional judgments of need, since these criteria themselves change through time.
4. Sometimes needs are defined in terms which preempt debate about whether they could more advantageously be met in one way or another, because what is estimated (directly) is "need for nursing" or "need for home help" or "need for income."

Each of these problems could be overcome, at an analytical level at least, with thought and effort, and there is no shortage of studies which have shown us how to do so. Spek (1972) has a simple but powerful taxonomy which is very useful in fighting our way through jungle (1),

---

[1] For a much fuller critique, see Williams (1974a) and the references cited therein.

and which involves posing only two basic questions to each of three parties (society, the experts, and the individual), namely: (a) Is the individual sick? (b) Is the individual in need of public care? In addition, he would ask a third question, which is more one of fact: (c) Does the individual demand public care? By this route I am sure we could eliminate much of the verbiage, noncommunication and misunderstanding between the citizenry, politicians, administrators, the medical fraternity, economists, sociologists, and social workers, which is so much of a hindrance to progress and effective cooperation in this field.

As regards (2) we are in more trouble, because whereas many of the cross-currents in (1) could be channeled more productively by semantic and taxonomic discussions, we face here some rather deep philosophical issues. Thus both Tribe (1972) and Rawls (1971) have recently argued for the absolute primacy of certain social objectives, though Tribe goes on to get into such a strange position, conceding so great a redefinition of this notion at the margin, that he effectively ends up in a relativist position, asserting that as your position gets more desperate you assign higher marginal values to what you have left, which is not at all a startling assertion to an economist. I believe that more harm is likely to be done by the closure of analysis which is likely to flow from the lexicographic approach than from any tradeoff errors we are likely to make in trying to give effect to the "all-things-are-substitutable-at-the-margin" approach, especially if we permit some things to take on very high values.

Points (3) and (4) together point strongly to a notion of need which is related directly to client state, and not to the state of the services the client uses. This distinction is clearly recognized in some studies, but unfortunately not in all, as the fusion of the two notions moves the discussion of "priority" rather too quickly to the service level and away from "quality of life" concepts.

6. Social Indicators as Measures of the Quality of Life

One way forward, which is currently receiving a great deal of attention, is the search for valid indicators of quality of life which could be made operational by compiling and comparing statistical series. The collection of such series is relatively straightforward in the current state of knowledge. The idea is that these series would give a broad indication of the state of society, and provide warning signals when things were going awry, thus stimulating debate on whether social priorities needed revision, or better mechanisms for intervention needed to be established, and so on.

There is a vast literature on this and related subjects which cannot possibly be reviewed here, so I will concentrate on one practical manifestation into which a great deal of effort has been put by individuals and governments in many countries, namely, the OECD Social Indicator Development Programme (1973). At the outset, it faced up squarely to the problems we have just been discussing, and asserted boldly (1973):

> The term "social concern" in the programme denotes an identifiable and definable aspiration or concern of fundamental and direct importance to human well-being as opposed to a matter of instrumental or indirect importance to well-being. . . . This focus means . . . that. . . some important social problems and particular government programmes . . . are excluded . . . (because) . . . they involve *means* rather than ends. This. . . is considered to be very important in differentiating the highly selective OECD social indicator programme from the more comprehensive social statistics programmes of other international organisations.

After discussing the various reasons why some possibilities are omitted from the list (among which are aesthetic values, love and comradeship, the family, international relationships), it is further stressed that the program concentrates on present quality of life and does not explicitly or systematically include notions of resource conservation or ecological balance, which have an investment perspective.

The basic list of social concerns emerging from this process comprises health, individual development through learning, employment and quality of working life, time and leisure, command over goods and services, physical environment, personal safety and the administration of justice, social opportunity and participation. Each of these factors is further subdivided. For instance, health is divided into (1) the probability of a healthy life through all stages of the life cycle and (2) the impact of health impairments on individuals. The latter, in turn, is further subdivided into (2a), the quality of health care in terms of reducing pain and restoring functional capabilities; (2b), the extent of universal distribution in the delivery of health care; (2c), the ability of the chronically impaired and permanently handicapped to participate more effectively in society.

Similar processes of refinement and differentiation are carried out for the other major concerns, but I propose to stick with health because it is one of the crucial concerns for the elderly, it contains within it all the problems to which I wish to refer, and it is the one that interests me most and with which I am most familiar.

I have always believed the distinction between "the probability of a healthy life" and "the impact of health impairments" to be unworkable, the real problem (common to both) being to devise a set of measures, directed firmly at 2a, related to pain and functional capabilities. These could then be used to see what has been achieved for "the chronically impaired and permanently handicapped" (2c), or (under 2b) for the population at large, divided by age/sex/race/socioeconomic class or whatever variable happens to excite attention or concern at the time.

Thus, when we look at the likely candidates for inclusion in any battery of social indicators for health, they fall into the following categories: (1) Measures of mortality and life expectation. (2) Measures of the incidence or prevalence of sickness or handicap. (3) Measures of the consequences of sickness or handicap. (4) Measures of the level of capacity or utilization of health-care services. (5) Measures of inputs into health-care services.

In principle, the "delivery of care" indicators in (4), and the resource-use indicators in (5) should be excluded under the (proper) self-denying ordinance enunciated earlier about "ends" and "means." I would argue further that (2) is not really very useful, because handicap can only be recognized in terms of its consequences and because "sickness" is a "fundamental concern" only to the extent that it generates loss of life expectation (which will be in 1) or pain and/or loss of function (which will be in 3).

It is this kind of argument which led two of my colleagues and me (Culyer, Lavers, and Williams, 1972) to argue very strongly for all social indicators in the health field to be related clearly and explicitly to a health index based essentially on these variables, plus a time dimension which would have a prognostic/probabilistic quality (just as loss-of-life-expectation does). The difficulties raised by this approach are not inconsiderable, however, and include: agreeing on relevant and operational definitions of social functioning, pain, and so on; finding some feasible way of getting data on the prevalence of these states in the community; getting operational agreement on the relative weights to be attached to different components in the "index"; and establishing the causal connections between policy instruments or activities and the present and future course of the index for the affected groups.

It is, however, clear that attempts to measure the quality of life for the elderly along the lines indicated will have to go far beyond the statistical series currently available to governments, and will require considerable development work at a much less aggregative level. This is not just a matter of collating such information for a smaller geographical jurisdiction,[2] useful though this may be, but of collating information

---

[2] For example, Chartered Institute of Public Finance and Accountancy (1974) and Flynn, Flynn, and Mellor (1972).

more microscopically at the level of the individual respondent. It is to this problem I turn next.

7. Assessment of Client State as a Quality of Life Measure

When arguing on earlier occasions (Williams, 1974b) for measures of quality of life which start from data collected about a broad range of activities for a single individual (and preferably repeated longitudinally), the usual retort is that it cannot be done, for any one or all of the reasons set out above. Since I have always believed that the greatest obstacle to getting things done is people who believe that they can't be done, I have not allowed myself to become daunted by that list of difficulties, and have sought (and am still seeking) to discover work which has already overcome one or more of those hurdles, in order to demonstrate that it *can* be done. Not all of the nuggets I have located in this prospecting activity are relevant to this paper, but I will present a few that are, primarily with the object of illustrating some approaches which seem worth emulating, but also in the hope that the reader may be able to help fill in the gaps, or reinforce my armory, by letting me know of others which seem relevant and actually or potentially productive.

It turns out that in the medical–social field there are literally hundreds of assessment schedules in operational use which purport to measure social functioning, pain, and so on, usually for diagnosis or treatment assignment, but occasionally as part of a study of prevalence. Because they vary so much in purpose, they also vary enormously in the range of information sought, the fineness of detail, mode of analysis, ease of application and focus of attention, and the manner in which the scaling and weighting of different variables is handled. With respect to the elderly, much of the published work has been surveyed by my colleague, Ken Wright (1974, pp. 258–259) whose conclusion is that

> It is frequently possible to enumerate the dimensions on which a comprehensive measure would be based. However, it is difficult to quantify or assess changes or collect reliable information on some of these dimensions and so an inconsistent picture emerges of considerable progress being made in measurement along one dimension, little or no progress...along others and some between these extremes. ...
> In the case of the elderly, useful work has been done on the assessment of disability and on the feeling of loneliness as a reaction to isolation and bereavement.... However, more work is needed in developing the outputs relating to...emotional state,... the relationships in families caring for their parents and in the standards of warmth, comfort and cleanliness of the domestic en-

vironment, in a way which is communicable between and intelligible by various professional staff, administrators and politicians.

This conviction has also led us to embark (with the help of a London-based survey research organization, Social and Community Planning and Research) on the field testing of a measuring instrument of our own, which is designed to serve as the vehicle by which one could test the relative effectiveness of a variety of support regimes. It builds up a longitudinal profile of differential outcomes in terms of patient state that can be applied by any ordinary intelligent person with minimal training.

The basic elements are as follows:

1. An assessment schedule, which covers three key dimensions: (a) physical mobility (e.g., whether bed-ridden, housebound, only short distances outdoors); (b) capacity for self-care (feeding, washing, dressing, housework); (c) mental state (intellectual capacities, mood). This information is later compressed into four scalings with respect to each dimension, giving sixty-four possible combinations.
2. Background information which concerns personal socioeconomic details, present domestic environment, social contacts, medical conditions, usage of services.
3. Three-monthly updating of all this information for the people in the sample.
4. The construction of a transitions matrix which shows the movement of respondents over time between the sixty-four initial assessment classes and the sixty-five subsequent assessment classes (the sixty-fifth being "dead").
5. An attempt to "explain" differential transitions with respect to the "background information" mentioned.

As yet, we are only at the pilot testing stage of elements (1) and (2), though we have done one three-monthly reassessment on over 200 persons in our pilot sample, and we are testing out the computation process on this data, though the substantive results from this small sample will not be of any great policy interest. The interesting part of the process for us lies in demonstrating that assessors with a very wide range of skills and backgrounds can use this schedule; that it generates data of interest in a wide range of policy contexts, and is not limited to particular conditions, services, or organizational levels. These are necessary ingredients if we are to confront seriously the problem of policy choice between institutional and community care for the elderly;

between medical, nursing and social support; between public, voluntary, and familial sources of such support, and so on.

Writing, as I have, in this rather egocentric way about our own work should not be taken as implying that similar work is not going on elsewhere. Close to our own work, in both concept and operation, are similar activities in Sweden[3] and the United States,[4] the latter work being far more advanced in execution than our own.

8. The Valuation Problem

A primary "valuation" of elements in this measurement process occurs with the decision to exclude certain items as irrelevant or of minimal importance, for in so doing we are obviously assigning them a value of zero. But if we go on to consider the various approaches to valuation found (often implicitly) *within* such assessment schedules, they will be found to manifest characteristics which should be readily recognizable by economists well versed in the debates about the "new" welfare economics.

One popular technique is "Guttman scaling," the essence of which is the establishment of a stable ordering of (say) loss of function such that anyone reporting dysfunction i can reliably be assumed also to suffer dysfunctions 1 to $i - 1$, but not $i + 1$ to j, where $1,2, .. , i, .. j$ are the labels describing the ordered dysfunctional states.[5] Thus, if $i = $ "chair-bound," $i - 1$ might be "unable to negotiate steps," $i - 2$ is "unable to walk more than 100 yards outdoors," and so on, implying that anyone who is chairbound can reliably be assumed not to do these other things either. Going the other way along the scale, if $i + 1 = $ "bedfast but alert" and $i + 2 = $ "unconscious," then we can also reliably assume that a person in state i is *not* in either of these other states. Although it might start out as a useful way of categorizing people, it soon becomes an ordinal ranking of states, because it becomes interpreted, quite under-standably, as a valuation statement to the effect that $i + 2$ is *worse* than $i + 1$, which in turn is *worse* than i, which in turn is *worse* than $i - 1$, which in turn is *worse* than $i - 2$, and it is certainly in this manner that such scales are frequently used (and on which limited valuations there would undoubtedly be widespread agreement).

[3] For example, the Dalby Health and Medical Care Centre near Lund, Sweden (in progress—private communication from Per Nyberg).

[4] At the Duke University Medical Center, Durham, N.C. See also Maddox and Douglas (1974).

[5] See, for instance, Rosow and Breslan (1966).

Where the existence of such well-ordered progressions or regressions cannot be established empirically, the next stage in implicit valuation is represented by the use of scoring systems to distinguish the more from the less severely affected clients. This is common over a wide range of professional assessments, from educational attainments to housing quality, and in the field of the quality of life of the elderly usually takes the form of "counting" specific disabilities. A very simple example is the following index of social isolation for those living alone (Wager, 1972), which is constructed thus:

For living alone *per se*	1 point
No help from relatives or friends available when required	1 point
If visitors received infrequently	1 point
If mobile outside dwelling only with considerable difficulty	1 point

Thus, there is a scale from 0 to 4, which contains within it the implication that the remedying of any one of these attributes is as valuable as remedying any other, since each carries the same weight in the index. There are plenty of more complex examples (in the same study) which use differential weights, but all of which have the same additive quality and hence all of which carry the above implication in some form or other, often without the authors or practitioners realizing it.

A further stage of sophistication is reached when the interplay of particular elements is explicitly recognized (i.e., the elements are not treated as separable and simply additive). Here a whole complex of factors has to be "valued" as a unit, in relation to other complex combinations of the same basic ingredients. At the extreme, this means rating the multidimensional state of each individual client separately, and a complex example of this kind has been reported by Patrick and coauthors (1973, p. 243) in which "the high degree of agreement among the judges concerning the rank order and scale separation of the items supports the hypothesis that unidimensional judgements were obtained."

The natural next step for an economist would be to attempt to construct "indifference" maps of client states, the axes being the different attributes, and the "contours" representing equally valued combinations of those attributes. The study by Patrick and coauthors (1973, p. 244) found, however, that this "method of equivalence stimuli is too complex for use outside a laboratory-like individual interview. The unrealistic assumptions and the emotive nature of the task confused and offended some judges, . . . although they will continue to be useful for criterion purposes."

Finally, there are various methods by which we could move from "points" or "index" values to money values, without reverting to the market as a source of such values. First, by finding at what point administrative–political decisions establish a cutoff point in resource use, we could derive a *shadow price* for the marginal point. Second, we might investigate what *explicit values* other social agencies have placed on particular client states, for instance, by investigating how much the courts have awarded in compensation for differing degrees of pain, grief, suffering, and disability entailed in personal injury cases (excluding the elements relating to loss of income).[6] A third method is to ask those responsible for the agency concerned to articulate a value which represents their own policy preference, so that this can be used in a decentralized way by the subordinate parts of the agency in their own decisions. This *postulated value* approach is what is used in the valuation of the avoidance of pain, grief, and suffering in the investment appraisal routine for the British interurban trunk road network (Dawson, 1974), though I know of no examples yet in the field of health and welfare services.

Thus, in the social policy literature we find the full range of nonmarket valuation procedures at work, yet each can readily be reformulated (where necessary) within that part of the conceptual apparatus of neoclassical welfare economics concerned with consumer choice. It seems a fertile (and relatively untilled) field, which should be an attractive prospect for nonmarket-oriented welfare economists.

9. Conclusions

Measuring the quality of life of the elderly is going to be an increasingly urgent and worthwhile task because of the growing pressure on social and economic resources which this population group is going to generate in all advanced countries over the next decade or so. Because the job *has* to be done, it *will* be done, but it will not necessarily be done *well*. Economists have an important contribution to make to this work because they have special skills and experience in conceptualizing valuation problems, and have available the powerful array of tools generated by welfare economics, especially as manifest in the cost–benefit approach, to help formulate problems in a manner that will make them susceptible to systematic analysis.

[6] A good example is the work of Rosser and Watts (1972).

Provided that we do not insist, in a dogmatic and doctrinaire manner, on using only information from markets, or from simulated markets, or from market-oriented activities, we will be able to tap a very rich source of ideas and data from the fields of social medicine and social work in this quest, with the full collaboration and support of the many dedicated, experienced, and intelligent researchers in those disciplines who work in this same territory. In that way, too, we should be able to win their confidence and respect sufficiently to break down their suspicions that cost-effectiveness and cost–benefit analyses are merely ways of ensuring the dominance of crude concepts like loss of earnings or hospital expenditures as the major guidelines for resource allocation, and convince them that disciplined analysis of humanitarian objectives and the effectiveness of the system in achieving them is *our* prime objective as well as *theirs*.

References

Chartered Institute of Public Finance and Accountancy. 1974. *Local Government Trends 1973* (London, 1974).

Culyer, A. J., R. J. Lavers, and Alan Williams. 1972. "Health Indicators," in Andrew Shonfield and Stella Shaw, eds., *Social Indicators and Social Policy* (London, Heinemann Educational Books).

Dawson, R. F. F. 1974. "The Cost of Human Impairment from Road Accidents," in Lees and Shaw, eds., *Impairment, Disability and Handicap* (London, Heinemann Educational Books).

Flynn, M., P. Flynn, and N. Mellor. 1972. "Social Malaise Research: A Study in Liverpool," *Social Trends No. 3* (London, Her Majesty's Stationery Office).

Maddox, G. L., and E. B. Douglas. 1974. "Ageing and Individual Differences: A Longitudinal Analysis," *Journal of Gerontology* vol. 29, p. 555.

OECD Social Indicator Development Programme: 1. List of Social Concerns Common to Most OECD Countries. 1973. (Paris, OECD, Manpower and Social Affairs Directorate.)

Patrick, Donald L., J. W. Bush, and Milton M. Chen. 1973. "Methods for Measuring Levels of Wellbeing for a Health Status Index," *Health Services Research* vol. 8, no. 3, pp. 228–245.

Rawls, John. 1971. *A Theory of Justice* (Cambridge, Mass., Harvard University Press).

Rosow, Irving, and Naomi Breslan. 1966. "A Guttman Health Scale for the Aged," *Journal of Gerontology* vol. 21, no. 4, pp. 556–559.

Rosser, Rachel, and Vincent Watts. 1972. "The Measurement of Hospital Output," *International Journal of Epidemiology* vol. 1, no. 4, pp. 361–368.

Spek, J. E. 1972. "On the Economic Analysis of Health and Medical Care in a Swedish Health District," in M. M. Hauser, ed., *The Economics of Medical Care* (London, Allen and Unwin).

Tribe, Lawrence H. 1972. "Policy Science: Analysis or Ideology," *Philosophy and Public Affairs* vol. 2, no. 1 (esp. p. 90 et seq.).

Wager, Ray. 1972. "Care of the Elderly," pp. 17 ff. (London, Chartered Institute of Public Finance and Accountancy).

Williams, Alan. 1974a. "Need as a Demand Concept," in A. J. Culyer, ed., *Economic Policies and Social Goals* (London, Martin Robertson).

———. 1974b. "Measuring the Effectiveness of Health Care Systems," in Mark Perlman, ed., *The Economics of Health and Medical Care* (London, Macmillan).

Wright, K. G. 1974. "Alternative Measures of Output of Social Programmes: The Elderly," in A. J. Culyer, ed., *Economic Policies and Social Goals* (London, Martin Robertson).

15
Reflections on the Quality of
Working Life

HERBERT C. MORTON

MOST working-age Americans and Britons spend nearly half of their waking hours on the job or commuting to it. Thus it is not difficult to make the case that working conditions call for separate treatment in this book, which is primarily focused on consumption. Pay and hours of work, nonpecuniary rewards and dissatisfactions, and distinctive workplace hazards affect the worker's well-being quite as directly as does the consumption of goods and services outside of the workplace. Indeed, to a large extent they shape these consumption patterns and influence one's feelings of well-being off the job as well as on it.[1]

In focusing on the work environment, this chapter introduces some considerations beyond the consumption realm, but the discussion deals only with work in the market—omitting housework, do-it-yourself activities, hobbies, and other creative uses of leisure that could also be performed for pay in the marketplace. What follows should be regarded more as an agenda for inquiry and discussion than as a systematic analysis. The data are primarily from the United States, but the issues are also of concern in other countries as well. Most of the considerations also apply to the quality of working life among all employees, not just those who work or live in metropolitan areas, but it is among urban workers that the questions treated here have attracted greatest attention.

1. Dimensions of Working Life

"Quality of working life" is a relatively new term for a bundle of old issues that have long been of interest to philosophers, theologians, social

---

I am indebted to Lowdon Wingo and Irving Hoch for helpful comments on an earlier draft.

[1] Campbell, Converse, and Rodgers (1976, p. 287) offer a quantitative assessment of the importance of work: "Satisfaction with work . . . is one of the strongest pre-

scientists, workers, and employers. It is a broad term that can embrace every conceivable aspect of the work ethic and working conditions. It is also a protean term whose meaning takes different shapes, depending on the context of the discussion. Social scientists engaged in the development of social indicators for the past decade have sought to include quantitative dimensions of the quality of work life among their measurements, but in general the term is still used loosely. Reflections of their efforts, as will be discussed later, have appeared in studies by the Russell Sage Foundation, the Survey Research Center at the University of Michigan, and other private research groups, as well as in government reports and statistical studies, including *Social Indicators 1973*, annual editions of *The Manpower Report of the President*, and issues of the *Monthly Labor Review*.[2]

The growing interest in the quality of working life which has become apparent in recent years signals an enlargement of perspective that is widely shared. It offers an opportunity to pull together disparate data and different analytical approaches—objective measures of working conditions, workers' expressions of satisfaction and dissatisfaction, managerial concerns about efficiency of output, and broader considerations of social cohesion and stability. A fairly inclusive definition of the quality of working life would encompass a number of factors that affect the work experience in an advanced industrial society.

• First is the payment for putting one's time, talents, and energy at someone else's disposal, either as an employee or an independent professional. (Payment here is construed broadly to include all forms of compensation, such as deferred income, pay for time not worked, and health and related fringe benefits. Generally this payment does not specifically cover the costs of commuting to the job, an issue that will be considered separately later in this chapter.) Although income is not

---

dictors of our Index of Well Being, accounting for nearly one fifth of the variance of the general measure of the quality of life experience."

[2] Working conditions have been an explicit governmental concern at least since the establishment in 1884 of the Bureau of Labor, predecessor of the Department of Labor. But it was probably the 1968 edition of the *Manpower Report of the President*, which included a chapter on "Quality of Employment," that marked the emergence of government recognition of the concept now commonly called quality of working life. The publication of the Department of Health, Education and Welfare—*Toward a Social Report* (Washington, GPO, 1969) reflected a growing federal interest in social indicators, but none of its seven chapters was devoted to the workplace; some related questions are touched on, such as occupational mobility, noise on the job, and training. Issues of the *Monthly Labor Review*, published by the Bureau of Labor Statistics, have long dealt with virtually all aspects of working life.

always explicitly treated in discussions of the quality of work, it should not be overlooked. It has both objective and subjective dimensions. The former is measured by statistics on real spendable earnings, disposable income, and so on. (One aspect of this objective dimension is discussed in this volume by Irving Hoch, who demonstrates that wages tend to increase with city size because workers must be compensated for losses in quality of life associated with large urban scale.) The subjective dimension is the worker's attitude toward the wage. Where the payment for services is perceived to be fair, the worker is more likely to feel satisfied with the bargain. Where the payment for services is considered inadequate, a feeling of anger or resentment is likely to affect the worker's attitude toward the job.[3] The objective data may or may not seriously affect the subjective perceptions. Attitudes toward differentials in pay between jobs or among industries may be more significant in affecting a worker's perception of his value than the level of income or rate of increase. Serious dissatisfaction with pay, for whatever reason, can color all other aspects of the job environment.

• Closely related are the hours of work—full time, part time, shift worked, and, of growing interest in recent years, opportunities for flexible work schedules.

• Next is the nature of the job. Sometimes the activity itself is highly satisfying—not only for artists, musicians, writers, skilled craftsmen, scientists, physicians, and so on, but also for many others who find the demands of the job are well matched to their skills and preferences. Sometimes the activity is deadening or unsuited to a worker's ability or temperament. Sometimes the socializing, or the "nontask" aspects of work, more than compensate for whatever burden is imposed by the job. (Closely related is the worker's attitude toward work, which in the Protestant ethic is viewed as a source of satisfaction in itself.)

• Fourth, there are a number of physical aspects of the work environment that affect the quality of working life. Some of these—temperature, light, dirt, noise—may cause only incidental discomfort in some circumstances, but in others they may become seriously enervating, dispiriting, injurious to health, or fatal. In recent years, attention has centered on safety hazards and on health hazards from toxic substances that may cause immediate illness or that lead to serious health difficulties after a long latency period. Other important physical factors are the convenience of the plant location (distance to work and availability of

---

[3] The overriding historical importance of the notion of "fairness" in British labor negotiations and its implications for wage-push inflation in recent years is analyzed by Sir John Hicks (1975). See especially chapter 3 on wages and inflation.

transport) and the accessibility of tools and materials in the plant. Workers frustrated by a long trip to work through heavy traffic or whose efficiency on the job is hampered by poor plant layouts are less likely to be satisfied.

• Fifth are the institutional aspects of the work setting—within the firm and outside it. Within the firm these include job security and other conditions of work, such as the availability of rest and recreational facilities, cafeterias, and other amenities. The firm's managerial style, including its policies toward training, advancement, motivation, communication and so on can be especially important. Outside the firm, there is a broader institutional context—the labor market. Limitations to entry into a profession or trade union, discrimination in hiring and promotion, and the inequality of educational and training opportunities have a significant bearing on the quality of working life.

• Finally there are the political, social, and economic aspects of life off the job—the considerations discussed in other parts of this book.

There are advantages in separating out working life for analytical purposes, but doing so is artificial. For example, can the reports of worker alienation in the late 1960s and early 1970s be attributed wholly to workplace dissatisfaction or were the workers reflecting anger over such general social problems as the Vietnam war and discrimination?

An alternative way of identifying these factors affecting the quality of life is to classify them as costs and benefits of employment, from the worker's point of view, as illustrated in the list on page 302. Doing so helps guard against the simple notion that flexible hours, or more autonomy on the job, or any other single innovation is likely to enhance job satisfaction substantially and for the long run.

But such a listing tells nothing about the relative importance of such factors. Is pay a more important determinant of job satisfaction than hours worked? Is the job itself—what one does all day—more important than the supervisory or social atmosphere in which one works? And so on. How does one go about measuring such preferences? How much weight should be given to data on such quantitative factors as hours of work, for example, and how much to more subjective information on worker's perceptions. And how long will such data be valid? Is there any logic at all in trying to rank factors in order of importance, or does the relative importance vary with the nature of the community, with the condition of the economy (prosperous or depressed) and so on? There is a range of tolerances for each of these factors. Slight variations are not likely to affect an individual's overall job satisfaction. On the other hand, a substantial deterioration in any of them might conceivably outweigh general satisfaction with all the rest.

Costs and Benefits of Working Life: An Illustrative Listing

A. The costs of work from the worker's viewpoint can be identified as follows:

   Expenditure of time and effort at someone else's direction or to meet another's needs

   Time and money spent commuting to work

   Physical discomforts on the job not serious enough to cause illness (heat, noise, pollution, poor light)

   Physical hazards strong enough to cause loss of work time, prolonged time off the job, or death (dangerous equipment, dangerous situations such as heights)

   Psychological and emotional discomforts of work (rigid managerial environment, poor relations among workers)

   Monotony and boredom resulting from fragmentation of jobs into meaningless tasks

   Health hazards serious enough to shorten the working life span or total life span (carcinogens, mutagens, and other toxic substances)

   Obstacles such as limitations to entry, discrimination in hiring and advancement, lack of training and so on that make it impossible to achieve full working potential

B. Readily identifiable benefits that enhance quality of life on the job include the following:

   Good pay and fringe benefits (health care, vacations, recreation facilities)

   Job security and adequate pensions

   Meaningful work in an organization with a sense of purpose, leading to a sense of self-fulfillment

   Opportunity for advancement

   Flexibility in work time that makes it possible to achieve other objectives or meet other obligations

   Clean, safe, healthful surroundings that add to a feeling of well-being

   Good social environment. Sense of camaraderie in work team

   Status

3. Some Theoretical Considerations

Economic theory touches on matters affecting the quality of working life in a number of ways, including assumptions about mobility and knowledge in the labor market, the role of wages in equalizing differences among occupations, assumptions about the burdensomeness of work, the concept of human capital, and the relative importance of allocative efficiency and effort.

1. In the first chapter, Wingo alludes to the assumptions of perfect mobility and information that are essential to the efficient functioning of the labor market under fully competitive conditions. From the viewpoint of quality of life, it is the lack of mobility and of information in real markets that poses problems for public policy. If a worker is barred by discrimination or other factors from choosing an occupation or job he or she prefers, the result may be not only an inequity and a less efficient market, but also a lowering of the quality of working life. (An overinvestment in training and education, on the other hand, might improve a worker's lot but would be inefficient.) Similarly, if workers are unaware of alternative opportunities for selling their services, not only will labor be inefficiently allocated from an economic standpoint, but the quality of employees' working lives will likewise be diminished, either because they are not working in the occupation they prefer or are not getting the market wage for what they are doing. There is a complementarity here in economic thinking and in the approach to quality of working life, though it may be obscured by differences between the languages of the economists and the sociologists.

2. Wage theory generally rationalizes wage differentials by attributing them either to differences in ability (productivity) or to differences in the disagreeability or hazardousness of the occupation. Typically, it is stated that wages will vary to equalize the differences among jobs.

From a standpoint of public policy related to the quality of life, one might hypothesize that greater attention might be given to reducing the actual differences among occupations rather than offering money inducements to workers to perform excessively risky or dirty jobs. The Occupational Safety and Health Act of 1970, with its emphasis on safety and health standards to limit exposure to risk, illustrates the approach but does not exhaust the possibilities. Market pressures will themselves provide an incentive to change processes and practices that are excessively costly. Further research might show how taxes and subsidies can be effectively used to increase the incentive to make desired changes. If such changes in the workplace are not likely to pay off in the long run, the tradeoff between productivity and other values needs to be explicitly formulated: the public could then choose whether to improve health and safety at the price of lost production and consumption.

A number of situations in which reliance on the market may appear unsatisfactory from the viewpoint of quality of working life can be suggested. One is the situation where no amount of money is considered to be reasonable compensation for a risk. If the threat of disability or death is excessive, society may simply decide to shut down an operation. In this instance, the humanitarian motive may be buttressed by an economic one as well. That is, a full internalization of costs might show them to greatly outweigh benefits from the production. Reliance on the market may also be unwarranted when the worker does not have enough information to correctly assess the cost of risk. Although he may consider the risk reasonable, the costs of a disability that will have to be borne by his family or by society may exceed his estimate—assuming here that the wage is such that the firm does not pay the full costs of the accidents and illnesses for which it is responsible. In these cases, education of workers about hazards of various occupations and industries may be warranted.

Another situation calling for intervention in the market is one in which no single employer has sufficient incentive to pursue research that would lead to a lowering of work hazards because costs are high, results uncertain, and the benefits will be shared by all. Here, government support for research may be an appropriate way of spreading the risk over the entire community.

3. In the simplest conventional description of a competitive model, the worker is viewed as a seller of personal services whose decision about how many hours of work to offer at a given wage rate is determined by his relative preferences for income and leisure. Graphically, the worker's preferences are shown on an indifference map where the slope of curves represents the marginal rate of substitution between income or consumption and leisure time. For any given wage rate, there is a combination of leisure and income that affords the worker "the greatest satisfaction." In this formulation, the behavior of the worker is one element in the market model that may be shown to be socially efficient under the assumed conditions.

Such a formulation implies that labor and leisure are antithetical, that labor is a burden and leisure is desired as a relief from that burden (Scitovsky, 1951, p. 106) :[4]

> We can, if we like, think of work as a negative commodity, of its burden as a disutility, or negative satisfaction, and of the earnings received for work as a negative price. This approach has the advantage of bringing into focus the parallelism between a person's

---

[4] Scitovsky himself took a different position some twenty years later (1976, p. 91): "the economists' conclusion that work is unpleasant and performed only for income can be derived neither from economic data nor from economic theorizing, and even less can it be established through the psychologists' approach."

choice of consumer goods and services and his decision concerning the type and amount of work he wants to perform. . . .

It is much safer, as well as more natural, to look at the face of the medal and concentrate our attention on work and the burden it involves, rather than on freedom from work and the satisfaction it yields.

Single-minded preoccupation with these postulates of economic theory, however, may lead to neglect of a group of issues related to the quality of life at work. One might argue that the whole thrust of the concern for quality of working life can be viewed as a reaction against an approach that limits the analysis of work to a choice between income and leisure. Eric Hoffer echoes for his fellow workers a theme that dates back at least to biblical times and is echoed in the Protestant ethic—that work is essential to man. People need to work, he writes, because work enables them to fulfill their daily need for a confirmation of their "self worth" (Hoffer, 1967, pp. 64–65).[5] In Hoffer's opinion, only a relatively few people have the good fortune to find employment that enables them to realize fully their urge for creativity or achievement because of the limitations of most of the jobs that have to be done. But all who work can satisfy their need for self-worth.

E. S. Schumacher states a similar thesis in less conventional terms. He argues that modern, industrialized society turns the role of work on its head. He illustrates the point by contrasting work in developed nations with his view of the notion of work in a Buddhist society (Schumacher, 1973, pp. 54–55).

> The Buddhist point of view takes the function of work to be at least threefold: to give a man a chance to utilize and develop his faculties; to enable him to overcome his ego-centeredness by joining with other people in a common task; and to bring forth the food and services needed for a becoming existence. Again the consequences that flow from this view are endless. To organize work in such a manner that it becomes meaningless, boring, stultifying, or nerve wracking for the worker would be little short of criminal; it would indicate a greater concern with goods than with people, an evil lack of compassion and a soul-destroying degree of attachment to the most primitive side of this worldly existence. Equally, to strive for leisure as an alternative to work would be considered a complete misunderstanding of one of the basic truths of human

---

[5] Essentially Hoffer (1967) is saying in plain talk what Tolstoi said in moral language and Freud in psychoanalytical terms. A biblical view from Proverbs 12:9: "Better is a man of humble standing who works for himself than one who plays the great man but lacks bread."

existence, namely, that work and leisure are complementary parts of the same living process and cannot be separated without destroying the joy of work and the bliss of leisure.

It is this concern with work itself—with what goes on at the job—that has been at the core of interest about quality of working life and has characterized efforts at job redesign and worker participation in decisions affecting their work assignments.

4. Since the early 1960s there has been a growing volume of research and publication on the subject of human capital formation. Its purpose has been to differentiate consumption expenditures from expenditures that are undertaken for future rewards. Much of this economic research has centered on education, which was long treated by economists as a consumption good. Among the early conclusions of this research was that the higher earnings achieved by those with college and postgraduate education could largely explain the great postwar demand for higher education. Critics have pointed to other plausible explanations for this increase. As a result, the field has its eminent practitioners and defenders. It also has its skeptics. A recent survey of the literature by Mark Blaug finds very little that has been conclusively demonstrated by empirical work to date, though he does applaud its boldness in attacking "certain traditionally neglected topics in economics, such as income distribution. Moreover, it has never entirely lost sight of its original goal of demonstrating that a wide range of apparently disconnected phenomena of the world are the outcome of a definite pattern of individual decisions, having in common the features of foregoing present gains for the prospect of future ones" (Blaug, 1976, p. 849).

The perspective of the human-capital researchers also suggests some insights into questions related to the quality of working life. It suggests, for example, that if most people find greater satisfaction in having some autonomy on the job, a greater range of tasks to do, and an opportunity for advancement, then the payoff from investing in training, education, and so on, is not only a pecuniary one but a nonpecuniary one as well.

The human-capital view suffers, however, from a one-sided orientation to the supply side of the labor market. The relationship between earnings and schooling is partly payment for a scarcity typified by the time when only a small proportion of the population possessed college degrees, which established entree into certain well-paying jobs. What happens when the spread of education to a much larger proportion of the society eventually reduces the scarcity component of the earnings differential?

A look at the demand side of the market may help to explain the paradox of rising discontent in the job market in recent years, just when more people seem able to take on more interesting or demanding jobs. Young people, for example, find it increasingly difficult to find jobs equal to their talents, training, and education. Research is needed to explain why there appears to be such a glut of human capital. Has the technological requirement for highly trained people leveled off or has the baby boom of the 1950s merely caused a temporary imbalance? (We may consider some day turning the clock back and educating people, rather than training them.)

Suppose that quality of working life is affected largely by a balance between what working people want to do and are capable of doing, on the one hand, and what they are pushed into doing (or kept from doing) on the other. Then more training or education will not guarantee a higher level of job satisfaction for the entire labor force, despite the obvious advantages of training in particular cases.

5. Some recent economic research has tended to suggest that the importance of the allocative choices in economic theory may be greatly exaggerated—that even if monopoly and other market imperfections were eliminated, the welfare gains would be relatively modest. Summarizing studies of welfare losses from monopoly and restrictions on trade, Harvey Liebenstein (1976) finds that these losses are frequently less than one-tenth of 1 percent in output. Differences in output reported in repeated studies cannot be explained by differences in observable inputs. "The nature of management, the environment in which it operates, and the incentives employed are significant" (Liebenstein, 1976, p. 37).

Liebenstein's central thesis is that effort is always a variable in employment relations, sometimes but not always resulting in a difference in income. It is a variable because most employment contracts are "incomplete and open. Not every aspect of a job is specified in advance" (1976, p. 98). Liebenstein identifies four components of effort, each of which is usually subject to adjustment by the individual worker: the choice of *activities* composing the effort, the *pace* at which each activity is carried out, the *quality* of the performance of each activity, and the *time* pattern and length of activity. These he collectively labels the "APQT bundle."

In the context of this discussion, what is interesting is Liebenstein's analytical support for the view that productivity is much higher when workers have substantial autonomy—or, in his terminology, when workers are given a partial or complete control of their APQT bundles. The alternative is self-defeating. "To preset the APQT bundle normally requires a fantastic amount of knowledge of operations, exceptionally close supervision of the individual carrying out the activities and detailed quality control of the results. Presetting the APQT bundles is likely to require very high information costs, supervisory costs, and quality control costs as compared to non-preset or partially preset bundles" (1976, p. 101). One of his examples of how rigorous enforcement of rules in a bureaucracy can depress productivity was the decision of British railroad workers to "work to rule" in lieu of a strike. The full presentation and critique of Liebenstein's work is beyond the scope of this paper. But the work clearly merits attention as a systematic and analytical presentation of ideas that are similar to those held intuitively by business managers who have been experimenting with the autonomous work groups discussed later in this chapter.

4. Measuring the Quality of Working Life

Economic and social data—growing in quantity and sophistication year by year—offer many insights into the quality of working life and suggest further opportunities for research. Some of the data are refinements in long-established series on employment, hours, and earnings; some are relatively new social indicators that seek to assess other measures of welfare, including perceptions of well-being. The social indicators movement dates back at least a decade in the United States. In 1970, however, with the initial publication of *Social Trends,* the United Kingdom became the first nation to publish an annual statistical compendium of such indicators. (The seventh edition appeared in December 1976 and by that time twenty nations were issuing such reports regularly.) Publication of *Social Indicators 1973* marked the U.S. government's belated entry into the field.[6]

Employment and Earnings

Employment data provide a good starting point for a discussion of measurement results and problems. They are especially well developed and their potential for analyzing the quality of working life has not been

---

[6] The seminal work in the field is generally considered to be *Social Indicators,* edited by Raymond A. Bauer (Cambridge, Mass., MIT Press, 1966) based on a study undertaken by the American Academy of Arts and Sciences to "appraise the social impact of outer space exploration." The 1969 HEW study, *Toward a Social Report,* cited earlier, contributed to the development of a system of social reporting and indicated that a social report could be developed in two years. However, it was five years before *Social Indicators 1973* appeared. The second issue of *Social Indicators,* which was scheduled for 1976, was sidetracked by a short-lived effort to bring out a monthly chartbook of social statistics. Entitled *Status,* the chartbook appeared experimentally in the summer and fall of 1976.

fully exploited. If we consider job security, for example, as an important ingredient of the quality of working life, we may look at data on changes in the unemployment rate, labor turnover, and the frequency and length of the spells of unemployment in a somewhat different light—as more than indicators of how the economy is performing. They may also bear a relationship to job dissatisfaction—and may be a more pervasive influence than a glance at the unemployment rate would suggest. The unemployed are not a fixed group who never get off the unemployment rolls. Rather, their ranks are in flux. During the early 1970s, about one worker in six or seven experienced some unemployment during a year (about three times the number unemployed at any one time) and a third of them experienced two or more periods of joblessness. About only one in fifteen of the unemployed fall into the long-term unemployed category (out of work for 27 weeks or longer).[7]

Employment data shed light on long-run conditions and trends as well as on cyclical change. The persistence of high unemployment rates among teenagers (three times the adult rate), among blacks (twice the rate of whites), and among women (50 percent higher than men) may help explain why job dissatisfaction among members of these groups is higher than the average for all workers. On the other hand, contradictory inferences may be drawn from long-run changes in labor force participation, particularly the increase in women's participation rates from about 34 to 48 percent over the past twenty-five years.[8] An optimistic interpretation is that a growing number of women have been able to exercise the option of working for pay as an alternative to housework or volunteer activities. A pessimistic one can be derived from the comments of wives who say a single income can't keep up with rising costs, and from data showing an increase in the number of divorces.

Broad measures of earnings and income show the extent of the long-run improvement in this measure of working life, but they are sometimes ambiguous in some respects. Weekly earnings in constant dollars in-

---

[7] Table 70, *Handbook of Labor Statistics 1975*. In 1975 about 20 percent of those who worked at some time during the year experienced at least one spell of unemployment—about two and a half times the average number unemployed during the year (Young, 1976). However, the official unemployment rate does not include the so-called discouraged workers—persons who want to work but have stopped looking for jobs. If their numbers were added to the number of unemployed, the rate would rise by 0.5 to 1.0 percent. For most of these persons, the discouraged worker status is temporary. See Mincer (1973).

[8] For recent figures on unemployment by age, race, and sex, see *Handbook 1975*, table 59, and table 4 of the Current Labor Statistics section in later issues of the *Monthly Labor Review*. For labor force participation rates, see table 4, *Handbook 1975*.

creased nearly 50 percent from 1947 to 1967, and somewhat less in the ensuing decade. The index of average hourly earnings (adjusted for overtime and interindustry shifts and inflation) has shown an increase almost every year since the start of the series in 1964.

Disposable income figures show similar long-term gains. The worker clearly gets much more for an hour on the job now than he did twenty years ago. But workers today are increasingly concerned about shorter run changes, especially whether their wage increases keep up with the erosion of purchasing power resulting from inflation and from the larger bite taken out of increased earnings by a progressive tax system and rising payroll taxes. The Bureau of Labor Statistics (BLS) issues data on real take-home pay and this "spendable earnings" series has shown little gain over the 1964–75 period. This series has also been subjected to heavy criticism in recent years on methodological grounds, which has led to changes in methods as well as the search by BLS and others for alternative measures.[9] Further work on the interpretation of earnings trends is warranted, not only for aggregate measures, but for specific groups within the labor force.

Working Time

Data on hours are closely related to those on income as an objective indicator of the quality of working life. They have long been available both as an average of hours worked by all people in the labor force and those worked by full-time employees. The trends are clearly parallel and show about a one-third reduction in the work week from 1900 to 1950, and little change in the average for all employees since then, although there was a decline from about 40 to 37 hours a week for production workers.[10] This stabilization in the length of the work week reflects a shift of emphasis toward taking productivity gains in the form of more pay and fringe benefits instead of leisure. The strike against the Ford Motor Company in September 1976 over the issue of more paid days off, however, revived questions, for the first time since the 1930s, about whether the shorter work week might become a major issue in the years ahead. (Strike activity has been episodic, more closely related to postwar adjustments and other unusual situations than to any long-run

[9] Problems of measuring earnings and income have been discussed in the *Monthly Labor Review*. See, for example, Alterman (1971) and Stein and Ryscavage (1974). For an outsider's critique, see George Perry (1973).

[10] For hours worked by production and nonsupervisory workers on nonagricultural payrolls (who comprise about two-thirds of nonagricultural workers) see table 78, *Handbook 1975*.

trend in dissatisfaction. The latest bulge in time lost was a result of labor disputes that occurred in the 1967–71 period, when there was rising concern about worker alienation. For the next five years work stoppages declined to the level that prevailed in the 1950s and early 1960s.)

But if there has been little recent change in the length of the work-week, there has been considerable change in other aspects of time worked. One is the liberalization of vacation time—with a rapid rise in the number of workers who are getting two weeks of vacation after only one, two, or three years on a job. More interesting from the stand-point of the quality of life have been the experiments in staggered hours, four-day workweeks, flexitime, sabbaticals, and early retirement.

In large urban areas congestion produces a special incentive to encourage staggered work hours. One experiment in varying the predominant 9–5 schedule in New York and New Jersey was initiated in 1970. Some workers were required to begin a half hour earlier than the usual starting time, others a half hour later. The experiment was extended by steps from lower Manhattan, to mid-Manhattan and to upper Manhattan—gradually encompassing 220,000 workers. Advantages of the staggered hours cited in a 1975 report were "improved efficiency of business operations, reduction of vertical travel time in buildings and building lobby congestion, employee punctuality, better morale, and possibly less crowded lunch periods in restaurants" (O'Malley, 1975, p. 166). The special difficulties of urban work life may also be reflected in the market. Hoch has reported a pattern of a shorter work week and higher hourly rates with city size for a sample of female workers. The decline in hours worked "was about a half hour a day, consistent with the differential in journey to work time" for New York workers compared with others in the survey (Hoch, 1972, p. 317).

In the United States, experimentation with the four-day week began in small, predominantly nonunion manufacturing plants along the East Coast and the Midwest in about 1970 as part of an effort to combat dissatisfaction and boredom on the job. But despite the enthusiasm of proponents and a brief flurry of new plans for about three years—a period when short-run economic conditions could have been more influential than a long-run change in preferences—no evidence of a great swing to the four-day week became evident. A Bureau of Labor Statistics report on hours in 1975 indicated that fewer than 2 percent of full-time employees worked a shorter than five-day week, with 1.1 percent working a four-day week (Hedges, 1975).

Fewer workdays a week should have offered numerous inducements to workers—principally a reduction of 20 percent or more in commuting time and costs. For management, the improvement in worker morale might reduce absenteeism and raise productivity. But so far workers have shown no great interest in the tradeoff of a longer working day for a day's less commuting. Management has found that absentee rates are not noticeably lower in firms with fewer work days and that reported gains in productivity are uncertain. The shorter workweek seems, however, to have had a demonstrable impact on moonlighting. The BLS report shows that workers on a four-day schedule are about twice as likely to hold a second job as those on a five-day schedule.

A more radical effort to alter time patterns of work is flexitime—which offers workers an opportunity to set their schedules in accord with their need so long as they work an agreed number of hours per workweek or per month (Hedges, 1973).[11] Generally there is a prescribed "core time" in late morning or early afternoon when all workers are required to be present. But some more advanced forms of flexitime pioneered in Europe give workers a choice of working days as well as hours. The opportunity for workers to take care of personal business would seem to have considerable appeal to many workers, the element of choice in the allocation of time being a clear gain in quality of working life. For management, the inducement to permit this kind of flexibility is twofold: to increase worker morale, and to enable workers to perform more effectively at hours of their own choosing than at hours set by the enterprise. A gain in productivity is the expected payoff. Although evidence is still fragmentary, there is some indication of an initial reduction in tardiness, absenteeism, and unrecorded leave and sick leave.

If autonomy is widely accepted as a desirable attribute of one's working life, flexitime experiments address an important aspect of working life. How widely it can be adopted and in what forms without hampering work schedules in various types of organizations is not yet clear; nor is the relative appeal of it to workers—and to which workers—yet understood.

Health and Safety

Another dimension of the quality of working life—and one of growing importance—is health and safety at the workplace. Historically, neither health nor accident data have been adequate, though workmen's com-

---

[11] A substantial expansion of flexible hours in governmental agencies was predicted for 1977 by *The Washington Post*, December 21, 1976, p. 2. Employees will be permitted to come in late or leave early or take a midday break so long as they work eight hours within an eleven-hour day.

pensation data have been useful for assessing certain kinds of hazards. With the advent of the Occupational Safety and Health Act of 1970, an entirely new statistical system was established by the Bureau of Labor Statistics to cover accidents and disease. Some 5 million workplaces were required to keep a log of their experience based on clearly defined criteria of recordable accidents and illnesses. The maintenance of such a log and the reporting of results by those firms selected to participate in an annual BLS survey was made mandatory; BLS had previously relied on voluntary participation in its surveys. Beginning with preliminary data for 1973, BLS has been reporting the results of these annual surveys since then.[12] While no one—neither labor, management, nor government (including the BLS)—is yet satisfied with the effectiveness of the OSHA survey, especially with regard to data on illnesses, a kind of benchmark has been established at least for accidents.

The statistics on health are much more conjectural. First, there is evidence that the reporting of illnesses has not been as meticulous as the reporting of accidents. Second, it is very difficult to determine whether illnesses are uniquely related to the workplace rather than to the environment in general. Third, there are no data measuring a general loss of efficiency due to illness among workers who remain on the job. This may be especially important in regard to a fourth difficulty, the length of time between exposure to illness and the onset of identifiable symptoms. This latency period is a particular problem for various carcinogens. Cancers and other diseases, such as asbestosis, may not show up or be diagnosed until workers have gone to a different job or retired. How does one make statistical estimates of current trends that take into account future consequences of today's exposures?

Whatever the precise dimensions of the health problem, it is clear from Ashford's (1976) study that:

1. Industrially caused illness is widespread. One HEW study has put the number of new cases of occupationally related diseases detected each year at 390,000. Since these illnesses are slow to develop and tend to be chronic, but not fully disabling, for a number of years, the total number of workers suffering from industrial illnesses has been estimated at many times the number of ailments diagnosed in a year—totaling perhaps several millions at any one time.

2. Industrial illness comes from a number of sources. Chemical substances that are inhaled may cause black lung disease among miners, lung malignancies, or emphysema; toxic substances may lead to cancers,

[12] The 1976 report—covering experiences in 1975 and issued as a BLS press release, USDL-76-1474 (December 8, 1976)—showed that one worker in eleven experienced a job-related illness or injury, a slight drop from 1974.

or lesions, or nervous disorders. Some illnesses may be of biological origins from fungi and bacteria. Others may arise from physical hazards in the workplace, such as radiation or excessive heat and noise. Stresses on the job resulting from the demands of the occupation or from psychological pressures pose additional problems.

3. Illnesses may be synergistic. The combined effect of toxic substances and heat stress, for example, may be much more serious than the simple cumulative effect of these hazards if encountered one at a time. Thus the National Institute of Occupational Safety and Health has raised questions about the adequacy of standards governing single elements since the effects of one hazard may be multiplied by the presence of intense heat.[13]

So far perhaps the most significant accomplishment of the OSHA—which has both disappointed its supporters and angered management generally—has been to awaken employers, employees, and the general public to the seriousness of occupational hazards and to the enormity of the problem of reducing them.

It also sets up a framework for improving health and safety that goes beyond the gathering of statistics, which was incidental to the central purposes of the legislation. The act established procedures for promulgating standards to govern the work environment. It provided for the inspection of workplaces and penalties for violations of the act's provisions. It supported continuing research on the nature and causes of occupational illnesses. A broad so-called general duty clause stated that each employer has an obligation "to furnish to each of his employees employment and a place of employment which are free from recognized hazards that are causing or are likely to cause death or serious physical harm to his employees." The thrust of many of these provisions was to increase the internalization of health costs by making the firm bear the cost of preventive measures that would reduce illness and death rates.

Given the size of the problem and its pervasiveness, the area of occupational safety and health may well yield the greatest payoff in the coming decades for efforts to improve the quality of life in the workplace. The system of objective reporting being developed to measure these changes in health and safety, though still far from trouble free, may provide the basis of better estimates of whether progress is being made.

---

[13] These points are discussed in greater detail in Ashford (1976), especially chapter 3, "The Nature and Dimensions of Occupational Health and Safety Problems."

Workers' Perceptions

Two surveys financed by the Department of Labor and carried out in 1969 and 1973 by the Survey Research Center of the University of Michigan have provided a very extensive and thoroughly analyzed sampling of worker attitudes (Quinn and Mangione, 1973; Quinn and Shepard, 1974). The surveys measured worker response to questions related to five aspects of their jobs: challenge, financial rewards, comfort, relations with co-workers, and availability of resources to do their work.

Overall, the combination of all factors showed little change in workers' own assessments of their job satisfaction. In both 1969 and 1973, fewer than 10 percent said they were "not too satisfied" or "not at all satisfied" with their working conditions. The proportion of workers saying they were "very satisfied" or "somewhat" was 91 percent in both surveys, but the number calling themselves "very satisfied" fell from 31 to 24 percent.

At the same time, the survey did show a difference in job satisfaction by age and by occupation. Young workers, though on balance reasonably satisfied with their jobs, were more likely to express dissatisfaction than older workers. Similarly, women tended to be less satisfied than men, and blacks less satisfied than whites; operatives were less satisfied than other occupational groups, including service workers.

Reviewing these and other data on job satisfaction in a later assessment, Campbell and Kahn of the Survey Research Center reported their conclusion that data simply do not support the contention that there is a substantial increase in worker dissatisfaction with their jobs and the quality of their work life (Campbell and Kahn, 1976, p. 180).

> ... more than 2,000 studies of job satisfaction have been published and many more have gone deservedly unpublished. Despite differences in coverage and methods of measurement, there is a certain consistency in the response patterns: few people call themselves extremely satisfied with their jobs, but fewer still report extreme dissatisfaction. The modal response is on the positive side of neutrality—"pretty satisfied," and there is no evidence of significant change.

However, to say that workers may be reasonably satisfied with the total aspects of their employment may still not say how they feel about the tasks that must be performed. Questions raised by Daniel Bell some twenty years earlier in an analysis of the positive responses given by workers to questions of job satisfaction are still worth pondering—

though they relate to surveys that were less objective and sophisticated than those of the Survey Research Center (Bell, 1962, p. 249).

> The argument...misses two essential points: there are, of course, many other aspects of the work environment *other than the job* which provide satisfactions (such as the clique group, the joking, loafing, etc.) but this cannot be used to disprove the debilitating aspect of the organization of work and *its* failure to provide satisfactions; secondly, no question about satisfaction is meaningful unless the worker is *aware of alternative* possibilities of work.

If Campbell's assessment is hardly the last word, it does serve to dramatize the difference between the survey research group and the authors of *Work in America* (1973), discussed below, who interpreted expressions of discontent in the late 1960s as a drastic change in worker satisfaction.

On the other hand, a nagging imponderable persists. Taking numbers at face value can be misleading. We have no good measures of tolerance —no basis for judging whether the social fabric will rip when 10 percent, 20 percent, or 50 percent of the workers are greatly dissatisfied.

A Need for Synthesis

What strikes one forcibly in a review of this literature is the paucity of links from the objective data on employment, hours, earnings, health and safety and so on, to data on job satisfaction and perceptions of well-being. Exceptions include the research of Kenneth C. Land (1974), which suggests that an increase in the unemployment rate is associated with a drop in job satisfaction, and that of Campbell, Converse, and Rodgers (1976).

Government efforts to draw these data together in ongoing statistical compilations have been less than satisfactory. *Social Indicators 1973*, which was finally published after numerous delays, was short on discussion and integration of material. Most of the text is devoted to definitions and sources, and the selection of material on "Employment Opportunities" (unemployment and labor force participation) and "Quality of Employment Life" hardly breaks new ground except for the inclusion of two charts from the 1969 and 1973 working conditions surveys under the heading of "Job Satisfaction." The technical notes refer to Levitan and Taggart's (1973) efforts to construct an index of employment and earnings inadequacy as well as to the possible development of alternative measures of job satisfaction. But overall the presentation is partial and a weak reflection of the efforts that have been made to assess the quality of working life. Thoughtful studies of the problems involved in improving measurements of work quality appear in Biderman and Drury (1976).

5. Humanitarian and Management Perspectives

If concern for the quality of working life is not really new, the growing public visibility of the issue in the United States during the past decade must be considered something of a novelty. Equally novel is the fact that two groups with quite different perspectives—humanitarians and social critics, on one hand, and business managers on the other—have both embraced the cause of improving the quality of working life. Influenced in part by social research, both groups have encouraged similar kinds of experiments in the workplace—a convergence that would have been surprising fifty years earlier. The size and influence of these two groups should not be exaggerated. They merit attention, not because of their numbers, but because of their commitment, their proselytizing zeal, and their willingness to experiment.

For the social critics, the issue of working life gained visibility and a kind of official status with the widely publicized report on *Work in America* (1973) prepared by a task force appointed by the Department of Health, Education and Welfare, which reported a rising discontent among workers.[14]

The period of the late 1960s and early 1970s was viewed by many observers as a period of rising unrest in factories as well as in the nation generally. Wildcat strikes (the most dramatic was at the Lordstown plant of General Motors in March 1972), absenteeism, reports of sabotage and poor workmanship were translated into catchwords such as "worker alienation" and the "blue-collar blues," in the press and in social science journals. The Congress as well as the Executive became interested, as evidenced by a Senate subcommittee hearing on Worker Alienation.[15] The HEW report and the Senate hearings concluded that a decline in quality of working life was helping to undermine the family and the entire social structure of the United States. Worker alienation was also held responsible to a large extent for alcoholism, drug addiction, low productivity, and high rates of sabotage, and for the staggering national bill in the areas of crime and delinquency.

---

[14] Portions of the discussion in this section and the following section on job redesign are adapted from my article "Quality of Life in Work" in *Employee and Labor Relations*, vol. VI, part 3, edited by Dale Yoder and Herbert G. Heneman, Jr. (Washington, Bureau of National Affairs, Inc., forthcoming.)

[15] *Worker Alienation 1972*, U.S. Senate Hearings before subcommittee on Employment, Manpower, and Poverty of the Committee on Labor and Public Welfare, 92 Cong. 2 sess., July 25–26, 1972.

This unrest was attributed largely to a number of social changes: A rise in the educational level of the work force after World War II led to higher aspirations and expectations. . . . Equal rights movements made women, blacks, and other disadvantaged minorities increasingly dissatisfied with routine jobs that offered little opportunity for satisfaction and growth. . . . New technology, while it eliminated many tedious jobs, at the same time reduced opportunities for initiative and flexibility in other types of work. . . . The growth of large firms increased the bureaucratization of many work environments in the private sector as well as in government. Years of affluence preceding the 1973–74 recession created a widespread feeling of economic security that led a greater number of people to think more seriously about obtaining self-fulfillment from work.

The spreading symptoms of unrest—boredom, anger, and deteriorating workmanship—and the sources of unrest suggested to some social scientists that innovative approaches to work were needed. The question was how to restore the challenges and satisfactions that were thought to have been associated with a higher proportion of jobs in earlier days.

A number of new approaches that emerged, such as "job redesign" and "worker participation" will be discussed later. The rationale of the humanitarians was that the assembly line and factory work in general are dehumanizing and hazardous. Jobs should be more interesting and workers should be· given more autonomy. If workers become more interested and more responsible they will be more satisfied, which is good for them and for society. Also if workers are happy, their productivity will rise.

Among business leaders themselves and management researchers, there was also a growing awareness of discontent and its implications. Businessmen were drawn to the subject because they were worried about productivity. It wasn't rising fast enough. They were concerned about absenteeism and poor workmanship, which led to higher costs. They were troubled by reports of low worker morale, even in plants which had a reputation for high wages, good working conditions, and enlightened management. Was it time for some fresh thinking about management philosophy?

Within this century, at least two different managerial attitudes toward production workers have gained widespread influence. The scientific management approach was introduced at the beginning of the century by Frederick W. Taylor and his followers. It was an engineering approach designed to exact the utmost efficiency from each worker's every motion. Tasks were broken down into their simplest components and timed. Targets for performance were established and enforced.

Supervision was tight. Great advances in productivity were often achieved. Taylorism gained during World War I and spread during the 1920s.

Such a mechanization of people could not be extended indefinitely, however, without becoming counterproductive. An early clue to the limitations of scientific management emerged from the well-known research of Elton Mayo, a sociologist. Mayo's research began when he was called in to investigate excessive turnover rates in the mule-spinning section of a Philadelphia textile plant which had enjoyed rather high overall worker morale for many years. He observed that unlike other workers in the plant, the workers who tended the machines in the mule-spinning room were isolated from each other—working alone, without contact with other employees. At his suggestion, rest periods were introduced and a nurse was hired to listen to the workers' complaints. Turnover declined. Productivity began to increase.

Hunches growing out of this experience were pursued through nearly a decade of research after Mayo went to the Harvard Business School. This research—the so-called Hawthorne experiments at the Western Electric Company—led to increasing insights into the nature of how people behave in the work setting and to the development of the "human relations" approach to management in the late 1930s (Roethlisberger and Dickson, 1939).

The human relations approach enjoyed considerable vogue among consultants and in the universities. But over the years its limitations also became visible as business began operating in a different, rapidly changing industrial environment and with a younger group of workers who had higher expectations. The old remedies did not seem as effective as they had been. Some analysts became uneasy and dissatisfied with the manipulative implications of some of the human relations tactics. Critics stressed that the purpose of the human relations effort was simply to reduce opposition to the firm's policies and practices, a practice that if recognized could be resented.

The years after Hawthorne had seen the development of another set of theories associated with a number of social researchers, including A. H. Maslow (1954). Maslow sought to show that people have a hierarchy of needs. As one moves up in this hierarchy from the basic wants for food and shelter, one eventually reaches a level where the important motivator is "self-actualization." In an urbanized and industrialized society with a widely shared high standard of living (by historical standards) self-actualization becomes the key to employee satisfaction and also to productivity. In place of the placating techniques of the human relations school, Maslow's followers sought to find ways to encourage the worker's capacity for self-direction.

At about the same time, American managers were hearing about a wide range of management innovations in Europe, the success of which could be interpreted as a confirmation of the Maslow thesis. The Volvo plant in Sweden, for example, organized around small autonomous work groups rather than the traditional assembly lines, attracted great interest. In the mid-1970s the Kockums shipyards in Sweden made a film, "The Flame," which it showed abroad as a confirmation of the payoff to workers and management alike of the new managerial approach which gave workers a chance to have a greater voice in work scheduling and other company affairs that affected their welfare. Management theorists talked of a new phase in the development of managerial theory, which they described as the "human resources" approach, and it led them to similar conclusions that the humanitarians were reaching: human resources can be utilized more productively if jobs are more interesting and if workers are given a say in what they do.

6. Job Redesign and Worker Participation: Efforts to Improve Quality

Some observers contend that the workplace remains one of the nation's most rigid institutions. Despite rapid changes in all aspects of social life and attitudes during the past twenty-five years or so, conditions on the job, with notable exceptions, are about the same as they have been, especially life on the assembly line.

This widespread rigidity contrasts strongly with a growing number of experiments since the mid-1960s in the redesigning of work and in the sharing of responsibility for work assignments and definition of tasks. Some of these experiments have been motivated in part by humanitarian impulses, but the impetus for most of them has been the desire of management to raise productivity by raising worker morale.

What is job redesign? In its simplest form, job redesign means putting together sets of tasks so that every job will include functions that require some skill or mental challenge, or both. The objective is to eliminate monotonous and routinized jobs. A preferred model for putting such changes into effect is to organize small work groups that are rather autonomous—in which eight or a dozen workers decide on how the tasks composing a productive activity are to be broken down, who is to do what, and how decisions are to be made within the group. Workers generally learn more than one job, so that assignments within the group can be rotated for the sake of variety. Thus workers are given a chance to make their jobs more interesting, to have a voice in what they do, and to assume some responsibility for the outcome of their efforts. The more innovative job redesign projects link these changes to changes in the entire organizational style, which includes provision of job training and career paths for workers and training executives in new approaches to organizational development.

In the United States, job redesign efforts have been concentrated in nonunion plants in the manufacturing sector. Unions have historically been almost indifferent to issues of job satisfaction and have been much less interested in encouraging job restructuring than in efforts to improve wages and benefits. At the height of publicity over blue-collar discontent, the president of the Machinists' Union said the only sure-fire way to improve a worker's morale is to pay him more (Winpisinger, 1973).

The results of job restructuring efforts have aroused considerable enthusiasm, but a careful weighing of experiences in the United States leaves one with as many questions as answers about its widespread applicability. For example, the authors of *Work in America* are unequivocal in their endorsement of job redesign as a device that will bring greater variety to jobs, offer a measure of autonomy for the worker, and permit some participation in designing tasks and setting goals. Unfortunately for application to the American setting, their case rests on twenty-six experiments in the United States, seven of which were accounted for by two firms (American Telephone and Telegraph Co. and Monsanto Chemical Corp.). Almost all the experiments involved a small number of workers (fewer than 100 in a third of the cases). Most of the experiments were of such recent origin that longer term effects could not be assessed. The assertiveness of the authors' conclusions seems quite out of character with the limitations of the supportive evidence.

A more balanced and illuminating analysis appeared in *Worker and the Job*, a collection of papers prepared for an American Assembly conference in 1973 (Rosow, 1974). It contains a study of 11 experiments in manufacturing plants with fewer than 500 employees, half of which are unionized. The report indicates that all of the organizations involved reported initial gains in the quality of working life, but at the same time employees who were interviewed gave widely differing responses to questions about the desirability of the changes. Firms generally observed a drop in absenteeism and turnover, a reduction in waste and downtime, and improvements in the product. However, early improvements did not always persist. A few firms abandoned their job redesign experiments and several others modified them. The author's conclusions reflected optimism about the potential of restructuring work, along with a recognition of the limited achievements to date (Walton, 1974).

The failure of job redesign efforts to bring about consistently lasting improvements in morale and higher levels of productivity can be attributed largely to failure in execution of the projects. There is little reason to doubt that in certain circumstances, and for some periods of time, job restructuring can make a contribution to worker morale and efficiency in production. What is more difficult to assess is the generality of its contribution to quality of working life. In what kinds of firms, in what proportion of firms, in what kinds of occupations, for what kinds of workers does job redesign offer a significant opportunity for raising the quality of life in the workplace? It is not yet at all clear that this approach will affect more than a minority of workers.[16]

One type of situation in which it can be clearly beneficial is where the logic of the product and marketing situation also calls for a change in job structure. This is the essential lesson from the Olivetti experience reported in *The Quality of Working Life,* an especially useful collection of studies on managerial efforts to bring about improvement in the work environment (Butera, 1975). It illustrates a range of approaches that reflects wide variety in the impetus for change, in the locus of responsibility for change, and in the nature of the changes (which range from job redesign to changes in organizational structure, to provisions for greater worker participation in management).

The 1960s was a turbulent period for Olivetti as a result of extensive and rapid changes in its product mix. There was a substantial decline in the relative importance of typewriters and other office equipment and a dramatic increase in the importance of more sophisticated equipment, such as data processing systems. New products were introduced, and there were also rapid changes in models. The pace of change reached a climax in the three-year period from the beginning of 1969 to the end of 1971, when the work force rose more than 20 percent, more than a third of the manufacturing employees changed jobs, and nearly one out of seven workers took internal training courses.

The company's effort to cope with this revolution in the industry and to respond to rising union pressure for the upgrading of jobs included an experiment in which an assembly line of fifty to sixty stations was

[16] A great deal of research is continuing, especially on job redesign, worker participation, and labor–management cooperation programs in various workplaces. The National Center for Productivity and the Quality of Working Life in Washington, D.C., the National Quality of Work Center in Washington, D.C., and the Work in America Institute, Inc. in Scarsdale, New York (which publishes a monthly newsletter, *World of Work Report*) are among the American organizations encouraging experiments in this area.

replaced by a series of subassemblies in which each group of workers completed an identifiable and testable unit, such as a printer or tabulator. The change itself was not unusual, but the way it was put in place and the rationale were distinctive.

It was management's conclusion that large assembly lines are not appropriate in a market situation that is no longer characterized by (a) a few, stable products (b) produced in large quantities (c) for customers demanding reliable performance and reasonable prices. Today's rapidly changing environment calls for a more flexible organization with a more adaptable work force. This is the "true cause" of the changes at Olivetti. "Really new job design cannot be undertaken only on the vague expectation of reduced absenteeism or started with only a new managerial philosophy" (Butera, 1975, p. 195). It can be undertaken successfully only in response to changes in technology and in the market.

Closely related to these experiments are experiments in worker participation, in defining work tasks, and in managerial decisions. Frequently job redesign experiments include an element of participation as well. But participation merits separate treatment.

Experiments in worker participation in management have been much more widespread in Europe than in the United States, and especially in socialist countries. A study of a wide variety of participative experiments in ten nations was conducted by the International Institute for Labor Studies in 1974 (Walker, 1974). Here, too, the results are mixed. Achieving a broad base of participation—extending it throughout the workforce and not just limiting it to a few representatives—has been difficult. To some extent, this is a reflection of a characteristic observable in organizations generally: a few people willingly and effectively assume leadership and responsibility. And it is a reflection, too, of individual differences in personalities, education, and capacities. Participation in management does not come naturally to everyone.

Even within participative bodies, where representatives presumably have been selected from among the most interested workers, active participation may be difficult to achieve because workers are intimidated by the setting, overwhelmed by the volume of statistics, puzzled by unfamiliar problems, or unaccustomed to the procedures adopted. Where workers do want to take an active part, they may be troubled by the lack of a guide on how to behave in a way that will assure their credibility with both workers and management.

If the representative views himself primarily as an expert—advising on matters affecting workers and on the probable reaction of workers to a proposed change—he may become regarded as a collaborator or member of the management team. If he views himself as a delegate who actively tries to persuade management to take steps in the workers' interests, he may be regarded by the rest of the board as a partisan interested only in workers' problems rather than in the broader long-range interests of the firm. In either instance, his effectiveness will be diminished.

If, despite these uncertainties, one decides on balance that participation in management is a promising avenue for improving the quality of working life for some workers, the question naturally arises: What are the costs in terms of management authority and what is the overall impact of participation?

The ten-nation study suggests that there is more evidence available for impact on productivity and managerial concerns than on the quality of life. The study indicates that the participation of workers in decision making does not necessarily lessen managerial prerogatives (indeed, quite the contrary, worker cooperation can sometimes heighten managerial leverage) or lessen efficiency. In areas such as safety, where close management–labor cooperation is essential, participative achievements are reported. Where workers have been given an opportunity to participate in the redesign of their jobs or in the planning of their working group, a strong sense of involvement and satisfaction has been reported. Generally, the effects on worker morale have tended to reflect the relative success or failure of that participation once the initial enthusiasm has worn off. Participation is just the beginning of an activity that may yield an improvement in the quality of working life.

What is missing from this analysis is a comprehensive estimate of the costs of achieving an improvement in quality of working life—one that includes not only the costs of worker time devoted to consultations but also the costs of some other worker objectives forgone. This is equally true of the experiments on job restructuring.

7. Concluding Comment

The issues identified in this discussion have been shown to have two dimensions. The first is a direct one—the impact on the individual workers, their perceptions of the job itself and how it affects them, which in turn affects the overall quality of their lives. The second is indirect—the impact of job satisfaction or discontent on workers' performance and the viability of the firm. Both dimensions are of important concern to workers, to unions, to employers, and to the general public or policy makers. Where innovations can improve both the quality of the work environment and productivity, adjustments are more likely to be made without public policy confrontations; managerial initiative and collective bargaining should offer possibilities for progress. Where improvements in the work environment do not improve productivity (especially where costs formerly externalized are internalized), serious confrontations are more likely to arise. Health is one such area of internal cost increase and conflict. But matters of job redesign and of worker participation in decisions on work issues may also be serious areas of conflict leading to public intervention.

So far, the literature on the quality of working life has provided some new evidence on matters that have been treated in the past under different headings, such as morale, motivation, and productivity in management's lexicon; or dignity, fair wages, and decent working conditions in the language of workers and trade unions. The quality of working life, defined broadly as in this essay, also suggests the need for an approach which can embrace data from different disciplines and link them to broad issues of social policy.

References

Alterman, Jack. 1971. "Compensation per Man-hour and Take-Home Pay," *Monthly Labor Review* (June).

Ashford, Nicholas A. 1976. *Crisis in the Workplace,* A Report to the Ford Foundation (Cambridge, Mass., MIT Press).

Bell, Daniel, 1962. *The End of Ideology: On the Exhaustion of Political Ideas in the Fifties.* Rev. ed. (New York, Free Press).

Biderman, Albert D., and Thomas F. Drury, eds. 1976. *Measuring Work Quality for Social Reporting* (New York, Wiley-Halstead).

Blaug, Mark. 1976. "Human Capital Theory: A Slightly Jaundiced View," *Journal of Economic Literature* (September) p. 849.

Butera, Frederico. 1975. "Environmental Factors in Job and Organizational Design: The Case of Olivetti," in Louis E. Davis and Albert B. Cherns, eds., *The Quality of Working Life* vol. 2 (New York, Free Press).

Campbell, Angus, and Robert L. Kahn. 1976. "Measuring the Quality of Life" in *Qualities of Life, Critical Choices for Americans* vol. 7 (Lexington, Mass., Lexington Books, D. C. Heath).

————, Philip E. Converse, and Willard L. Rodgers. 1976. *The Quality of American Life: Perceptions, Evaluations, and Satisfactions* (New York, Russell Sage).

Davis, Louis E., and Albert B. Cherns, eds. 1975. *The Quality of Working Life* vol. 2 (New York, Free Press).

Hedges, Janice Neipert. 1973. "New Patterns for Working Time," *Monthly Labor Review* (February).

————. 1975. "How Many Days Make a Workweek?" *Monthly Labor Review* (April).

Hicks, John. 1975. *The Crisis of Keynesian Economics* (New York, Basic Books).

Hoch, Irving. 1972. "Income and City Size," *Urban Studies* (October) p. 317.

Hoffer, Eric. 1967. *Ordeal of Change* (New York, Harper & Row, Perennial Library).

Maslow, Abraham H. 1954. *Motivation and Personality* (New York, Harper & Row).

Land, Kenneth C. 1974. "Two Preliminary Models for the Analysis of Changes in a Social Indicator of Job Satisfaction." (American Statistical Association, Proceedings of the Social Statistics Section).

Levitan, Sar, and Robert Taggart. 1973. "Employment and Earnings Inadequacy: A Measure of Worker Welfare," *Monthly Labor Review* (October).

Liebenstein, Harvey. 1976. *Beyond Economic Man: A New Foundation for Microeconomics* (Cambridge, Mass., Harvard University Press).

Mincer, Jacob. 1973. "Determining the Number of Hidden Unemployed," *Monthly Labor Review* (March).

O'Malley, Brendan W. 1975. "Work Schedule Changes to Reduce Peak Transportation Demand," *Better Use of Existing Transportation Facilities* (Washington, Transportation Research Branch).

Perry, George. 1973. "Real Spendable Weekly Earnings," *Brookings Papers on Economic Activity*, 3, 1972 (Washington, Brookings Institution).

Quinn, Robert P., and T. W. Mangione. 1973. *The 1969–70 Survey of Working Conditions*, Chronicles of an Unfinished Enterprise (Ann Arbor, University of Michigan Survey Research Center).

————, and Linda J. Shepard. 1974. The 1972–73 Quality of Employment Survey, Report to the Employment Standards Administration, U.S. Department of Labor (Ann Arbor, University of Michigan Survey Research Center).

Roethlisberger, F. J., and W. J. Dickson. 1939. *Management and the Worker* (Cambridge, Mass., Harvard University Press).

Rosow, Jerome M., ed. 1974. *The Worker and the Job: Coping with Change*. Published for the American Assembly (Englewood Cliffs, N.J., Prentice-Hall).

Schumacher, E. F. 1973. *Small Is Beautiful: Economics as if People Mattered* (London, Blond & Buggs) pp. 54–55.

Scitovsky, Tibor. 1951. *Welfare and Competition: The Economics of a Fully Employed Economy* (Chicago, Irwin).
————. 1976. *The Joyless Economy: An Inquiry into Human Satisfaction and Consumer Dissatisfaction* (New York and London, Oxford University Press).
Social Indicators 1973 (U.S. Office of Management and Budget, 1974).
Stein, Robert L., and Paul M. Ryscavage. 1974. "Measuring Annual Earnings of Household Heads in Production Jobs," *Monthly Labor Review* (April).
U.S. Bureau of Labor Statistics. 1975. *Handbook of Labor Statistics, Reference Edition* (Washington, Bulletin 1865).
U.S. Office of Management and Budget. 1974. *Social Indicators 1973.* (Washington, GPO).
Walker, Kenneth F. 1974. "Workers' Participation in Management—Problems, Practices and Prospects," Bulletin, International Institute for Labour Studies (December).
Walton, Richard E. 1974. "Innovative Restructuring of Work," in Jerome M. Rosow, ed., *The Worker and the Job: Coping with Change.* Published for the American Assembly (Englewood Cliffs, N.J., Prentice-Hall).
Winpisinger, William W. 1973. "Job Enrichment: A Union View," *Monthly Labor Review* (April) p. 54.
Work in America. 1973. Report of a Task Force to the Secretary of Health; Education and Welfare (Cambridge, Mass., MIT Press).
Young, Anne M. 1976. "Work Experience of the Population in 1975" *Monthly Labor Review* (November) p. 47.

Library of Congress Cataloging in Publication Data

Main entry under title:

Public economics and the quality of life.

   1. Externalities (Economics) 2. Environmental
policy. 3. Public goods. 4. Cities and towns.
I. Wingo, Lowdon. II. Evans, Alan
III. Resources for the Future. IV. Centre for
Environmental Studies.
HB99.3.P8   330'.01   76-47393
ISBN 0-8018-1941-5

www.ingramcontent.com/pod-product-compliance
Ingram Content Group UK Ltd.
Pitfield, Milton Keynes, MK11 3LW, UK
UKHW020859280225
455677UK00006B/107